Emplacing
a Pilgrimage

*The Ōyama Cult
and Regional Religion
in Early Modern Japan*

Harvard East Asian Monographs 297

Emplacing a Pilgrimage

The Ōyama Cult
and Regional Religion
in Early Modern Japan

Barbara Ambros

Published by the Harvard University Asia Center
and distributed by Harvard University Press
Cambridge (Massachusetts) and London, 2008

Printed in the United States of America

The Harvard University Asia Center publishes a monograph series and, in coordination with the Fairbank Center for Chinese Studies, the Korea Institute, the Reischauer Institute of Japanese Studies, and other faculties and institutes, administers research projects designed to further scholarly understanding of China, Japan, Vietnam, Korea, and other Asian countries. The Center also sponsors projects addressing multidisciplinary and regional issues in Asia.

Library of Congress Cataloging-in-Publication Data

Ambros, Barbara, 1968–
    Emplacing a pilgrimage : the Ōyama cult and regional religion in early modern Japan / Barbara Ambros.
        p. cm. -- (Harvard East Asian monographs ; 297)
    Includes bibliographical references and index.
    ISBN 978-0-674-02775-6 (cloth : alk. paper)
        1. Mountain worship--Japan--Oyama (Kanagawa-ken) 2. Oyama (Kanagawa-ken, Japan)--Religious life and customs. I. Title.
    BL2211.M6A46 2008
    299.5'61350952136--dc22

                                                                                                    2007050303

Index by David Prout

An earlier version of Chapter 3 was published as: "Localized Religious Specialists in Early Modern Japan: The Development of the Ōyama *oshi* System." *Japanese Journal of Religious Studies* 28, nos. 3–4, (2001): 329–72.

An abbreviated earlier version of Chapter 6 was published as: "Reconfiguring Ōyama's Pantheon." *Kōyasan Daigaku Bulletin of Research of the Institute of Esoteric Buddhist Culture* 2 (Special Issue, 2003): 27–45.

♾ Printed on acid-free paper

Last figure below indicates year of this printing

18 17 16 15 14 13 12 11 10 09 08

To Alex Lee

a friend and great inspiration

to all who knew him

Acknowledgments

This study had its beginning in the kind suggestion of Tamamuro Fumio. I had worked on pilgrimage in the Heian period previously, which had piqued my interest in the topic of pilgrimage. However, the promise of abundant source material led me to consider shifting to the early modern period. Furthermore, Allan Grapard's work on sacred sites had impressed me deeply and inspired me to write my dissertation on a specific sacred site, preferably a mountain. When I was not quite sure which site to choose, my doctoral advisor, Helen Hardacre, suggested that I talk to Tamamuro Fumio. When I asked him whether he knew of any early modern pilgrimage center that needed further study, he recommended that I study the Ōyama cult.

All shortcomings of this study are, of course, my responsibility, but I would like to acknowledge the kindness and assistance of the many scholars and friends in the United States, Europe, and Japan who allowed me to complete this project. First and foremost, I would like to thank Helen Hardacre, my doctoral advisor at Harvard University, without whose unwavering support this study would have been impossible. Her insightful advice during the research phase of this project and her patient comments on the various drafts of the manuscript constituted the greatest encouragement. Tamamuro Fumio of Meiji University made important documents available to me along the way. His constant support and his willingness to share his masterful expertise in early modern religion were invaluable.

Throughout my work on this project, I was fortunate to receive the support of Matsuoka Takashi, Miyake Hitoshi, the late Miyata Noboru, Nishigai Kenji, Sugane Yukihiro, Suzuki Masataka, Umezawa Fumiko, and Shimazono Susumu. I would also like to express my gratitude to the many scholars at the local archives that provided the bulk of the source material for this dissertation: the municipal archives of Isehara City, the town of Samukawa, Atsugi City, and Setagaya Ward. I am particularly indebted to Mr. Ōnuki at the Isehara City Archives, who selflessly devoted hours of his time to answering my many questions and making documents available to me. Thanks are also due to Takahashi Atsumi and Yamamoto Akiko, who helped me read and transcribe some of my sources.

At Harvard, Harold Bolitho and Mikael Adolphson read and gave substantive comments on my manuscript. Robert Gimello gave me much needed insight from a Buddhist studies perspective. Many helpful suggestions also came from scholars at other universities, including Professors Gail Bernstein, Richard Gardner, Allan Grapard, F. G. Notehelfer, Paul Swanson, Sarah Thal, Ronald Toby, Constantine Vaporis, Anne Walthall, and Kären Wigen. In addition, Professor Charles Hallisey and the graduate student members of the Harvard Buddhist Studies Workshop gave me valuable feedback in the beginning stages of this project. I owe endless gratitude to the dissertation support group in Tokyo whose members included Michael Burtscher, Steve Covell, Betsy Dorn, Michael Eastwood, Terry Jackson, Hiromi Maeda, Reiko Sono, Alex Vesey, Duncan Williams, and Noell Wilson. Their comments on my early drafts greatly improved the manuscript. I would also like to thank Mark Byington and Gray Tuttle, who participated in a similar group at Harvard, as well as Paula Maute, Susan Oehler, and again Duncan Williams, who meticulously worked through my manuscript to improve it stylistically. I would also like to thank all the students in my sacred mountains and pilgrimage seminar, who helped me continue to approach this topic with fresh eyes.

My research in Japan could not have progressed without affiliations with the Institute of Religious Studies at the University of Tokyo during 1998 to 2000 and with the Faculty of Comparative Culture at Sophia University from 1999 to 2000. I must also acknowledge the institutes and fellowships that made this research possible: the Harvard Center for the Study of World Religions, which gave me the opportunity to receive considerable advice from many international scholars of religion during my two years of residency from 1995 to 1997; the Edwin O. Reischauer Institute of Japanese Studies, which provided me with financial support for summer research in Japan and during my penultimate year at Harvard; the Japanese Ministry of Education, whose grant allowed me to pursue my research in Japan from 1998 to 2000; the Japanese Society for the Promotion of Science, which supported me as a postdoctoral fellow at the Historiographical Institute of the University of Tokyo from 2002 to 2003; and the University of North Carolina University Research Council, which provided financial support during the final stages of the publication process from 2006 to 2007.

Contents

Reference Matter

Table and Figures

Table

Figures

Emplacing
a Pilgrimage

The Ōyama Cult
and Regional Religion
in Early Modern Japan

INTRODUCTION

The Ōyama Cult in Regional History

In their *Handbook for Travellers in Japan* (1891), Basil Hall Chamberlain and William Benjamin Mason recommended Ōyama, a sacred mountain in central Kanagawa Prefecture, as a convenient tourist excursion from Yokohama, about 22 miles west of the port. From the 1860s, a number of Americans living in Yokohama began to visit the mountain to experience its natural beauty.[1] Towering above the western edge of the Kantō plain, Ōyama had attracted countless visitors even before the arrival of Western-style alpine mountaineering. Chamberlain and Mason wrote:

This celebrated mountain, about 4,000 ft. high, . . . is a favorite goal of pilgrims, who continue to be attracted to its shrine, although the old Buddhist objects of worship have here, as in so many other parts of the country, been replaced officially by comparatively obscure Shinto deities. . . . The people of the neighboring countryside often call the mountain by the name of Sekison-san.[2]

From the late seventeenth century on, Ōyama flourished as a popular pilgrimage site dedicated to the esoteric Buddhist Wisdom King Fudō Myōō and the *honji suijaku* deity Sekison Daigongen, a local rock deity understood as an emanation of Fudō Myōō or of the bodhisattva Kannon. Even in Chamberlain and Mason's time, its strong Buddhist flavor was still palpable despite the official disassociation of *kami* and Buddhas in the early Meiji period (1868–1912). This is evident in the continued use of the *honji suijaku* name for the deity on its summit—Sekison—as a designation for the site as a whole.

In the study of Japanese religion, the early modern period was once regarded as a time when Confucianism and Nativism flourished and Buddhism became degenerated, but in recent years this image has changed. Following the lead of recent Japanese scholarship, some Western scholars have reevaluated the role that Buddhism played in early modern culture and society while others have traced the development of Shinto outside Nativist circles.[3] As Herman Ooms notes, in addition to Neo-Confucianism the religious landscape of early modern Japan included "Shinto and Buddhism as well as eclectic and folk traditions."[4] This religious pluralism, Ooms points out, presents a dilemma for the researchers when trying to select a subject for their studies that will be representative of early modern religion as a whole: does one select a "representative" tradition, does one choose a panoramic view of all traditions, or does one trace a theme across multiple traditions? While many researchers—including recent revisionist scholars—have chosen the first option of selecting a representative tradition, Ooms argues that this obscures the plurality of the religious landscape.[5] Ooms's suggestion not to single out one tradition as representative is helpful in conveying the rich religious diversity of the period, but his characterization of the early modern Japanese landscape might convey the impression that Shinto and Buddhism somehow existed as clearly distinct traditions even before the Meiji era. Given the highly combinatory nature of premodern Japanese religions, this still raises methodological problems.

Focus on a particular region or locality provides an alternative solution to this dilemma. Michel Foucault has noted that the nineteenth century was preoccupied with history whereas in the twentieth century, space became an important paradigm, leading to ideological debates between "pious descendants of time and the determined inhabitants of space."[6] Edward Soja argues:

So unbudgeably [*sic*] hegemonic has been this historicism of theoretical consciousness that it has tended to occlude a comparable critical sensibility to the spatiality of social life, a practical theoretical consciousness that sees the lifeworld of being creatively located not only in the making of history but also in the construction of human geographies, the social production of space and the restless formation and reformation of geographical landscapes: social being actively emplaced in space *and* time in an explicitly historical *and* geographical contextualization.[7]

The parallel in the field of Japanese religions would be the juxtaposition of sectarian or tradition-based narratives, with narratives that focus on a particular region or site. In recent years, several scholarly works have appeared that are emplaced in specific local contexts. In her study of Japanese religion in the nineteenth century, Helen Hardacre, for example, chooses to examine a specific region—parts of the Musashi and Sagami Provinces—rather than a specific religious tradition. Alternatively, Nam-lin Hur discusses a specific site, the Buddhist temple Sensōji in Edo; and Sarah Thal closely analyzes the historical development of the cult of Mt. Konpira in Shikoku.[8] Recognizing the importance of place over sectarian affiliation or tradition in Japan, Allan Grapard has argued eloquently that we need more studies focused on a specific institutional complex:

First, Japanese religiosity is grounded in specific sites at which beliefs and practices were combined and transmitted exclusively within specific lineages. . . .

Second, Japanese religiosity is neither Shinto nor Buddhist nor sectarian but essentially combinative. . . .

Third, those combinative systems, which evolved in specific sites, were indissolubly linked, in their genesis as in their evolution, to social and economic structures and practices as well as concepts of legitimacy and power, all of which were interrelated and embodied in rituals and institutions marking those sites.[9]

Inspired by Grapard's three hypotheses, this monograph focuses on how the Ōyama cult, which transcended sectarian divisions and traditions, fit into the socioeconomic landscape of the Kantō-Tōkai region. The Ōyama cult is a particularly instructive case because of its highly combinatory nature as well as its role as an important pilgrimage center that affected the entire Kantō region. The word "cult" is used here not in the sense of a fanatical, unorthodox, spurious religious movement or "sect" but as a translation of the Japanese word *shinkō*, indicating the beliefs, practices, and infrastructure associated with a sacred site (e.g., a mountain) or a particular deity. This usage approximates more closely its Latin root, *cultus*, in the sense of worship, veneration, or observance of religious obligations.[10]

The Ōyama cult serves as a lens through which to view the early modern Japanese religious landscape. During the early modern period, Ōyama (literally, Big Mountain)—also known as Afurisan (Wild Moun-

tain or Rain Falling Mountain)[11]—developed into a flourishing pilgrimage site that was well known throughout Edo and its hinterland, the
Kantō region. The mountain had a wide appeal ranging from rainmaking
and business success to faith healing. Once its early modern institutional
structures were established through patronage from the Tokugawa *bakufu*, Ōyama was able to attract large numbers of pilgrims due to its proximity to the city of Edo, then one of the largest urban centers in the
world. Even though it was officially affiliated with the Kogi Shingon
School as a branch temple of Mt. Kōya—and served as an important
regional center of that school—its devotees included adherents of all
forms of Buddhism. Even at the mountain itself, several other Buddhist
schools were also involved in the management of the site, including
the Rinzai Zen school and Honzanha *shugendō*, a branch of *yamabushi*
(mountain ascetics) affiliated with the Tendai school. Ōyama's *oshi*
(former mountain ascetics and shrine priests serving as innkeepers
and proselytizers) disseminated the cult among one million devotees
throughout the Kantō region, leading to the development of tens of
thousands of Ōyama pilgrimage associations (*kō*). At the height of its
popularity in the early nineteenth century, Ōyama's mountain slopes
were covered with over twenty temples, multiple shrines, and about 160
inns in two temple towns (*monzenmachi*): Sakamoto Village and Minoge
Village. These numerous institutions controlled access to Ōyama's deities and its sacred sites—its waterfalls, caves, and peaks. This sacred
multiplex flourished over the course of the early modern period both
as a sectarian Shingon center as well as a non-sectarian pilgrimage destination until the early Meiji period when the new regime's policy disassociating *kami* and Buddhas (*shinbutsu bunri*) changed the Ōyama cult
into a Sect Shinto organization, Ōyama Keishin Kōsha (Association of
Reverence and Humility).

It is important to note that Ōyama was a regional site. It illustrates
the high degree of regionalization and localization of the premodern
Japanese religious landscape. Even today, the mountain has little name
recognition beyond the Kantō region, but it is a regional landmark that
serves as a favorite destination for hiking and school trips by residents
of the surrounding Kantō Plain. The mountain gained the status of a
regional landmark in the early modern period. Located only about 45
miles from the city of Edo, it is thought to have had about one million

parishioner households in the Kantō-Tōkai region at the height of its popularity in the eighteenth and nineteenth centuries.[12] The pilgrimage to Ōyama during the Sixth and Seventh Months was an integral part of the region's annual ritual calendar. The system of roads to Ōyama— though perhaps not quite on the level of the Tōkaidō, a major highway between Edo and Kyoto—shaped the cityscape of Edo and the landscapes of the Musashi and Sagami Provinces in significant ways. What were once the pilgrimage routes to Ōyama had become major regional arteries of transportation in Tokyo and Kanagawa Prefecture.

The Development of the Oshi System

In Japanese scholarship, the Ōyama cult falls under the rubric of *sangaku shinkō*, which can be translated as "mountain veneration" or "mountain cult." Despite the common association of mountain cults with the tradition of mountain asceticism (*shugendō*), this category also includes other elements, such as monastic Buddhism and pilgrimage. In fact, formal mountain asceticism was nearly eradicated at Ōyama in the 1660s and remained only a minor component of the Ōyama cult from then on. At that time, most of the mountain ascetics at Ōyama turned into *oshi*. To recognize them as a separate type of religious professional, their name, *oshi*, has been left in Japanese throughout this monograph, which devotes several chapters to their development and activities at Ōyama.

In early modern Japan, the *oshi* emerged as a major type of religious specialist that played an essential role in the popularization of mountain cults and pilgrimage sites. *Oshi* were present at sites such as Ōyama, the Ise Shrines, and Mt. Fuji and had their counterparts in Kōya *hijiri* and Zenkōji *shūto* and *tsumado*. Such religious professionals were found at many large-scale sacred sites and pilgrimage destinations across Japan. They were usually not celibate, ran inns to lodge pilgrims, and maintained parishes to which they distributed amulets and from which they collected regular donations. *Oshi* have sometimes been regarded as a subcategory of shrine priests or mountain ascetics. Occasionally, they have also been likened to peddlers. Although it is true that the *oshi* often originally derived from shrine priests and mountain ascetics, and were itinerant like peddlers, these descriptions do not aptly characterize the central role that the *oshi* played in the popularization of sacred sites in the early modern period. Even though they emerged at some sites, such as the Ise Shrines, before the early modern period, they grew into a distinct category of religious professionals at many regional sites, such as Ōyama, during the late seventeenth century.

One of the earliest detailed historical studies of the *oshi* appeared in Shinjō Tsunezō's work on the socioeconomic development of pilgrimage in Japan, *Shinkō Shaji sankei no shakai-keizai shiteki kenkyū*. Shinjō delineates the emergence of the *oshi* systems in premodern Japan, focusing on Kumano and Ise, where the earliest and the most extensive *oshi* systems developed. His findings—though embedded in a nostalgic narrative of a medieval golden age and early modern decline common in scholarship of his generation—apply in many ways to similar systems at other sacred sites and are useful to review.

According to Shinjō, the oldest *oshi* system developed at Kumano. From the early twelfth century, the Kumano *oshi* provided lodging and performed ritual prayers for pilgrims who were brought to their doors by mountain ascetics and Buddhist priests acting as pilgrimage guides (*sendatsu*). Through the *oshi-sendatsu* system, the pilgrimages to Kumano expanded to levels of society outside the aristocracy, even when pilgrimages to other shrines and temples were still largely limited to the nobility.[13] Shinjō argues that in the Kamakura period, the *oshi*'s patrons began to include not just aristocrats but also warriors. At first the bond between an *oshi* and a pilgrim was only temporary and limited to the duration of the pilgrimage, but eventually deeper ties developed whereby pilgrims from a specific warrior conglomerate became regular patrons (*dan'otsu* or *danna*) of a specific *oshi*. These patrons came from diverse geographic regions, including Tōtōmi, Musashi, Dewa, and Kai Provinces. By the late fourteenth century, the *oshi*'s patrons included kin groups from the wealthy peasantry from the provinces around the capital, where the peasantry's standard of living was improving markedly. Around 1400, the *oshi* served patrons from the most distant regions of Japan, including northeastern Honshū and the southern tip of Kyūshū. As the number of patrons from among the peasantry increased in the mid-fifteenth century, the *oshi* began to shift their attention away from the kin groups to the village unit, which began to emerge in the late medieval period.[14] Perhaps this clear shift in patron constituencies is partially illusory due to selective source materials. The hypothesis that the circle of patrons of religious institutions gradually widened from aristocrats in ancient Japan to warriors in the early medieval period, and to the peasantry and merchant class in the middle and late medieval and early modern periods, has been questioned by recent scholarship.[15] Nevertheless, evidence suggests that gradually the *oshi* came to rely on merchant and peasant patrons to a much greater degree than they had initially.

In the Kamakura and Muromachi periods, *oshi* systems also developed at the Ise Shrines, the Matsuo Shrine, the Mishima Shrine, Mt. Fuji, and at Hakusan. At the Ise Shrines, the *onshi* developed from the large number of low-ranking shrine priests who needed to supplement their income by providing accommodation for pilgrims. The system began at the Outer Ise Shrine in the early Kamakura period based on aristocratic and warrior patrons, but it did not start to flourish until the late Kamakura period when patronage expanded to whole warrior conglomerates. The Ise Shrines were able to forge ties with warriors in eastern Japan through the shrines' extensive land holdings there. It was primarily the *onshi* who spread the Ise cult in these areas. In contrast to the Kumano *oshi*, the Ise *onshi* tended to deal with their patrons directly without the *sendatsu* acting as middlemen. Once the patrons extended out to peasant villages by the early sixteenth century, the *onshi* relied on village elders as middlemen in order to maintain their ties. These patrons collectively made up "parishes," which the Ise *onshi* considered property that could be passed down from generation to generation or even sold. The same practice has also been documented at Kumano, sporadically in the Kamakura period and more frequently in the Muromachi period. Throughout the sixteenth century, the Ise *onshi* also kept careful records of their parish rounds, detailing their journeys and listing patrons' names. On their rounds of patron households, the Ise *onshi* not only administered purification rituals and distribute amulets but also collected funds and distributed small trinkets, tea, and local souvenirs. The records also show regional differences in the composition of parishes: some consisted primarily of warriors and wealthy peasants whereas others comprised large numbers of ordinary peasants.[16]

In the early modern period, the *oshi* at Kumano declined in number because the Kumano *sendatsu*, on whose mediation the *oshi* relied, virtually disappeared by the mid-eighteenth century. However, the Ise *onshi* prospered since they had more direct, personal contact with their patrons. By the 1590s, 145 *onshi* operated inns at the Outer Ise Shrine. In

order to quell the fierce competition among the *onshi*, the *bakufu*'s Tōtōmi Province office, near the Outer Shrines, regulated the interactions
of the Ise *onshi*, recognizing parishes as hereditary possessions of the
onshi and the household (*ie*) as the basic unit of a parish. The Ise *onshi*
system expanded until the mid-eighteenth century but then declined into
the mid-nineteenth century. In 1738, the number of *onshi* at the Outer Ise
Shrine peaked at 592 but fell to 370 in 1832. Similarly, the number of *onshi*
at the Inner Ise Shrine reached 271 in 1777 but dropped to 181 by 1866.[17]

Shinjō concludes that the interactions of the Ise *onshi* with their
parishioners became increasingly mercantile, with the *onshi* acting more
as peddlers than religious professionals, and that their numerical decline
indicates the decreasing religious importance of the profession.[18] However, Shinjō's pejorative association of *oshi* with peddlers reflects not
so much an actual degeneration as it does the scholarly inclinations of
his generation as well as the prejudices and suspicions of the sedentary
population toward vagrants, mendicants, itinerant religious professionals, and other marginals; and this is commonly reflected in the historical
sources.[19]

The mercantile activities of the *oshi* were not necessarily linked to a
degeneration of the profession but were linked to their religious functions and helped them reaffirm their social networks. In the late seventeenth century, the German physician Engelbert Kaempfer wrote of the
interactions between pilgrims and the Ise *onshi*—or, as he called them,
negi or *kannushi* (shrine priests)—observing that the *onshi* served both as
innkeepers and guides for pilgrims at Ise and maintained customary
ties with their patrons in their territories by distributing amulets and
small trinkets in exchange for annual donations. The more prestigious
the recipient of the talisman, the larger his donation; but in return,
the recipient would also receive more elaborate trinkets.[20] Based on
Kaempfer's description and parallel evidence from Ōyama, the distribution of trinkets emerges in a different light. The distribution of trinkets
and small gifts went hand-in-hand with the dissemination of amulets
and the collection of donations. The practice of distributing gifts is
therefore not indicative of the *oshi*'s degeneration into a mere peddler
without religious functions. The data from Ōyama further suggest that
a parallel numerical decline of the *oshi* was caused by the increasing
formalization of the profession, which narrowed the pool of those

eligible for the title. Even though the Ōyama *oshi* had their roots in the medieval period, they only fully emerged as a distinct category of religious professionals in the early modern period.

The Ancient and Medieval Periods

One reason to focus on Ōyama's early modern history, rather than its ancient or medieval history, is the lack of source materials about these earlier periods and, conversely, the relative abundance of material on the site from the early modern period. Prior to the early modern period there is very little documentation of the actual conditions of the community on Ōyama, a fact that was already bemoaned by Sudō Shigeo (1826–1886), the Nativist author of the *Afurijinja kodenkō* (A treatise on the old legends of the Afuri Shrine, 1849). He wrote about medieval Ōyama: "Because there are no official records from that time, hardly anything is known except for legends told by the elders."[21] The kind of artifacts and documents that survived from earlier periods are limited to a few archeological finds, legends concerning the founding of the temple on the mountain slope, and sporadic mention of contact with the imperial court and military leaders in the Kantō region.

As a result, very little is known about Ōyama in the ancient period. Excavations on Ōyama's summit in 1879 and 1960 indicate that the site was indeed a center of worship dating back to antiquity. In addition to finding Jōmon pottery, the archeological surveys unearthed several other artifacts, the oldest of which dated back to the ninth century.[22] Medieval legends of the founding of Ōyama's Buddhist institutions, particularly those in the *Ōyamadera engi* (The founding legend of Ōyamadera),[23] claim that the Buddhist monk Rōben (689–773), the second patriarch of Kegon Buddhism in Japan and a founder of the central state-sponsored temple Tōdaiji in Nara, established a Buddhist temple at Ōyama in 755 when he returned to Sagami, the province of his birth. Rōben is said to have chosen Ōyama because it was known as one of the mysterious places in the region. Through his close connection with the imperial court, Rōben was supposedly granted funds from Sagami, Awa, and Kazusa Provinces to support the newly founded Buddhist temple.[24] The historicity of this legend is questionable. Even if we assume that a Buddhist temple was founded on Ōyama in the late eighth century, it could hardly have been more than one of many remote sacred places in the distant provinces from the perspective of the imperial court in Kyoto. Legend has it that other famous monks also visited Ōyama including Kōzō, a disciple of Gyōki (668–749); Kūkai (774–835), the founder of the Shingon school; and Annen (841–890s), a famous Tendai monk.[25] These claims probably also lack historicity and were merely attempts to convey pedigree on the site. However, the *Ōyamadera engi's* assertion that the shrines on the summit were built in 890 under Emperor Uda (r. 887–897) is at least corroborated by the *Engi shiki*, compiled under Uda's successor Emperor Daigo (r. 897–930), which does indeed list the Afuri Shrine, the principal shrine on Ōyama's summit, as one of twelve minor provincial shrines in Sagami Province.[26] Unfortunately, this source contains no details about the institutional dimensions of the site.

Once the Kantō Plain became the seat of government for the new military regime during the Kamakura period, Ōyama began to appear more frequently in historical documents. Throughout the medieval period, the religious at Ōyama aligned themselves with local warlords who controlled the region, receiving their patronage and land in exchange for military service and ritual assistance. The warlords relied on the military support of local warriors and *yamabushi* from Ōyama, who were able to provide valuable intelligence during military conflicts because of their familiarity with the local terrain. Naturally, the warlords also sought divine assistance through Ōyama's ritualists, who used their prayers and rites to afford sacred protection to the petitioners and victory in war.

Concretely, Ōyama's importance began to rise with the establishment of the Kamakura *bakufu* in the east. Previously a mere distant, provincial site, Ōyama suddenly gained national importance through its proximity to the military headquarters in Kamakura, which sought the sacred assistance of Ōyama's ritualists. In 1184, Ōyamadera, the main temple, was awarded a small village in its foothills by Minamoto no Yoritomo, who became shogun in 1192. In return, according to the medieval *Azuma kagami*, monks from Ōyamadera gave the shogunate their ritual support by participating in memorial rites for Retired Emperor Go-Shirakawa, in 1192 and 1193, and by reciting the *Daihannyakyō* (Great Wisdom Sūtra) to ensure safe childbirth for Yoritomo's wife, Masako, in 1192.[27]

From at least around this time, Ōyama was associated with the Shingon school, specifically the Shingon Ritsu school. One factor that contributed to Ōyama's rise in stature during the Kamakura period was the work of the Shingon Ritsu monk Kenjō (?–1296), popularly known as Gangyō Shōnin. Gangyō received the patronage of the Hōjō, who acted as regents to the shogun in Kamakura, and their patronage enabled Gangyō to commission esoteric rituals at Ōyama. He eventually revitalized Ōyama and installed a large iron statue of the Buddhist deity Fudō as the temple's main image of worship.[28] In his efforts to spread faith in Ōyama's Fudō and, thus, to raise funds for the reconstruction of the site, Gangyō might have propagated, if not created, the legends of the founding of the temple described in the *Ōyamadera engi*, first mentioned in a document around 1300. Gangyō was in many ways a typical representative of Kamakura-period Ritsu monks, who were particularly active in raising funds for the reconstruction of Buddhist temples. Since Ritsu monks were particularly known for their strict observance of the Buddhist precepts, they had the ethical credibility to solicit donations.[29] Gangyō's personal emphasis on monastic orthodoxy also explains why a figure such as Rōben, an eminent eighth-century Kegon monk closely associated with Tōdaiji and thus the Buddhist orthodoxy in Nara, plays such a central role in the founding legends of the temple. Gangyō was not the only Shingon Ritsu cleric interested in Ōyama and the story of its foundation. In 1307, another Shingon Ritsu cleric, Ken'a (1261–1338), who was highly active in neighboring Musashi Province, made a pilgrimage to Ōyama and viewed a copy of the *Ōyamadera engi*.[30] Ken'a and his circle of students had a strong interest Ryōbu Shinto associated with the Ise Shrines and *kami* matters in general.[31] Hence the founding legend of a combinatory multiplex like Ōyama might have been of great interest to him.

Several decades later, the Ashikaga shogunate also sought Ōyama's allegiance. Even though the military government was based in Kyoto, Ōyama was important to the Ashikaga because they also maintained an eastern outpost in Kamakura not far from Ōyama. Ashikaga no Takauji rewarded a local strongman, Satō Chūmu, for his service in battle by making him *bettō* (head administrator) of Ōyama in 1350, a testimony to Ōyama's growing importance as a religious institution in the region. He also donated to the temple a small piece of land in the foothills in return for pacification prayers conducted by Ōyamadera in 1352 during the Ashikaga's struggle to maintain control over the Kantō region. Between 1350 and 1422, the Ashikaga repeatedly turned to Ōyamadera to commission pacification prayers and prayers for victory in battle. In return, they rewarded the temple with land, monetary donations, and resources for construction projects. In 1490, the Ashikaga were the first to extend their rule of law over the Ōyamadera's homestead when they admonished the residents of the temple and the villages at the foot of the mountain to obey the law.[32] However, they made no attempt to regulate the affairs of the temple in as concrete detail as the Tokugawa would about two hundred years later.

From 1530 to 1590, Ōyama aligned itself with the Later Hōjō clan, based in Odawara, southwest from Ōyama, who had gradually managed to take control of the Kantō region, beginning with Izu, Sagami, and Musashi and eventually also large parts of Kōzuke, Shimotsuke, and Shimōsa. Like the Ashikaga, the Odawara Hōjō supported construction projects and donated land to the temple complex. In return, they counted on Ōyama's ritual and military support during the mid-sixteenth century, commissioning prayers for military success and relying on *yamabushi* from Ōyama to act as scouts in battle.[33] Ōyama also became involved in the wars that preceded the unification of Japan under the Tokugawa. The Hōjō felt increasing pressure from Toyotomi Hideyoshi and Tokugawa Ieyasu after the former issued an edict demanding that the Hōjō submit to his authority as his vassals. To defend their autonomy, the Hōjō mobilized capable villagers in Sagami and in southern Musashi and Izu Provinces, threatening those who failed to comply with capital punishment and promising rich rewards for loyal service.[34] When Hideyoshi raised his forces and attacked the Hōjō in 1589, Ōyama became embroiled in the struggle. As the Hōjō fought their last battles against Hideyoshi, from 1589 to 1590, forces from Ōyama fought on the side of the losing Hōjō.

After his victory, Hideyoshi issued orders to curb the military activities of Ōyama's anchorites[35] and asserted his authority over the land by commissioning cadastral surveys in the 1590s. Ōyama and its foothill villages were surveyed between 1591 and 1593, providing us the first concrete image of the mountain: Ōyama's slopes were shared by several large temples, multiple hermitages of *yamabushi* as well as the houses of a shrine priest, a shrine carpenter, and several laymen who may have been Ōyama's first *oshi*—innkeepers catering to pilgrims.[36] The site was administered by a *yamabushi* of warrior background who acted as *bettō* and resided at a temple called Godaiin Hachidaibō.[37]

Thus it is only with the coming of the Tokugawa to the Kantō region in the 1590s that much more tangible evidence of the institutional structures of Ōyama and its cult is extant, although much information is still missing even for this later period. For example, it is regrettable that detailed sources containing the concrete experiences of pilgrims are rather limited because hardly anyone kept narrative records of the relatively short pilgrimage to the mountain.

The Early Modern Transformation

Emplacing Ōyama in the early modern Kantō region requires, in Clifford Geertz's parlance, a "thick description" of its regional and local contexts. This is made possible by the ready availability of documents from the early modern period. This study is largely based on regional and local sources—such as regional gazetteers, document collections compiled by contemporary municipal archives, and previously unpublished documents in private collections. This monograph is also greatly indebted to the work of local Japanese historians. With the rise of interest in local history since the 1970s and subsequent surveys of available documents in the 1980s, scholarship on the early modern Ōyama cult has grown in volume and in scope during the past few years. Despite the virtual absence of Western scholarship on the site, Japanese scholars have recognized the importance of Ōyama in the early modern Kantō region. Tamamuro Fumio has divided Japanese publications on the Ōyama cult into three large categories: one, the organization of Ōyama's *oshi* (innkeeper-proselytizers) and their relationship with their parishes; two, pilgrimage routes to Ōyama; and three, the development of the Ōyama cult in the Meiji period.[38] In order to provide a comprehensive picture of the cult in the culture of early modern Kantō region, this monograph not only expands on these three aspects in Chapters 3, 5, and 7, respectively, but also adds chapters on Ōyama's sacred geography, its role as a Shingon institution, the ritual activities associated with the pilgrimage cult, and the development of the legends about its deities. The cult of Ōyama defies easy definition because it cuts across the lines of demarcation between religious traditions and specific schools of Buddhism. Therefore, this study focuses on thematic elements of the cult as they developed over the course of the early modern period.

Chapter 1 introduces Ōyama's sacred geography to provide a spatial, material, and symbolic context for the Ōyama cult and its institutions. The classical Eliadian definition of sacred space tends to locate sacrality in constant physical and symbolic features of a site, but Ōyama serves as an example of a sacred place (rather than merely an abstract space) whose significance was assigned in various, sometimes competing, ways that shifted along with institutional and historical changes. The chapter traces Ōyama's transformation from a medieval *yamabushi* site that was understood as an earthly manifestation of Maitreya's Tuṣita Heaven into a complex Shingon academy and popular pilgrimage site in the early modern period.

Chapters 2 and 3 examine Ōyama's institutional complexities. A typical premodern cultic site, Ōyama presented an integrated mixture of traditions that were inseparable but not always entirely harmonious. Ōyama comprised Buddhist, Shinto, *yamabushi*, and *oshi* institutions of various sectarian affiliations. Chapter 2 focuses on the line of seventeen abbots who managed the mountain during the early modern period. This chapter discusses the ways in which the Shingon Buddhist clergy assumed control over Ōyama, maintained its hold over this sacred site, and simultaneously turned it into a major regional Kogi Shingon academy. As a regional Shingon academy that was necessary to train clerics for the growing number of temples established by the temple registration system of early modern Japan, Ōyama was able to become a leader in a regional network of Kogi Shingon temples even though it had few branch temples of its own. As a sacred site, Ōyama was controlled institutionally and ritually by the Shingon clergy, whose twenty-plus subtemples on the mountain cooperated in the administration of the site, led by the abbot of Hachidaibō, its main Shingon temple. Ōyama's Shingon institutions therefore had dual functions that alternately reinforced and stood at odds with each other. The growing popularity of the site and the influx of pilgrims enhanced the Shingon temples' wealth but also created rifts among them. These factors contributed to the gradual weakening of the Hachidaibō abbots' control over the site.

Chapter 3 traces the development of the *oshi* system at Ōyama. In the first half of the seventeenth century, the *oshi*, managed large parishes of devotees throughout the Kantō region. By the nineteenth century, about 160 *oshi* were administering one million parish households across the entire Kantō-Tōkai region with an average of about 6,000 households per *oshi*. Some of the most powerful *oshi* had as many as 12,000 parishioner families. These parishes were different from those of Buddhist temples in the temple registration system, which might ideally have had one hundred to a thousand parish households with obligatory ties to the temple through the performance of funerary and memorial rites. Instead of providing funerary rites, *oshi* distributed amulets and collected yearly donations from their parishioners, housing them in inns at Ōyama when they came on pilgrimage. In order to lessen competition from inns in nearby villages, Ōyama's *oshi* were specially licensed by the local Shingon clergy at Ōyama, but in the early nineteenth century many *oshi* began to seek additional Shinto licenses from the Shirakawa house, a sacerdotal lineage associated with the imperial court in Kyoto. These Shirakawa licenses, together with a growing interest in national learning among the *oshi*, became important factors in the disassociation of *kami* and Buddhas in the Meiji period.

The next two chapters examine the development of the pilgrimage to Ōyama. Chapter 4 explores how Ōyama's ritual specialists, clergy and the *oshi*, jointly managed the pilgrimage cult, which became centered on the summer festival: The clergy officiated at rituals within the Buddhist precinct, i.e., Ōyama's principal cultic sites, whereas the *oshi* lodged pilgrims, acted as intermediaries between pilgrims and clerics, and maintained active relationships with their parishioners through parish rounds to distribute amulets and collect first-fruit donations. By the early nineteenth century, Ōyama had become a highly complex and active site whose influence extended across the entire Kantō region. The Ōyama cult had successfully adapted its economy from one based primarily on state patronage during the medieval period to one based on the donations from a broad social base—its parishioners in villages and urban areas.

Chapter 5 discusses the impact of the Ōyama cult on the Kantō region as a popular pilgrimage destination. During the early modern period, some lengthy pilgrimages, such as mass pilgrimages to the Ise Shrines or solitary pilgrimages by impoverished travelers around the island of Shikoku, had a reputation for running counter to the orderly social ideals of the *bakufu*—they represented in some respects what Victor Turner termed an antistructure to everyday life. Pilgrimages to Ōyama, however, reinforced rather than undermined social structures. The pilgrimage shaped the regional identity and inspired numerous woodblock prints, popular travel guides, and other works describing the ritual calendar of Edo residents and travel in the Kantō-Tōkai region. Overland and sea-borne pilgrimage routes developed that linked Ōyama to the Kantō region. Since pilgrims from Edo took only about one week to complete the pilgrimage, and pilgrims from the northeastern provinces in the Kantō took only about twice as long, the *bakufu* posed little opposition to the pilgrimage. Moreover, most pilgrims traveled in confraternities based in rural villages or urban neighborhoods, or organized around professional groups or businesses. Such pilgrims did not abscond from their communities; instead, they were usually dispatched as annual representatives. Confraternity members pooled their funds to finance the pilgrimage, and therefore the pilgrims were not a burden on communities along the route but fueled the regional economy.

Chapter 6 examines imaginary representations of the mountain. Changing and competing legends concerning Ōyama's pantheon developed in conjunction with institutional and geographic changes at Ōyama. This chapter covers a variety of texts produced by religious professionals at Ōyama. This intertextual universe of competing narratives created and copied by the Buddhist clergy and *oshi* reflects the underlying tensions and complexities at the site. The *Ōyamadera engi*, whose origins lie in the medieval period, depicts a typical *yamabushi* pantheon centering around the fierce Buddhist Wisdom King Fudō Myōō and was later incorporated into early modern versions of Ōyama's pantheon promoted by the Shingon clergy. However, the Shingon clergy also produced new legends on the one hand linking Ōyama's deities to native deities featured in the ancient national chronicles and, on the other, embedding them in Shingon's Ryōbu Shinto theories, which identified all deities with the cosmic Buddha Dainichi. With the influx of Shirakawa Shinto into Ōyama beginning in the late eighteenth century, new legends emerged aimed at linking a particular sacerdotal lineage with the ancient imperial court and its mythology. Through this last process, Ōyama's sacred rock deity Sekison, which had been identified with Fudō in the medieval period and later with Kannon, gained an increasingly distinct identity as a native deity. Last but not least, the presence of Nativists in the mid-nineteenth century brought about an unprecedented shift away from earlier models of layering and accretion toward attempts to recover Ōyama's "original" Shinto deities before the arrival of Buddhism, foreshadowing the tensions that led to the disassociation of *kami* and Buddhas in the early Meiji period.

The final chapter examines an important turning point in Ōyama's history: the disassociation of *kami* and Buddhas and Ōyama's transformation into a Sect Shinto organization during the first two decades of the Meiji period. During this period Ōyama changed fundamentally—in its sacred geography, in its physical layout and institutional structures, in the nature of its deities, and in its rituals. Set in motion through legislation issued by the new Meiji regime and implemented through local initiatives, Ōyama's early Meiji transformation changed the mountain from a thoroughly combinatory complex into a dual site with distinct Shinto and Buddhist spheres. Even though the Meiji regime provided the legal basis for the changes, their implementation was determined by local forces, which were even able to adapt orders that fundamentally challenged the economic basis of the Ōyama cult, such as the prohibition of *oshi* in 1871. Because of local efforts, Ōyama's new institutions and rituals were partially indebted to structures that had been developed during the early modern period while the clear disassociation of *kami* and Buddhas as well as attempts to standardize the organization of believers throughout the Kantō region changed the basic nature of the Ōyama cult.

The Ōyama cult illustrates that location or place, an aspect of a religious site that is often ignored, constitutes a central force in shaping religion. Premodern Japanese religion, like Japanese society in general, was largely emplaced in specific locales and regions. As a pilgrimage site, Ōyama was consciously constructed as a remote place far from human habitation; in fact, it was a place marked by its proximity to a major urban center and by great accessibility—pilgrims visiting the mountain, Ōyama's innkeepers traveling through the region to collect donations and distribute amulets, and Shingon clerics from temples in the region training at Ōyama in order to return to their home temples after the completion of their training period. In its ordinariness, the

Ōyama cult occupied a middle ground that was neither at the center of political power nor at the margins of society. The cultic site that initially survived on patronage by the *bakufu* came to depend almost exclusively on the donations' broad social base—villagers, townspeople, and low-ranking officials. The Ōyama cult was not used by the *bakufu* to mobilize human resources or to suppress resistance to the regime, but neither was it a movement to subvert the existing social order. The cult flourished precisely because it was based on and upheld the social structures that shaped village and urban life. Therefore, it can serve as a useful case study of mainstream early modern religion and society.

ONE

From a Mountain Retreat
to a Pilgrimage Center

This chapter traces the transfigurations of Ōyama's spatial symbolisms and practices from the medieval through the early modern periods and links them with the political dynamics involved in the appropriation of the terrain. The medieval Ōyama cult combined the cults of Maitreya and Fudō, according to which Ōyama was both a representation of Maitreya's Tuṣita Heaven and simultaneously the embodiment and residence of Fudō. The distinction between *yamabushi* and Buddhist monks was not clearly delineated as both trained and lived as anchorites on Ōyama's slopes and in caves and hermitages at the foot of the mountain. In the early modern period, however, this landscape became more clearly compartmentalized, reflecting the new regime's penchant for clear social hierarchies. Married mountain ascetics were classified as *yamabushi* and were forced to settle at the foot of the mountain, while celibate Shingon clerics were cast as "pure monks." The latter continued to reside on the mountain slope and took over the management of the major cultic sites. The most sacred area, the uninhabited land around the summit, became Ōyama's major pilgrimage attraction. The location of its major cultic sites—the Fudō Hall and a waterfall on the central slope, as well as the shrines to Sekison on the summit—may not have changed dramatically over the centuries, but the ways in which the landscape was inhabited, traversed, and interpreted did.

Sacred Mountains in Japan

Mountains have been venerated for various reasons throughout Japanese history. They appear in the ancient national chronicles, the *Kojiki* (712) and the *Nihongi* (720), as places where heavenly divinities (*kami*) descended to earth, where human beings could encounter supernatural beings, and where sovereigns went to view their land. In the medieval *engi* literature on sacred sites, Buddhist deities were often said to have manifested themselves on mountain peaks that had purportedly flown from India or China to Japan.

Writing from a folklorist's perspective, Hori Ichirō delineates three basic types of mountain cults in Japan. One is the veneration of volcanoes and other conically shaped mountains. Renowned for their awesome destructive as well as creative powers, such mountains were regarded as the residence or even the embodiment of the divine. In some cases, they even took the place of man-made shrine buildings as the object of worship on the mountain side. Often fishermen prayed to mountain deities to grant them a bountiful catch. The second type of mountain cult is the veneration of mountains as watersheds and sources of water. The mountain deity (*yama no kami*) was believed to descend to the rice paddies in the spring and become the nurturing deity of the field (*ta no kami*) until the fall. This reflects the central role that mountains played in an agricultural society that was heavily dependent on a steady water supply for rice cultivation in paddy fields. The third type casts mountains as the realm of spirits and the dead, reflecting the function of mountains as burial grounds and the existence of ancient hill-shaped tombs (*kofun*). As an extension of the belief that mountains were the abode of divinities, spirits, and the dead, mountains were regarded as portals to other worlds or as an *axis mundi*, the embodiment of the entire universe like the mythical Buddhist peak Mt. Sumeru.[1]

In many respects, Ōyama is the embodiment of a sacred mountain. The mountain has a conical shape, is the source of a river, and has been regarded as the realm of the dead. It belongs to a mountain range on the southeastern edge of the Kantō Plain, near what is now Tokyo (see Fig. 1.1). At 1,246 meters, it is not exceptionally tall, but, bordering a coastal plain, it rises steeply from sea level between the ocean of Sagami Bay to the south and the Tanzawa Mountain Range to the north.

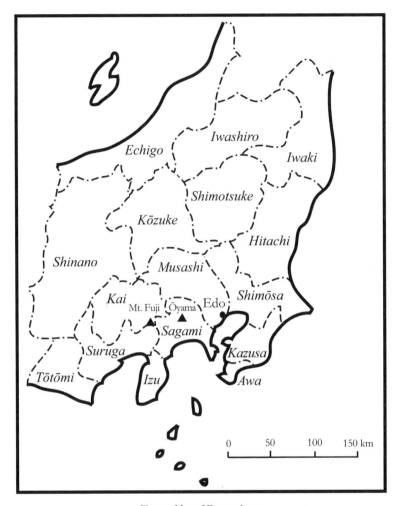

Fig. 1.1 Map of Eastern Japan

The *Sōyō Ōyama fu* (A genealogy of Sagami Ōyama; 1792) contains a typically hyperbolic description that makes this mountain appear much more majestic than its actual height would suggest:

On the eastern road in Japan, there is a tall mountain . . . called Ōyama. It is tall and steep. To the east, one sees the sea. To the west, many desolate mountains pile up. Ōyama is veiled in clouds and mist. There is no path through the forests and woods. Its circumference is many scores. It is over 100 quadrillion feet tall. The mountain holds the land in the four directions in its grip. On its seven sides, there are impenetrable mountain forests. Not even the song of a single bird breaks the complete silence on the summit. In the front flows a great river called Ōfusagi River. The summit is very steep and cragged, and its rocky cliffs are desolate. Its valleys are deep, and there are many strange rocks. Grass and trees grow abundantly. The heavens are covered in mist and the ground is overgrown with vegetation. The cries of animals ring out constantly so that people of all walks of life are in awe of it. Many people have climbed it to pray for a miracle.[2]

Ōyama appears as an archetypal sacred mountain, whose majesty dominates the landscape, functioning as an *axis mundi*. Stock descriptions of the mountain, like the one in the *Sōshū Ōyama fu*, usually comment on its rugged steepness, dense forests, and tranquil summit veiled in clouds, a sign of its other-worldliness. However, as William Powell notes, though sacred mountains are often depicted as timeless and share archetypal features, each mountain exists in its socio-cultural context, which may give rise to multiple, even competing, discourses about its sacred space.[3] This is an aspect that is largely absent from Hori's work on sacred mountains. His notions of the sacrality of mountains, particularly his discussion of the mountain as an *axis mundi*, are clearly indebted to Eliadian phenomelogical notions of sacred space.[4] As insightful as Hori's observations on mountain veneration in Japan are, they convey abstract aspects of such cults rather than emplacing them in actual locally specific socio-historical contexts.

To merely state that Ōyama is an archetypal sacred mountain because it has the topographical marks of a sacred mountain is to imply that its spatial practices are somehow inherent to its topography and emerged organically from the beliefs of the inhabitants of its territory and surrounding areas. Such a limited analysis veils how the meanings of its sacred space were produced by a variety of social forces. Throughout its history, Ōyama was, in Michel Foucault's parlance, a "heterotopia." Foucault defines heterotopias as "real places . . . which are something like counter-sites, a kind of effectively enacted utopia in which the real sites, all the other real sites that can be found within the culture, are simultaneously represented, contested, and inverted. Places that are outside of all places, even though it may be possible to indicate their location in reality."[5] As Foucault points out, heterotopias are not necessarily static but their meanings are often adapted by societies to accommodate historical changes.[6]

Henri Lefebvre's notions of the construction of space and the political motivation behind this process are useful for decoding Ōyama's sacred territory. According to Lefebvre, religious spaces are representational spaces charged with potent symbolism that speak to the imagination and can be used by its inhabitants to form "more or less coherent systems of non-verbal symbols and signs."[7] Religious space displays a complex intertwining of religious and political dynamics. Religious specialists in particular make use of what Lefebvre calls "absolute space" and gain legitimization and political authority in the process of consecrating a sacred space in imitation of a utopian ideal. Meanwhile, even though places regarded as sacred are often selected based on inherent natural features, once they have been identified and consecrated those features are often obliterated.[8] However, Lefebvre assumes a juxtaposition of religious specialists aligned with political powers and the populace at large that is dominated by political and religious forces. In contrast, in the case of early modern Ōyama, struggles over spatial practices, though often backed or prohibited by political authorities, mostly occurred between different types of religious specialists.

Since the medieval period, Ōyama has been marked with boundaries between pure and impure space, and between the mundane village, the ritual training ground, and the most sacred inner sanctum. While the sacred site has incorporated physical features such as rocks, caves, and waterfalls, its spatial practices were not just determined by the topography itself. Despite the continuities in its topography, the meanings of its imagined and symbolic boundaries have changed throughout its history, reflecting its changing religious institutions and the impact of political forces from local to national levels. Ōyama shifted from an otherworldly paradise that was the training ground of recluses and mountain ascetics to a popular pilgrimage center and sectarian training center.

Allan Grapard has argued that from the medieval to the early modern period a shift occurred from "geognosis," mystical, esoteric spatial knowledge that served soteriological purposes, to "geopiety," protosecular practices and beliefs directed toward space. Whereas geognosis was available only to trained religious specialists and educated elites, the general populace engaged in geopiety. This trend, Grapard argues, became particularly pronounced in the early modern period.[9] However, at Ōyama this shift was not so much from soteriological knowledge to protosecular practices as from an emphasis on soteriological practices toward one on devotional practices and sectarian concerns. The change was not one that grew spontaneously out of popular religious practices but was deliberately promoted by Ōyama's religious specialists due to changes in the early modern religious landscape.

A Medieval Mountain Retreat

The most complete description of Ōyama in the Muromachi period—albeit idealized and embellished with Chinese and Japanese aesthetic conventions—is provided by the poet-monk Shinkei in his *Oi no kurigoto*, written between 1471 and 1475 during his retirement in the foothills of Ōyama. A refuge from the destruction and turmoil of the Ōnin War that had spread to the eastern provinces, Ōyama represented to Shinkei an idyllic, peaceful retreat. Drawing on well-known Chinese poetic images, he likened Ōyama to the Chinese mountain Lu-shan, visited by the famous poet Bo Juyi during his exile, and to Penglai, the realm of Daoist immortals. As a temporary visitor at a hermitage on the fringes of Ōyama, Shinkei indicated little of the spiritual significance Ōyama had for the resident mountain ascetics. His allusions to Ōyama's temples and shrines are couched in poetic imagery. He alludes to the rainmaking deities on Ōyama's summit veiled in mist and the dragon deity on its slope only in passing. Reminiscent of Chinese literati-style ink paintings of mountain landscapes that dwarf a human figure, Shinkei's account captures Ōyama as a pristine wilderness with a tumbling river and dense cedar and pine forests on its slopes that overlooked the Tanzawa Mountains in the west and the Kantō Plain in the east. In an age fraught with warfare and destruction, Ōyama represented a paradisiacal haven where a lonely recluse could find solace. The image of Ōyama as a place of salvation from the misery of the world is pervasive in Shinkei's account.[10]

Military turmoil, natural disasters, and socio-political changes destroyed many historical documents, leading to the paucity of historically reliable sources from Ōyama's ancient and medieval past. When dealing with a site of mountain asceticism, the researcher is faced with an additional impediment. As Grapard has noted, the *shugendō* tradition was largely esoteric and left few documents regarding its doctrines.[11] Hence it is difficult to reconstruct the exact layout and meaning of many medieval *shugendō* sites. Given the lack of concrete historical documents, scholars have turned to medieval religious texts that were used for proselytization and often contained mythical, symbolic descriptions of the site. For example, Ian Reader and George Tanabe argue that despite its lack of historicity and propagational purposes, *engi* literature presents a valuable resource as "mythistory," claiming the sacred powers of places and icons, and hence take a central place in the development of pilgrimage cults.[12] Similarly, Max Moerman argues that the *engi* "are as much spatial as historical narratives. They are territorial legends, genealogies of places, and, as such, are concerned with locality and displacement."[13] Hence, they tend to contain detailed information about the symbolic meanings of places.

This applies very directly to the *Ōyamadera engi*, which may have only limited historical veracity and reflects more about the religious culture and spatial practices at the time of its composition (probably the late Kamakura period) than about the period in which it is set (the mid-eighth century). There are two basic versions of the *Ōyamadera engi*, one in *kanbun*, the Japanese hybrid form of literary Chinese, and the other, an illustrated version in the vernacular. The earliest extant version of the former, which comes in a single scroll, dates from 1637, whereas the latter's two scrolls date from 1532. The exact origins of the texts and which of the two is the older are difficult determine, but the earliest reference to a one-scroll version of the *Ōyamadera engi* dates from 1307. Another text mentions a copy made by Emperor Go-Komatsu (r. 1393–1412; lived 1375–1432), but whether this claim was merely an effort to gain prestige rather than historical fact is unclear. The vernacular version from 1532 is the oldest text to survive to the present, but a one-scroll version was apparently lost during the tumultuous Keichō era (1596–1615).[14] Based on the few extant historical documents and several versions of the *Ōyamadera engi*, it is possible to create a tentative reconstruction of the site's physical and symbolic layout from the late thirteenth to the late sixteenth centuries.

The image of Ōyama as a distant and majestic retreat for hermits and mountain ascetics emerges in all versions of the *Ōyamadera engi*. The 1532 *Ōyamadera engi* describes the mountain nestled between the Sakai River to the west and the Tanzawa Mountain Range in the north as overlooking the Kantō Plain in the east and Sagami Bay in the south:

Isn't [Ōyama] truly the greatest mountain in Japan? . . . All views of this mountain are the most wonderful in the country. To the east, it allows a clear view of 10,000 villages. 3,000 worlds lie at its foot. To the south the expanse of the ocean is limitless. To the west, a great river flows from the Dragon Gate. To the north, one hundred mountains pile up to the sky. This sacred mountain cannot but be the Pure Land. In front of the Golden Hall, there are the four-sided corridor, the bell tower, the scripture storage hall, the three-storied pagoda, the shrine of the Ōyama Myōō, and various Buddha [halls]. The roofs of 49 temples and hermitages stand closely lined up. The bell of the practice of the three mysteries sounds continuously. The sound of votive water offerings (*aka*) has never stopped in the 90 days of summer. It is a place where one can enter the first stage of *samadhi* through meditation as well as concentrate on the contemplation of the One Principle. Before entering the study of scholastic learning, one works hard practicing the exoteric and esoteric teachings. It truly is a sacred place removed from worldly attachments and suffering.[15]

This late medieval text identifies the mountainscape as training ground for esoteric Buddhist practice and interprets it as a paradise on earth. The *kanbun* version of the *Ōyamadera engi*, extant as a copy from 1637, contains a similar description of the mountain:

Ōyama in Sagami on the Tōkaidō in the great country of Japan is the shield of the nation. . . . It is also said that [Ōyama] is the body of the Five Great Wisdom Kings. . . . The mountain has seven sides. Resembling an *uṣṇīṣa*, it symbolizes the entire body of the King of Esoteric Wisdom [*myōō*]. In the front it faces the blue ocean; in the back it passes into deep forest. On the left there are desolate ravines; on the right there are deep caves. In the center is an unusually dense forest. Mysterious cragged rocks and boulders litter the steep slope. Strange rocks and boulders lie in irregular patterns as if cut in pieces with a sword. It is as if the tall and pointy mountain had the 3,000 worlds at its feet and valleys large enough to swallow eight or nine misty clouds are on its chest. It is as if it held boundless surrounding plains clutched in its fist and from its two eyes sprang the Han River. Like Mt. Kunlun, it is veiled in mist and like Penglai, it is surrounded by swirling clouds. Sometimes, its jeweled pagodas and golden halls are lined up like stars. Sometimes, its heavenly palaces circle and drift slowly like fog. Spirits and ghosts come to this place uninhabited by humans. Noise does not penetrate the mountain. It is a place that is far removed. Immortals roam here and sages live here as recluses in caves.[16]

The 1637 version interprets the mountainscape in Buddhist terms and personifies the entire mountain as an embodiment of Fudō Myōō.

Again Ōyama, which is compared to famous Daoist sacred paradises, appears as an otherworldly, mysterious place inhabited by spirits and sages and far removed from the mundane world of ordinary humans.

Sacred Space in the *Ōyamadera engi*

In addition to a general description of the mountain, the *Ōyamadera engi* contains a legendary account of how the monk Rōben (689–773), the second patriarch of the Kegon school and scholar-monk, who was intimately involved in the founding of Tōdaiji in Nara, founded Ōyama's first Buddhist temple in 755 and spent three years in residence on the mountain. Although the historicity of this story is doubtful, it was widely accepted in the premodern period. The narrative of the *Ōyamadera engi* portrays the mountain as an earthly manifestation of Maitreya's Pure Land, promising the faithful, especially anchorites, instant salvation in this age of *mappō* (the latter days of the Buddhist law). In addition, the cult of Maitreya was interwoven with the cult of Fudō.

Many sacred sites in medieval Japan featured a Maitreya cult when the concept of *mappō* made many yearn for a better existence in a Buddhist paradise such as Amida's Western Pure Land or Maitreya's Tuṣita Heaven. At Kasagidera, which also centered on the cult of Maitreya, monks engaged in fundraising activities to supplement the income from their small land holdings and revitalize the temple in the Kamakura period. These fundraising monks promised their patrons rebirth in Tuṣita Heaven and predicted that the reconstructed temple and its images would last until Maitreya's distant descent in the future.[17] Likewise, throughout the medieval period, Ōyama had several small landholdings scattered through nearby villages in the area but not limited to the immediate foot of the mountain.[18] The estate was perhaps sufficient to support a small monastic community but not to fund large-scale reconstruction projects, which were necessary periodically to maintain the compound. For such projects, the temple had to rely on fundraising campaigns. When the temple complex was in disrepair in the late thirteenth century, Gangyō (?–1296), a Shingon Ritsu monk active in Sagami Province, reconstructed the temple complex and dedicated an iron sculpture of Fudō that became Ōyama's central image of worship.[19] The Ashikaga and the later Hōjō financed other reconstruction projects in 1432 and in 1586 respectively.[20]

Illustrated versions of founding stories of temples were one of the many genres used by *etoki* performers for their sermons and *etoki* performances by itinerant practitioners were often closely tied to fundraising campaigns.[21] It is thus no coincidence that the earliest reference to an *Ōyamadera engi* dates from 1307, only shortly after the Shingon monk Gangyō had made efforts to revitalize Ōyama.[22] The *Ōyamadera engi* was an effective tool to spread the Ōyama cult, reassuring pilgrims that a visit would bring them good fortune in this life and salvation in the next. It was on such visits that pilgrims viewed, borrowed, and copied the *Ōyamadera engi*.[23]

The legendary account of how Rōben first set foot on Ōyama in the eighth century conveys Ōyama's symbolic meaning. According to the 1532 version of the *Ōyamadera engi*, the monk Rōben opened up Ōyama as a Buddhist center for religious training in 755 and trained at his new temple for three years until he received the patronage of the imperial court.[24] The *engi* describes Rōben as a charismatic cleric who leads the residents of Sagami Province to Ōyama's summit. Before he ventures onto the mountain, it is a complete wilderness, void of human settlement. Wild animals and spirits inhabit the mountain, making it a dangerous place for humans. In awe of the mountain, people have venerated it as a sacred place only from afar. As Lefebvre argues, "magic and sorcery . . . too have their own spaces, opposed to (but presupposing) religio-political space; also set apart and reserved, such spaces are cursed rather than blessed and beneficent."[25] The narrative of the *Ōyamadera engi* reflects a Buddhist perspective. Places of pre-Buddhist local spirit worship are portrayed as threatening, dangerous, and hence in need of taming by the Buddhist clergy. Once tamed, they can become beneficent religious spaces rather than places of evil magic. This is a recurrent theme in the *Ōyamadera engi*.

Rōben repeatedly tames the dangerous spiritual powers he encounters in this volatile place. A mysterious light emanating from the summit at night attests to the sacrality of the mountain (see Fig. 1.2). Under Rōben's guidance and protection, the local villagers cut a path to the summit to investigate the mysterious light. They dig into the ground beyond a stone *torii* and find a golden stone statue of Fudō. When they worship Fudō, all except Rōben are struck dead because they have

Fig. 1.2   A mysterious light shines from the summit veiled in clouds.
Ōyamadera engi. Courtesy of Hiratsuka-shi hakubutsukan.

Fig. 1.3   Rōben leads the villagers to the summit in 755.
Ōyamadera engi. Courtesy of Hiratsuka-shi hakubutsukan.

violated the rule against ritual pollution on the summit. Luckily, Rōben is able to resuscitate them (see Fig. 1.3). Fudō then reveals to Rōben that Ōyama had originally been the left side of a mountain in India but that it had flown to Japan, and he had come with it.

In search of suitable wood to make a statue of Fudō, Rōben locates a sacred zelkova tree on the southern slope of the mountain. A branch of this tree breaks off and flies miraculously to what is to become the site of the Golden Hall. Rōben sculpts a statue from the branch, and it begins to bleed before Rōben has even completed it, which purportedly proves that it is a living statue that needs no consecration to bring it to life (see Fig. 1.4). Rōben worships the sacred statue for three weeks, and suddenly 49 temples appear on the mountain slope (see Fig. 1.5). The statue of Fudō reveals to Rōben that even during this age of the decline of the dharma, anyone with faith in the mountain will prosper in this world and be reborn into Tuṣita Heaven in the next. Fudō further identifies Rōben as a human incarnation of Maitreya.[26]

While Rōben has tamed the volatile landscape, it remains marked by prohibitions, as many sacred or taboo places tend to be. These are, in Lefebvre's words, "made up of areas set apart, reserved—and so mysterious."[27] During Rōben's encounter with Fudō, Fudō recites a verse telling Rōben that a triangular area of eighteen *chō* around the summit is restricted ground to be kept pure and that the five Buddhas, in the form of the Five Wisdom Kings (*myōō*), will grant protection to any pilgrim:

> Because this place is pure, it is restricted ground
> Deluded sentient beings shall not inhabit
> Eighteen *chō* to the east, south, and west.
> You have made a statue in my likeness and
>   installed it as the main image of worship.
>
> On this mountain, the Five Buddhas took form
> And grant protection as the Five Wisdom Kings.
> Should somebody make a pilgrimage just once,
> His household will be safe from harm and he will
>   be shielded from illness.[28]

Even though this medieval text already encourages pilgrimages to the temple dedicated to Ōyama Fudō, it does not invite the uninitiated to climb to the summit. On the contrary, the fate of the villagers on the summit seems to warn ordinary people not to attempt to climb to the summit but to leave this to religious professionals. Interestingly, the summit was not the only taboo spot on the mountain. Ikazuchidake (Thunder Peak), a secondary peak on the central slope near Nijū no Taki, was permanently off limits and never became the focus of a pilgrimage cult in the early modern period. According to the *kanbun* version of the *Ōyamadera engi*, Ikazuchidake was one of five peaks on the central slope that were associated with the Five Wisdom Kings (*myōō*). A waterfall in the area by the name of Ikazuchidaki (Thunder Falls) was

Fig. 1.4　Rōben carves a living statue of Fudō Myōō.
Ōyamadera engi. Courtesy of Hiratsuka-shi hakubutsukan.

Fig 1.5　Rōben worships Fudō at the Forty-Nine Halls.
Ōyamadera engi. Courtesy of Hiratsuka-shi hakubutsukan.

the focus of a rainmaking cult, requiring consistent worship to prevent endless rainfall. At the foot of the peak, a seemingly bottomless cave inhabited by bats was so deep and dark that was impossible to reach its farthest recess. Ikazuchidake itself was considered dangerous territory: anyone who dared to climb it would be killed by lightning.[29] This echoes a theme that also appears in the story of Rōben's first ascent to the summit and his encounter with the sacred statue of Fudō. In both cases, the stories seem to warn people to stay away rather than try to encounter the deities directly by climbing to the summit.

The theme of a dragon and an associated rainmaking cult also appears in the *Ōyamadera engi* from 1532. Here again Rōben encounters volatile, pre-Buddhist forces on the mountain. Practicing austerities for another seven days by a cave near the Golden Hall on the central slope, Rōben is granted a further miracle: a serpent by the name of Shinja Daiō (Great Serpent King) appears and claims to be the protective deity of the mountain after having been saved by Rōben (i.e., Maitreya) from its existence as an unruly deity (see Fig. 1.6). This typical motif reflects the Buddhist incorporation of a pre-existing local cult through the story of the conversion and harnessing of the local deity.[30] The dragon explains to Rōben that the 49 temples, which earlier appeared to Rōben, prove that the area on the slopes was the inner sanctum of Tuṣita Heaven. He also tells the monk that the waterfalls on Ōyama have the power to purify all beings from pollution and bring enlightenment and liberation to them. Upon Rōben's request for clear, cold water on the mountain—probably for ritual use for votive offerings—the dragon makes a waterfall appear in a valley that was previously dry.[31] This motif resonates with the common East Asian association of dragons with water and rainmaking.[32]

The *Ōyamadera engi* marks three sites on Ōyama as particularly sacred: Ōyama's summit, where Rōben encounters Fudō; Ōyama's central slope, where he sculpts and enshrines a wooden statue of Fudō and has a vision of 49 temples; and a waterfall near the central slope, where he encounters a dragon deity. On the most literal level, the *Ōyamadera engi* thus introduces the most important cultic sites on the mountain to potential visitors, from which it is possible to deduce their layout. The central slope appears the most important and accessible of the three sites and is

Fig. 1.6　A dragon deity appears to Rōben at Nijū no Taki. *Ōyamadera engi*. Courtesy of Hiratsuka-shi hakubutsukan.

Fig. 1.7　The medieval temple complex, with the gate, main hall, three shrines, and a pagoda. *Ōyamadera engi*. Courtesy of Hiratsuka-shi hakubutsukan.

rendered quite realistically in the earliest extant version of the vernacular *Ōyamadera engi* from 1532, which may well reflect Ōyama's layout during the sixteenth century: "In front of the Golden Hall, there are the four-sided corridor, the bell tower, the scripture storage hall, the three-storied pagoda, the shrine of the Ōyama Myōō, and various Buddha [halls]. The roofs of 49 temples and hermitages stand closely lined up."[33]

The text also includes an illustration that shows several of the landmarks mentioned in the description (see Fig. 1.7): the corridor, the three-storied pagoda, and a central Golden Hall with three shrines behind it (the center one probably being the Ōyama Myōō Shrine). In addition, it also shows a gate with two protective deities at the entrance of the complex. According to this description, the cultic center appears to have been a central hall dedicated to Fudō,[34] which was paired with a trio of shrines dedicated to *honji suijaku* deities. As an indication that the site was open to a variety of religious specialists, the illustration depicts two Buddhist clerics with shaved heads and in monastic robes next to the main hall, a long-haired mountain ascetic in a loincloth under a waterfall outside the gate, and En no Gyōja, the legendary founder of *shugendō* (the tradition of mountain asceticism), with two demonic attendants near the pagoda. Still, the peripheral placement of the symbols of mountain asceticism compared to the placement of orthodox monks near the main cultic center is perhaps foreshadowing the developments of the early seventeenth century.

The *Ōyamadera engi*'s description of the mountain slope as a space shared by celibate monks and *yamabushi* is corroborated by evidence from the late sixteenth century. In 1591, over a decade before the site was completely reconstructed by the Tokugawa, it was surveyed under Hideyoshi. The survey does not include the central temple complex dedicated to Fudō but suggests that there were indeed about 50 hermitages and temples on the mountain slope—to be exact, 12 hermitages of *yamabushi*, 36 lay residences, and 7 temples on the mountain. The largest establishments were two temples—Hachidaibō, housing, according to other sources, the head administrator of the site; and Daiyōji, later identified as a Rinzai Zen temple; as well as the residences of two shrine priests.[35] According to a nineteenth-century source, the lay residences reached all the way to the Gate of the Two Kings, which marked the entrance to the Golden Hall enshrining Fudō.[36]

An Earthly Paradise

The *Ōyamadera engi* not only gives us an approximate idea what the site might have looked like in the sixteenth century, but it also conveys the symbolic meaning of Ōyama's sacred landscape. Ōyama was considered sacred, first of all, because it was thought to have originated in India. Moreover, the mountain was also viewed as the Wisdom King Fudō's chosen place of residence and even as his personified embodiment surrounded by four other Wisdom Kings. As a Buddhist statue usually faces south and is viewed from the front or perhaps the sides but not from the back, Ōyama's sacred ground encompassed its front and sides (east, west, and south) but not its back, which was joined to the Tanzawa Mountain range in the north. In addition to the cult of Fudō, it was also associated with the cult of Maitreya, both of which were often intertwined in medieval Japan. Fudō played the role of an intermediary who protected and helped the faithful reach Maitreya's Tuṣita Heaven.[37]

The *Ōyamadera engi*, in fact, echoed scriptural themes from Maitreya's future encounter with Mahākāśyapa, one of Śākyamuni's foremost disciples, known for his accomplishments in meditation and asceticism and for having a golden-colored body due to his great merit, as described in the most important Maitreya scriptures. According to the *Miroku geshō kyō* (Sūtra on Maitreya's Birth in This World), Mahākāśyapa awaits the future arrival of Maitreya in a cave on a mountain summit in Magadha to transmit his golden robe to Maitreya. According to the *Miroku jōbutsu kyō* (Sūtra on Maitreya Attaining Buddhahood), Maitreya ascends to the summit of Wolf-Track Mountain on Vulture Peak, opens up the mountain, and finds Mahākāśyapa, who transmits his golden robe to Maitreya.

In the *Ōyamadera engi*, Rōben assumes the role of Maitreya, whereas Ōyama's golden-bodied Fudō is Mahākāśyapa. Rōben, heralded as a living reincarnation of Maitreya, is described as so powerful that he even tamed a wrathful dragon deity residing on the mountain slope and converted him to Buddhism. A Fudō-shaped sacred rock on Ōyama's summit plays the role of Mahākāśyapa, who sits enveloped in a rocky cave in India in the Maitreya scriptures. This is a variant on the Maitreya theme, in which a monk or mountain ascetic usually assumes the role of Mahākāśyapa, such as in the case of the Shingon monk Kūkai, who was said to await Maitreya's coming while seated in meditation on

Mt. Kōya. However, these two roles were often conflated in the minds of the devotees.

Accordingly, the most sacred ground on Ōyama was on the summit, a feature that Ōyama shared with most sacred mountains in Japan. The summit was often believed to be either an earthly Buddhist paradise or a Buddhist pure land associated with specific Buddhist deities. Ōyama's summit was one such "pure" land. A triangular area of 18 *chō*—east, south, and west around the summit and on the slopes—was to be kept ritually pure. The peak was sacred because it harbored a particularly powerful statue of Fudō (i.e., Mahākāśyapa) that was so sacred that those who viewed it and were ritually impure would be struck dead. Even though the text clearly speaks of a "pure land" (*jōdo*), it identifies Ōyama with Tuṣita Heaven, the heaven in which Maitreya resides. Maitreya was believed to reside in this heaven awaiting his future descent onto earth in about five billion years. Technically, Tuṣita Heaven is not a pure land, but the *Ōyamadera engi* does not make such a subtle distinction and calls the mountain "Maitreya's Pure Land."[38]

The mountain slope below the summit was equally efficacious and gave physical evidence that Ōyama was indeed Maitreya's Tuṣita Heaven. According to Foucault, a "heterotopia is capable of juxtaposing in a single real place several spaces, several sites that are themselves incompatible."[39] Likewise, Ōyama's space was interpreted as multidimensional: an earthly manifestation of a utopian space. Buildings and physical features on the mountain were seen as concrete correspondences with Maitreya's heaven. Ōyama's central slope was seen as an earthly representation of the inner sanctum (*naiin*) of future Buddha Maitreya's heaven.[40] The inner sanctuary of Tuṣita Heaven contained 49 halls (*shijūkuin*), 12 Heavenly Palaces in each of the four directions—which equals 48 palaces—and the Jewel Hall at the center.[41] These 49 halls were said to have manifested themselves directly on Ōyama's slopes. During Rōben's ascetic training in Ōyama, 49 hermitages, which corresponded to 49 halls in Maitreya's heaven, miraculously appeared to Rōben. These halls were a clear sign of the other world: they appeared only temporarily and only to the initiated. This was presented as direct proof of the sacred powers of Ōyama's landscape. The *kanbun* version of the *Ōyamadera engi* gave the halls a more tangible existence by naming each of them. Yet despite this apparent realism, the halls had primarily a symbolic, esoteric meaning. Not a single name of the 49 halls appears to have corresponded to an actual temple, hermitage, or lay residence in the late medieval period. According to Lefebvre, this mixing of the physical and utopian, social and mental elements is common in religious spaces.[42] Because of the resonances between textual and iconographic representations of Maitreya's paradise and Ōyama's topography, visitors had the chance to experience Maitreya's presence in a localized context and to establish a karmic connection with Maitreya that guaranteed them salvation in the future.

Yet the *Ōyamadera engi* did not invite pilgrims to take their visits lightly, and the text cautioned ordinary people to fear the wrath of Ōyama's fierce and powerful deities. Many of Ōyama's waterfalls, caves, and springs were said to have been created or inhabited by deities and to have awesome powers (e.g., to wash away impurities and grant wisdom). Similarly, the summit was described as a dangerous wilderness, inhabited by deities who could easily become volatile if visitors approached them with the incorrect rituals or in a state of ritual pollution. Unlike contemporaneous texts from other sacred sites, which often limited this warning to women, the *Ōyamadera engi* emphasized that all uninitiated human beings—men *and* women—were considered polluted. Only specially trained practitioners like Rōben could channel the sacred powers of the mountain to elicit revelations and miracles that would benefit ordinary beings.

Thus Ōyama was a potent landscape in which caves, waterfalls, and peaks could serve as places of training for esoteric practices by initiated anchorites, including both Buddhist monks and *yamabushi*. This sacred space was not limited to the summit and the central slope. According to the *kanbun* version of the *Ōyamadera engi*, the hills, caves, and waterfalls in Ōyama's foothills were incorporated into the sacred landscape. Three areas in particular—to the west, south, and north—appear as training grounds and settlements of anchorites.[43] Since Ōyama was likened to a Buddhist icon facing south, the entire northern side of the mountain was considered peripheral as well. *Yamabushi* and other religious recluses like the poet monk Shinkei, who lived at a small temple in Ōyama's foothills, could settle in this periphery. The hermitages and temples on the immediate mountain slope and in the foothills indicate that Ōyama was already a regionally important sacred site by the late medieval period.

Nevertheless, the complex was still considerably smaller than the huge complex of over twenty temples and numerous small shrines and chapels on the mountainside, as well as over 150 *oshi* inns in the villages below it, that it became during the early modern period.

New Boundaries in the Early Modern Period

After 1600, Ōyama's reputation as a remote mountain retreat changed dramatically when it became a bustling pilgrimage destination and a hierarchically ordered space in which only the celibate Shingon clergy wielded absolute ritual authority. In the late sixteenth century, the chaos of the Warring States period ended, bringing tremendous changes in the way that religious institutions interacted with the new regime, particularly in the region around Edo, which consisted primarily of land belonging to the Tokugawa *bakufu* and *hatamoto* ("bannermen"). In 1605, the *bakufu* issued laws that demarcated Ōyama along clear lines, separating the monastic precinct and village.

Ōyama and the villages at its foot emerged as a highly ordered space that was divided into three distinct zones (see Fig. 1.8): two temple towns at the mountain's foot, the Shingon precinct on the slopes, and uninhabited wilderness around the summit.[44] The entrance to each of these areas was marked by a gate or a *torii*, except for the entrance to the monastic precinct, which was marked by a hall dedicated to Fudō. Gates are a common element on sacred mountains in Japan. They not only demarcate spatial boundaries but also symbolize the passage from one spiritual realm to the next.[45] Foucault notes that heterotopias tend to "presuppose a system of opening and closing that both isolates them and makes the penetrable. In general, the heterotopic site is not freely accessible like a public place. Either entry is compulsory . . . or else the individual has to submit to rites and purifications."[46] Like its medieval predecessor early modern Ōyama was still a heterotopia, but its meanings and spatial organization changed over the course of the early modern period. Ōyama's slopes were governed by new rules of permanent and temporary exclusion based on gender, ritual purity, occupational qualifications, and monastic affiliation.

Early modern Ōyama's heterotopic space resembled that of a nested doll, which stacked one heterotopia within the other. The first zone

Fig. 1.8 Panoramic view of Ōyama in the early nineteenth century.
Shinpen Sagami no kuni fudoki kō (1840). Courtesy of the National Archives of Japan.

comprised the temple towns where Ōyama's *oshi* had their residences. The second zone was the monastic precinct of the Shingon clergy, which was subdivided into three sections on the main ascent on the southeastern slope. The first section was the area between the Outer Fudō Hall and the Gate of the Two Kings. This was the outer boundary of the monastic precinct, and the ascent was lined with fourteen shrines and twenty chapels.[47] The second section was the area between the Gate of the Two Kings and the Tower Gate, where the resident Shingon clergy had thirteen temples, which later increased to nineteen.[48] The third section was the area beyond the Tower Gate around the Main Hall, where Ōyama's famous Fudō Myōō was enshrined.[49] Last but not least, the third zone was the area between the copper *torii* and the summit. This zone was a deliberate wilderness with steep, cragged paths periodically marked by gates, stone markers, and Buddhist statues but void of buildings except for a single shrine near its entrance and the five shrines on the summit. This gave pilgrims the impression of having entered a remote, wild landscape far from human settlements.[50]

Despite the new sense of order and the predominance of the Buddhist orthodoxy, Ōyama retained its combinatory nature, which drew no line between Buddhism and Shinto. The amalgamation of *kami* and Buddhas was more complex than the forging of a relationship between a Buddhist temple on the mountain slope and a shrine on the summit. Ōyama, from the village at its foot to its summit, was covered by a multitude of temples, chapels, statues, shrines, and *torii*. The deities at these shrines were conceived of in combinative terms and were mostly administered by the Buddhist clergy.

The Village

In 1605, the Tokugawa regime forced Ōyama's *yamabushi* to resettle at the foot of the mountain in the transitional zone between the mundane space of the outside world and the sacred space of the mountain. Two villages served as mountain-ascetic/*oshi* settlements and accommodated the growing pilgrimage business as Ōyama's temple towns (*monzenmachi*): Minoge Village and Sakamoto Village. The marginal status of the villages, from the point of view of their new landlords, the Shingon clergy, was embodied in the name Sakamoto (piedmont), usually used for the southeastern settlement but even occasionally as Nishisakamoto (western piedmont) for Minoge Village in the southwest, and the term *yamashita* (below the mountain), occasionally used for residents of the temple towns.[51]

Sakamoto Village, on Ōyama's southeastern slope, was nearly four times as large as Minoge Village on the southwestern slope because Ōyama's front and main ascent led through Sakamoto Village. In 1609, the *bakufu* awarded one hundred *koku* at the foot of the mountain in Sakamoto Village and the adjacent Koyasu Village to the Shingon clergy as Ōyama's temple land. Since Sakamoto Village was located within the boundaries of the temple land, it was under the jurisdiction of the Shingon temples. For example, within Ōyama's temple land, hunting was prohibited for ordinary villagers, based on the Buddhist prohibition against the taking of life. This led to an increase in the number of deer and boar in the area and made farming virtually impossible.[52] Unlike Ōyama's secondary temple town, Minoge, which was primarily a farming village, Sakamoto came to rely primarily on the pilgrimage business.

Visitors from the east, residents of the populous Kantō Plain—the city of Edo as well as Musashi, Awa, Kazusa, Shimōsa, Kōzuke, Shimotsuke, and Hitachi Provinces—found Sakamoto more convenient since it was about 45 miles from Edo, 5 miles closer than Minoge, which was only conveniently located for pilgrims from the west—from western Sagami, Izu, Suruga, or Kai Provinces, or from Mt. Fuji. These factors gave Sakamoto an advantage over Minoge and explain why Sakamoto was the larger settlement in the early modern period.

Sharing a focus on sources of water, both Sakamoto and Minoge developed along mountain streams that originated on the slopes of Ōyama: the Kanai River in the case of Minoge and the Ōyama River in the case of Sakamoto. Both villages included springs and waterfalls that were used for rituals connected to the cult of Ōyama. In Minoge, a spring on Mt. Harutake was used for votive water offerings to the deities on Ōyama's summit. Pilgrims used another spring for purification rituals.[53] In Sakamoto, four of the six village sections had waterfalls that were administered by *oshi* and used by pilgrims for purification rituals before they ascended the mountain: Ōdaki, Atagodaki, Rōbendaki, and Motodaki.[54] Since the temple towns constituted a transitional zone between the sacred and the mundane, pilgrims could shed their ritual pollution and purify themselves by taking ablutions and changing into clean clothing.[55] By the early nineteenth century, the waterfalls in Sakamoto had become the most popular motif of Ōyama. Among woodblock prints, depictions of the waterfalls in Sakamoto, such as Rōbendaki and Ōdaki, outnumbered the prints of Ōyama's monastic precinct and the summit (see Fig. 1.9).[56]

The Monastic Precinct

The monastic precinct was managed by Shingon clerics, who received legal and judicial backing by the *bakufu* and its head temple, Mt. Kōya. Between 1605 and 1608, the *bakufu* sponsored the reconstruction of the temple complex, which gave it the basic shape it retained throughout the early modern period. The layout appears to reflect earlier spatial arrangements in regard to Ōyama's major cultic sites on the summit and the central slope (see Figs. 1.10 and 1.11). On the central slope, the Main Hall, dedicated to Fudō, was surrounded by a joint shrine of Myōō

Fig. 1.9 "Sōshū Ōyama Rōben no taki," Katsushika Hokusai, *Shokoku taki mawari*.
Courtesy of Kanagawa kenritsu reshikishi hakubutsukan.

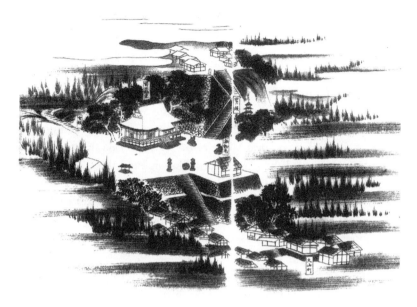

Fig. 1.10   The area around the Outer Fudō Hall in the early nineteenth century.
Shinpen Sagami no kuni fudoki kō (1840). Courtesy of the National Archives of Japan.

Fig. 1.11   The main hall and entrance to the summit in the early nineteenth century.
Shinpen Sagami no kuni fudoki kō (1840). Courtesy of the National Archives of Japan.

(Rōben's living wooden statue of Ōyama Fudō), Kashima Myōjin, and Sekison Gongen; a Treasure Hall; seven shrines dedicated to various *honji suijaku* deities; the Honjidō housing Dainichi; and a Mikoshidō, a chapel for a sacred palanquin. Below the Main Hall, between the Tower Gate and the Gate of the Two Kings, were the Scripture Hall, the bell tower, and a Hachidaiōji Shrine, as well as the Shingon clergy's temples, including Hachidaibō, the residence of the head abbot. In addition, the Nijū Hall enshrined the dragon deity of Nijū no Taki, a waterfall east of the Main Hall, and the Outer Fudō Hall marked the entrance to the monastic precinct at the foot of the mountain. This basic spatial layout remained intact throughout the early modern period, even though the complex expanded as the mountain developed into a popular pilgrimage destination.[57] By the 1830s and 1840s, Ōyama had developed into an impressive multiplex. The buildings initially constructed with the financial support of the *bakufu* had been supplemented by numerous smaller shrines, chapels, and monuments erected by ordinary donors such as pilgrimage associations.

As with most sacred mountains in premodern Japan, early modern Ōyama had areas of restricted access (*kekkai*). As noted above, the roots of this arrangement lay in the medieval period. According to the *Ōyamadera engi*, the reasoning behind the restricted ground was primarily based on notions of ritual pollution—such as death, illness, menstruation, and childbirth—and the identification of the landscape with a pure inner sanctum or Maitreya's Tuṣita Heaven. As Allan Grapard notes in his discussion of the sacred geography of Mt. Hiko, the term *kekkai*, which he translates as "bounded realm" or "perimeter," had several meanings:

This term referred to three related practices, which had their origin in India, where it signified the construction of an area in which deities were invoked. By extensions, it went on to refer to the establishment of a consecrated zone for the construction of temples. In Japan, the term referred to these two phenomena, but also, from the ninth century, to entire geographical areas that were set aside as the exclusive property of (Shinto-) Buddhist institutions.[58]

In addition, as Grapard shows, Mt. Hiko was vertically divided into four zones (*shido kekkai*), "four superimposed layers in which life was subjected to growing constraints on behavior."[59] Ōyama was similarly divided into zones, but its *kekkai*, the perimeter of its monastic precinct, became associated with one particular constraint. Officially, entry to the monastic precinct was prohibited for women (*nyonin kekkai* or *nyonin kinsei*). In this case, the prohibition was not based on ritual pollution but was meant to ensure that the Buddhist clergy kept their precepts.

In his discussion of the exclusion of women from sacred mountains, Ushiyama Yoshiyuki notes this bifurcation into two basic types of restricted ground. He gives early examples from the Heian period for the two types of *kekkai*: one based on ritual purity such as the case of Mt. Kinpusen, which not only barred women from entering but also required men to keep a three-month fast before their ascent, and one based on the maintenance of monastic precepts such as in case of Mt. Hiei, which barred women to prevent them from leading astray the monks in training.[60] With early modern Ōyama, both forms of restricted ground were present, but in both cases purity and pollution or the observance of monastic precepts were not the only considerations involved. Economic considerations also played a role in the application of the prohibition.

The prohibition against women entering the monastic precinct was also linked to the ban against married anchorites' right to inhabit the mountain slope. It appears the restricted ground determined in the *bakufu*'s regulations from 1609 was determined by the Buddhist clergy taking over the sacred site with the sanction of the *bakufu*. To establish the authority of the Shingon clergy over non-celibate *yamabushi*, women and, by implication, married *yamabushi* were barred from the mountain. Whereas medieval Ōyama was inhabited by non-celibate *yamabushi* and celibate Buddhist monks, both of whom served as ritual specialists and trained on the mountain, the regulations decreed by the Tokugawa *bakufu* and by Ōyama's head temple Mt. Kōya in 1609 gave the "pure," (i.e., celibate) Kogi Shingon clergy authority over Ōyama.[61] The regulations issued by the *bakufu* in 1609 changed the meaning of the restricted ground by drawing the border at the Outer Fudō Hall, the entrance to the monastic precinct, and settling everyone but celibate clerics at the foot of the mountain:

Item: That the area above the Outer Fudō Hall is restricted to pure monks shall be firmly obeyed in perpetuity.

Item: The former quarters and residences of married clerics and *yamabushi* shall be divided among the pure monks at the discretion of Hachidaibō.[62]

The *bakufu*'s directives were only an abbreviated form of more practical, detailed regulations issued by Mt. Kōya, Ōyama's head temple, that specified how these restrictions were actually enforced. Remarkably, the directives issued by Mt. Kōya denied full religious authority to the *yamabushi* and married clerics but lifted the restriction against women pilgrims during the day.

Item: The area above the Outer Fudō Hall is of course prohibited for women (*nyonin kekkai*). However, women making a pilgrimage to Fudō are allowed to do so between the hour of the dragon [around 7 or 8 AM] and the hour of the monkey [around 4 or 5 PM]. Attachment: The practice of women from the foot of the mountain who enter monastic quarters to bring daily supplies and for other kinds of business shall cease. If old women who say that they are relatives come to visit, the monk in question is to step outside the temple.[63]

Similar temporal enforcement of the restriction against women already appears in the monastic *ritsuryō* codes of the eighth century, which prohibited women from spending the night at monks' quarters and men from doing the same at nuns' quarters. In addition, monks and nuns were only allowed to enter each other's quarters for special rituals, instruction, and in cases of death and illness.[64]

The example of early modern Ōyama suggests that the extent of limitations placed on women's access to the site was also based on economic considerations and that it was the orthodox celibate clergy rather than married *yamabushi* who had an interest in their enforcement. Ōyama's Shingon clergy sought to balance the role of the site as a pilgrimage destination and a place for monastic training. The restricted ground set up in the early seventeenth century denoted the training ground and property of the Shingon Buddhist clergy at Ōyama. Barring women from spending the night also implied that married *yamabushi* could not settle with their families within the boundaries of the monastic precinct. Women pilgrims *per se* did not challenge the authority of the clergy. On the contrary, the clergy who controlled services carried out in the Main Hall relied on pilgrims' donations, including those made by women. Based on the law codes of 1609, the clergy at Hachidaibō and the other Shingon temples were the only ones allowed to live on the mountain and to collect donations from pilgrims left at the halls, chapels, and shrines that had been reconstructed between 1605 and 1608. They also managed

Fig. 1.12   The summit in the early nineteenth century.
Shinpen Sagami no kuni fudoki kō (1840). Courtesy of the National Archives of Japan.

other small chapels and shrines on the mountain as well as Raigōdani, a valley near the summit, where pilgrims used to view the sunrise on their way to the summit. After 1609, the *yamabushi* only maintained exclusive control over one of three Gyōja Chapels dedicated to En no Gyōja, the legendary seventh-century founder of the tradition of mountain asceticism.[65] In her study of the prohibition against women, Miyazaki Fumiko notes that the prohibition against women was also adjusted at Mt. Fuji, where women were allowed to enter the restricted area every 60 years during the early modern period when pilgrimage to the mountain became very popular. As at Ōyama, the motivation behind this practice was in part economical.[66]

The Summit

Yet notions of ritual pollution remained important in the early modern period. From the late seventeenth century, even though pilgrims came to worship Ōyama Fudō in the Main Hall throughout the year, Ōyama's predominant pilgrimage season was during the summer, when the summit was open to pilgrims for a three-week-long festival. The summit housed the shrines of Sekison, Daitengu, Shōtengu, and Tokuichi and the Wind and Rain deities (see Fig. 1.12). The area around

Ōyama's summit attained an aura of sacredness through inaccessibility. It remained a virtual wilderness with a steep path, littered with boulders. Pilgrims, who were admitted for only three weeks in the summer, had to overcome the walk through rugged terrain and wilderness before reaching the summit. Ironically, it was the deliberate remoteness of the summit, closed most of the year, that attracted pilgrims, in much the same way as periodic displays (*kaichō*) of particularly sacred Buddhist statues attracted thousands of pilgrims. Because of limited access to the area, the pilgrimage became all the more attractive when entry was only periodically granted.

Evidence from the late eighteenth and early nineteenth centuries indicates that the boundary of the restricted ground that excluded all women, considered permanently polluted by nature, and any man deemed ritually stained by temporary pollution began behind the Main Hall dedicated to Fudō. To ensure that pilgrims observed the restricted ground around the summit, the boundary was marked by gates or stone posts where paths entered the zone. Behind the Main Hall, it was identified by a copper *torii*. Those who were prohibited from ascending further worshiped the shrines on the summit from afar at the Votive Picture Hall, near the copper *torii*.[67] A gate also marked the ascent from Minoge Village.[68]

This distinction between permanent and temporary exclusion is also found at other sacred sites and ceremonial spaces. Suzuki Masataka distinguishes between two different notions of ritual pollution: temporary forms of pollution caused by pregnancy, childbirth, menstruation, and death, which could be lifted after a certain period, and permanent pollution, which was thought to stain women *per se* and therefore barred them permanently from entry into ceremonial space, shrines, temples, and sacred mountains.[69] As an example of notions of permanent pollution, Suzuki cites cases from northeastern Japan, where hunters often explain the permanent prohibition by arguing that the female mountain goddess hates menstrual blood and easily feels jealous when women enter her domain.[70] Conversely, Bernard Faure cites the legend of Toran, common to many *shugendō* sites: a nun defies the prohibition against women, angers the mountain god, and is turned into a stone. Faure interprets the tale as an attempt by the male Buddhist clergy to displace the ancient tradition of female shamans in the service of predominantly female mountain deities so that the clergy could take control of the territory.[71]

In comparison, early modern Ōyama presents an interesting case. Ōyama's deities were officially identified as male, not female. Nevertheless, women were permanently barred from the summit while men only encountered temporary restrictions, being allowed onto the summit during the summer festival, except when they had a death in the family.[72] Male pilgrims also had to observe rules regarding ritual pollution and, ideally, were to maintain ritual purity starting with their dress. In one story from the *Ōyama Fudō reigenki* (A record of miracles of Ōyama Fudō; 1792), a young pilgrim was dressed in white robes (*jōe*) and refused to eat food that he considered ritually impure because it had been prepared by a woman.[73] The custom was reflected in the mountain code from 1713, which gave *oshi* the responsibility to ensure that pilgrims wore pure robes and were not stained by ritual pollution.[74] Interestingly, there is no evidence that women ever challenged this prohibition. If they did, no records remain of their transgressions. For example, when a couple from northeastern Japan visited Ōyama in the Second Month of 1863, their pilgrimage was limited to Ōyama Fudō because the summit was of course closed during that season. The husband noted no special restrictions against his wife but mentioned that the ascent to the Main Hall enshrining Fudō was physically difficult for women. Neither husband nor wife appears to have sought to climb to the summit without authorization.[75]

In contrast, the theme of men violating the taboo against ritual pollution appears in a variety of sources—often threatening that noncompliant behavior leads to divine punishment. Already in the medieval *Ōyamadera engi*, male villagers accompanying Rōben are struck dead when they encounter the awesome power of Ōyama Fudō on the summit because they are not ritually pure. Despite this warning, quite a few pilgrims who were considered ritually polluted seem to have ignored the prohibition, especially in the early eighteenth century, when the pilgrimage during the summer festival first gained increased popularity. In 1713, the temple issued the following injunctions concerning the summer festival:

Item: Every year there are some among the pilgrims who have not kept a fast, whose garments are stained by pollution, or who are polluted themselves. Last year, there were especially many cases like this. From this year, the *oshi* shall pay attention that they will not allow those affected by pollution to make the pilgrimage.[76]

Even though the clergy determined the boundary of the restricted ground, they obviously depended on the cooperation of the *oshi* since they actually had the most direct contact with pilgrims. As inhabitants of the transitional zone at the foot of the mountain, the *oshi* had to ensure that pilgrims were ritually pure when they ascended the mountain, that they wore pure robes and took ablutions for purification, and that those who did not fulfill those conditions were prevented from ascending.

Such efforts of policing seem to have been largely ineffective. Instead, tales of transgression and divine punishment served to promote faith in the power of Ōyama's deities. The *Ōyama Fudō reigenki*, a collection of 125 miracle tales that date primarily from the mid-eighteenth century, compiled by the Shingon monk, Shinzō, a resident at Ōyama, includes several stories on the topic as if to frighten potential violators of the ban: ritual purity had to be maintained on the summit to avoid the wrath of Ōyama's deities. In these tales, pilgrims were prevented from climbing to the summit because they had violated the ban against ritual pollution by being in mourning or having incurred a social taboo. As the compiler Shinzō of the *Ōyama Fudō reigenki* explains: "Pilgrims who try to climb the mountain despite being tainted by pollution are punished."[77] In one story, the wife of a pilgrim from Edo died while he was away on a pilgrimage to Ōyama in the summer of 1776. After he had worshipped at the Main Hall, he set out to climb to the summit to visit the shrine of Sekison. In front of the *torii* marking the entrance to the summit his heart started beating violently, and he felt dizzy so that he could not enter the gate. His friend, however, was able to ascend without any problems. Shinzō believed that the man could not enter the sacred grounds of Sekison because of the pollution incurred through his wife's death.[78] In another story, a pilgrim from Azabu in Edo who had sold his daughter into prostitution to finance his prodigal lifestyle was unable to ascend to the summit.[79] In both cases, it is not the gender of the relatives (both of whom happened to be women) that prevents the pilgrim from ascending but the stain of death or the pilgrim's own immoral conduct. Another pilgrim was struck by sudden madness in Koyasu Village at the foot of Ōyama and died upon his return to Edo for attempting to climb to the top of the mountain despite being in mourning for his uncle.[80] A pilgrim from the same family who also attempted to make a pilgrimage at this time fell off his horse near the town of Nagatsuta in Musashi Province and pierced his stomach with his dagger, which forced him to return to Edo.[81] Another pilgrim from Madarame Village in Sagami Province tried to ascend to the summit via Minoge Village several times, but palpitations prevented him from climbing above the central slope, which the compiler Shinzō again interpreted as a result of ritual pollution.[82]

In these cases, the ritual pollution was not so much physical but symbolic: none of the pilgrims attempted to bring physical remains of the dead into the restricted zone and often had not even had direct contact with a dead body. They were merely polluted by familial association. By contrast, scholarly literature on this topic has often explained the careful restrictions as efforts to guard against physical pollution by decomposition and bodily fluids, such as blood and excrement. This vigilance has been interpreted as a means to maintain the purity of rivers originating in mountains and serving the entire region as a source of irrigation for paddy fields. For example, Allan Grapard notes in his discussion of the sacred geography of Mt. Hiko in Kyūshū that the orientation of the restricted ground was adjusted so that it would contain the sources of several important rivers. Mt. Hiko was divided into four zones with progressively severe measures to preserve the natural environment: prohibitions against killing and agriculture in the outermost zone, prohibitions against giving birth in the second zone, prohibitions against large animals such as horses and oxen and against death in the third zone, and, finally, prohibitions "against the release of excrement, urine, saliva, phlegm, or mucous from the nose."[83]

Ōyama was not a complete exception from this pattern. Its triangular temple land encompassed the sources of a river that nurtured several agricultural villages at its foot; hunting and killing were banned on the temple land; and the summit was an area associated strongly with the taboo against death. However, once Ōyama became a major pilgrimage destination, the area around the summit could not be kept completely free from physical pollution by human body fluids. By 1777, the summit featured two toilets to accommodate the masses of pilgrims. Practical considerations seem to have overruled blanket restrictions. The toilets were perhaps an effort to contain the extent of the inevitable pollution by human excrement. The *Ōyama Fudō reigenki*, which mentions their presence, describes the lavatories as islands of pollution. When a fire destroyed the shrines on the summit that year, it left the toilets unscathed, leading contemporaries to conclude that the blaze had been a divine fire because it had not touched the place of pollution.[84] The managers of the site must have realized that to the common pilgrim the summit may have conveyed the image of a pristine wilderness, but it was not an idealized Buddhist paradise, where conventional time stood still, death and rebirth ceased, and ordinary bodily functions were suspended. For the early modern religious institutions on the mountain, the site was first and foremost a pilgrimage center. Just as the exclusion of women was handled flexibly within the boundaries of the monastic precinct, a practical approach was adopted to handle the human waste from the masses of pilgrims on the summit. In both cases, some degree of temporal or spatial containment was adopted to keep the pollution in check without hindering the operation of the pilgrimage site.

Conclusion

In the medieval period, *yamabushi* and fully celibate Buddhist clerics inhabited and trained on Ōyama's slopes and in caves and hermitages at its foot. Ōyama was viewed as a distant mountain retreat that was an earthly representation of Maitreya's Tuṣita Heaven and harbored a sacred statue of Fudō. The few available documents suggest that the differentiation between *yamabushi* and ordained clerics and between their respective spaces was less demarcated in this period. Consequently, space was organized far less hierarchically and experienced in a less linear fashion. That is, practitioners did not simply enter the mountain for a short visit to the major cultic sites but also inhabited and wandered through Ōyama's heterotopic space following the principles of an esoteric tradition.

In the early modern period, Ōyama came to reflect existing social and religious hierarchies with its distinct spaces reserved for the divine (Sekison on the summit and Fudō on the central slope), the Shingon clergy (on the central slope below the divine), and by the *oshi* and villagers (in the periphery of the mountain's base). The closer the space was to the summit the less accessible it was to the public. In the seventeenth century, Ōyama's institutions and its sacred geography were completely restructured to reflect a new hierarchy through spatial arrangements. The previous order did not disappear completely but was interpreted in radically different ways. Over the course of the early modern period, Ōyama was transformed from a remote training ground of anchorites into a popular pilgrimage destination. Pilgrims to Ōyama were encouraged to traverse the mountain site quickly, progressing in a straight line from one famous cultic center to the next, rather than training in the esoteric caves hidden in the valleys of Ōyama's lower slopes. Ōyama remained a training center but only for Shingon monks who engaged in scholastic and ritual training; Ōyama's *oshi* were marginalized spatially.

Ōyama's boundaries also reflected larger societal ideals of hierarchy prevalent in the early modern period: between different Buddhist sects, between lay and ordained, between Sakamoto and neighboring villages. Both the Buddhist clergy and the *oshi* learned to coexist symbiotically within the early modern system. Over the course of the period, the temple towns at the foot of Ōyama, particularly Sakamoto, flourished with inns and shops while the sacred precincts on the mountain, initially established with *bakufu* patronage, had been supplemented with small monuments, shrines, and chapels by ordinary devotees.

In 1855, however, the strict physical order was shaken, literally, by an earthquake and ensuing fires that severely damaged the temples, shrines, and chapels on the mountain slope and the temple towns below. The exact impact of the fires is discussed in the following chapters, but suffice to say that the monastic precinct and the temple towns were slowly rebuilt in the 1850s and 1860s. Even though Ōyama's early modern boundaries remained intact until the Meiji Restoration, natural disaster had proved the transience of Ōyama's geography, thereby setting the stage for the dramatic changes brought about by the disassociation of *kami* and Buddhas in the early Meiji period.

TWO

A Regional Kogi Shingon Academy

One of the most important institutional factors in Ōyama's early modern transformation was its role as a regional Kogi Shingon academy, endowed with land by shogunal patronage. It functioned to train clerics to staff Kogi Shingon temples in villages throughout the Kantō region. As a Shingon institution within this new system, Ōyama played a dual role: a sectarian educational facility and an intersectarian pilgrimage destination, not unlike its head temple, Mt. Kōya. Like Mt. Kōya, the site was also a conglomerate of several Shingon temples—initially thirteen and later nineteen—among which one, Hachidaibō, played the role of the administrative center.

This chapter focuses on the succession of Hachidaibō's abbots under whom Ōyama's Shingon institutions developed during the early modern period (see Table 2.1). Of course, the fortune of the Ōyama cult as a whole was not always synonymous with the fortune of the Hachidaibō abbots, who must have administered the site not only personally but also through an ecclesiastical bureaucracy. However, in extant documents, the abbots often emerge as the only recognizable individual faces and serve as a synecdoche. As symbols of power and authority, the Hachidaibō abbots provide a measure of Ōyama's institutional development. Based on Ōyama's institutional growth and the control the Hachidaibō abbots wielded over its numerous Shingon institutions, Ōyama's early modern history can be divided into two periods: a formative period from 1600 to 1750, during which the Hachidaibō abbots created the

Table 2.1

The Hachidaibō Abbots, 1605–1878

Generation	Name	Abbotship	Death Date
1	Jitsuō	1605–1618	Genna 4 (1618)/2/2
2	Jitsuei	1618–1625	Kan'ei 2 (1625)/6/24
3	Kenryū	1633–1654	Jōō 3 (1654)/8/14
4	Ryūkei	1654–1687	Jōkyō 4 (1687)/1/2
5	Kūben	1687–1700	Genroku 13 (1700)/5/2 *
6	Kaizō	1700–1731	Kyōhō 16 (1731)/2/28 *
7	Shusō	1731–1746	Enkyō 3 (1746)/1/21 *
8	Hōnyo	1746–1757	Hōreki 7 (1757)/7/5 *
9	Seinyo	1757–1761	Hōreki 11 (1761)/11/14 *
10	Myōjū	1761–1763	Hōreki 13 (1763)/4/29 *
11	Kōga	1763–1766	Meiwa 3 (1766)/7/28 *
12	Kanga	1766–1790	Kansei 2 (1790)/12/17 *
13	Jakushin	1790–1801	Kyōwa 1 (1801)/9/3
14	Jakudō	1801–1822	Bunsei 5 (1822)/12/7
15	Shōdō	1822– ?†	Genji 1 (1864)/8/16
16	Kakkyoku	1855–1865	Keiō 1 (1865)/3/7
17	Ōjū	1865–1867	Keiō 3 (1867)/9/5
18	Jitsujō	1867–1878	Meiji 11 (1878)/3/3

* buried at Raigōin on Ōyama; † dismissed from abbacy
SOURCE: Tōma, "Ōyama shi," 52–131, especially 126–27.

institutional frameworks that brought Ōyama prosperity, and a period of fragmentation between 1750 and 1868, during which the Hachidaibō abbots became less able to provide Ōyama with sectarian cohesion and stability. Until the end of the seventeenth century, Ōyama's institutions relied largely on significant donations by the shogunate, but from the early eighteenth century, when such donations were becoming less plentiful, Ōyama's institutions were financed by direct donations from the population of the Kantō region.

A study of Ōyama as a Kogi Shingon temple not only illuminates the development of the early modern institutional structures of the cultic site but also sheds light on the early modern history of Shingon Buddhism and early modern Buddhism as a whole. In the early modern period, Buddhism fully penetrated all levels of Japanese society through the establishment of the head-branch temple system (*honmatsu seido*) and the temple registration system (*terauke seido*). To facilitate the development of the two systems, many new temples were founded and older temples changed sectarian affiliation or chose a single one among several present at the site, just as Ōyama was taken over by the Kogi Shingon school. In most cases, however, Shingon, Tendai, and *shugendō* temples were taken over by the Zen, Nichiren, and Pure Land schools.[1] Yet this does not mean that the Shingon and Tendai schools became insignificant during this period. The Tendai temple Kan'eiji and the Jōdo temple Zōjōji were the ancestral temples of the Tokugawa while the imperial family had their funerals and memorial services performed by the Shingon school. Moreover, despite the blows dealt to the Tendai and Shingon schools during the late sixteenth century, the two schools remained the most highly endowed Buddhist schools in terms of their land holdings bestowed by shogunal patronage even though the total number of their temples was far exceeded by the Jōdoshin and Sōtō schools.[2]

By the late eighteenth century, the Shingi Shingon school, with approximately 15,000 temples, was larger than the Kogi Shingon school, with approximately 10,000 temples. Whereas the former was primarily concentrated in eastern Japan, the latter was numerically strong in the west, where it held several important large temples, including Mt. Kōya, Ninnaji, Tōji, Daigoji, and Takaosanji. Pilgrimage to Mt. Kōya—the Kogi Shingon school's sectarian headquarters—was widely popular, giving the Kogi Shingon school significance throughout Japan despite its smaller size. In the Kantō region—with the exception of Edo and Sagami Province—the two Shingon schools combined held the largest number of temples among the Buddhist schools. Sagami was the only province in eastern Japan in which the Kogi Shingon school outnumbered the Shingi Shingon school, and it was where the eastern Kogi Shingon schools developed a strong regional network of head-branch temples. As a regional academy, Ōyama was a part of this network.[3]

The history of Ōyama's Shingon temples and abbots illustrates that the first century of the early modern period was marked by sectarian expansion facilitated initially by a careful balance between sectarian interests and the political interests of the new Tokugawa regime. The hierarchical sectarian frameworks created in the early seventeenth century allowed temples and sectarian networks to grow. Eventually, these structures were supported not only by state patronage but also by the monetary contributions from a much broader constituency. In this new system, Ōyama's Shingon temples served dual functions: they trained Kogi Shingon novices for later appointment at Shingon temples in the Kantō region, and, simultaneously, they were in charge of the sacred site and its rituals. Ōyama's status as an academy contributed to the spread of the Ōyama cult through the Kantō region. Most of the early modern period yields ample evidence for the advantageous interplay of the two aspects.

Especially in the first half of the early modern period, the Hachidaibō abbots were able to assert their control over Ōyama's former *yamabushi* turned *oshi* and the Shingon clergy. However, Ōyama's heightened prestige and popularity occasionally posed a challenge to its stability and institutional cohesion. The flourishing pilgrimage business fostered competition among the Shingon clerics, which undermined the authority of the Hachidaibō abbot because it increased the independence of the Shingon subtemples under his control. Moreover, at the end of the early modern period, Hachidaibō abbots held their tenure for very brief spans of time. The prestigious office of the Hachidaibō abbot was given only to senior clerics as a lifetime appointment. Unfortunately, several of these senior clerics, who were of an advanced age, died soon after their appointment and therefore provided little institutional stability and leadership, which had debilitating consequences. This situation was exacerbated by several natural disasters that afflicted Ōyama at end of the early modern period.

Furthermore, one of the primary sources of Ōyama's revenue would eventually turn out to be another institutional weakness in the transition to the modern period. Ōyama, like many Shingon temples, derived much of its income from the administration of an adjunct shrine and from its temple land, which made it particularly vulnerable during the disassociation of *kami* and Buddhas in the early Meiji period. Yet despite their misfortune at the end of the early modern period, it would be a mistake to characterize Ōyama's Shingon institutions as moribund. During a long period of institution building that lasted through the seventeenth century, Ōyama's Buddhist institutions were remarkably stable.

Restructuring the Monastic Complex, 1590–1618

Ōyama was completely transformed under Tokugawa rule from a site of mountain asceticism to an orthodox Kogi Shingon training monastery.

At the end of the sixteenth century, a local warrior held the hereditary appointment as *bettō* (head administrator) of Hachidaibō, the largest hermitage on the mountain. After the defeat of the Hōjō by Toyotomi Hideyoshi in 1590 and the establishment of Tokugawa Ieyasu as the new ruler of the Kantō region, Ieyasu did not immediately try to change Ōyama's administrative structures. Ieyasu controlled six provinces in the Kantō—Izu, Sagami, Musashi, Shimōsa, Kazusa, and Awa Provinces— and was ordered to move his seat from Suruga to Edo, at the center of the region. As he asserted his power in the region, he shrewdly recruited vassals who had previously served the Hōjō and recognized their prior status.[4] Similarly, the new regime surveyed the mountain in 1591 but left its institutional structures in place. One of Ieyasu's vassals even married the daughter of the local warrior in charge of the mountain.[5] This reflects a larger pattern in Tokugawa Ieyasu's policy toward Honzanha *yamabushi* in the Kantō region, who were also represented at Ōyama. As Udaka Yoshiaki notes, Honzanha *yamabushi* had received the patronage of the Odawara-based Hōjō. Therefore, they had grown into a powerful network of ritual specialists in the Kantō region. When Ieyasu first established his base in Edo, he pursued a policy of compromise toward the Honzanha ascetics, but once his power had been firmly established he proceeded to take away their monopolies on certain purification rites.[6]

Beginning in the mid-fifteenth century, the Kogi Shingon school had established a solid base in southeastern Sagami Province, about one century before other rival schools.[7] With the establishment of Tokugawa rule, the Kogi Shingon school was among the first Buddhist schools to gain recognition and patronage from the Tokugawa regime. Perhaps uneasy about the regime's ability to maintain control over Ōyama's local warriors and *yamabushi*, all of whom were local men with local interests, Ieyasu eventually stripped them of their control over the mountain once he had firmly established his authority. Tokugawa Ieyasu became shogun in 1603 but retired to Sunpu Castle in Suruga in 1605 and transferred the office to his son Hidetada, thereby securing the succession of his heir. Ōyama was now wedged between the seat of the Tokugawa regime in Edo and Ieyasu's castle in Suruga. At the beginning of 1605, Ieyasu issued an order that forced Ōyama's *yamabushi* to resettle at the foot of the mountain and turn the mountain itself over to the Kogi Shingon clergy to ensure that Ōyama would not undermine the Tokugawa regime's authority:

When the Shingon monk Gangyō revitalized Ōyama [in the thirteenth century], the clergy was diligent in their practice of the three mysteries, making continuous incense and water offerings. In recent years, the light of the dharma no longer continues to shine, and the esoteric teachings have been neglected, a situation that we shall henceforth rectify. Instead of having clerics engage in frivolous behavior, only orthodox monks, who observe the precepts and the teachings, shall reside on this famous mountain. Those who notoriously violate the precepts shall swiftly rectify their misbehavior. Heterodox monks, who neither study nor observe the precepts, shall be cast out. Clerics who observe the precepts shall live and practice here. The teachings of the Kogi Shingon school shall be observed in perpetuity henceforth.[8]

According to this edict, ritualists at Ōyama were guilty of immoral conduct and neglected their duties. The edict drew a clear distinction between orthodox monks (literally, "pure" monks), who kept the precepts, and heterodox monks, who violated the precepts. This created a distinction between supposedly celibate Shingon clerics and married *yamabushi*, who were assigned a lower status as religious professionals. Henceforth, Ōyama was to be the domain of orthodox Kogi Shingon clerics, a move justified by pointing to Ōyama's connection with a thirteenth-century Shingon precept specialist, the monk Gangyō.[9] The order was couched in the language of rectifying the local ritualists' neglect of proper religious services by returning to scholastic learning and adhering to the precepts, but it effectively stripped the *yamabushi* of their right to live on the mountain. The so-called return to orthodox Buddhism actually created a new order. It took away power from potentially subversive local forces, embodied by the married mountain ascetics who had lived and trained on the mountain for generations, and transferred it to relative outsiders, the Shingon clergy, who came to Ōyama from the larger region rather than the local setting.

  To replace the *yamabushi*, the shogunate installed Jitsuō as the abbot of Hachidaibō—the head administrative temple at Ōyama—as well as 25 other clerics, about two clerics for each of the thirteen Shingon temples on the mountain slope. Jitsuō was a high-ranking Kogi Shingon cleric, born in central Sagami Province as the son of a local warrior.[10] As a young boy, he took the tonsure at Hōkongōji in Kōzu Village,

Lower Ashigara District. Even at a young age, he was active in the promotion of the Kogi Shingon school in Sagami Province. In the 1570s, he revitalized several smaller temples in the area, which later became branch temples of Hōkongōji.[11] Before becoming the abbot of Hachidaibō, he served as the abbot of Jōchiin in Hiratsuka, Ōsumi District. Both Hōkongōji and Jōchiin were among seven important Kogi Shingon temples in Sagami Province affiliated with Tōji, a major Kogi Shingon temple in Kyoto, since 1557.[12]

Through Jitsuō's appointment, Ōyama became firmly incorporated into the orthodox Kogi Shingon fold. Since it had not been an exclusively Shingon institution previously, Ōyama needed to be completely restructured, both physically and institutionally. The basic groundwork for this process took place between 1605 and 1610 and resulted in Ōyama becoming a shogunal prayer temple and an immediate branch temple of Mt. Kōya, the headquarters of the Kogi Shingon school. In 1605, three months after Jitsuō's appointment as Ōyama's chief abbot, the *bakufu* directed Ina Tadatsugu, an important vassal of Ieyasu in the Kantō region, to undertake a large reconstruction project, an effort that took about three and a half years. The project gave Ōyama the basic architectural layout that it retained throughout the early modern period. Located on the central mountain slope, Hachidaibō was the chief administrative temple surrounded by eleven other subtemples (see Fig. 2.1).[13] To give Jitsuō sufficient financial power to control the mountain as abbot, he was awarded 57 *koku* as a personal stipend and authority over the temples and forests on Ōyama itself.[14] This meant that Hachidaibō held ritual and financial control over the temple compound and had the exclusive right to the mountain forest. The clerics could give the villagers the right to gather firewood, building materials, and weeds for fertilizer, but the use of prime timber was restricted.[15]

Jitsuō proved to be an able and influential abbot. His appointment to a newly converted Kogi Shingon temple at a regionally important sacred site enhanced his status in the Kogi Shingon school. He was one of twelve eminent clerics, including four representatives of Kogi Shingon, invited to attend a debate between the Jōdo and Nichiren schools in the winter of 1608.[16] Together with his successors Jitsuei and Kenryū, he was also invited to Ieyasu's castle at Sunpu in Suruga to lecture on

HACHIDAIBŌ

(two branches: one in monastic precinct, one in Sakamoto)

WITHIN THE MONASTIC PRECINCT		IN SAKAMOTO AND OTHER VILLAGES
Subtemples	*Lamp Duty*	*Branch Temples*
1. Daikakubō	Daikanjin	1. Raigōin (Sakamoto, Sagami)
2. Kaminoin		2. Kannonji (Sakamoto, Sagami)
3. Nakanoin	*Wakibō*	3. Kōmyōin (Ōtake, Sagami)
4. Jōenbō	*(since the late 17th century)*	4. Fukusenji (Marushima, Sagami)
5. Hashimotobō	1. Shinrikibō	5. Daijōin (Koishikawa, Musashi)
6. Hōjuin	2. Kōenbō	*(4 and 5 added between 1630 and the late 1700s)*
7. Jitsujōbō	3. Hōkōbō	
8. Jutokuin	4. Chōjunbō	
9. Yōchiin	5. Sengakubō	
10. Kōtokuin	6. Yūjunbō	
11. Kirakubō		

WITHIN SAKAMOTO AND MINOGE	
Attendants	*9 Shrine priests/*
1. Iwamotobō	*spirit mediums*
2. Genchōbō	
3. Yūsenbō	*Approx. 140 oshi*
4. Shōhonbō	

Fig. 2.1 The institutional structure of the temple complex in the early modern period.

the Buddhist teachings.[17] In 1609, Ōyama was further awarded almost 100 *koku* of temple land—72 in Sakamoto Village and 27 in Koyasu Village—to give it a sound financial base. The village settlement on the temple land later developed into Ōyama's primary temple town.[18] For a Kogi Shingon temple in the Kantō region, the award was extensive, placing Ōyama, with combined temple landholdings of 157 *koku*, in second position among Kogi Shingon temples behind Kongōōin at Hakone (200 *koku*) and before Anrakuji in Ichinomiya (100 *koku*) and Ryōzenji in Hinata (64 *koku*).[19]

Ōyama was, of course, not the only institution that received the attention of the Tokugawa regime. Between 1605 and 1620, the shogunate issued numerous new law codes (*hatto*), such as those governing aristocratic families (in 1613 and 1615) and one governing warrior families (in 1615).[20] This was also the period in which all schools of Japanese Buddhism saw extensive institutional restructuring. The first and foremost of these developments was the issuing of law codes governing religious institutions issued by the *bakufu* and by newly recognized head temples of various sects. Even though regional warlords of the Warring States period and the unifiers Oda Nobunaga and Toyotomi Hideyoshi had occasionally sought control over specific, powerful religious institutions, the Buddhist sects had not yet been organized into unified systems encompassing the whole of Japan. The Tokugawa's earliest attempts to standardize sectarian regulations were likewise limited to major temples in the Kantō and Kansai regions—in other words, both the region closest to Edo and directly under shogunal control and the region containing the most powerful temples near Kyoto and Nara.[21] Between 1601 and 1615, for the Shingon school alone, the *bakufu* issued the *Kōyasanchū hatto* (1601), *Kantō Shingonshū Kogi hatto* (Kantō Kogi Shingon School Code), *Daigoji hatto*, *Sagami Ōyama hatto*, the *Tōji hatto* (all four in 1609), another set of *Kōyasanchū hatto* (1610), the *Hasedera hatto* (1612), *Chisekiin hatto* (1613), *Kantō Shingi Shingonshū hatto* (1613), and *Shingonshū shohatto* (1615). Only the last of these codes covered the entire Shingon sect throughout Japan. In addition to clarifying the specifics of individual Shingon institutions, these codes regulated the training of clerics, fees for the performance of certain rituals *vis-à-vis* Honzanha and Tōzanha *shugendō*, and the wearing of monastic robes.[22]

Around this time the *bakufu* also designated a central head temple for each sect and established a hierarchical system of head and branch temples.[23] According to Udaka Yoshiaki, Kogi Shingon head-branch temple relations in the late sixteenth century had still been fluid and based on personal lineage ties and the temples' relationship with the authorities, but in the early seventeenth century head-branch temple relations came to be based on the temples' ranks.[24] Mt. Kōya functioned as the central administrative head temple of the Kogi Shingon school, but Tōji and Daigoji—later also Ninnaji and Takaosanji—in the Kyoto area, the stronghold of the Kogi Shingon school, were given secondary head temple status for the training of clerics in 1609.[25] Likewise, a system of regional academies (*dangisho*) was set up in the same year to create sectarian cohesion and hierarchy in the Kantō region.[26] Ōyama became one of 33 Shingon academies in Sagami, Musashi, and Izu Provinces, gaining religious authority throughout the Kantō region.[27]

The Kantō academy system elevated the ranking of Ōyama in the Kogi Shingon school in the Kantō region. This may have been due to the fact that the Ōyama Hachidaibō abbot Jitsuō was involved in drafting the law codes. Even though the *bakufu* provided the initial impulse for the development of sectarian regulations, the guidelines were essentially drafted by high-ranking clerics of the Kogi Shingon school and later approved by the *bakufu*. According to a nine-article code issued by the *bakufu* for the Kantō Kogi Shingon school in 1609, clerics who were to serve as abbots had to spend at least three years of training at an academy where they were to devote themselves to the study of the teachings of the Kogi Shingon school before being awarded the title *nōke* (teacher). This nine-article code was an abstract of a more detailed code issued on the same day by the Shingon clerics Raikei (Kōyasan Henshōkōin), Jitsuō (Sagami Ōyamadera Hachidaibō), and Kaiun (Izusan Hannyain): the *Kantōchū honji hōrongi shokeshū sadamesho* (Regulations for the Scholarly Training of Novices at Head Temples in the Kantō).[28]

The same pattern of issuing law codes was repeated for Ōyama: in 1609, the *bakufu* issued a three-article code that was simultaneously issued in much greater detail by the scholar-monk Raikei from Mt. Kōya. These codes spelled out the implied meaning of Ieyasu's edict from 1605 more directly. Only pure monks (i.e., celibate clerics) were to reside above the Outer Fudō Hall, and *yamabushi* and lay households were to turn over their residences to the abbot of Hachidaibō for reassignment to the clerics. Similarly, all assets—patrons, the mountain forests, the chapels and shrines on the mountain, and all donations—were to be administered by the Shingon clerics residing in twelve temples on Ōyama.[29] The *bakufu*'s orders were but a summary of more detailed regulations issued by Mt. Kōya, which clarified the duties of the clergy and their authority over the *yamabushi* at Ōyama. Since the regulations were issued by the head temple Mt. Kōya and were addressed to the branch temple Ōyama, represented by Hachidaibō, the laws were primarily concerned with the authority of the Shingon temples at Ōyama. To maintain order at the mountain, they clarified the primary ritual activities of the clergy, the distinction between ordained and lay ritualists, and the management of the precinct. They also gave Hachidaibō increased leverage to control both clerics and *yamabushi*. In addition, they were intended to create cohesion among the Shingon clerics by preventing factionalism and by creating a sense of sectarian identity. This was achieved by giving the Shingon clergy exclusive control over key rituals, making monastic attendance in communal Shingon rituals mandatory, rotating ritual and administrative duties among clerics at Hachidaibō and eleven other subtemples, and granting Hachidaibō increased representation and legal powers.[30]

While these regulations served to establish a sense of hierarchy at Ōyama, they did not specify the place of the non-Shingon Buddhist clergy, the *yamabushi*'s role in yearly festivals, and the distribution of ritual duties and donations from the multitude of smaller shrines and Buddhist chapels at Ōyama. To avoid further ambiguity, Raikei issued another code later in 1609 that curtailed *yamabushi*'s participation in rituals on the mountain and banished clerics of other sects from residing on Ōyama.[31] Moreover, income from the temple land and donations from the majority of the Buddhist chapels and shrines were to be exclusively collected by the conglomerate of twelve Shingon temples, led by Hachidaibō. A few shrines and chapels were exempt from this rule and were managed by a select number of hereditary shrine priests and ritualists in the service of Hachidaibō.[32] Among the clergy, Hachidaibō was given individual control over the largest number halls (6 of 22), but the majority of the remaining halls were administered jointly by the clergy rather than by a specific subtemple. To further ensure the administrative supremacy of the Hachidaibō abbot over the clerics at the other eleven temples, he was also given the right to investigate clerics at the subtemples who did not devote themselves to scholarly study.[33]

The Shingon clergy's attempt to assume total control over Ōyama's ritual space and the income derived thereof was perhaps most clearly embodied by a signboard with prohibitions regarding the main sanctuary dedicated to Fudō, which Raikei issued on the same day as the above-mentioned monastic codes. It included the following items: only the clerics on duty were to be allowed in the inner sanctuary, and only they could give pilgrims a tour of the sanctuary; sales within the Buddhist halls were prohibited; and inns at the foot of the mountain were required to turn over offerings received for *tenaga* services (a complex central offertory rite at Ōyama) to the Shingon clergy.[34] The main hall dedicated to Fudō was Ōyama's primary cultic site and yielded to highest income from pilgrims, particularly through the performance of *tenaga* services commissioned by the pilgrims. These involved elaborate vegetarian food offerings and were the most expensive rite conducted on their behalf.

However, that the *bakufu* and a high-ranking cleric from Mt. Kōya continued issuing orders over a period of four years indicates that change came only slowly and was only reluctantly accepted by Ōyama's *yamabushi*, shrine priests, and non-Shingon Buddhist clerics. Although detailed evidence is sparse, records indicate that Hachidaibō was involved in at least two disputes during this decade. In 1616, Hachidaibō found itself locked in a dispute with local *yamabushi* over the right to guide pilgrims to Ise and Kumano—an indication that Ōyama had not yet attained its later popularity as a regional pilgrimage site. Rather than catering only to local pilgrims, its ritualists acted as guides to more famous historical pilgrimage sites in western Japan. In 1618, the year that Jitsuō passed away and was succeeded by his disciple Jitsuei, who proved to be a weak leader, Hachidaibō was engaged in a confrontation with Ōyama's shrine priests, an incident that prompted the Tokugawa regime to intervene on behalf of the clergy.[35]

The *bakufu* had an interest in seeing the Shingon temple Hachidaibō prevail over its rival institutions at Ōyama. Through its patronage of the Shingon clergy, the shogunate could simultaneously assert its image as the righteous restorer of the Buddhist teachings, eliminate politically subversive powers, and reap the spiritual rewards of Ōyama's efficacy as a sacred site much in the same way that medieval regional lords had harnessed Ōyama's sacred powers for their military success. Like their predecessors, the Ashikaga and the Odawara Hōjō, the Tokugawa shogunate had sponsored the physical reconstruction of the site and commissioned prayers for the new regime. As a shogunal prayer temple, Ōyama not only carried out regular prayers for the Tokugawa regime but also received high-ranking pilgrims representing the shogunal interests in times of national crisis.[36]

Unlike their medieval counterparts, however, the Tokugawa took a much greater regulatory role in the shaping of the monastic complex. By 1615, Ōyama had evolved from a potentially hostile institution with ties to the Odawara Hōjō to one supportive of the Tokugawa regime. It was led by a *bakufu*-appointed Shingon abbot, had been completely rebuilt with *bakufu* funding and institutionally restructured through *bakufu* legislation, and had been appointed as an academy and shogunal prayer temple serving as a site for official prayers for continued shogunal succession and military success of the Tokugawa. In this process,

Jitsuō's personal acquaintance with Raikei and the Tokugawa regime made him an ideal candidate to see to the *bakufu*'s interests as well as the interests of the Shingon school.

Consolidating an Early Modern Shingon Temple Complex, 1618–1690

When Jitsuō passed away three years later in 1618, he was succeeded by his disciple Jitsuei,[37] whose tenure lasted from 1618 until his death in 1625. Little is known of Jitsuei's abbotship except for the above-mentioned dispute between Hachidaibō and a shrine priest in 1618. Jitsuei seems to have lacked Jitsuō's charisma and failed to designate a successor. After his death, Hachidaibō continued for eight years without a designated abbot, during which the remaining clerics at Ōyama's subtemples presumably took charge of the daily affairs.

The *Kantō Shingonshū Kogi honmatsuchō* (Head-Branch Temple Register of the Kogi Shingon Sect Temples in the Kantō Region), compiled in 1633, illustrates both Ōyama's elevated position within the Kogi Shingon school of the early seventeenth century and how quickly Ōyama could lose its powerful influence within the sect without a Hachidaibō abbot. Similar registers were compiled in the early 1630s by other Buddhist schools in response to an order by the *bakufu*, which attempted to further organize them into a hierarchical head-branch temple system.[38] According to the register, Ōyama was one of the five great Shingon temples in the Kantō region after Izusan Hannyain in Izu, Hakonesan Kongōin in Sagami, Shōgon'in, which was one of the temples at the Kamakura Hachiman Shrine in Sagami, and Ōji Konrinji in Musashi. All five temples functioned as shogunal prayer temples and were ranked as academies. Even though Ōyama's temple land was smaller than three of the other temples, only Ōyama and the temples at the Hachiman Shrine in Kamakura held the rank of a *jōhōdanjo* (permanent academy). The two *jōhōdanjō* were thereby lifted in status above the other larger temples, which were merely given the title of *hōdanjo* (academy).[39] According to the same record, Ōyama's Hachidaibō was a branch temple of Mt. Kōya. Its remaining eleven subtemples were treated not as branch temples of Hachidaibō but as one unit belonging to Ōyamadera together with Hachidaibō. These twelve temples there had 25 official clerics. In addition, Hachidaibō had three branch temples, Raigōin and Kannonji in Sakamoto Village and Kōmyōin in Ōtake Village.[40]

Yet despite its elevated status in the sectarian hierarchy, Ōyama had temporarily lost its influence within the regional Kogi Shingon school due to the vacant Hachidaibō abbacy. The head-branch-temple register was compiled by six clerics from Kogi Shingon academies in the Kantō region, including two whose temples ranked below Ōyama, but Ōyama's clerics did not participate in the compilation.[41] Moreover, the absence of a scholarly abbot from Hachidaibō violated the sectarian regulations for Kantō Kogi Shingon academies from 1609, a situation that may have come to the attention of the compilers as they conducted their survey, which familiarized them with the institutional structure of Ōyama. As Udaka Yoshiaki notes, the Kogi Shingon school—like the larger Shingi Shingon school—was controlled by several powerful temples in the Kantō region, which took on the role of liaisons (*furegashira*) with the authorities in the seventeenth and early eighteenth centuries. Ōyama's Hachidaibō was usually counted among these "Five Great Kantō Temples."[42] Without an abbot, however, Hachidaibō could not take on this administrative role.

Ōyama needed the Hachidaibō abbot not only to maintain its influence within its sect but also to maintain full shogunal patronage. When a strong earthquake struck Sagami, Izu, and Suruga Provinces in 1633, Hachidaibō was still without an abbot. The earthquake was severe enough to cause structural damage to Odawara Castle.[43] Ōyama was probably also damaged by the quake but was not rebuilt until 1638 after the appointment of Kenryū, the former abbot of the Hakonesan Kongōōin, as the new Hachidaibō abbot in the summer of 1633.[44] While the resident clergy was able to run Ōyama under ordinary circumstances, they seem to have lacked the necessary leadership to conduct a major fund-raising and reconstruction project without a charismatic abbot.

Soon after his appointment, Kenryū took various steps to restore Ōyama's predominant position in the Kantō Shingon school and remove incongruities regarding its land holdings. In 1636, three years after Kenryū's appointment, Ōyama was granted shogunal approval to incorporate the 57 *koku* in Kominoge Village, initially granted to the Hachidaibō abbot as a personal stipend, into the general temple land. This step appears to have addressed problems Ōyama probably incurred when it was without an abbot for eight years.[45] Kenryū also initiated renewed contact with the *bakufu*, which led to an official visit to

Ōyama by Eizō, at the time a high-ranking cleric at Mt. Tsukuba and later abbot of Konshōin, Yushima, Edo, as a shogunal representative in the spring of 1637. About a year later, in 1638, the magistrate of temples and shrines sent an order of complete reconstruction of the temple precincts. The magistrate of temples and shrines followed up on its order by sending carpenters and budgeting 10,000 *ryō* to cover the costs of construction in the winter of 1639. The construction work lasted nearly two years, from the spring of 1640 to the winter of 1641. Its completion was marked by a ridgepole-raising ceremony and the installation of the Buddhist statuary. A ceremonious Great Mandala service was held and was attended by important Shingon clerics from Musashi, Sagami, and Izu Provinces. At around this time, Kasuga no Tsubone, the former wet-nurse of Tokugawa Iemitsu, visited Ōyama twice as a shogunal representative—once in the autumn of 1640, to pray for a son for Tokugawa Iemitsu, and once in the summer of 1643, to mark the completion of the construction project. Similarly, Eizō was again dispatched as a representative of Iemitsu's newborn son in 1642. Clearly, during Kenryū's tenure, which lasted sixteen years until his death in 1650, Ōyama enjoyed close relations with the *bakufu*.[46]

The next three abbots of Ōyama also provided strong leadership during their long tenures and secured essential *bakufu* patronage. Ryū-kei, who had become a monk and Kenryū's disciple at Ōyama, served as abbot for 37 years until early 1687. Through his family background, Ryūkei was able to gain support from the authorities. He was apparently related to the Tokugawa through the Mito branch, which secured him leverage with the magistrate of temples and shrines. For example, Hachidaibō still had not solidified its authority firmly. When *yamabushi* and *oshi* in Sakamoto Village kept challenging Hachidaibō's authority, the magistrate of temples and shrines sided with Ryūkei and Hachidaibō. In 1663, a dispute erupted between the Shingon temples and the *yamabushi*, which appears to have been caused by a disagreement over hereditary stipends.[47] The magistrate of temples and shrines issued ordinances to settle the dispute between the two parties, judging that the *yamabushi* and others who opposed Hachidaibō were members of an "evil faction." Five *yamabushi* and six *oshi*, including highly placed ritualists, were first jailed for opposing Hachidaibō in the previous year and then exiled from Sakamoto Village.[48] Most of Ōyama's many *yama-*

bushi were forced to give up their status as *yamabushi* and become *oshi*.[49] Only three *yamabushi* were allowed to remain in Sakamoto Village because they had not participated in the resistance. Furthermore, the Rinzai clerics at the Daiyōji—the second largest temple on Ōyama in the late sixteenth century—and two smaller temples were also banished.[50] The outcome of the dispute was of great significance for Ōyama's early modern development and is discussed in greater detail in the following chapter, which addresses the *oshi*'s development from *yamabushi*. The dispute gave Hachidaibō an opportunity to banish *yamabushi* and clerics in the village who had outside affiliations with Honzanha *shugendō* or the Rinzai school. Hachidaibō was thereby able to secure fully its authority over Ōyama.[51]

Ryūkei continued his efforts to implement the new order in the temple towns by issuing a mountain code in 1674, which aimed to regulate the hereditary rights of *oshi* to their parishioners and reduce the competition between the *oshi* and innkeepers for pilgrims. Ryūkei also secured the *bakufu*'s support when natural disasters such as floods and fires struck Ōyama's temple land, causing heavy damage to the town and temple buildings. When the Ōyama River flooded and washed away valuable land from Sakamoto Village in the summer of 1666, Ryūkei petitioned assistance from the *bakufu* in the spring of the following year. In response, the *bakufu* transferred about two-and-a-half acres of land from the neighboring Koyasu Village, which became Sakamoto Village's Shinchō (New Town).[52] After fires destroyed the Scripture Hall and the Outer Fudō Hall, in 1668 and 1673, respectively, Ryūkei secured 200 *ryō* and lumber from the *bakufu* for repairs of the major temple buildings at Ōyama in 1676.[53] However, his request in the spring of 1687 for funds for further reconstruction was not granted.[54] Eventually, his successor Kūben, who became the Hachidaibō abbot in 1687 about one month after Ryūkei's death, secured the funding for a large-scale reconstruction.

Full Institutional Formation, 1690–1750

By Kūben's time, Ōyama had become a leader among the Kogi Shingon temples in the region. Hachidaibō's abbots, including Kūben, came from one of the 33 academies in Sagami, Musashi, or Izu Provinces. Jitsuō's, Kenryū's, and Kūben's appointments took place after they had been promoted to the position of abbot of an academy of equal or lower rank than Ōyama's Shingon complex. In contrast, Jitsuei and Ryūkei were direct disciples of their predecessors at Hachidaibō and could be considered insiders for the high post. In either case, the appointment as Hachidaibō abbot was a final promotion since they held their offices until their deaths. But Ōyama's regional importance was due not only to the high rank of the office of the abbot.

Under Abbot Kūben, Ōyama also flourished as a major Shingon center in Sagami Province and was reconstructed physically and institutionally. Kūben was a native of Nichiren Village (Tsukui District, Sagami Province) and became ordained and served as abbot at Renjōin in Makino Village (also in Tsukui District). He later transferred to Ishikawa Hōshōji, an academy in Musashi Province with 44 branch temples.[55] From there he moved to Ōyama, where he held his post as abbot for thirteen years until his death in the summer of 1700. Kūben maintained close contact with the shogunate. Three weeks after his installation, he had an audience at Edo castle, which became a custom for newly appointed abbots at Ōyama. From 1692, he also paid visits to the magistrate of temples and shrines for the New Year, which also became customary for Ōyama's abbots. Ōyama was one of five Kogi Shingon temples—the *de facto furegashira*, or sectarian liaison in administrative matters—in the Kantō region that paid regular tribute to the shogunate.[56]

From 1688, about one year after his installation, Kūben continued his predecessor's request to the magistrate of temples and shrines to repair Ōyama's temple buildings. It had been 48 years since the last major reconstruction. In his requests, Kūben reminded the magistrate of temples and shrines that the *bakufu* had sponsored reconstruction at Ōyama under Ieyasu, Iemitsu, and Ietsuna. He filed three further requests over the next two years but without positive results. In 1692, Kūben renewed his request, citing previous shogunal patronage and pointing out that Ōyama was in such grave need of repairs that Ieyasu's orders to Ōyama's 25 clerics to hold rites on behalf of the shogunate could not be carried out safely. Three months later, the magistrate of temples and shrines dispatched a delegation to Ōyama to assess the necessary repairs and granted the Shingon temples over 6,000 *ryō*, lumber, and lacquer. Construction began the following year in the summer of 1693 and lasted five months. Again the completion of the construction work was celebrated with a Great Mandala Service, which included representatives from other Kogi Shingon academies and their branch temples in Sagami Province. The service marking the complete reconstruction of a Kogi Shingon academy like Ōyama brought together clerics from throughout the area, cementing sectarian and head-branch temple relations.[57]

Furthermore, Ōyama's Hachidaibō represented sectarian interests and acted as a spokesperson for Kogi Shingon temples in the region. Rituals such as the Great Mandala Service and Ōyama's status as an academy helped to cultivate sectarian ties, which were helpful when the sect faced internal conflict. In 1697 and 1698, Hachidaibō's abbot Kūben became embroiled in a dispute over the performance of purification rites for the pilgrimage to Ise and Kumano, which pitted Kogi Shingon temples in Sagami Province not only against Tendai-affiliated Honzanha *yamabushi* but also another faction within the Kogi Shingon school. Hachidaibō under Kūben acted as a representative of the Kogi Shingon temples, which included twelve temples whose clerics had attended the Great Mandala Service at Ōyama in 1692. None of the clerics in the opposing Kogi Shingon faction from three temples had participated in this event.[58] During the dispute, Ōyama acted as the leader (*tōnin*) of the Kogi Shingon school in Sagami Province, which was represented by seventeen regional academies, much in the same way that Gyokurō-bō, a Honzanha mountain-ascetic temple in Odawara, represented Honzanha temples even though Ōyama was not the head temple of the other Kogi Shingon branch temples. The Kogi Shingon academies acted in concert by holding assemblies at one of the academies to decide their course of action in the beginning of the case and to sum up their position shortly before the conclusion of the legal proceedings. The actual Kogi Shingon *furegashira* (liaison temple) Zenshūin, which was supposed to act as the liaison between Kogi Shingon temples and the *bakufu*, entered into the dispute only once: to convey the renegade Shingon temples' apology to the magistrate of temples and shrines for having sent impertinent letters to the authorities.

During the dispute, Ōyama acted as the regional leader, coordinating the legal effort against Honzanha. Kūben, the Hachidaibō abbot, filed the initial counter-suit against Honzanha and represented the school during most of the case, even staying in Edo for about seven months. Ōyama's clerics issued correspondence on behalf of the Shingon school to the magistrate of temples and shrines, enforced orders affecting the regional Shingon school, argued the case before the *bakufu*, and took charge of controlling smaller temples that violated the sectarian policy or acted without sectarian authorization. Ōyama's clergy could take this position due to the academy's high rank in the Kogi Shingon school, its direct connection to Mt. Kōya, its close connection to the *bakufu*, and its considerable endowment of temple land and income through pilgrims. However, eventually, this administrative system based on five great Kogi Shingon temples in the Kantō region disappeared in the mid-eighteenth century.[59]

After his death in 1700, Kūben was succeeded by Kaizō, Ōyama's last major abbot in the eighteenth century, who held the office of Hachi-daibō abbot for 31 years until 1731. During Kūben's and his successor Kaizō's tenures, Ōyama underwent structural reform that extended to Sakamoto Village.[60] At the beginning of his tenure, Kaizō faced several difficult challenges, ranging from natural disasters to disputes between the villages at the foot of the mountain, but he was ultimately able to surmount all these problems. Ōyama's temple complex had survived a severe earthquake in 1697 unharmed, but in the winter of 1703, only three-and-a-half years after Kaizō's appointment, Ōyama's temples were devastated by another major earthquake that destroyed more than 6,300 buildings in Sagami Province.[61] This must have been a crucial test of Kaizō's leadership, but he was able to meet the difficult challenge through important institutional changes. Indeed, it may have been precisely the destruction of the temple complex that allowed him to make such drastic structural reforms. Kaizō was fortunate to receive immediate support from the magistrate of temples and shrines, who sent an emissary to investigate the damage in the spring of 1704, followed by an order for reconstruction and a grant of 2,000 *ryō* and 25,000 pieces of lumber. Similarly, when a flood damaged Sakamoto Village in the following year, the *bakufu* contributed 300 *ryō* in the summer of 1705.[62] The *bakufu*'s continued financial support of Ōyama was extraordinary, considering that other institutions were finding it increasingly difficult to obtain funding from the shogunate by this time. The newly reconstructed buildings proved to be highly earthquake resistant, surviving major quakes in 1706, 1707, and 1782, even though the latter two were strong enough to cause severe damage in Odawara.[63] When the temple finally was destroyed due to an earthquake in 1855, it was not the tremor itself but subsequent fires that caused the damage. Despite major earthquakes and a devastating eruption of Mt. Fuji in 1707 that covered large parts of Sagami Province in 20 to 60 centimeters of volcanic ash that clogged rivers and destroyed crops,[64] Ōyama flourished under Kaizō.

During his tenure, Kaizō consolidated important institutional structures that bolstered the authority of Hachidaibō's abbots over Ōyama. He established a new cemetery for Hachidaibō's abbots on the lower slopes of Ōyama, which was to house the tombs of the Hachidaibō abbots since Kūben (fifth generation) during the early modern period— with the exception of the thirteenth-, fourteenth-, fifteenth-, and seventeenth-generation abbots in the late eighteenth and early nineteenth centuries, when the ties of the Hachidaibō abbots with Ōyama weakened.[65] Kaizō also named as his representatives (*wakibō*) six newly established temples on the mountain (see Fig. 2.1). These temples were all founded in the second half of the seventeenth century. Even though they were located in the same area as the other twelve subtemples, they seem to have had a different administrative function, which was to serve the needs of the Hachidaibō abbot. For example, when the shrines on the summit burned down in 1719, clerics from three of the six *wakibō* assisted Kaizō in a purification ceremony after the fire.[66] It was probably also during his tenure that Ōyama received official recognition for identifying Sekison Daigongen and Tokuichi, two deities venerated on Ōyama's summit, with the ancient deities Tori no Iwakusufune no Mikoto and Ōyamazumi no Mikoto. As noted in Chapter 6, Kaizō may have used the *Ōyamajiki*, which he compiled to clarify the ancient origins of Ōyama's deities, to achieve his goal.

Under Kaizō, the institutionalization of Ōyama was completed. He not only reconstructed the entire compound but also issued three sets of mountain codes and set up an important administrative system to handle the growing numbers of pilgrims. The codes were devised to lend support to *oshi* residing in Sakamoto Village *vis-à-vis* their competitors in Koyasu Village.[67] Sakamoto faced trouble with its neighbor Koyasu. Pilgrims from Edo and the eastern Kantō region passed through both villages. Although Sakamoto was located completely within the boundaries of Ōyama's temple land, parts of Koyasu lay outside it. This did not prevent the residents of Koyasu from catering to pilgrims and claiming parishioners just like their neighbors in Sakamoto. The competition for pilgrims caused severe tension between the villages. Kaizō attempted to settle the dispute by issuing Ōyama's second mountain code in 1702, which established a licensing system for *oshi* under the control of the Shingon temples.[68] However, neither Hachidaibō nor the other subtemples disapproved of Koyasu handling pilgrims *per se*. As long as the residents fought among themselves without challenging the clergy's authority, the latter had little to lose by offering special licenses and privileges to the *oshi*, even though they continued to accept the services of unlicensed innkeepers in Koyasu in bringing pilgrims to their doors. Kaizō issued two further sets of mountain codes in 1713 and 1721 that were intended to accommodate the rising numbers of pilgrims through the extension of the summer festival. They also clarified the handling of pilgrims and defined the position of an *oshi* and his rights.

Once Ōyama became a popular pilgrimage destination from the late seventeenth century, it was necessary to regulate the performance of Buddhist rituals for the pilgrims. For example, performance of fire rituals (*goma*) by the twelve subtemples on the mountain was controlled by a system of mediation (*toritsugi*), which was finalized under Kaizō. As Matsuoka Takashi explains, this system was devised to regulate concretely how the Ōyama clergy directed *goma* rituals performed before the main image of worship for the benefit of pilgrims who were parishioners of *oshi* at the foot of the mountain. The idea that only the ordained clergy should perform rituals at the Main Hall had been set up already by Raikei's regulations from 1609.[69] In the late seventeenth century, the clergy devised a system regulating which of the subtemples would handle pilgrims based on the *oshi* with whom they were affiliated and so ensured that the subtemples' handling of increasing numbers of pilgrims proceeded smoothly.

In 1718 and 1730, under Abbot Kaizō, registers were compiled detailing which of the twelve subtemples provided *goma* services for the parishioners of which *oshi* or the guests of which inn in Sakamoto Village and in Minoge Village. The *oshi* and other villagers running small inns were divided into upper, middle, and lower levels. Some of the *oshi*, especially those ranked as upper level, relied on two subtemples, but the system essentially eliminated competition among the temples for pilgrims staying at inns at the foot of the mountain.[70] The mediation system also secured income for the clerics, but pilgrims were not divided equally among the subtemples. Hachidaibō, which controlled a large percentage of the donations from the halls and temples on the mountain and the temple land, did not need to rely primarily on income from rituals commissioned by pilgrims. Therefore, Hachidaibō served only three percent, mostly medium-level households. The remaining eleven subtemples, however, had to supplement their income with fees collected from pilgrims. Nakanoin, Daikakubō, Jutokuin, and Hōjuin together served about 53 percent of the households.[71] Although it did not create complete equality among the twelve subtemples, the mediation system essentially provided enough stability to prevent excessive competition.

By the end of Kaizō's tenure, Ōyama had become such a popular pilgrimage site that enough funds were raised to partially cover small reconstruction projects. Fortunately, Ōyama did not face any large-scale reconstruction until 1855; it only had to finance the reconstruction of the shrines on the summit on three occasions during the eighteenth century. In the spring of 1719, Kanbei, a man from Kawaguchi Village in Musashi Province, climbed to the summit during the off-season and set two of the five shrines on fire. He claimed upon his arrest that Heaven had instructed him to commit arson so that the shrines would be rebuilt. About ten days later, Kaizō set out to Edo to report the case to the magistrate of temples and shrines and to request funds for repairs. Reconstruction, which took three months and lasted through the summer, was partially funded by a grant of 200 *ryō* from the magistrate of temples and shrines. However, the grant proved to be insufficient. Donations from the Sekison Shrine (15 *ryō*), Daitengu Shrine (9 *ryō*), and Shōtengu Shrine (9 *ryō*), as well as funds from Hachidaibō (10 *ryō*), were to be collected each autumn over the course of the next twelve years, totaling 516 *ryō*. Since the shrines on the summit were administered collectively by the Shingon clerics, who had the right to the donations, the remaining costs were borne by the Shingon clergy.[72] On another occasion, when the shrines on the summit burned down in a brush fire at the beginning of 1732, during the first year of the tenure of Kaizō's successor Shusō, who served as Hachidaibō abbot for fifteen years until 1746, the shrines were rebuilt in the spring of the following year. Ōyama's Shingon temples seem to have covered the costs of the reconstruction on their own, under the management of a *wakibō* cleric and with the support of nearby villages through donations of timber.[73]

Institutional Tensions, 1750–1867

By the late eighteenth century, Ōyama's fame as a popular pilgrimage center was firmly established, and its function as an administrative Shingon center with close contact with the magistrate of temples and shrines continued. But the dual aspects of Ōyama as a pilgrimage center and a Shingon academy no longer reinforced each other as smoothly as before. In this period, Hachidaibō's hold over its Shingon subtemples at Ōyama waned. This was due partially to the relatively short periods of tenure of the Hachidaibō abbots, who frequently died before they could establish a personal power base. Over the course of the early modern period, Hachidaibō had seventeen abbots whereas its subtemples on Ōyama on average had only thirteen abbots each, indicating that their tenure at Ōyama lasted longer and allowed them to form stronger local bonds than the chief abbots at Hachidaibō.[74] The situation was exacerbated by long-term absences of the Hachidaibō abbot for audiences in Edo, which weakened his influence over the subtemples even further. In addition, natural disasters took their toll on Ōyama.

Ōyama maintained its influential position within the Kogi Shingon sect and continued to serve as an academy until the end of the period. When a register listing the ranks of important temples was compiled in the early nineteenth century, Ōyama was listed as one of 27 highly ranked scholar temples of the Kogi Shingon school, apart from Mt. Kōya, and as one of the upper-level temples with land holdings larger than 35 *koku*.[75] An updated head-branch-temple register compiled in the late eighteenth century revealed that most other head temples were more firmly incorporated into the parish temple system and had a widespread network of branch temples in Sagami and Musashi Provinces. In contrast, Ōyama had only five, mostly local, branch temples and therefore could not rely on its branch temples to exert its influence within the regional Kogi Shingon school.[76]

The academy at Ōyama achieved its influence over other Kogi Shingon temples by attracting regional clerics from other regional academies by virtue of its high rank in the sectarian hierarchy. The abbots and clerics drawn from other Shingon academies in the region helped to establish a network centered around Ōyama, even though Ōyama had few direct branch temples itself. Whereas some clerics appear to have come as young trainees only to obtain qualifications to become abbots of their home temples, others became the subabbots of one of Ōyama's subtemples and spent considerable time on the mountain.[77] Records covering the last generation of clerics at Ōyama's subtemples during the early modern period illustrate that they were, typically, second, third, or fourth sons of peasants from Sagami or Musashi Provinces. The clerics were ordained at Ōyama or another regional academy nearby between the ages of 7 and 11, went to Mt. Kōya to train for two to five years between the ages of 18 and 21, and were installed as abbots of Ōyama's subtemples in their early twenties. For this particular generation, only the chief abbot at Hachidaibō had a warrior background. He was also considerably older: he had trained at Mt. Kōya for eighteen years and was appointed at Ōyama at the age of 52.[78] Ōyama's Shingon temples were representative of the Kantō region. According to the same document, about 75 percent of the Kogi Shingon clerics in the Kantō region were of peasant background about 12 percent came from warrior families and about 5 percent from merchant families. About 82 percent had received their initiation to become certified as abbots at Mt. Kōya, 5 percent at Ōyama, and 9 percent at other academies in Sagami Province.[79]

In addition to training at Ōyama, local Shingon clerics promoted the Ōyama cult by performing prayer rituals dedicated to Fudō, Ōyama's central Buddhist deity, for local villagers and sending them to Ōyama on thanksgiving pilgrimages. The *Ōyama Fudō reigenki*, a miracle tale collection published by Shinzō, one of Ōyama's clerics, in 1792, contains several anecdotes that illustrate how the Ōyama cult was promoted by local clerics. As miracle tales, the full historicity of the tales is difficult to prove. Nevertheless, since most of the tales are set within a few decades of the publication when at least some of the clerics still would have been alive, it is likely that they were based on actual people and events. For example, a monk called Chōō, who had trained at Jutokuin, was known as a powerful Ōyama Fudō devotee: in 1740 he purportedly cured the wife of Itō Kinzaemon from madness through performing 30,000 spells and incantations and encouraging her family to pray to Ōyama Fudō.[80] Similarly, Fukushuin, a cleric from the local Shingon temple Jōenji, assisted a family affiliated with the Nichiren school—to which the other two village temples belonged—in curing their son of smallpox in 1764. The family sent representatives to Ōyama on a pilgrimage and vowed to make yearly pilgrimages thereafter.[81] In 1771, Jitsunyo from Ōyama's Nakanoin Province gave a desperate pilgrim from Hirama Village an old rope that had been replaced by a new one on the statue of Fudō and that he had worn as an amulet. The pilgrim used small pieces of the rope to cure his daughter and others in need.[82] In 1775, Hakujitsu from Kaminoin performed a *goma* rite to cure a boy from Susugaya Village of diarrhea. Upon his instruction, the boy's parents came to Ōyama to have another *goma* ritual performed and to fast and go on retreat for seven days once the boy recovered.[83] As these tales of healing and worship of Ōyama Fudō indicate, local Shingon clerics served as intermediaries between the Ōyama cult and lay believers.

However, at Ōyama itself the relationship between Hachidaibō and the other subtemples was becoming increasingly fragmented. Officially, the subtemples still functioned as a unit and were bound together by communal observances and administrative structures. The mediation system remained in effect, but alternate routes of establishing direct ties with parishioners developed by the late eighteenth century.[84] These parishioners were not local villagers in the temple registration system but villagers scattered through the Kantō region like the parishes of Ōyama's *oshi*, as discussed in the following chapter. How the temples administered these parishes is not always clear, but in some cases, they provided *goma* services and collected first-fruit donations (*hatsuho*) from their parishioners in cooperation with village headmen.[85] In others, they handed their parishes to specific *oshi* under the terms of a contract that gave them continued access to the parishioners for *goma* services at Ōyama, regardless of the *oshi*'s official affiliation in the mediation system.[86] In either case, the arrangement undermined the stability of the mediation system by circumventing the established temple-*oshi*-parishioner relationships and by allowing specific subtemples at Ōyama to supplement their income.

Moreover, other Shingon temples at Ōyama sought additional income by establishing special contact with pilgrims, which was not covered by the mediation system. By 1835, the subtemple Yōchiin had taken control of the Outer Fudō Hall and the adjacent waterfall, which had previously been managed by an *oshi*.[87] Yōchiin was incorporated into the mediation system but did not have the lion's share of *oshi* parishioners, nor did it seem to have its own parishioners. Therefore, it may have been in need of the additional income derived from its role of managing the Outer Fudō Hall and controlling access to the waterfall, which was probably used for ritual ablutions by pilgrims.

Furthermore, Raigōin, which was located on the lower slopes of the mountain just above the Outer Fudō Hall, and the *wakibō* Kōenbō, located near Hachidaibō, had taken up a new function. Both Raigōin and Kōenbō had been closely associated with Hachidaibō: Kōenbō as Hachidaibō's *wakibō* and Raigōin as Hachidaibō's branch temple, which provided funerary rituals for the abbots and functioned as a parish temple for the *oshi* at Ōyama. By the nineteenth century, as Hachidaibō's authority was weakening, both became known as Chatōdera (Tea Temple) because peasants in the region would come to visit either temple one hundred days after a family member had passed away to offer tea for the repose of the deceased.[88] Neither was part of the mediation system and therefore lacked a steady source of income from the *oshi*'s parishioners. With the weakened leadership of Hachidaibō, however, the two temples successfully sought income from other sources.

Hachidaibō's lack of control over the remaining eleven subtemples is illustrated by a case involving Kirakubō, which was one of the temples that held its own parish outside the mediation system and, by the late eighteenth century, housed the most senior cleric, second only to the Hachidaibō abbot.[89] Early in 1793, the Hachidaibō abbot Jakushin, who had been appointed three years earlier, returned from a lengthy stay in Edo. He discovered that Kirakubō, one of the eleven subtemples under Hachidaibō's authority, had hired the Ōyama carpenter, Tenaka Myōōtarō, to construct an elaborate Chinese-style gate without obtaining prior permission from Hachidaibō. Kirakubō had not only violated sumptuary laws but also caused trouble for Hachidaibō, which had sent a detailed, official map of the temple precinct to the *bakufu* a few months earlier. The construction of the gate made the map obsolete.[90] Even though the construction of a gate may not seem an important violation to modern thinking, a gateway was a spatial symbol of Kirakubō's independence from Hachidaibō: it established a physical barrier between the two institutions. Furthermore, a highly decorative Chinese-style gate was a status symbol that could not easily be ignored by Hachidaibō.[91]

Hachidaibō's weakened influence was a result of the high turnover rate of Hachidaibō's abbots starting around 1750 and a series of natural disasters from the 1770s. As mentioned above, Ōyama had gone through a similar phase of institutional weakness in the early seventeenth century after Abbot Jitsuei's death. Despite its institutional prestige, the academy at Ōyama had temporarily lost its influence within the regional Kogi Shingon school and had been unable to respond to crisis when a natural disaster struck in the early seventeenth century. In the late eighteenth century, the academy faced a similar situation when several abbots died after only two to three years in office. Between 1750 and 1770, few records exist for the four successive abbots who had little time during their brief tenures to make a lasting imprint on Ōyama's history. Shusō's successor Hōnyo held his office for about eleven years until 1757. He was succeeded by Seinyo (d. 1761), who held his office for four years; Myōjū (d. 1763), who held his office for about one and half years; and Kōga (d. 1766), who held his office for three years.[92] After Kōga's death in 1766, he was succeeded by Kanga (d. 1788), whose tenure lasted for 24 years.

Although Kanga brought stability to the Hachidaibō abbotship, his tenure and that of his successor was marked by upheaval and natural disasters. Trouble began in 1771, when a riot broke out in protest of Hachidaibō's appointment of a village official in Sakamoto. Then, as if to make matters worse, a brushfire destroyed four of the five shrines on the summit. In 1774, another fire broke out near the border of the village and nearly destroyed the entire town. Without sufficient funds, the rebuilding of the shrines did not occur until 1777, when the *bakufu* contributed 100 *ryō*. Disaster struck again in 1780 when a flood claimed many casualties in Sakamoto. In 1792, another flood suddenly struck the town.[93] The problems during this period affected not only Ōyama and its *monzenmachi* but the whole Kantō region as well. Floods and earthquakes reduced the number of pilgrims in the 1780s. In particular, the eruption of Mt. Asama in 1783 caused massive starvation in the Kantō region, consequently harming the local economy.[94]

Hachidaibō's abbots were increasingly unable to consolidate their position at Ōyama. Whereas previous Hachidaibō abbots had been buried on the mountain for eight generations to mark their strong link to the site, the practice ceased with Jakushin (d. 1801). Shōdō, who succeeded Jakushin's disciple Jakudō in 1822, was even banished from his office during his lifetime. Shōdō was originally from Hadano Village at the foot of Ōyama. He was forced to retire suddenly as abbot of Hachidaibō because of a riot at Ōyama, the causes of which are unclear. He initially resettled at an academy called Tōkakuin (Hiratsuka), then moved to Kongōchōji's branch temple Hōshūin in Sakato (Isehara), and finally obtained permission to return to Kannonji in Sakamoto, where he passed away at the age of 79 in 1864. Despite his return to Ōyama, he was not given an abbot's grave.[95]

The repercussions of Shōdō's dismissal were magnified because the office of the Hachidaibō abbot remained unfilled when Ōyama was reduced to ashes in the wake of a great earthquake in early 1855. Without an abbot at Hachidaibō, the clerics from the demolished subtemples had to cope with the immediate consequences of the fire.[96] The *bakufu* provided limited support for the reconstruction, but both *oshi* and clerics had to raise funds for the reconstruction project. Upon an emergency order by the *bakufu*, Kakkyoku, the former abbot of the Hakonesan Kongōin, was appointed as Hachidaibō abbot and moved to Ōyama immediately after the disaster. Kakkyoku oversaw the gradual process of reconstruction but passed away in 1865 without completing the construction project and was laid to rest at Ōyama. His successor Ōjū, the former abbot of the Ichigaya Hachiman Shrine in Edo, passed away only two years later in 1867 and was not buried at Ōyama. During the following years, Ōyama went through a particularly difficult process of disassociating *kami* and Buddhas that could not be mollified by the newly appointed Hachidaibō abbot Jitsujō.[97]

Conclusion

The early modern period was marked by great institutional restructuring and expansion. With the establishment of the head-branch temple system and the universal temple registration system in the seventeenth century, Buddhist schools developed the institutional frameworks that supported the extensive demand for clerics to staff village temples. This affected even institutions like Ōyama, which had few branch temples but trained clerics for abbotships of smaller temples. Ōyama became a Shingon training center with the support of the Tokugawa *bakufu* in the early seventeenth century. Its institutional structures grew slowly under the strong leadership of the Hachidaibō abbots until the site was fully formed by the mid-eighteenth century and became a leader among Shingon temples in the region. By the late eighteenth century, Ōyama had become a highly complex institution that required clear leadership from the Hachidaibō abbots in order to maintain cohesion.

However, natural disasters and the untimely deaths of successive abbots undermined Hachidaibō's authority. This was one of Ōyama's structural weaknesses: much of the administration rested in the authority of Hachidaibō abbot, but by the end of the period the abbots' control over the mountain became diminished and Ōyama's Shingon institutions increasingly fragmented. Ironically, it was Ōyama's popularity as a pilgrimage site that spurred on this process because it created opportunities for Ōyama's Shingon subtemples to further their individual interests on income derived from pilgrims rather than exist merely as subdivisions of a sectarian training monastery. Yet the need to develop a flourishing pilgrimage industry at Ōyama had been created by *bakufu* orders that gave full ritual authority and control of the temple land to the Shingon clergy, leaving the expelled *yamabushi* to seek other means of income, which they did by expanding and maintaining extensive parishes of believers in the Kantō region. Even the Shingon clergy ultimately needed the pilgrimage business. How else could they support a major Shingon academy without a significant number of branch temples to provide financial contributions? The temple land and periodic monetary grants from the *bakufu* were equally insufficient to sustain the multiple Buddhist institutions on the mountain. Unlike Ōyama's earlier temple land during the medieval period, which had been in fertile agricultural villages and needed to support a much smaller number of temples on the mountain, the temple land granted by the Tokugawa consisted only of rugged mountain terrain, most of which was not arable. Over the course of the early modern period, the *bakufu* became increasingly reluctant to grant funds for reconstruction projects. Instead, the clerics had to rely on donations from a broad constituency. The clergy augmented their income by controlling Ōyama's cult of Fudō and of the *honji suijaku* deities on the summit. Ōyama, like many Kogi Shingon temples, was a combinatory multiplex where Shingon clerics controlled the ritual life of a local shrine.[98] This combinatory arrangement would make Kogi Shingon temples in Sagami Province particularly vulnerable during the disassociation of *kami* and Buddhas during the early Meiji period but sustained the temples during the early modern period.

Throughout Japanese history, successful Buddhist institutions depended financially on patrons. Before the early modern period, many large temples relied predominantly on their extensive estates and on their ties with the aristocracy and local warlords for funding, while supplementing their income through occasional fundraising campaigns. During the early modern period, however, with its proliferation of Buddhist institutions, these traditional sources were no longer sufficient. Even large temples that did not function as funeral temples had to turn to a broader constituency as their primary, regular source of funding. Ōyama is one example of an institution that was able to navigate this shift successfully. After all, its Shingon clergy came primarily from the same peasant background as many of Ōyama's devotees. However, Ōyama's two dozen Shingon clerics on their own could hardly have developed the mountain into a major pilgrimage institution with over one million affiliated devotees. The next two chapters examine how the clerics were assisted in the management of the Ōyama cult by the *oshi* system, which developed at Ōyama in the seventeenth century.

THREE

The Emergence of the Ōyama Oshi

This chapter examines the rise of the Ōyama *oshi* during the seventeenth century under the Shingon clergy, their full institutionalization and symbiotic relationship with the Shingon clergy during the eighteenth century, and their eventual fragmentation and Shintoization in the nineteenth century under the influence of the Shirakawa Shinto and the Hirata school of Nativism. The *oshi* were the key players in Ōyama's early modern transformation into a highly popular pilgrimage destination and again in Ōyama's transformation from a Buddhist into a Shinto site during the early Meiji period.

In early modern Japan, many famous pilgrimage sites were dependent on hereditary religious specialists who provided accommodations for pilgrims at their inns, acted as guides, distributed amulets, and collected donations. These sites included the Ise Shrines, Dewa Sanzan in northern Honshū, Enoshima and Ōyama in Sagami Province, Mt. Mitake in Musashi Province, Mt. Fuji in Suruga and Kai Provinces, Mt. Minobu in Kai Province, Zenkōji in Shinano Province, the Tsushima Shrine in Owari Province, Tateyama in Etchū Province, Hakusan in Kaga Province, the Taga Shrine in Ōmi Province, Mt. Atago in Yamashiro Province, Mt. Kōya in Kii Province, and Mt. Hiko in Bizen Province.[1] These were akin to, and in many cases developed from, *yamabushi*, shrine priests, or low-ranking Buddhist monks. Although initially developed from other types of religious professionals, these hereditary specialists developed a distinct identity.

In many instances, this differentiation occurred in the early modern period and was linked to the development of guild-like associations that guaranteed members their distinct status through licensing mechanisms, even though the authorities and the public often viewed them as members of an eclectic group of itinerant proselytizers and performers that fulfilled similar functions such as the distribution of talismans and the solicitation of alms. The associations of mendicant monks (*gannin bōzu*) in Edo and Osaka are a similar case. To protect themselves from competitors, the mendicants formed an association affiliated with Daizōin or Enkōin at Mt. Kurama and approved by the city magistrate. Over the course of the early modern period, these officially recognized mendicants contested the rights of outcasts, *yamabushi*, and unlicensed mendicants to perform similar activities within their territory. Comparable associations of mendicants were found in Kyoto, Edo, and even smaller towns in eastern Japan, such as Sunpu, and Kōfu.[2] *Kumano bikuni*, mendicant nuns whose public image was as eclectic as that of their male counterparts, employed a similar licensing system through affiliation with Myōshinji, a temple associated with the Kumano Shingū.[3]

Even as religious specialists such as *yamabushi*, *gannin bōzu*, and *Kumano bikuni* came to rely on such transregional patterns of affiliation, others sought local affiliations with popular pilgrimage sites in whose vicinity they settled. At many sites, including the Ise Shrines, Mt. Fuji, Mt. Haruna, Enoshima, Mt. Mitake, and Ōyama, they were called *oshi*—pronounced *onshi* at Ise—which literally means "venerable master" and originally appears to be short for *kitōshi* (prayer master). In the mid-Heian period, the term *oshi* was first used at Buddhist temples and later at shrine-temple multiplexes near the capital, such as the Iwashimizu Hachiman Shrine.[4] Subsequently, the *oshi* associated with the Ise and Kumano Shrines developed into a distinct category of religious specialist beginning in the late-Heian and medieval periods. By the early modern period, *oshi* had become indispensable because they contributed to the growth of pilgrimage cults. Ōyama was one such regional pilgrimage site at which a complex *oshi* system developed from *yamabushi* and shrine priests during the early modern period.

Ōyama's *oshi*, who descended from its medieval *yamabushi* and shrine priests, as well as local artisans and merchants, gradually developed into a distinct form of religious professional in the early modern period.

Even though the Shingon clergy, who controlled Ōyama, established a regional Kogi Shingon network, they alone could not sufficiently spread the Ōyama cult. Ōyama owed its popularity to its *oshi*, who developed parishes in the Kantō region. Beginning in the late seventeenth century, the *oshi* expanded the mountain's most important asset—customary parishioners. Using similar methods as the Ise *onshi*, the Ōyama *oshi* made rounds to their parishioners to collect first-fruit donations (*hatsuho*)—originally, the first harvested crops, this later became an equivalent amount in cash. The Ōyama *oshi*, like their Ise counterparts, also distributed gifts and amulets and provided housing for pilgrims who came to Ōyama. The *oshi* were usually not celibate and passed their profession and parishes on to their heirs, just as merchants, artisans, or performers would pass on their family trade.

As in the case of Ise, the expanding number of Ōyama *oshi* reflects a pattern of growth until the mid-eighteenth century, which then leveled off until the mid-nineteenth century. These fluctuations are more a reflection of the increasing professionalization of the *oshi* rather than of a decline in Ōyama's popularity. The *oshi* entered into a symbiotic relationship with the Shingon clergy, who guaranteed their status when faced with competitors. To limit the pool of contenders eligible to become *oshi* and thus curb the competition among them, the Shingon clergy provided the *oshi* with licenses that distinguished those living in Ōyama's *monzen-machi* from residents of neighboring villages keen on sharing the profits of a growing pilgrimage industry. In return, the *oshi* served as liaisons between pilgrims and the Shingon Buddhist clergy on the mountain. The Shingon clergy also employed a number of villagers for the administration of Ōyama and for the performance of certain ritual functions, which contributed to status distinctions between the *oshi*.

By the late eighteenth century, new developments undermined the authority of the Shingon priesthood over the *oshi*. Many *oshi* challenged the authority of the Shingon clergy by obtaining shrine-priest licenses from the Shirakawa, a sacerdotal lineage who served as the hereditary heads of the Department of Divinity (Jingikan) at the imperial court, and by joining the Hirata school of Nativism. Together with the impact of famines in the 1780s, 1830s, and 1840s, and repeated natural disasters such as an earthquake in 1855 and the political instability of the *baku-matsu* era, social ferment grew, which ultimately escalated in the early

Meiji period during the disassociation of *kami* and Buddhas. Through this process, the *oshi* emerged as an important factor in the early modern development of the Ōyama cult.

From Yamabushi *to* Oshi, *1600–1670*

In the sixteenth century, Ōyama was inhabited jointly by *yamabushi*, shrine priests, and Buddhist monks. Since the Muromachi period, Ōyama had been the training ground of regional *yamabushi*. *Yamabushi* from Ōyama went to nearby Mt. Hasuge to attend dharma lectures and to train in caves or hermitages in its valleys. Likewise, until 1560, *yamabushi* from nearby Mt. Hasuge practiced *mine'iri* (a retreat into the mountains) twice a year in the spring and the fall, along a route leading from Mt. Hasuge via Iiyama (another nearby *shugendō* site) across mountains and valleys to Ōyama's summit, ending the retreat at the Fudō Hall. After 1560, the retreat was held only in the spring despite failed attempts to revive the fall practice in 1617 and 1637. Suzuki Masashi has argued that the route, which led the ascetics from its starting point at Mt. Hasuge in the northeast to its endpoint at Ōyama in the southwest, was a symbolic journey to a western paradise. The retreat initially took 49 days—the length of the first period of mourning after death—but was shortened to 35 days in 1557. The last stretch of the route was shared with the route that led *yamabushi* from Mt. Hinata, Ōyama's direct neighbor, to Ōyama.[5]

In the first decade of the seventeenth century, as the Shingon clergy took control of the mountain with the blessing of the new Tokugawa regime, all other residents such as *yamabushi* were ordered off the mountain and resettled in the two villages of Minoge and Sakamoto. The former was situated on the southwestern side of the mountain facing toward Odawara and Mt. Fuji, and the latter on the southeastern side facing Edo and the Kantō plain. Since the city of Edo grew rapidly, Sakamoto prospered, with the pilgrimage business as its mainstay. Sakamoto also differed from Minoge as it was located within the boundaries of Ōyama's temple land and thus under the jurisdiction of the Shingon clergy on the mountain.

Only a few extant documents shed light on the activities of Ōyama's *yamabushi* and shrine priests living in these two villages in this early period. In the first two decades of the seventeenth century, the transition from a site that allowed multiple traditions to exist side by side to one that was dominated by the Shingon clergy led to recurrent conflicts. According to the law codes (*hatto*) issued in 1609 by Ōyama's head temple, Mt. Kōya, *yamabushi* practiced their own rites in the yearly festival held in the Second Month, but because the elaborate rituals and offerings interfered with the Shingon clergy's control, they were sharply curtailed and placed under the supervision of the clergy. The *yamabushi* also had little access to the income from pilgrims because they each were permitted to collect the donations at only one chapel on the mountain and had to turn over their patrons to the Shingon clergy.[6] Because of the paucity of documents, it is difficult to tell how quickly and to what extent the shrine priests and the *yamabushi* accepted these new power structures. There is some indication that the transition was not entirely smooth. In 1618, Ōyama's shrine priests became involved in a dispute with Hachidaibō, the temple of the Ōyama abbot, but unfortunately we do not know the exact nature of the dispute.[7]

Another issue of contention was whether the Shingon clerics could act as guides (*sendatsu*) for pilgrims to Ise and Kumano. Between 1613 and 1616, *yamabushi* in the area near Ōyama disputed the right of Ōyama's Shingon clergy to guide pilgrims to Ise and Kumano as *sendatsu*, acting as a liaison between pilgrims and the Kumano or Ise *oshi*. According to Ōyama's law codes issued by the *bakufu* in 1609, the *yamabushi* at Ōyama had been forced to turn their patrons over to the Shingon clergy. *Yamabushi* in the area, who were affiliated with the Tendai Honzan branch of *shugendō*, acted as pilgrimage guides (*sendatsu*) for such patrons when they went on to western Japan to enter the mountains at Ōmine. They also took them to Ise and Kumano—entrance to which the Honzan branch claimed exclusive privilege by *bakufu* decree. When Ōyama's Shingon clergy assumed similar roles upon taking over the patrons from the *yamabushi* at Ōyama, 24 Tendai-affiliated Honzanha *yamabushi* in the area, including Enzōbō from Mt. Hasuge, appealed to the *bakufu* to assert their privilege with the support of Gyokurōbō, their immediate head temple in Odawara.[8]

The dominance of the Shingon clergy over the *yamabushi* and shrine priests, however, did not lead immediately to the formation of a complex *oshi* system; that began only about 50 years later. In the 1660s, the tradition of mountain asceticism largely disappeared from Ōyama, and most of its practitioners became *oshi* in the aftermath of a dispute between the Shingon clergy on the one side and a number of *yamabushi*, Rinzai Buddhist clerics, and *oshi* on the other side. In 1663, the magistrate of temples and shrines settled a dispute over land titles between Hachidaibō and a group in Sakamoto Village consisting of five *yamabushi* and seven *oshi* who ran small inns and three Rinzai temples. The dispute ended with the banishment of the ringleaders from Ōyama's temple land. All other *yamabushi*, except for three who were not involved in the dispute, were prohibited from maintaining their status as ascetics. About 35, therefore, opted to become *oshi* whereas some of the banished parties resettled in nearby villages such as Koyasu Village.[9] Therefore, 1663 basically marked the end of the tradition of *yamabushi* at Ōyama, the majority of whom had settled in Sakamoto Village. It is also clear that even though there are no documents referring to Ōyama *oshi* prior to 1663, some *oshi* must already have been present at Ōyama because documents regarding the dispute mentioned the title *oshi* in reference to some of the involved parties. These *oshi* and the newly transformed former *yamabushi* may have modeled themselves after the *oshi* in Ise and Kumano Shrines since the *oshi* systems in both places were likely familiar to them through their activities as pilgrimage guides.

What benefit did the Shingon clergy derive from having most *yamabushi* become *oshi*, and why did conversion occur in the 1660s? Beginning in the second half of the seventeenth century, *bakufu* and domainal laws increasingly required autonomous itinerant religious, *yamabushi*, and shrine priests to form translocal affiliations with well-known Buddhist temples or Shinto sacerdotal houses. Ōyama's *oshi* were also affected by these developments but, in contrast to *yamabushi* and shrine priests, were only locally affiliated with Ōyama's Shingon temples.

In the seventeenth century, *yamabushi* and some shrine priests were forming translocal affiliations, which gave them special ritual qualifications and access to external advocates in local disputes. *Shugendō*, the tradition of *yamabushi*, had been organized since the early seventeenth century into a sectarian system similar to the Buddhist sects based on *bakufu* decrees. Most *yamabushi* were affiliated with either the Tōzanha (Shingon) or Honzanha (Tendai). These *shugendō* branches were subject to regulations issued by the *bakufu* in 1609 and 1613, respectively. In 1609, Shōgoin in Kyoto became the headquarters of the Honzanha affiliated with the Tendai school of Buddhism. In 1613, Sanbōin, a hermitage at Daigoji in Kyoto, became the headquarters of the Tōzanha affiliated with the Shingon school. The *yamabushi* at Mt. Haguro in northeastern Japan were considered an independent branch.[10]

From the 1660s, the *bakufu* and the various domains intensified their efforts to limit the autonomy of peripatetic monks, nuns, and *yamabushi*. Such marginal religious specialists were required to seek affiliation with Buddhist temples, particularly those belonging to the Shingon and Tendai schools. Urban areas such as Edo and Osaka, with high concentrations of itinerant preachers, were first to develop guild-like networks of mendicants. Soon after the Meireki fire destroyed Edo in 1657, municipal authorities attempted to rid the city of unauthorized mendicants.[11] For example, in 1662 and 1673 Edo authorities required religious itinerants to show documents proving their affiliation with a Buddhist temple before they were hosted at a lay devotee's home, which was a common practice on fundraising and proselytizing rounds, or allowed to settle in a neighborhood.[12] In the 1660s and 1680s, the Edo authorities also sought to curb the unauthorized establishment of Buddhist temples, the private installation of Buddhist icons, and the performance of rituals for fundraising purposes by itinerant preachers and *yamabushi*.[13] The authorities periodically issued similar restrictions throughout the early modern period, an indication that the regulations were only partially effective.[14]

Other domains soon followed suit. The most extreme case was that of the Mito Domain. In the 1660s, the domainal authorities began to crack down on what they regarded as spurious preachers and temples. The policy led to the closure of thousands of Buddhist establishments, especially those run by *yamabushi*, mendicants, and other religious specialists considered illegitimate by the authorities.[15] By the 1700s, efforts to regulate mendicants also occurred in northeastern domains such as Morioka and Yonezawa.[16] In a social climate that questioned the official status of autonomous religious figures, Ōyama's Shingon clergy found support from *bakufu* authorities during the dispute in the 1660s.

Yamabushi and Buddhist monks of other schools had a certain measure of institutional autonomy from Ōyama's Shingon clergy because they were developing translocal ties. Consequently, the Shingon clergy sought to eliminate them or turn them into *oshi* when possible. The clergy had secured control over the monastic precinct on the mountain since 1609, but both clerics of all other Buddhist schools and *yamabushi* remained active at the site. Some Buddhist clerics of other schools chose to adapt to the changing religious landscape by finding their place in the emerging temple registration system rather than in the dissemination of the Ōyama cult. Three Jōdo temples that remained in Sakamoto Village developed into funeral temples for the merchants, artisans, and tenants at the foot of the mountain and did not run afoul with the Shingon clergy.[17] However, fourteen Rinzai Zen temples did not become incorporated into the temple registration system but were quite similar to the *yamabushi* hermitages in the village. Consequently, the Shingon clergy banned three of them in 1663 during the above-mentioned dispute that forced most of Ōyama's *yamabushi* to become *oshi*. Ten other Rinzai temples seem to have gone out of business by the early 1700s. Only one remained, with the resident monk acting as an *oshi* until the nineteenth century.[18]

The *yamabushi* that remained at Ōyama beyond the purge of 1663, including three in Sakamoto Village and five to seven in Minoge Village, were all Honzanha *yamabushi* affiliated directly with Shōgoin and not with the locally powerful Gyokurōbō, with which at least some of Ōyama's *yamabushi* appear to have been affiliated earlier in the seventeenth century. They maintained contact with their *shugendō* hierarchy by performing ascetic exercises in the Ōmine mountain range—by which they advanced in the *shugendō* ranks—until a lack of disciples and successors forced them to abandon the practice by the late eighteenth century.[19]

This pattern of affiliation contrasted sharply with other Honzanha *yamabushi* in the area, such as twelve Honzanha *yamabushi* at neighboring Mt. Hinata, who were affiliated with Gyokurōbō in Odawara. That such external affiliations could be used for leverage against the Shingon clergy in disputes and power struggles is illustrated by the above-mentioned dispute of 1613–1616 between the clergy and Gyokurōbō-affiliated *yamabushi* from the area. In another dispute, centered on Honzanha *shugendō* privileges in 1697, the Shingon abbots of Ōyama and Mt. Hinata found themselves again in opposition to Gyokurōbō.[20] This dispute, however, did not involve the *yamabushi* at Ōyama because they had no ties with Gyokurōbō. By forcing the majority of Ōyama *yamabushi* to renounce their status and convert to *oshi*, the clergy had successfully kept them out of a powerful regional network. The remaining *yamabushi* were also not part of this network because of their distinct affiliation with a temple in Kyoto, which may have offered them some protection through its prestige as a famous temple but few personal ties due to its physical distance.

The situation of the shrine priests shows parallel developments. However, despite efforts by the Yoshida House to extend its control over shrines in various regions, many shrine priests chose to remain independent. Translocal affiliations were far less common than among *yamabushi* and Buddhist clerics until the nineteenth century when large numbers of shrine priests sought affiliation with the Shirakawa House. The Yoshida had managed to win the patronage of the Tokugawa *bakufu* in the early seventeenth century and had taken on a role that resembled that formerly played by the Jingikan at the Heian court in certain Shinto state rites (e.g., in the rebuilding of the Ise Shrines or the dispatch of imperial messengers).[21] Based on earlier practices of shrine priests seeking certification and advancement in rank from the Yoshida and Shirakawa Houses, the *bakufu* issued a five-article law code entitled *Shosha no negi kannushi hatto* (Law Code for Shrine Priests and Head Shrine Priests) in 1665, which recognized these roles of the sacerdotal houses as official. The code defined shrine priests as those serving as hereditary ritualists at shrines. Most importantly, it required unranked shrine priests to wear white robes. Shrine priests who wished to wear colored robes had to obtain permission through the Yoshida. Perhaps to mollify the imperial court and keep the Yoshida in check, shrine priests seeking court ranks were required to rely on customary channels of mediation—that is, the Shirakawa House—in their dealings with the court.[22] However, the legislation did not make such affiliations mandatory for unranked priests. It only affected those seeking to acquire the status associated with higher ranks, which usually raised them above the general peasantry and granted them warrior-like privileges. These benefits initially made the Yoshida licenses more popular among shrine priests than court ranks issued through Shirakawa mediation.[23] As Hiromi Maeda has argued, shrine ranks obtained through the Yoshida became a common status symbol for small shrines in eastern Japan, where their influence was particularly strong with the exception of parts of Sagami Province and the southern

Bōsō Peninsula. Among status-conscious villagers, rank became a convenient means to gain prestige for village shrines that were of relatively recent vintage.[24] In order to eliminate a loophole that could have allowed peasants to shed their cultivator status and escape the burden of taxation, the *bakufu* tried to limit the number of those eligible for Yoshida licenses not only by requiring permission from the magistrate of temples and shrines and village officials but also by excluding certain types of religious specialists at shrines, such as spirit mediums.[25]

While the Yoshida House extended its influence also to Ōyama, only one or two ritualists established an affiliation. Satō Chūmu, who traced his lineage back to a warrior occupying the position of Ōyama *bettō* in the medieval period, obtained a Yoshida license in 1652, thirteen years before the above-mentioned decree. Yano Seitayū, another *oshi* who claimed warrior heritage, was able to obtain a Yoshida license in 1729. Most Ōyama shrine priests, however, chose to remain independent or were prevented from forming an affiliation by law. The other nine shrine priests, five of whom were spirit mediums (*kannagi*), had no Yoshida licenses but were commissioned by Hachidaibō to perform *kagura*.[26] This placed them in a similar relationship with the Shingon clergy as the *oshi*. Therefore, Hachidaibō held the same authority over shrine priests as over *oshi*. Later in the early modern period, many shrine priests sought affiliation with other sacerdotal houses, such as the Shirakawa. This development also occurred at Ōyama. In the early nineteenth century, when large numbers of *oshi* claiming to be shrine priests sought affiliation with the Shirakawa, Hachidaibō strongly resisted these attempts that clashed with its interests.

These categories of religious specialists were not completely mutually exclusive. In fact, there existed several hybrid religious professionals. Some *oshi* also maintained their status as Buddhist monks of non-Shingon sects or as *yamabushi*. Some *oshi* served simultaneously as shrine priests or shrine carpenters and even obtained Yoshida or Shirakawa Shinto licenses. However, until the turn of the nineteenth century their number was fairly limited.[27] Most *oshi* were only locally affiliated. The *oshi* soon discovered that a licensing system had its benefits because its guild-like nature provided protection from competitors. Moreover, a single affiliation with the local Shingon institution could also be advantageous compared to a dual affiliation. It is probably no accident that most of the Rinzai temples and some of the remaining *yamabushi* went out of business while *oshi* without external ties prospered. Not only may the latter group have had a better relationship with the Shingon clergy, but they also escaped having to pay high fees for dual affiliations. Certification as *yamabushi* or shrine priests or a position as a Buddhist branch temple had its price because of the dues that needed to be paid to head temples or sacerdotal houses.

Parishes as the Basis for Oshi *Status, 1670–1700*

The outcome of the 1663 dispute served the interests of the Shingon clergy, but other beneficiaries were those who had been *oshi* even before the dispute. Once most *yamabushi* were banished or had become *oshi*, a large segment of the village population had been given equal status. It is actually possible that the initial dispute was not between the Shingon clergy on the one side and a coalition of *yamabushi*, Rinzai Buddhist clerics, and *oshi* on the other side. In the early modern period, it was common to punish both parties involved in a dispute. It is therefore conceivable that this dispute, which, according to the *Afurijinja kodenkō* (1849), may have been over hereditary family stipends (*karoku*), was actually waged between a coalition of *yamabushi* and Rinzai Buddhist clerics on the one hand and several *oshi* who contested the privileges of the former on the other.[28] As Hermann Ooms has argued, in the late seventeenth century, changing village dynamics led to an increasing number of disputes between the village leadership and a growing number of landholding peasants who were seeking greater political participation. In other words, the latter sought to see their economic status reflected by their political status within the village.[29] Similarly, in the case of Sakamoto Village, a growing number of *oshi* may have pressured the *yamabushi* and Rinzai clerics for a leveling of their status-based roles within the village.

In regard to ritual function and status, what was the difference between the earliest *oshi*—the so-called "lay" *oshi*—and *yamabushi* and shrine priests? Minoge, the agricultural village that doubled as Ōyama's secondary *monzenmachi* at the southwestern foot of the mountain, was not affected by the dispute in 1663. Therefore, a handful of *yamabushi* who had settled there instead of in Sakamoto remained *yamabushi* and were not forced to become *oshi* in the 1660s. Hence the ratio between *yamabushi* and *oshi* was 1 to 3 rather than 1 to 50.[30] A document from

1703, signed by six *yamabushi* and sixteen lay *oshi* from Minoge Village, outlined their different duties during festivals at Ōyama. *Yamabushi*, who had religious names based on their hermitages (so-and-so -*in* or -*bō*), performed sacerdotal duties, such as special rituals during the yearly festival, consistent with their role in the early seventeenth century whereas lay *oshi*, who did not have religious names, were responsible for menial duties, such as cleaning the pilgrimage paths on the mountain, to which one can also add lodging pilgrims.[31] These early lay *oshi* appear closer in status to ordinary cultivators than ritualists who had the right to carry distinctive names. In this document, households with shrine priestly functions were left out of this division of labor even though they were clearly present in the village. Hondaibō, one of three *kannagi* (spirit medium) households in the village, appears in the position of village headman alongside a peasant. Other documents indicate that *kannagi* in Minoge Village bearing names similar to the *yamabushi* hermitage names—so-and-so -*bō*—were charged with the performance of ritual dances.[32] This suggests that those with special sacerdotal duties were in the same privileged category as older landed peasants whereas *oshi* ranked lower in the village hierarchy.

Once the *oshi* became the most numerous religious specialists on the mountain in the 1660s, their rights and duties became increasingly professionalized and delineated *vis-à-vis* competitors of peasant stock, a process that lasted until the 1750s. The development is documented by a series of five codes that were promulgated by Ōyama's Shingon clergy in 1674, 1702, 1713, 1721, and 1753. These codes were issued to quell the competition among *oshi* and non-*oshi* villagers, which led to fierce disputes in 1702 and 1752 between the residents of Sakamoto Village and neighboring Koyasu Village on the route from Edo. The major sources of contention among the residents at the foot of Ōyama involved issues concerning the handling of pilgrims and parishioners, such as who could claim the title "*oshi*," what constituted a violation of the bond between the *oshi* and his parish, who could run inns and cater to pilgrims providing lodging and meals, who could sell amulets and collect *hatsuho*, and who could operate waterfalls for purification.[33]

Initially, ownership of a parish gave the holder the status of an *oshi*. The mountain code in 1674, issued to quell disputes between villagers accusing one another of stealing their customers, used the term *oshi* in a very vague sense. Pilgrims were divided into those who had and those who did not have *oshi*. Not only were innkeepers to avoid luring their neighbors' customers into their inns and to refrain from engaging in price wars, they were also obligated—as were noodle shop owners—to determine whether potential customers had customary ties to a specific *oshi* before catering to them. If a pilgrim had ties with an *oshi*, only that *oshi* could house or provide meals for him. If a group of pilgrims consisted of patrons of different *oshi*, each of these *oshi* could house the entire group as long as they could lay claim to at least one parishioner among the group. If the group contained no fixed parishioners, anyone could house them. Violators were punished with stiff fines.[34] This suggests that the claim to be an *oshi* hinged primarily on an innkeeper's claim to have a customary parish.

These *oshi* parishes were different from the funeral parishes developed by Buddhist temples in the temple registration system, even though both were called by the same name. *Oshi* neither provided mortuary rites for their parishioners nor was the affiliation mandated by the Tokugawa authorities. Nevertheless, the concept of the parish appears to have developed at Ōyama at approximately the same time as the emergence of the funeral parishes through the temple registration system in the latter half of the seventeenth century. Regular patrons (*danna*) are first mentioned in the regulations covering Ōyama issued by the *bakufu* in 1609, in which married *yamabushi* were ordered to turn their *danna* over to the Shingon clergy. From the 1660s, patrons (*danna*) or, from the early 1700s, parishioners (*danka*) appear frequently in documents—mountain codes, sales certificates, and parish registers. Even though the associations between *oshi* and their parishes were not obligatory but voluntary, their ties had an element of permanence and exclusivity. *Oshi* even treated their parishes as valuable commodities that could be bought and sold. The earliest extant sales document dates from 1665, two years after the term *oshi* appeared for the first time in documents from Ōyama.[35]

Unlike funeral parishes, *oshi* parishioners did not tend to live in the same village but in villages that were often separated from Ōyama by great distances. Initially *oshi* developed ties with villagers closer to Ōyama. Extant records indicate that the *oshi* first developed parishes in Sagami Province, where Ōyama was located, and then gradually spread to neighboring provinces such as Musashi, Kazusa, Awa, and the city of

Edo and finally throughout the Kantō region. The earliest extant parish registers and certificates of parish sales between 1665 and 1730 cover areas in the vicinity of Ōyama. They are concentrated in western Sagami (Ōsumi, Aikō, Kōza, and Miura Districts), including farming villages and coastal fishing villages. There are also records of parishes outside Sagami, in Musashi and Kazusa Provinces, and very limited evidence of parishioners in Edo from around 1700.[36]

Licensing Systems and Increasing Professionalization, 1700–1750

A parish did not remain the only element that distinguished an *oshi* from a non-*oshi* innkeeper. To avoid too many *oshi* competing for parishes, the Shingon clergy established other limitations. The first indication that the place of residence played a role in who was allowed to call himself an *oshi* appears in documents regarding a dispute between Koyasu and Sakamoto Villages and the mountain code from 1702. Originally, Ōyama was awarded about 72 *koku* in Sakamoto and 27 *koku* in Koyasu, making both villages part of Ōyama's temple land, which totaled 100 *koku*. In 1666, a section of Koyasu was transferred to Sakamoto to replace land that had been washed away during a flood.[37] It is likely that Koyasu as a whole ceased to be part of Ōyama's temple land around the time of this transfer because by the mid-nineteenth century Sakamoto alone comprised Ōyama's one hundred *koku*. Sakamoto and Koyasu were very different kinds of villages. The former had virtually no land for cultivation whereas the latter was a farming village.[38]

By the early 1700s, rivalries between the residents of Sakamoto and Koyasu erupted. In the spring of 1702, a dispute was brought before the magistrate of temples and shrines over whether residents of Koyasu had the right to call themselves *oshi* and to print and sell amulets. The residents of lower Sakamoto, identifying themselves as "those who serve as *oshi* in the temple land of Ōyama," contrasted their position with peasants acting as innkeepers in Koyasu. Pointing out the relative absence of fields in Sakamoto, the innkeepers argued that catering to pilgrims and parishioners was the only business to sustain them. Their work also included distributing amulets, collecting first-fruit donations, and acting as go-betweens for the Shingon clergy and pilgrims who wanted to have rituals performed by the temples. The residents of Sakamoto took issue with the villagers from Koyasu who usurped the rights of the Sakamoto *oshi* by setting up new inns and claiming to be *oshi*, dispensing amulets, and collecting first fruits. In response, the residents of Koyasu claimed a lack of fields to justify that its villagers needed to operate inns and denied having appropriated the privileges of the *oshi*. The magistrate of temples and shrines supported Sakamoto's claim that Koyasu's villagers had sold unauthorized amulets. The authorities ordered the confiscation of printing blocks for amulets and prohibited unauthorized sales. The magistrate also recognized the rights of traditional inns in Koyasu but banned newly opened inns from conducting business and pulling in customers off the street.

Similar disputes involving villagers from Koyasu and even neighboring Kamikasuya Village continued through the summer of 1702.[39] To alleviate the tension between the residents of Sakamoto and neighboring towns over rampant competition, Hachidaibō, under Abbot Kaizō, issued another mountain code in the early autumn of 1702. Sumptuary regulations were aimed at preventing extravagance at the inns as well as the soaring prices for lodging and palanquins. In addition, the code gave *oshi* the exclusive right to provide lodging and sell goods to their parishioners and to make agreements to share this right with other *oshi*.[40]

The code also regulated the *oshi*'s relationship with the Shingon temples, giving them the role not only of innkeepers but also of intermediaries between pilgrims and clerics for the dissemination of amulets and the performance of rituals. *Oshi* could distribute amulets to any pilgrim, but these amulets were to be consecrated by the Shingon temples. The *oshi* were reminded to follow the system of mediation for *goma* rituals held for pilgrims, which meant that specific *oshi* served as liaisons for a designated Shingon temple and its parishioners. They were also forbidden to overcharge pilgrims or to withhold the pilgrims' donations from the Shingon temples.

Above all, the code established the criteria for who could claim to be an *oshi*. The status of an *oshi* no longer hinged only on the ownership of a parish but on the *oshi*'s ancestry and a clearly defined licensing system administered by the Shingon clergy. One could no longer become an *oshi* simply by purchasing a parish. The title *oshi* was granted exclusively to those whose families had traditionally performed ritual prayers (*kitō*) or were skilled in matters of the *kami*:

Item: *Oshi* who have not traditionally practiced *kami* matters or ritual prayers are not to serve as *oshi*. Henceforth, *oshi* are to request licenses from the temples on Ōyama.

Attachment: Lately there have been some who became *oshi* by buying parishioners (*danna*). This practice is to cease.[41]

Since the Shingon clergy licensed only residents of Ōyama's temple land and allowed only those who had been licensed to issue amulets consecrated by the clergy, the temples had an effective means of controlling the growth of *oshi* households. Hence the number of *oshi* remained stable throughout the rest of the early modern period. There were about 130 oshi in Sakamoto in 1718. After a brief spike of 153 in 1730, the number fell to just over 140 in 1735 and remained fairly constant for the next one hundred years.[42] The *oshi* of Sakamoto Village benefited from this arrangement because it gave them the exclusive right to the title *oshi*.

Subsequent mountain codes from 1713 and 1721 defined the duties and privileges of the *oshi* even further. In the former, the role of the *oshi* as an intermediary was expanded: *oshi* were responsible for pilgrims during the yearly summer festival and had to make sure that pilgrims were not stained by ritual pollution. The latter code contained the following definition that clearly stated the status and function of an *oshi*:

Item. An *oshi* is neither a peasant nor artisan nor merchant but an itinerant. He makes a living by keeping the customs of the Buddhas and the *kami*; performing spells and incantations; maintaining parishioners (*danna*) in various places, for whom he provides lodging should they come on pilgrimage; handing out amulets on several occasions; and receiving first-fruit donations (*hatsuho*).[43]

Oshi were not considered members of the three occupational groups— peasants, artisans, and merchants—that formed the basis of the early modern society headed by the warrior class. In this, *oshi* resembled Buddhist monks, *yamabushi*, and Shinto priests, who were also excluded from the occupational groups.

In the first half of the seventeenth century, it became common practice among peasant, merchant, and artisan households to adopt a hereditary name for the head of the household, which would be passed to the successor once he assumed the family headship.[44] Similarly, in order to indicate their unique position and status as religious specialists, many *oshi* adopted special names often ending with *-tayū*, a suffix also customarily used by Ise *onshi* and performers. According to Engelbert Kaempfer, the Ise *onshi* used the title *tayū*, which he translated as "ambassador" or "evangelist."[45] By the 1730s, 71 Ōyama *oshi* used such names. By 1744, five more adopted a name ending with *-tayū*. Many others, even though their names did not contain the suffix *-tayū*, adopted names that were clearly different from ordinary merchant and peasant names. One of the earliest examples of this is an *oshi* who went by the name of Utsumi Jirōemon until 1682 but suddenly adopted the name Utsumi Yūkei in 1683 after acquiring a large number of parishioners, reflecting the very process that the Shingon clergy would later prohibit: namely, becoming an *oshi* by purchasing a parish.[46] In addition, many *oshi* ran inns with names that sounded like mountain-ascetic hermitages—so-and-so *-bō* or *-in*—regardless of whether their ancestors had actually been *yamabushi* or not.

Through the tightly controlled licensing system, the number of Ōyama *oshi* eventually stabilized at 144, remaining virtually unchanged between 1735 and 1824. Licenses and *oshi* names were passed on from generation to generation, but could also be sold or passed on to adopted heirs, which still gave those coveting a license a way to acquire one even though the total number was limited. An *oshi* name and with it an *oshi* license could be acquired by marriage, as in the case of the bean curd vendor Denbee, who became Ogasawara Shōnosuke upon marrying the *oshi* Ogasawara Yūkei's daughter.[47] It could also be obtained through purchase, as Kanzaki Hantayū did in 1803.[48] In several cases, new licenses were awarded by the Shingon temples upon official appointments. Tenaka Myōōtarō—the Ōyama carpenter—served as Ōyama's intendant under Hachidaibō abbot Hōnyo (1746–1757). He received a license to adopt the *oshi* name Ogawa and henceforth was also known under his *oshi* name, Ogawa Ranbutsu. Similarly, Masuda Gennosuke and Nakayama Naiki were given their *oshi* licenses when the former was appointed as Ōyama's intendant and the latter became a village headman.[49] The licensing system, therefore, provided the Shingon temples with a means to reward those serving their interests and created a symbiotic relationship between *oshi* and clerics.

However, the licensing system had two weaknesses. One, it guaranteed no protection against inns outside Ōyama's temple land taking in pilgrims and was only partially successful in limiting competition from neighboring villages. Two, it limited the number of innkeepers who could bring pilgrims to the Shingon clergy's doors, thus running counter to the temples' own interests because they relied on income from pilgrims' donations. According to a dispute during the 1750s, small seasonal inns had sprung up in Koyasu and Kamikasuya that drained customers away from Sakamoto. Since both villages were outside Ōyama's temple land—being on *bakufu* and *hatamoto* lands—the Shingon temples had no authority to outlaw such establishments. The Sakamoto residents could find no redress from the Shingon temples and, therefore, had to turn to the magistrate of temples and shrines for judgment. What contributed to the problem was that, despite the licensing system established by Hachidaibō, the Shingon temples apparently continued to accept the Koyasu residents as go-betweens for the arrangement of services instead of making this service the monopoly of licensed *oshi*. The Shingon temples appear to have been more eager to attract large numbers of pilgrims and their donations than they were to protect the interests of the *oshi* on Ōyama's temple land.[50]

The Shingon clergy, however, did recognize special privileges for *oshi* acting as intermediaries. Even though the clerics were legally entitled to all the donations made by pilgrims for rituals performed at the temples, *oshi* received a percentage of the donations. If pilgrims did not stay with *oshi* but in Koyasu or came to the temples on their own accord, the *oshi* might miss their opportunity to claim their share. Therefore, the Shingon clergy issued a mountain code in 1753 that addressed the *oshi*'s interests by regulating the distribution of pilgrims' donations among their *oshi*, the Shingon temples, and the village office. *Oshi* were required to turn over the appropriate share to the temples and the village office, whereas the temples had to ensure that the *oshi* was given an opportunity to claim his share of the offerings should the pilgrims fail to use his services as go-between.[51] Over the course of 50 years, the *oshi* had therefore developed from parish-holding innkeepers to tightly regulated religious professionals who had the privilege to collect donations from, and distribute amulets to, their parishioners and who acted as intermediaries between the Shingon temples and pilgrims, from which they also derived a guaranteed source of income.

The Saturation of the Kantō Region and Status Differentiation, 1750–1800

In addition to the competition the Sakamoto *oshi* faced from neighboring villages, a second important factor made it necessary to restrict the pool of *oshi*. Until the early eighteenth century, when the Ōyama cult's popularity was on the rise and the *oshi* developed new parishes across the Kantō region, the expanding sphere of the Ōyama cult was able to sustain a growing number of *oshi*. However, by the second half of the eighteenth century, the Kantō region was saturated with *oshi* parishes, thus hindering the *oshi*'s expansion of their territory. Therefore, it was essential to limit the number of licenses.

Extant parish registers and parish sales documents from between 1730 and 1780 indicate that the first parish holdings of the Ōyama *oshi* were concentrated in Sagami, Musashi, and Kazusa Provinces.[52] Over the course of the eighteenth century, increasing evidence points to parishes in Edo. These parishes were attractive because they were more convenient for *oshi* to manage than parishes in more distant areas. The *oshi* collected first-fruit donations (*hatsuho*) from their parishioners and distributed amulets to them. In nearby villages, they also collected first-fruit donations several times per year but in smaller amounts. Distant villages were more difficult to reach, and first-fruit donations were accordingly collected more infrequently. Nearby parishes therefore provided a small but steady source of income.[53] When *oshi* acquired new parishioners, they kept such practical considerations in mind. When buying parishioners from other *oshi*, for example, they would not simply buy large numbers of parishioners scattered across a wide area but parishioners in neighboring villages. Often they would buy parishioners from the same villages repeatedly, gradually increasing their holdings.[54]

The number of extant parish records increased dramatically after 1780. Again, Sagami Province had the highest number (i.e., the highest concentration of parishes), followed by Musashi, Edo, and Kazusa. However, due to the high number of existing parishes in these regions, it was difficult to establish new parishes. Therefore, should *oshi* seek to expand their parishes in these regions, they had to shift parishes from one *oshi* to another through sales and pawning as indicated. Indeed, most transactions like this were limited to Sagami, Musashi, and Kazusa Provinces.

Parishioners then became an ever-more treasured possession. Tamamuro Fumio even argues that the price of parishioners increased toward the beginning of the *bakumatsu* period, but his evidence is limited because it is based only on documents from one *oshi*.[55] A broader survey of extant sales certificates suggests not a price increase for parishioners but that the *oshi* were less willing to part with their parishes permanently. Instead, the practice of pawning and leasing one's parish to another *oshi* grew over the course of the eighteenth century. In 1733, for example, Utsumi Shikibu lent money to Yano Izumo, who used parts of his parish as collateral:

Monetary Loan

A total of 2 *ryō* 26 *monme* in Edo *koban* coins.

This certifies the receipt of the amount stated above [seal]. In exchange, I have handed over 45 of my parishioners (*danna*) [seal] in Tsuchiya Village. The money shall be promptly returned before the twentieth of the seventh month of the coming Year of the Tiger (1734). If the payment is overdue in the least, the guarantor will immediately confiscate the pawned item. This document also bears the seal of the *gonin gumi* representative and the guarantor.

Kyōhō 16 (1733)/7/19

Borrower	Yano Izumo [seal]
Gonin gumi Representative	Gohee [seal]
Guarantor	[illegible] *tayū* [seal]

To Utsumi Shikibutayū[56]

The first such practice is documented in 1730. Pawning and leasing of parishioners continued into the early Meiji period, taking place with increasing frequency from the 1830s. Similarly, from 1757, there is evidence that *oshi* began to rent out parishioners for a limited number of years (usually ten) to another *oshi* who would have the exclusive right to the parishioners for that time period. From the 1810s, pawning and renting out parishioners became far more frequent even than the final sale of parishes.[57]

By the late eighteenth century, the Ōyama cult had spread to regions further away from Sagami Province. Even though Ōyama *oshi* may have preferred nearby parishes, the scarcity of available parishes forced them to expand their holdings in distant areas, where they could control larger parishes in larger areas. Eventually, their total holdings of parishioners in regions more distant from Ōyama outnumbered their holdings in closer areas. From 1778, there are records of parishes in Shimōsa Province and, after 1790, in Awa, Hitachi, Suruga, Izu, Kai, Kōzuke, Shimotsuke, and Mutsu Provinces.

Despite the high number of documents from this period, it is impossible to gain a comprehensive sense of the exact spread of parishes for the early modern period based on scattered parish registers. The *Kaidōki* (1877), an early Meiji survey of households affiliated with Ōyama, reflects the distribution of earlier holdings and allows us to estimate the range of Ōyama's cult in the pre-Meiji era (see Fig. 3.1). The data from the *Kaidōki* have their limitations. The documents were compiled in the early Meiji period, when the Ōyama cult was reshaped as a Sect Shinto organization, Ōyama Keishin Kōsha. Furthermore, the documents do not contain data about all former *oshi*, who may have either gone out of business or refused to participate in Ōyama Keishin Kōsha. However, even though the *Kaidōki* is not completely comprehensive, it allows us to gain a general impression of the spread of the Ōyama cult in the nineteenth century.

An estimate of the number of affiliated households is about 930,000 (or about 7,860 per *oshi*) concentrated in Sagami and Musashi Provinces (about 40 percent). Although the number of parishioners in Sagami Province was not the highest, the province, especially the districts closest to Ōyama, had the highest density of affiliated households. More distant regions were shared among fewer *oshi* and contained larger parishes but a lower concentration of them. This evidence supports the hypothesis that these nearby areas were the earliest regions covered by *oshi*, whereas more distant regions were explored later. Furthermore, while *oshi* from Sakamoto managed parishes in all provinces in the Kantō region, *oshi* from Minoge had parishes primarily in Sagami, Musashi, Izu, and Suruga Provinces and scattered holdings in Kai and Shinano Provinces. Minoge lay along the western pilgrimage route to Ōyama, so Minoge *oshi* tended to cultivate parishioners who would pass through Minoge rather than Sakamoto on their pilgrimages to Ōyama.[58]

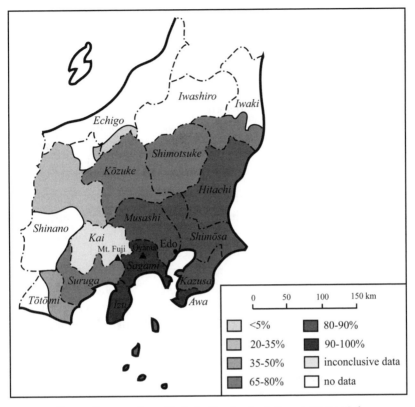

Fig. 3.1 Ōyama confraternities in the Kantō region in the early Meiji period

Initially, the presence of such parishes gave the *oshi* their status, but since the early eighteenth century, licenses and ancestry became equally important. These marks of distinction created the basis for status differences among the *oshi*. The number of licensed *oshi* was fairly stable, which limited the competition between them, but not all *oshi* had the same prestigious ancestry, parish size, or relationship with the Shingon clergy. One way to distinguish between different levels of *oshi* was a ranking system determined by the Shingon clergy based on the *oshi*'s parish size. The mediation system—used by the Shingon temples from 1718 to classify *oshi* who came to their temples for *goma* rituals—divided *oshi* into three levels: upper, middle, and lower rank. The upper and middle ranks were occupied by about 140 fully licensed *oshi* with proper *oshi* names. Those in the lower ranks had no *oshi* names and were shopkeepers and artisans who ran inns and acted as go-betweens in a fashion similar to full *oshi*.[59] The second way of differentiating between grades of *oshi* was family ancestry, which may also have played a role in the assignment of rank. A document from 1786 distinguished between several types: (a) those who were plain *oshi* with a long family tradition, (b) those who were related to 60 former mountain-ascetic families, (c) those who were *yamabushi*, (d) those who were shrine priests, (e) those who were servants of Hachidaibō, and (f) new *oshi* who were of merchant or artisan stock and had acquired licenses recently. Many of these new *oshi*, who made up about one quarter of all *oshi*, came primarily from a merchant background—several had run rice wine, bean curd, or noodle shops, and a few had been artisans (e.g., carpenters or wheelwrights) before becoming *oshi*.[60] A third means of creating status differences between *oshi* was the award of village offices by Hachidaibō, such as intendant or administrative duties at Hachidaibō. Sakamoto Village consisted of six sections divided into an upper part (Sakamotochō, Inarichō, Kaisanchō) and a lower part (Fukunagachō, Besshochō, Shinchō). Three-fifths of the *oshi* in Sakamoto resided in the lower part of the village, clustered around the lower Hachidaibō branch.[61] The upper part of the village was primarily populated with merchants, artisans, and tenants.[62] There were six village heads and six village elders, one for each section. In addition, the upper and lower parts each had an intendant and an overseer.[63] Hachidaibō assigned these offices to villagers who belonged to the *oshi* population because *oshi*—especially if they had large parishes—were wealthier than small-scale merchants, artisans, or tenants who accounted for the remaining non-*oshi* population in Sakamoto. If they were not *oshi* before the appointment, village officials were given an *oshi* license upon their appointment.

Shintoization of the Oshi, *1800–1868*

In this climate of social differentiation, a period of natural disasters and misfortunes led to social ferment in the late eighteenth century and again in the mid-nineteenth century. In 1771, a riot in Sakamoto Village was sparked by the appointment of Negishi Gondayū as intendant of upper Sakamoto. This was the first time in over one hundred years that Sakamoto's villagers were in open disagreement with Hachidaibō. As with many uprisings in this period, however, their criticism was not directed at Hachidaibō itself but against a fellow villager and his appointment to office. In the aftermath of the riot, the magistrate sentenced the three village headmen from Lower Sakamoto to be expelled from the village and ordered the 130 or so other *oshi* to pay a fine.[64]

As noted in Chapter 2, Ōyama and Sakamoto Village, and even the entire Kantō region, were struck by a series of natural disasters in the 1700s and 1780s that caused destruction and economic upheaval, leading to a decline in the number of pilgrims. The *oshi* felt the resulting economic pressure. They requested grain assistance in 1783 and, in 1784, a delay in the payment of taxes. In 1787, the village officials resigned from their offices after filing another request to delay tax payments.[65] Even though the total number of *oshi* remained stable, we can only presume that events led to considerable ferment in the village, heightening the disparities between rich and poor.

In this climate of social unrest, several *oshi* and artisans traditionally affiliated with the Shingon temples sought outside affiliation, independent from Hachidaibō. As noted above, the Yoshida House had been able to gradually expand its control over shrine priests beginning in the seventeenth century. However, many shrine priests remained independent either by choice or because they were prevented by law from seeking such an affiliation. Beginning in the late eighteenth century, an increasing number of ritualists turned to the Shirakawa, whose affiliates rose from about 50 in the mid-eighteenth century to almost 300 by 1816. In Sagami Province, the number of Shirakawa affiliates among shrines more than doubled and among shrine priests rose from 10 to 71 between 1816 and 1868. In contrast, in the 1830s only 31 (about 26 percent of all shrine priests in the province) had been affiliated with the Yoshida. By that time, the Shirakawa affiliates already were concentrated in Ōsumi District, where they equaled the number of Yoshida affiliates.[66] Their concentration in Ōsumi District is significant because Ōyama was located there.

The Shirakawa not only rivaled the Yoshida in their appeal to shrine priests but also attracted a much wider circle of affiliates. Since the 1790s, the Yoshida had been repeatedly admonished not to issue licenses to peasants who had not traditionally acted as shrine priests and could not supply the necessary documents issued by domain officials proving their traditional status.[67] By contrast, the Shirakawa were not limited by such restrictions but could issue licenses to anyone who could claim a connection with the imperial house, however tenuous. By the mid-nineteenth century, Shirakawa affiliates not only included shrine priests but also many village heads, peasants, and artisans such as carpenters, wood-cutters, roofers, and sweet-makers, who eventually came to outnumber Shinto priests with Shirakawa licenses.[68] Among this diverse group were *oshi* affiliated with sacred mountains such as Mt. Fuji, Mt. Mitake, and Ōyama.[69]

At Ōyama, what began as a way to obtain permission to wear special ritual robes and hats during carpentry rituals evolved into a way to defy the authority of the Shingon clergy. To Ōyama *oshi* who sought an alternative to the licensing system of Ōyama's Shingon clergy, the model set by shrine priests seeking to escape the control of the Yoshida was appealing. Before the nineteenth century, only three households at Ōyama held Shinto licenses: two *oshi* had obtained Yoshida licenses in 1652 and 1729,[70] respectively, and Ōyama's shrine carpenter, Tenaka Myōōtarō, held a Shirakawa license from 1773. The first holder of a Shirakawa license, the Ōyama shrine carpenter, did not find himself in conflict with the Shingon clergy because he obtained the license in his position as a carpenter, not as an *oshi*, though he held both titles. The Tenaka Myōōtarō carpenters passed their licenses on from generation to generation—having them occasionally renewed in 1811, 1821, 1827, and 1854. In 1811, the Tenaka carpenter also arranged for one of his apprentices to receive a license.[71] As long as these licenses were limited to a few members of the community, causing limited but not entirely disruptive friction among the *oshi* and posing no direct challenge of Hachidaibō's authority, the Shingon clergy did not oppose such licenses.

The carpentry rituals performed by the Tenaka Myōōtarō demonstrate how he used his Shirakawa license to distinguish himself from other carpenters in the community. He was after all not the only carpenter in the village, which had a total of five in 1735.[72] The shrine carpenter played a ceremonial role during the reconstruction of Ōyama's shrines even before obtaining a Shirakawa license. During the 1690s and 1770s, the carpenter served in similar capacities, but there was an important difference between the two occasions: the source of his authority to carry out special rituals. In the 1690s, his qualifications were primarily based on local tradition and precedent. During the reconstruction of Ōyama's temple complex in the late seventeenth century, Tenaka

Myōōtarō served as head carpenter at the shrines on the summit. He and his assistants made offerings and wore priest-like ceremonial robes and hats during rituals held at some of the shrines on Ōyama.[73] Tenaka Myōōtarō's role was very similar during the reconstruction of the shrines on the summit in the 1770s; it was also based on local tradition and precedent, but, in addition, he also held a newly acquired Shirakawa license that distinguished him from other villagers serving as carpenters. Again he served as head carpenter, but he used the Shirakawa license as his qualification to recite liturgy, some of which had been transmitted to him by a shrine priest with a Shirakawa license from a neighboring village. This suggests that family heritage was no longer enough to secure special privileges in the village and that licenses were needed to prove one's qualifications. The Shingon clergy saw no reason to object to his new Shirakawa license and recognized his elevated status as head carpenter, attended the rituals held by him, and eventually granted him the highest payments for his services among carpenters.[74]

Hachidaibō's attitude toward Shirakawa licenses changed, however, when large numbers of *oshi* sought affiliation with the Shirakawa family. By the end of the early modern period, a total of 52 *oshi*, or about 35 percent of Ōyama's *oshi*, held Shirakawa licenses, even though Hachidaibō initially resisted the surge. The first of these obtained a license in 1818, followed in 1828 and 1837 by two *oshi* who had been in charge of Shinto rituals as shrine priests previously but had not held licenses from an external institution. These licenses granted the holders the right to wear special ceremonial robes.[75] After Ōyama's temple complex and Sakamoto Village were destroyed by fires in the aftermath of a disastrous earthquake in 1855, two more carpenters obtained Shirakawa licenses through an introduction by Tenaka Myōōtarō. They too could perform ridgepole-raising ceremonies and wear ceremonial robes and hats. Their pursuit of licenses was directly linked to rituals during the reconstruction of the shrines on Ōyama's summit and slopes, a practice that does not seem to have disturbed Shingon clerics at Ōyama, even though one of the carpenters was also an *oshi* just like Tenaka Myōōtarō. As long as their Shinto ritual duties were limited to carpentry rituals, they posed no threat to the Shingon temples.[76]

Eventually, however, large numbers of *oshi* who were not involved in the reconstruction work sought to obtain Shirakawa licenses. Hachidaibō resisted when in 1855 seven applicants claimed to be shrine priests (*shikan*) requested licenses to perform *shinpai* (*kami* worship) ceremonies at their home altars and wear ceremonial robes and hats. These seven included members of two households who had indeed previously held positions as shrine priests, a *kannagi* in 1856 and the head shrine priest in 1857, but the others were ordinary *oshi*.[77] Hachidaibō refused to issue the necessary documents for the *oshi* to have their licenses officially recognized, and those who applied between 1856 and 1859 were also unable to obtain official recognition. In 1860, Hachidaibō prohibited all *oshi* from joining outside schools, such as the Shirakawa, which led the *oshi* to appeal to the magistrate of temples and shrines with the support of the Shirakawa in the summer of 1860.[78] The Shirakawa representative argued that the Sekison Shrine was in fact originally a Shinto shrine since it had appeared in the tenth-century *Engi shiki* under the name Afurijinja but had later become a mixed Buddhist-Shinto site under the *honji suijaku* theory of the Buddhist clergy. The Shingon abbot who denied the claims and refused to issue the necessary documents to make their Shirakawa licenses official argued that the Shingon clergy had been granted authority over Ōyama's land and that the Shingon monk Gangyō had revitalized the temple on Ōyama in the Kamakura period, setting a strong precedent for the exclusive authority of the Shingon clergy over the site. According to the Shirakawa, the abbot's argument was faulty because the Shinto faction based its claim on the authority of tenth-century *Engi shiki*, which predated Gangyō's late thirteenth-century connection with Ōyama and proved that Ōyama had once been under the authority of the Jingikan and that the Buddhist elements were a later accretion. In addition, there was precedent for the presence of other schools at Ōyama, such as the shrine priests affiliated with the Yoshida and the *yamabushi* affiliated with the Tendai school. Based on the Yoshida precedent, the Shirakawa claimed, the Shingon abbot should have issued the necessary documents.[79]

In the spring of 1861, the Hachidaibō abbot Kakkyoku was summoned to the magistrate of temples and shrines to settle the dispute. The *oshi* were represented by three Shirakawa-affiliated *oshi*, two of whom had obtained their Shirakawa licenses before the dispute (1818 and 1828). Two of the three *oshi* (Utsumi Shikibu and Sudō Shigeo) had also become members of the Nativist Hirata school in 1847. The Shirakawa-affiliated *oshi* made their case using strong, polemical language and claimed, for example, that the evil monks at Ōyama had unfairly wrenched control over the *oshi*'s parishes from the *oshi* and monopolized rituals and the issuing of amulets at the Sekison Shrine and the Fudō Hall. They said that the *oshi* were prohibited from serving what they claimed was their traditional function as shrine priests, including the right to issue amulets of the deity at the Sekison Shrine and conduct Shinto rituals.[80] In the fall of 1860, the situation escalated when the *oshi* tried to hold a Shinto funeral for an *oshi* who sought a Shirakawa license. The Shingon clergy was vehemently opposed to the performance of a Shinto funeral[81] because virtually all *oshi* in Sakamoto Village were parishioners of Raigōin and Kannonji, the two funerary Shingon temples in Sakamoto Village that were branch temples of Hachidaibō.[82] A Shinto funeral was an open rejection of the Shingon clergy's authority over the *oshi*. In the following year, the *oshi* renewed their appeal, represented by Shirakawa-affiliated *oshi* Yamada Hyōma, who had also been affiliated with the Hirata school since 1857. The controversy remained unresolved for several years until after the death of Abbot Kakkyoku in 1865: six more *oshi* joined the Shirakawa school, and Hachidaibō finally gave its official permission to recognize the Shirakawa licenses of 48 *oshi*.[83]

The Impact of Nativism

What made Hachidaibō so defensive against outside affiliation with the Shirakawa? And what led these *oshi* to adopt such a strong anti-Buddhist stance and suddenly challenge the authority of the Shingon clergy? In the first instance, the Shingon temples probably felt already that this was a time of crisis. The Buddhist precinct and Sakamoto Village had been completely destroyed in fires during the aftermath of a great earthquake in 1855. Reconstruction of the Buddhist precinct was progressing slowly. The *bakufu*, which had ordered the confiscation of temple bells around Japan to manufacture cannons in defense of a foreign threat in 1854,[84] only provided nominal funding for the project. The authority of Ōyama's abbots had gradually been undermined by their brief terms of tenure in the first half of the nineteenth century—due to, variously, their untimely deaths or local disputes. In fact, when the earthquake struck in 1855, Ōyama was without an abbot, and a new one was appointed hastily. In addition, even though the Shingon clergy also had official permission to raise funds for the reconstruction, their means were quite limited. The majority of the costs was actually borne by nearby villages that donated lumber and by the parishes of Ōyama's *oshi*.

The sense of economic and social upheaval was not limited to Ōyama but also extended to the national level. According to Anne Walthall, international pressure and domestic tensions led to the growth of Nativism in rural areas. Internationally, Japan was experiencing increased contact with Russian, British, and American vessels, which culminated in the arrival of Commodore Matthew Perry in 1853 and Consul Townsend Harris's call for trade treaties in 1858. Domestically, the ruling warrior class was divided on how to deal with the foreign threat, which gave low-ranking warriors an opportunity to promote change in the name of the motto to "revere the emperor and expel the barbarians (*sonnō jōi*)." The economic impact of the opening of ports such as Yokohama in 1859 further contributed to the turmoil by destabilizing the currency. As international pressure mounted, local village elites joined the Nativist Hirata school.[85] Walthall is referring to the growth of Nativism in the Ina Valley of Shinano Province, but the same circumstances apply to Sagami Province. Indeed, the inhabitants of Ōyama were probably even more keenly aware of the foreign threat because of their proximity to Edo and Sagami Bay as well as to Yokohama. Furthermore, the flow of pilgrims was affected as the shogunate occasionally closed the seaborne pilgrimage routes to Ōyama in order to contain local revolts and the mobility of masterless samurai.[86]

In this climate of political uncertainty and social instability, several *oshi* gravitated to the Nativist movement. Three of the four leaders of the anti-Buddhist Shirakawa faction—Sudō Shigeo, Utsumi Shikibu, and Yamada Hyōma—had a strong connection with the Nativist Hirata school founded by Hirata Atsutane (1776–1843), who had himself become licensed by the Shirakawa in 1840. Among the various schools of national learning, all of which examined Japan's classical literature and ancient writings to find the "truly" indigenous roots of Japan, the Hirata school had a strong focus on Shinto cosmology and offered religious professionals such as Ōyama's *oshi* and shrine priests an appealing alternate view on a subject that was dominated largely by Buddhist concepts. The brand of national learning at Ōyama is perhaps best exemplified by the *Afurijinja kodenkō*, the overtly anti-Buddhist work authored by Sudō

Shigeo one year after he joined the Hirata school and six years before he became licensed by the Shirakawa. Sudō Shigeo's interest in Nativism went far beyond a mere interest in literature. Through an examination of the *Kojiki* (712), *Nihongi* (720), and *Engi shiki* (927), and a critical analysis of works that he attributed to the Shingon clergy (e.g., *Ōyamadera engi*, and *Ōyama Fudō reigenki*), Sudō attempted to reconstruct Ōyama's pre-Buddhist roots—its deities, places of worship, names, and rituals before the monk Rōben's arrival. He accused the Shingon clergy of deceiving Japan's rulers and villagers in the Kantō region with evil magic and argued that the Buddhist site should revert to its pre-Buddhist form, the Afuri Shrine. In the process, Sudō also reevaluated the mountain codes issued under Kaizō, which he saw as oppressive even though they had initially protected the rights of *oshi* in regard to their parishes and licenses *vis-à-vis* competition from Koyasu Village: "The sixth abbot Kaizō laid down various regulations for the mountain. These were all ways to take away the power of those who had served as *shishoku* (shrine priests) since days of old. Once the monks had come to power, they set up regulations and charged various people with duties."[87]

To Sudō, the mountain codes did not protect the rights of the *oshi* but merely served to take away their power in the same way the Tokugawa legislation did in the beginning of the seventeenth century. Sudō considered the *oshi* the rightful heirs to the original shrine priests, whom he thought had served at the Afuri Shrine before the arrival of Buddhism at Ōyama. He expressed their connection by using *shishoku*, meaning shrine priest, rather than the more usual way of writing *shishoku*, meaning *oshi*, with the same *shi* as in *oshi*. He argued for the restoration of original Shinto ceremonies based on the *Engi shiki* under the leadership of the descendants of the shrine priests.[88] This was essentially the argument used by the Shirakawa faction in their dispute against the Shingon clergy at Ōyama.[89]

Sudō, Utsumi, and Yamada were not the only Nativist *oshi* at that time. Sakamoto Village was the foremost center of the Hirata school in Sagami Province: before the Meiji period, 12 of 22 members in Sagami were Ōyama *oshi*. In the area, the school recruited most of its members through a network of Shinto priests in the Kantō region. Ten of the twelve *oshi* also already held or later acquired Shirakawa licenses, indicating a close relationship between the *oshi*'s Shintoist and Nativist interests.

Between 1847 and 1857, the first Hirata school members at Ōyama were introduced with the help of outside shrine priests. The first two *oshi* to join the school were Utsumi Shikibu and Sudō Shigeo—who joined in 1847, four years after the death of Hirata Atsutane, the founder of the school. Both Utsumi and Sudō were introduced to the Hirata school by a shrine priest (*kannushi*) at a Hachiman shrine in Shimōsa. As in the case of the rush to acquire Shirakawa licenses after the fire in 1855, several other *oshi* joined the Hirata school then. In 1857, about two years after the great fire, Yamada Hyōma and another *oshi* were introduced to the Hirata school by a native of Shinano Province who later became the head shrine priest (*gūji*) at the Atsuta Shrine in Owari Province. At that time, Yamada and the other *oshi* both had already attempted to obtain Shirakawa licenses, as had six of the eight other *oshi* who joined subsequently between 1858 and 1865 after they were introduced to the school by one of their peers at Ōyama. [90]

The overlap between those holding Shirakawa licenses and those who became members of the Hirata school indicates a strong leaning toward Nativism within the Shinto specialist contingent of the *oshi*. Twenty percent of the *oshi* licensed by the Shirakawa had become members of the Hirata school.[91] Fifty-three percent of the *oshi* who held Shirakawa licenses and/or were members of the Hirata school can be identified as *oshi* who ranked as upper-level in the mediation system for *goma* rituals. This suggests that these were rather well-to-do *oshi* with large parishes.[92] For these wealthy *oshi*, the great fire in 1855 had provided a fertile ground in which they could prosper at Ōyama. The anti-Buddhist rhetoric of the Nativist Hirata school provided ammunition on ideological grounds whereas their Shirakawa affiliation gave them the necessary institutional backing to oppose the authority of the Shingon clergy. These Nativist scholars, including Sudō Shigeo, and holders of Shirakawa licenses were to become instrumental leaders in the disassociation of *kami* and Buddhas during the early Meiji period.

Conclusion

The return to ancient ways envisioned by these Nativist *oshi* was not simply a return to medieval Ōyama but a mythical, pre-Buddhist site. They did not seek a reinstatement of Ōyama's *shugendō* but a pure Shinto tradition. They attempted to reject their status as *oshi* and redefine themselves as Shinto shrine priests. Ironically, however, they took for granted the highly popular Ōyama cult, which had resulted from the *oshi*'s symbiotic relationship with the Shingon clergy during the early modern period.

It had been their role as *oshi* that contributed to the spread of the Ōyama cult in the Kantō region in the seventeenth and eighteenth centuries. Over the course of the seventeenth century, the *oshi* developed primarily out of *yamabushi* who had lost much of their authority to the Shingon clergy on the mountain in the first decade of the seventeenth century. Eventually, the tradition of mountain asceticism largely disappeared from Ōyama in the second half of the seventeenth century and left the former *yamabushi* to seek new means of income, forcing them to run inns and develop parishes throughout the Kantō region. These parishes, from which most of Ōyama's pilgrims came, became the single most important source of income for Ōyama. The system spread from areas near Ōyama across the entire Kantō region. It was these *oshi* who sustained the bonds between parishioners and the mountain through making yearly rounds of their parishes and providing accommodations for pilgrims. Despite their conflict-laden genesis, the *oshi* were not in constant opposition to Ōyama's Shingon temples. They developed customary networks with temples to handle pilgrims and received licenses from the head Shingon temple, Hachidaibō, which helped them to distinguish themselves from their competing innkeepers in neighboring villages. Another reason why the *oshi* did not voice a united opposition to the temples was that they were in fact a fairly diverse group with different heritages and levels of wealth. Some *oshi* were in the employ of Hachidaibō and therefore shared the temples' interests. It was only in the mid-nineteenth century that several wealthy *oshi* began to seek affiliation with external sources of authority such as the Shirakawa House and to engage in anti-Buddhist rhetoric culled from the Nativist Hirata school. This rhetoric eventually led to friction between the Shingon temples and the *oshi*, and provided the basis for the disassociation of *kami* and Buddhas in the early Meiji period.

As travel increased in the early modern period, pilgrimages to various sacred sites became popular throughout Japan. Religious specialists like the *oshi* contributed to the growth and continued popularity of these pilgrimage centers. Rather than relying on sporadic, haphazard pilgrims, the *oshi* and their parishes stabilized the sites by forming systems of pilgrimage management. That is why the most popular early modern pilgrimage centers such as sacred mountains (e.g., Ōyama, Mt. Fuji, and Tateyama) or famous temples and shrines (e.g., Zenkōji and Ise) had *oshi* or comparable systems. The concrete organizational structures differed from site to site. While Ōyama's *oshi* were controlled by the Kogi Shingon clergy, Mt. Fuji's *oshi* were organized in self-governing guilds, and at Zenkōji, low-ranking Buddhist clerics (*shūto*) at subtemples serving as inns were controlled by the Tendai abbot of Zenkōji. Like Ōyama's *oshi*, all these religious professionals also owned parishes, collected donations, and distributed amulets. These proselytizing innkeepers provided the pilgrimage sites with a comparatively stable base of income from their parishioners. They also helped to stem competition and strife by limiting the pool of contenders who could participate in the system and by strictly regulating the interactions with pilgrims and parishioners. Even though these religious specialists were usually not officially in charge of administering the cultic site, they represented the key to success for the majority Japan's early modern pilgrimage cults.

FOUR

Managing the Mountain

This chapter examines how Ōyama's ritual specialists—the Shingon clerics and the *oshi*—managed the pilgrimage cult. In the seventeenth century, Ōyama's ritual life changed from one focused on rites to benefit the Tokugawa regime to one focused on providing rituals for large numbers of pilgrims. Even though Ōyama's Shingon clergy continued to carry out state-sponsored rites on behalf of the Tokugawa regime, Ōyama's religious institutions came to depend on many small-scale donations from pilgrims and parishioners rather than single large payments or land grants earned through state patronage. In other words, Ōyama changed with the larger religious landscape of the early modern period, in which religious institutions relied increasingly on parish systems for their income rather than on large estates, state patronage, and a few wealthy patrons.

Ōyama's deities, primarily Fudō and Sekison, attracted pilgrims from the entire Kantō region and from all walks of life. They came to pray for healing, business and agricultural success, a good catch of fish, and protection from natural disasters and misfortune. During the seventeenth century, Ōyama's Shingon clergy created the mountain's principal festival in the Seventh Month to match the end of the monastic summer retreat. This summer festival drew large numbers of pilgrims because Ōyama's summit was only accessible for the three weeks of the festival. The summer festival employed a strategy similar that of a *kaichō* (display of a concealed sacred image), which was adopted by many temples with a hidden main image of worship during the same period: by prohibiting access to the sacred most of the time, the temples were able to attract large numbers of pilgrims during short periods when access was granted.

Simultaneously, the *oshi*, having lost their status as *yamabushi* and their right to officiate at rituals held on the mountain, developed parishes throughout the Kantō region. The *oshi* ensured the continued flow of pilgrims by personally visiting their parishes and lodging parishioners in their inns at Ōyama on their pilgrimages. By the dawn of the eighteenth century, the new system was firmly established and remained stable until the end of the early modern period. Once the Ōyama cult's early modern ritual cycle became established, both the Shingon clergy and the *oshi* managed to coexist in a symbiotic relationship that benefited them both.

A Shogunal Prayer Temple

Once the Shingon clergy took control of Ōyama by order of the Tokugawa regime in the early seventeenth century, only fully ordained Kogi Shingon clerics could officiate at rituals within the monastic precinct, particularly at those dedicated to Fudō Myōō, the main image of worship in the central hall. In return for the Tokugawa regime's backing, Ōyama's Shingon clergy was expected to provide spiritual support to the Tokugawa shogunate. Ōyama's temples had performed a similar function since before the early modern period. The Ashikaga shogunate commissioned prayers for the safety and peace of the realm on several occasions. Likewise Ōyama developed ties with the Hōjō in Odawara and performed prayers for their victory in battle.[1] Similarly, the Tokugawa shogunate also harnessed Ōyama. Tokugawa Ieyasu designated Ōyama as a sacred place offering protection to Edo in 1605—local tradition even has it that he visited Ōyama in person, but there is no supporting evidence for this claim.[2] Therefore, Ōyama's temples carried out rites for the protection of the state to ensure the continuation of the shogunal regime and the reign of the emperor. After the death of Tokugawa Ieyasu, Ōyama came to hold a special service dedicated to his deified spirit, Tōshō Gongen, on the seventeenth of each month.[3] Even in the late eighteenth century, daily rituals included prayers for good fortune for the *bakufu*, peace of the nation and the prosperity of the people, the growing spread of Buddhism, and the successful training of the Shingon clergy. The prayers highlighted the roles of Ōyama's purported founder, Rōben, and its restorer, Gangyō, in the establishment of the cult but also named Tokugawa Ieyasu's "firm orders"—in other words, the legislation that assured the authority of the Shingon clergy—as the essential basis for the continued ability of the clergy to carry out such prayers.[4]

As a reward for state-protection rites, Ōyama's Shingon clergy received shogunal backing in the management of the Ōyama cult and financial assistance for reconstruction projects. In the first decade of the seventeenth century, the shogunate recognized the Shingon clergy's authority over the site, granted the Shingon temples land, and funded the reconstruction of the entire complex. The close contact with the *bakufu* lasted through the seventeenth century. In the 1630s, visits of shogunal representatives were often related to a massive reconstruction project, which the *bakufu* funded and assisted by providing craftsmen. The shogunate contributed 10,000 *ryō* to another full-scale reconstruction project in the 1640s and granted 200 ryō and 5,000 pieces of lumber for repairs in the 1670s.[5]

Eventually, financial support from the *bakufu* began to wane. While the Tokugawa regime continued to recognize its initial land grant to the Shingon temples, its support for repairs slowly dwindled. In 1692, the Hachidaibō abbot Kūben was desperate for funds and pointed to the customary patronage of the *bakufu* and the clergy's responsibility to perform prayers on behalf of the shogunate. He hoped to motivate the *bakufu* to provide financial support to repair the wooden temple buildings that had become so dilapidated that the monks found it difficult to continue their residency. Following Kūben's persistent pleas, the Tokugawa regime reluctantly sponsored large-scale repairs. Ōyama received 4,251 *ryō* and 48,630 pieces of lumber for reconstruction of the entire complex.[6]

For the rest of the early modern period, the financial support for such projects from the *bakufu* steadily decreased. After the precinct suffered severe damage during an earthquake in the early 1700s, the shogunate donated 2000 *ryō* and 15,000 pieces of lumber. When the shrines on the summit were destroyed by a fire about twenty years later, the shogunate contributed 200 *ryō*. However, in similar circumstances in the 1770s, the shogunate only granted 1.7 *ryō*. When the entire precinct was destroyed by an earthquake in the 1850s, the shogunate—itself under financial pressure—donated less than one *ryō* and instead gave Ōyama's clerics permission to raise funds in the Kantō region, but in a region devastated by the quake this proved to be a difficult task.[7] Rituals dedicated to the benefit of the shogunate continued, but they no longer constituted the primary focus. Ōyama clerics and *oshi* filled the gap by appealing to a broad constituency as a popular pilgrimage cult.

Pilgrimage to Ōyama

Ōyamamairi, the pilgrimage to Ōyama, gained great popularity in the early modern period. Scholars have given various reasons for Ōyama's ability to attract such large numbers of pilgrims. In his study on early modern travel, for instance, Constantine Vaporis notes the agricultural significance of the pilgrimage to Ōyama. He suggests that peasants in the Kantō regions visited Ōyama for rainmaking rites (rainmaking and thanksgiving for rain) and therefore the authorities were not likely to prohibit pilgrimages to Ōyama.[8] Yet the Ōyama cult was not only famous for agricultural rites. It attracted large numbers of pilgrims from Edo and from coastal villages, who were merchants, artisans, fishermen, and boat operators not engaged in agriculture. Tamamuro Fumio has argued that it was the cult of Fudō with its focus on healing and protection from fire that made Ōyama so vastly popular in the early modern period.[9] Hartmut O. Rotermund has highlighted Ōyama's importance as a center of healing, especially from smallpox.[10] Suzuki Shōsei has argued that pilgrims were drawn to Ōyama for different reasons depending on the region where they lived: cultivators from Sagami and Musashi Provinces worshipped its agricultural deity; pilgrims from the seacoast in Awa and Izu Provinces came for protection at sea; some pilgrims from Sagami, Musashi, Shimōsa, and Kazusa Provinces came to practice austerities; other pilgrims from Sagami came to pacify the spirits of the dead; while pilgrims from Edo sought good fortune and protection from disasters.[11] Appropriately, the mountain was also known as Nyoizan (Mt. Wish Fulfillment) because it promised to fulfill any kind of wish.

Ōyama's wide appeal is reflected in premodern texts meant to advertise the Ōyama cult. The medieval *Ōyamadera engi* (1532) already promoted pilgrimages to Ōyama as means to solve any imaginable kind of problem:

Should somebody make a pilgrimage just once, his household will be safe from harm, and he will be free from illness. . . . If there is ever a time when the realm is in disorder and the country is not at peace, if there is ever trouble with wind and rain or water and fire, commission Buddhist services at this mountain and concentrate on your faith and pray. Then disasters shall soon abate, and the country will be pacified. . . . Those who have faith in this mountain and make a pilgrimage here shall be granted benefits during their lives and shall be reborn in the Pure Land after death.[12]

During the early modern period, Ōyama's deities were also known for their universal efficacy. According to the *Ōyama Fudō reigenki*, compiled by the Shingon cleric Shinzō in 1792, the purported benefits of Ōyama included relief from a large variety of problems by ensuring the physical and economic well-being of believers. Only about 10 percent of the stories address spiritual issues such as salvation after death or the attainment of wisdom. The largest number of tales deals with illness (36 percent), suggesting that Ōyama was especially known for its healing efficacy. The second most common problem addressed in the *Ōyama Fudō reigenki* is fire, usually through amulets and talismanic swords obtained on pilgrimages to Ōyama. Protection from fire was particularly important to urban residents in Edo, where fires periodically destroyed whole sections of the city. Raging fires had only recently ravaged Edo in the 1770s, which provided the compiler, Shinzō, with several exemplary tales of Sekison's and Fudō's power to ward off fire.[13] Ōyama's talismanic swords and amulets not only granted fire safety but warded off harm and misfortune in general: the retrieval of lost persons and items as well as protection from physical harm and natural disasters.[14] Agricultural concerns such as protection from droughts and insects were important to believers residing in agricultural villages, and safety at sea was a major issue for ferrymen and fishermen.[15] Ōyama became so popular precisely because it could accommodate such a wide range of concerns.[16]

If Ōyama was renowned for such powers since medieval times, why did the pilgrimage to Ōyama not gain much momentum until the late seventeenth century? The *Ōyama Fudō reigenki*, in fact, contains examples of two types of pilgrimages to Ōyama: those to Ōyama Fudō, which occurred throughout the year, and those to Ōyama during the summer festival of Sekison. The first type comprised primarily thanksgiving pilgrimages and spontaneous pilgrimages motivated by special wishes often related to protection from agricultural disasters or to healing. As in the medieval period, pilgrims continued to be motivated by spontaneous need in the early modern period. As with illness, agricultural disasters such as droughts or pests gave the pilgrims a sense of urgency that often could not wait until the next Sekison summer festival. In Story VI.7, Shichibei from Madarame Village in Sagami Province prayed to Fudō in the Fourth Month of 1770 to save his sprouting soybeans from mice. After a successful harvest, he immediately went to Ōyama to offer his first fruits.[17]

These pilgrimages were directed only at Ōyama Fudō, enshrined at Ōyama's Main Hall on the central slope, to which pilgrims could gain access regardless of the season or their gender. According to the *Ōyama Fudō reigenki*, these pilgrimages often emphasized physical mortification and strong devotion to Fudō. Pilgrims who wanted to affect the fulfillment of a wish tended to emphasize in their pilgrimages an ascetic ideal and strong faith. As John Eade and Michael Sallnow have observed, pilgrimage is often marked by an "overtly transactional ethic" according to which "physical suffering and penance are exchanged for material and spiritual favours."[18] If worshippers were particularly devout, they sometimes chose to make monthly pilgrimages. Story VI.9 in the *Ōyama Fudō reigenki* gives the example of Hanzaemon from Ochiai Village, who chose to make monthly pilgrimages to Ōyama Fudō. A pilgrim who wanted to make a difficult wish come true would go on a retreat and fast for seven days. Story II.2 explains: "In days of old, some people fasted for 7 or even 21 days, but, lately, perhaps because people's energy has declined, sick people and those without much strength come and wish to stay overnight. It has become a rule that the practice is limited to three days and three nights or two nights and three days. No one has been allowed to fast for seven days. Therefore, those who wish to continue for seven days have to take a break after two nights and three days."

Visits of shogunal representatives during the early seventeenth century—though not entirely representative of ordinary pilgrims due to their high rank—represent the only documented cases of pilgrimage in the early seventeenth century and had no connection with the summer festival. Kasuga no Tsubone, the wet-nurse of Tokugawa Iemitsu, visited Ōyama as a shogunal representative in 1615, 1640, and 1643. In the Fourth Month of 1615, Kasuga no Tsubone was dispatched to Ōyama as a shogunal representative to pray for military success for the campaign in Osaka in the summer of that year. About 25 years later, Kasuga no Tsubone visited Ōyama twice as a shogunal representative—once in the

Eighth Month of 1640 to pray for a son for Iemitsu and once in the Fourth Month of 1643 to mark the completion of the reconstruction of Ōyama. Similarly, several high-ranking clerics of the Kogi and Shingi Shingon Schools visited Ōyama in the 1640s and 1650s. Eizō, a high-ranking cleric at Mt. Tsukuba and later abbot of Konshōin in Edo, was dispatched as a shogunal representative in the Second Month of 1637 and again as a representative of Iemitsu's newborn son in the Ninth Month of 1642. That each visit occurred on the 28th of the month, Fudō's *ennichi*, indicates a strong connection with Fudō. The aristocratic cleric Sonshō from Daikakuji, an important Kogi Shingon academy in Kyoto, visited Ōyama in 1643 and offered a plaque commemorating Iemitsu's reconstruction of Ōyama. Another aristocratic cleric, Chūsha from the Shingi Shingon Rokuharamitsuji in Kyoto, made a pilgrimage in the Eleventh Month of 1647 and donated a votive plaque at Ōyama's Gate of the Two Kings. In the First Month of 1653, the aristocratic cleric Eiyo went on retreat at Ōyama for seventeen days as a shogunal representative, had a *goma* ritual performed and offered gold and silver to pray for the well-being of the thirteen-year-old Tokugawa Ietsuna.[19] Apart from these high-ranking state representatives and anecdotal evidence in the *Ōyama Fudō reigenki*, relatively few documents survive that cover such sporadic pilgrimages to Fudō. This suggests that Ōyama did not attract high numbers of pilgrims apart from the summer festival.

The second type of pilgrimage, which appears more frequently in documents, was less focused on asceticism than on ritual purity and combined the cult of Fudō with the cult of Sekison. This type of pilgrimage was limited to the summer festival of Sekison, which was held between 6/28 and 7/17, during which the summit was open to male pilgrims. Pilgrimages during Sekison's festival are well documented not only because of the high number of pilgrims but also because pilgrims usually traveled in small groups, namely pilgrimage confraternities, which occasionally left behind detailed records of their journeys. These pilgrimage confraternities gave the pilgrimage social and economic stability. Village or neighborhoods pooled their funds to dispatch several members of the community as representatives to Ōyama. These representatives would commission rituals on behalf of the community at Ōyama and return with amulets for the entire village or neighborhood. According one story in the *Ōyama Fudō reigenki*, villagers from a neighborhood in Odawara went on a pilgrimage to Ōyama at the start of the summer festival in 1746. The group had brought back a golden seal of Sekison for Zenjirō, a devoted Nichiren adherent, who venerated only the 30 central deities of the Nichiren School. Zenjirō accepted the group's ordinary souvenirs but did not enshrine the amulet and discarded it irreverently. Suddenly, there was a loud noise as if the roof of his house were pelted with thousands of stones. The noise continued for several days until Zenjirō retrieved the amulet and enshrined it properly. In commemoration of the event, people from the neighborhood and nearby villages made their pilgrimages every year during the first days of Sekison's festival.[20]

Zenjirō's story also points to another important aspect of the pilgrimage during the summer festival: Sekison and the summit were associated with taboos against ritual pollution. Hence Zenjirō was punished for failing to enshrine the amulet properly. Because of its focus on ritual purity, the pilgrimage during the summer festival was more attractive to men than women, who were considered ritually impure and barred from the summit. By contrast, the pilgrimage to Fudō attracted both men and women. Even though women did not have access to the summit, they could visit the Main Hall of Fudō on the central slope. In fact, villages near Ōyama depended on pilgrims to Ōyama Fudō once the yearly Sekison's summer festival had passed. Therefore, these villages objected vehemently to the removal of the sacred statue of Fudō during disassociation of *kami* and Buddhas in the early Meiji period. If Fudō were removed, they argued, there would be no pilgrims during the rest of the year.[21] However, the summer festival drew much larger numbers of pilgrims than sporadic pilgrimages to Fudō throughout the year. It is not surprising then that only 21 (16.8 percent) of *Ōyama Fudō reigenki*'s 125 stories, particularly those about Fudō rather than Sekison, deal with women's connections with the Ōyama.

Evidence from eighteenth-century travel literature supports the idea that ritual purity was an important issue during pilgrimages during the summer festival: pilgrims prepared for their journey with ritual ablutions and purifications. The *Zoku Edo sunago onko meisekishi* (1735) described how pilgrims, about to visit Ōyama for the summer festival, took ritual ablutions in the Asakusa River, contemplated on Sekison, and recited the words "*Sange, Sange, rokkonshōjō*" (Penitence, penitence!

Purification of the Six Senses!) and the names of the deities at Ōyama, "*Hachidai Kongara Dōji, Ōyama Daishō Fudō Myōō, Sekison Daigongen, Daitengu, Shōtengu.*"[22] According to the *Edo sōganoko meisho taizen* (1747), pilgrims who wished to visit Ōyama during the summer festival were encouraged to take ablutions in the Sumida River at Ryōgokubashi and warned not to take these rituals lightly but practice them with a sincere heart. The *Tōsei zamochi banashi* (1766) explained that one could make even difficult wishes come true if one kept a restricted diet for one hundred days and performed seven sets of thousand-fold ablutions. The *Tōto saijiki* (1838) explained that pilgrims to Ōyama took ablutions in the Sumida River.[23] Once pilgrims came to Ōyama, they used waterfalls at the foot of the mountain—Ōtaki, Atagodaki, Rōbendaki, Motodaki, and Fudōdaki—for ritual ablutions, which became a favorite motif of woodblock print artists in the nineteenth century.

The summer festival was wedged between the end of the monastic summer retreat (4/15–7/1) and the *obon* festival (7/15). Since this was the only time when the summit was open to ordinary pilgrims, it became the major pilgrimage attraction. Ōyama's deities were known to be wrathful; therefore, they could only be exposed to public view with the protection by the special magic powers of the Buddhist clergy, a theme that already appears in the *Ōyamadera engi*. The gate-opening rituals during the festival reenacted the legend of Rōben's ascent of Ōyama. According to the *Ōyamadera engi*, the monk Rōben was said to have led the people of Sagami to the summit where they discovered a sacred stone statue of Fudō by digging in the ground. The statue was so powerful that all who viewed it were struck dead. Miraculously, the monk Rōben escaped death and resuscitated the others with his powerful spells. In a similar way, the Shingon clergy symbolically asserted control over the sacred area around the summit and reenacted Ōyama's sacred history through the rituals of the summer festival.[24]

The summer festival had a mixture of agricultural and Buddhist components. It took place around the time of the *obon* festival (7/15), which marked the beginning of the harvest season. The festival had originally started on 7/1, the end of the summer retreat. In 1713, the period from 6/28 to 6/30 was added and later came to be known as *hatsuyama* (first mountain). One article in the mountain code from 1713 states:

Item: The gate-opening (*kaichō*) for the main shrines is held on 6/28. In the past, pilgrims have been permitted to pay their respects from 7/1, but recently, the power of the deity and the number of pilgrims has been increasing year by year. Therefore, from this year on, it will be permissible to make an early pilgrimage after the gate opening on 6/28.[25]

The three days were added to cope with the increasing popularity of the pilgrimage. Conveniently, the addition meant that the festival now began on Fudō's *ennichi* (auspicious day to establish a karmic connection) on the 28th day of the month. The festival began with a prayer service and a gate-opening ceremony that opened the path to the shrines on the summit to male pilgrims.[26] The remaining eighteen days of the festival were divided into three periods: *nanokadō* (7/1–7/7), *ainoyama* (7/8–7/14), and *bon'yama* (7/15–7/17). During and immediately after the festival, the clergy also held *kaichō* (displays of hidden images of worship) at the three shrines behind the Main Hall (7/7) and at the Nijū Chapel at Nijū no Taki (7/18).[27]

The summer festival harnessed the esoteric powers that the clergy acquired during their summer retreat (4/15–7/1). The Shingon clergy began their preparations early in the Fifth Month. According to the list of yearly ceremonies, 10,000 recitations of scriptures dedicated to Fudō Myōō and Kannon were performed on 5/7, 5/8, 6/2, and 6/3 to consecrate the amulets and golden seals.[28] The consecration ceremonies were held twice, in sets of two, at about three-week intervals during the monastic summer retreat. They coincided with the completion of ritual segments during the retreat, which also lasted about three weeks each and would have heightened the ritual powers of the clerics on retreat, allowing them to charge the amulets with efficacy through the chanting of scriptures and meditation.[29] This was done on four consecutive occasions, indicating that there were a large number of amulets. Pilgrims bought such amulets when they came to the festival.[30]

The connection between the summer festival and *obon*, when rituals to memorialize one's ancestors are held at ancestral altars and cemeteries, is apparent in the name *bon'yama* (*obon* mountain) for the period of the festival between 7/15 and 7/17. Even though the Japanese *obon* festival is celebrated considerably differently from the Chinese *yu lan pen* (Japanese: *urabon*) festival, the reason for the timing of the Chinese and Japanese festivals is identical. In his discussion of the Chinese celebration, Stephen Teiser notes the connection between the end of the monastic summer retreat and the *yu lan pen* festival on 7/15. In the lunar calendar, the day coincided with the full moon between the summer solstice and autumn equinox, and marked the beginning of harvest in north China.[31] Furthermore, *yu lan pen* took place at the end of the summer retreat of the monastic community, when the monastic community could harness the powers acquired during the summer retreat and put them to use for the good of lay supporters and their ancestors.[32]

Similarly, during Ōyama's summer festival, the clergy harnessed the powers accumulated during the summer retreat to open the summit to pilgrims. During the interlude of *ainoyama* (7/8–7/14), they held daily meditative *sanmai* services in preparation for the final phase of the festival during *bon'yama* (7/15–7/17). Even though the *obon* festival and *sanmai* services were usually associated with funeral and memorial rites during the early modern period, Ōyama's *bon'yama* had no association with death rites, but strict prohibitions against those in mourning were observed. Such pilgrims were prevented from ascending to the summit during the festival. The focus of the festival was to obtain various blessings for this world.

The opening of the summit was called *kaichō* (literally, opening of the curtain). This use of the term is somewhat curious as the rite is usually called *yamabiraki* (opening of the mountain). Use of this terminology was intended to make an obvious parallel between the opening of the summit and a display of a sacred icon. *Kaichō* and the related terms, *kaihi* (opening of the door) and *keigan* (opening of the alcove), usually referred to the practice of opening the front doors of the small shrine cabinet or alcove that holds the statue of a Buddhist or Shinto deity or other sacred treasures. One can loosely define *kaichō* as a temporary public display of a sacred object such as a *hibutsu* (concealed Buddha) or other sacred treasures that are otherwise hidden from public view. During the early modern period, *kaichō*—especially those held at host temples in urban centers—became major fund-raising events for temples in order to cover the costs of construction and repairs.[33]

Kaichō were carried out to allow the worshipper to establish a karmic bond (*kechien*) with the image by viewing it. For example, during *kaichō* at Zenkōji, a large pillar is erected in the open space in front of the main hall. A colored string tied to a hand of the sacred Amida triad on display is attached to a thick rope that leads to the pillar, which pilgrims then have the opportunity to touch to form a karmic bond. The *kaichō* shared this concept with the *ennichi*, which often commemorated the making or discovery of the sacred image in question. On such a day, visitors could multiply the spiritual merit gained through their pilgrimage. At Sensōji in Edo, for example, visitors could multiply their merit by up to 46,000 times through a pilgrimage on a special festival day.[34] During a *kaichō*, which gives visitors direct access to an image of worship otherwise hidden from view, the karmic connection is not just symbolic but visible and sometimes even palpable. Because of its heightened spiritual efficacy, a *kaichō* bears a powerful attraction for pilgrims. Sacred mountains like Ōyama, which opened their summits to pilgrims for a limited time, employed a similar rationale. In place of a sacred image, Ōyama's summit itself was on display and drew large numbers of pilgrims.

The Clergy's Contact with Pilgrims

During the festival, the Shingon clergy used their spiritual energy to perform rituals commissioned by pilgrims, such as *tenaga* and *goma* rituals dedicated to Fudō. According to ordinances issued in the early seventeenth century, only Shingon clerics were authorized to perform these rites in the hall dedicated to Fudō. Fees for those rites collected at the pilgrims' inns had to be turned over to the clergy. [35] The clergy made a symbolic claim to Ōyama's space, history, and deities by performing the *tenaga* rite. According to a document from 1795, the rite was held in memory of Rōben, who purportedly founded Ōyama's first Buddhist temple and performed esoteric rituals for three weeks after which the Fudō and his attendants appeared to him promising pilgrims longevity, prosperity, health, and familial harmony. To symbolize the five peaks and seven sides of Ōyama, the officiant presented 75 different trays decked with food of the five flavors to the deities of Ōyama at the altar in the main hall. The officiant also offered cloth and recited prayers (*norito*) before the main image of worship while *kagura* music was performed. This ritual was designed to bring peace to the world, make grain grow abundantly, and guarantee prosperity for many generations.[36]

Tenaga rites were expensive because of the large number of food offerings involved. A single *tenaga* rite cost about seven *ryō*—one *ryō* in cash for the performance as well as rice and vegetables worth six *ryō*.[37]

In the early seventeenth century, wealthy pilgrims commissioned the rite. When Kasuga no Tsubone and the high-ranking Shingi Shingon cleric, Eizō, visited Ōyama as shogunal representatives in the 1630s and 1640s, they had *tenaga* services performed and offered money.[38] As the early modern period progressed, *tenaga* rites were routinely commissioned by pilgrims who formed confraternities to be able to afford the expensive rites by pooling their resources.[39]

Another extremely important ritual held by Shingon clerics for the benefit of pilgrims was the *goma* ritual, a common esoteric ritual practiced by Shingon and Tendai clerics and mountain ascetics. During a *goma* rite, which is often performed before Fudō, the practitioner performs visualizations, *mantras,* and *mudras* while offering water, incense, oil, honey, rice, the five grains, and wooden slats in a fire ceremony. The ritual is usually meant to guarantee the sponsor material, physical, or spiritual benefits or to convey the sponsor's gratitude for benefits previously received.[40]

Goma rituals had a long history at Ōyama. The Ashikaga sponsored the construction of a *goma* chapel in 1400 when Ōyama was still a vibrant site of mountain asceticism.[41] Under the new monastic code of 1609, the performance of the rite in honor of Ōyama Fudō became the Shingon clergy's exclusive privilege. When the high-ranking cleric Eiyo from Konjōin, an imperially sponsored temple, made a seven-day pilgrimage to Ōyama on behalf of the shogunate, commissioning *goma* rituals and offering flowers and money in 1653, the ritual was performed by Shingon clerics.[42]

With the growing popularity of the pilgrimage to Ōyama, large numbers of pilgrims commissioned *goma* rites. As noted in Chapters 2 and 3, the Shingon temples established a mediation (*toritsugi*) system that linked the parishioners of one *oshi* and pilgrims at one inn with one or two specific subtemples when pilgrims commissioned *goma* services in order to regulate the flow of pilgrims between the temples and inns.[43] The *goma* rite (but not the *tenaga* rite) was subject to a carefully regulated system because *goma* rites were more frequently held than *tenaga* rites. This was because they cost only a small fraction of *tenaga* rites. For example, a *gomakō* (confraternity dedicated to commissioning *goma* rituals) from Hachiman Village in Sagami Province spent 500 *mon* on the rite, less than 2 percent of the costs of a *tenaga* rite.[44] Since this ritual was less costly, it was even affordable for individual pilgrims. In the *Ōyama Fudō reigenki*, for example, the wife of Zenbei, a greengrocer from Edo, performed fervent prayers that culminated in the vision of a flame and, the following night, a vision of Fudō inside the flame. Within a few days, her eyesight was restored. In order to express their gratitude, both the husband and wife set out from Edo to make a thanksgiving pilgrimage to Ōyama in the Ninth Month. They stayed with the *oshi* Hachidayū and commissioned a *goma* ritual at a Buddhist temple.[45]

Not all Shingon subtemples within Ōyama's Buddhist precinct were incorporated into the mediation system for *goma* rituals but only the original twelve subtemples. Six additional subtemples (*wakibō*) and Daikanjin on the central slope, as well as Raigōin, a Shingon ancestral temple near the border of the Buddhist precinct and Sakamoto, were excluded. Yet, despite their exclusion, two of the other Shingon temples, Raigōin and Kōenbō (a *wakibō*), attracted pilgrims from nearby villages by offering memorial rites for deceased family members one hundred days after their death. Since the rite included an offering of tea, Raigōin and Kōenbō became known as Chatōdera (literally, tea temple).[46] The origins of the practice are unclear, but it is likely that the two temples introduced this ritual in the early nineteenth century. The Shingon temples that conducted only prayer rituals (*kitō*) did not become involved in death rituals, but Raigōin and Kōenbō were not incorporated into the mediation system for *goma* rites and therefore did not have to preserve their ritual purity to ensure their efficacy. They were allowed to perform mortuary rites to generate income.

The Oshi's *Contacts with Pilgrims*

Because the Shingon clergy monopolized the major rituals at the most sacred sites within the Buddhist precinct and the income derived thereof, Ōyama's *yamabushi*, shrine priests, and *oshi* had to rely on other sources on income. Among the *oshi*, participation in Shingon-controlled rituals was limited to a few hereditary sacerdotal families who had ritual duties as *yamabushi* and shrine priests. The 1609 monastic regulations placed four sacerdotal shrine priest families (*shinke*)[47] in charge of the *mikoshi* chapel near the Main Hall and gave the *yamabushi* control over the Gyōja Chapel, dedicated to their legendary founder En no Gyōja. This gave these shrine priests and *yamabushi* the right to collect the donations made at these halls. In return, the shrine priests and *yamabushi* had to fulfill ritual duties. For the *yamabushi*, as noted above, ritual duties consisted of participation in the *shinji* festival in the Second Month, for which the clergy set concrete parameters and paid the *yamabushi* in rice and cash.[48] Even though the tradition of mountain asceticism virtually disappeared from Sakamoto Village, these rituals lasted at least into the early eighteenth century, when the Shingon clergy seems to have relied on *yamabushi* from Minoge.[49] In addition, despite the clergy's monopoly on presiding over *tenaga* rituals, five shrine priests performed dance rituals (*kagura*) associated with the rite.[50]

Several *oshi* households also came to control access to four waterfalls in Sakamoto Village that were used by pilgrims—for a fee—for purification during the summer festival.[51] In 1831, an *omikikō*, a confraternity devoted to the offering of sacred rice wine, visited Ōyama during the summer festival. The group spent 100 *mon* on their visit to Ōdaki, which equaled 33 percent of the fee for a single pilgrim's overnight accommodations or the price of three pilgrims' meals at the inn of their *oshi*, Murayama Hachidayū.[52] During a dispute between Sakamoto and Koyasu Villages from 1752, one of the charges was that villagers in Koyasu had opened new waterfalls for purification during the pilgrimage season without authorization from the Shingon temples.[53] Therefore, with limited ways to support themselves, the *oshi* staunchly defended their right to charge a fee for access to waterfalls.

Compared to the elaborate rites conducted by the Shingon clergy at Ōyama's primary cultic sites, most *oshi* were only authorized to perform small-scale rituals at their inns and on their parish rounds. The Shingon clergy did not oppose these practices but actually required *oshi* to be skilled in such rituals. The mountain code of 1702 specified that "In respect to *kami* matters and prayers (*kitō*), those who have not been transmitted such rituals should not act as *oshi*," and the code of 1721 declared that "*Oshi* . . . maintain the tradition of the Buddhas and the *kami* and perform prayers (*kitō*)."[54] The detailed nature of the rituals differed depending on the household, but they dealt with common concerns such as rainmaking rites, spirit pacification, divination, healing, fortune, and fertility. For example, in the early summer of 1786, villagers in Yotsu Village (Ashigara Shimo District, Sagami Province) called for Enkyōin, an *oshi* and mountain ascetic in Minoge Village, to perform rituals for protection from rodents.[55] Another *oshi*, Satō Oribe, owned a manual called *Sōden mitsuji* (Secret Matters Transmitted from Generation to Generation), which contained esoteric spells to cure burns, toothaches, fever, and smallpox; to dispel vermin; and to prompt the birth of a child.[56] He also owned a manual entitled *Uranai ninsō den* (Transmissions of Divination and Physiognomy; 1790), which gave detailed instructions on how to predict a client's fortune, physical condition, and reproductive potential by assessing the color of his *ki* (*qi* or energy), the back and front of his hands and feet, the sound of his voice, and facial features.[57] Similarly, an esoteric ritual manual of the *oshi* Utsumi Yūkei entitled *Kasō mitsuden* (Secret Family Transmissions; 1836), contained instructions inspired by *onmyōdō* (*yin-yang* theory) that linked directionality (the twelve animals and the ten stems) with the five elements and five colors to divine good fortune, illness, and disasters.[58]

What is of interest here is that these manuals are from the late eighteenth and early nineteenth century when diviniation activities in urban areas were increasingly controlled by the Tsuchimikado, a Kyoto-based lineage of *onmyōdō* diviners that traced itself back to the legendary Heian-period diviner Abe no Seimei. In 1791, the Tsuchimikado received official permission by the *bakufu* to license *onmyōdō* diviners after half a century of disputes with *yamabushi* over the right to perform divination. Officially, the Tsuchimikado had held this right by imperial and shōgunal decree since 1683 but had been unable to enforce their control over *onmyōdō* diviners beyond Edo, Owari Province, and the provinces around Kyoto. Before 1791, most diviners—including laymen, *yamabushi*, Buddhist clerics, and Shinto priests—operated without special licenses. After 1791, Tsuchimikado-affiliated diviners in Edo and Osaka attempted to force others engaged in the practice to obtain similar licenses.[59] Despite the frequent conflicts between *onmyōdō* diviners and *yamabushi* even after 1791, there is no indication of similar conflicts involving Ōyama's *oshi*. It is likely that the divination activities of the *oshi* were on such a limited scale that they escaped notice by Tsuchimikado-affiliated diviners even though their parish rounds frequently took them into Edo, where the diviners were particularly active.

The primary occupation of most *oshi* was to cater to pilgrims as innkeepers and proselytizers. *Oshi* provided food and lodging for pilgrims at Ōyama, but they also played the role of intermediary, visiting parishioners and arranging for rituals at the Shingon temples.[60] As noted in Chapter 3, the *oshi*'s most important right was that of parish ownership. In the 1676 mountain code, *oshi* were given the exclusive right to house and provide meals for their parishioners on pilgrimages, except during the festival when anyone could provide light meals during the daytime since the town bustled with pilgrims. In the 1702 and 1713 codes, the *oshi* were charged to act as intermediaries between pilgrims and the Shingon clergy for *goma* rituals and to monitor whether pilgrims were ritually pure and wore robes suitable for their ascent to the summit during the summer festival.[61] Mediation between pilgrims and the Shingon subtemples also brought in a welcome supplement since the *oshi* received a small percentage of the donations.

Considering how adamantly they defended their right to house pilgrims against competition in the villages of Koyasu and Kamikasuya, running inns and even bean curd, noodle, and artisan shops also provided the *oshi* with essential income. In the nineteenth century, *oshi* charged pilgrims 30 to 100 *mon* for meals and 250 to 1,000 *mon* for lodging, depending on the inn and the quality of service. In addition, confraternities tipped the *oshi* and his staff between 50 and 750 *mon* each, depending on their status within the inn. Income during the summer festival was substantial. During the summer festival in 1831, for instance, Hachidayū had 857 guests at his inn and collected about 60 *ryō* for lodging, meals, and sales of amulets, candles, sake, tobacco, and sandals.[62] Hachidayū's earnings were probably above average. Compared with other *oshi*, he had a relatively large parish and was therefore wealthier than many *oshi* with parishes only about 25 to 50 percent the size of his.

The Oshi's Parish Rounds

While the Shingon clergy's primary contact with devotees occurred during the performance of complex rites such as *goma* and *tenaga* services on the mountain, the interactions between pilgrims and *oshi* were not limited to those at the site. In addition to their work as innkeepers at Ōyama during the busy pilgrimage season, *oshi* went on parish rounds to distribute amulets during the off-season. The dissemination of amulets was one of the most carefully guarded privileges, an issue that appears in the mountain codes of 1702 and 1721 and was contested in disputes in 1702 and 1752.[63] The *oshi* sold amulets—which were consecrated by the Shingon clergy—to pilgrims during festivals and also distributed them on parish rounds (*dankai*) during months when no important festivals were held at Ōyama. In addition, the *oshi* used these rounds to collect *hatsuho* (first-fruit donations) and to cement their connection with their parishioners. Inomata Gidayū noted in his copy of the abridged *Ōyamadera engi* (1852): "Among the houses that are lined up tightly on both sides of the road at the foot of this mountain, there are many *oshi*. They have parishioners in many provinces to whom they distribute amulets in the First, Fifth, and Ninth Months."[64]

These months would have been particularly convenient for *oshi* to travel away from Ōyama. The main pilgrimage season was in the Seventh Month, but during the Fifth and Ninth Months the Shingon clergy held their summer and winter retreats (4/15–7/1 and 9/15–12/2).[65] The First Month provided the *oshi* with an opportunity to bear seasonal greetings to their parishioners and renew their relationships for the New Year. Conveniently, the Shingon clergy consecrated new amulets during first seven days of the New Year when special New Year's ceremonies were held at the Shingon temples.[66]

The distribution of amulets and the collection of first-fruit donations on parish rounds had a ritualistic character. The *oshi* would more or less follow a set course from one parish to another each season or each year. His contact with his parishioners involved a ritualized exchange of commodities: the *oshi* handed out amulets and gifts and received donations from his parishioners. This exchange also followed set patterns and reflected social hierarchies through the value of the gifts and the donations. Occasionally, the *oshi* also performed individual rituals on his route for the benefit of particular parishioners.

The example of Murayama Hachidayū, the above-mentioned wealthy *oshi* with close ties to Hachidaibō, illustrates the particulars involved in an *oshi*'s parish rounds. The frequency with which *oshi* visited their parishes depended on their distance from Ōyama. Nearby villages were easily accessible, and *oshi* could visit them several times a year and maintain close contact. For example, Murayama Hachidayū's parish rounds of Sagami Province took him multiple times to several villages in Sagami Province during 1854. Four times that year, he paid visits to seven villages in southeastern Sagami Province within a radius of 30 kilometers from Ōyama. Three times that year, he visited a village in southern Sagami Province, about 15 kilometers from Ōyama. Twice that year, he toured several villages 15 to 25 kilometers away in southwestern Sagami Province, 35 kilometers to the northeast in southwestern Musashi Province, and 50 kilometers in eastern Sagami Province.[67]

A register compiled in the same year contains a list of items he carried on his tour. In addition to standard travel documents, travel gear, and a few personal effects, he brought his parish register and donation register to assist him in finding his way around his parish and to account for the donations he received. He also carried boxes with amulets and gifts such as local specialties to be distributed among parishioners in exchange for their dues. Finally, he also brought along a booklet with prayers (*norito*), which suggests that he performed small rituals for some parishioners on his rounds.[68]

An earlier record of Hachidayū's rounds, in 1837, lists the amulets that he distributed in Edo as well as Musashi, Shimōsa, Kazusa, and Sagami Provinces. A similar record exists of his parish rounds to Edo, Kazusa, and Shimōsa Provinces in 1845, 1846, and 1847. These records all indicate that Hachidayū distributed thousands of amulets of various kinds and sizes as well as packages of medicine. The most common item was small amulets, which Hachidayū handed out about four times as often as he did large amulets and amulets printed on special paper. Depending on the recipients' needs, Hachidayū would also distribute a few special amulets for various professions, such as silkworm cultivators and boat operators.[69]

The 1837 record meticulously documents that Hachidayū also distributed to parishioners local specialties (rice crackers, rice cakes, seaweed, pepper in little bags, wheat noodles, and tangerines), useful household utensils (chopsticks and ladles), dishes (bowls, containers, stacked lunchboxes, trays, and saucers), and small accessories (fans, hair ornaments, tobacco cases, hand towels, and cloths)—all items that could be easily transported. To children, he would hand out pictures and tops—one of Ōyama's special products. Chopsticks, rice crackers, and rice cakes were given to almost every household that also received an amulet, but special Ōyama lacquerware (bowls, trays, and stacked boxes) was reserved for those who provided Hachidayū accommodations. In the parishes near Ōyama, which he visited several times per year, he always gave out chopsticks and seasonal gifts to convey his seasonal greetings: rice crackers and kelp in the spring, fans in the summer, women's hair ornaments in autumn, and rice cakes and ladles in the winter.[70]

A particularly important gift was medicine, packages of which Hachidayū distributed to almost every household. This indicates that the *oshi* combined their role as proselytizer with that of healer. Data from other *oshi* who prepared medicinal pills and powders based on family recipes suggest the various kinds of medicines these may have been. An *oshi* by the name of Takao Sachū distributed thousands of packages of oral medicine, powdered restorative, and ointment on his parish rounds in 1842 and the summer of 1852, respectively. Takao's medicines contained bark from the *ōbaku* (amur cork) tree and were used to treat burns and stomach ailments.[71] An earlier document from 1795 transmitted by Utsumi Shikibu also showed that *ōbaku*-based powders and pills to treat stomach ailments were distributed.[72]

The allocation of such commodities did not mean that *oshi* were essentially itinerant peddlers, as Shinjō Tsunezō has argued in the case of the *onshi* at the Ise Shrines, who according to Shinjō, devolved from low-ranking shrine priests into traveling vendors during the sixteenth century.[73] Although his descriptions of Ise *onshi* distributing trinkets along with amulets are very similar to those of the activities of the Ōyama *oshi* beginning in the late seventeenth century, data from the latter suggest a much closer connection between two aspects that Shinjō regards as distinct: the religious and the economic functions of *oshi* parish rounds. The distribution of commodities—amulets and gifts—in exchange for first-fruit donations (*hatsuho*) was linked. For instance, even though Murayama Hachidayū distributed food, accessories, and medicines, he did not act simply as a vendor. These items were gifts that he added to his amulets, the distribution of which was the main purpose of his parish rounds. The amulets and additional gifts were often handed out as sets whose value depended on the status of the recipient. Hachidayū distributed large amulets and more substantial gifts to his hosts—influential villagers (village heads, village elders, shrine priests, and temples)—and gave small amulets and less-valuable gifts to ordinary villagers.[74] In their studies of Hachidayū's rounds, both Tanaka Sen'ichi and Matsuoka Takashi point out that this *oshi* occasionally distributed amulets personally at each house (in 23 of 155 villages; 14 percent) but more often had the amulets distributed by important villagers or at local temples, where the *oshi* would leave amulets and gifts for the rest of the village.[75] These findings are mirrored by evidence from other *oshi*s' parishes. Parish registers, even very early ones, contain special marks next to the names of high-ranking villagers, as if the *oshi* needed to remind himself whom to give special gifts and amulets. Other registers list villagers who received special gifts individually but provide only a summary of the total number of households that received ordinary items.[76]

In most of his parishes, Hachidayū distributed plain small amulets (to ordinary parishioners) and special paper amulets (to village officials),[77] but in regions that specialized in particular occupations, he also handed out special amulets. In several villages around Hachiōji (Nishi and Minami Tama Districts, Musashi Province) that specialized in sericulture, for example, he distributed about 500 to 600 silkworm amulets in 1834 and 1844.[78] Another *oshi*, Takao Sachū, distributed about 300 silkworm amulets in the same region of Musashi in 1852.[79] On parish rounds in coastal villages, Hachidayū distributed boat amulets. As he did with large amulets and those specially inscribed, Hachidayū distributed boat amulets only on special occasions to important villagers. On his parish rounds of Kazusa Province in 1840, Hachidayū gave a boat amulet and a tobacco box to an official in a coastal village between the ports of Kisarazu and Futtsu. At the port of Futtsu, he spent the night at the house of the village head to whom he gave a boat amulet, a tobacco box, and two trays.[80] Similarly, Utsumi Yūkei marked boat owners in the same way as he would neighborhood leaders and village heads in his parish register of two coastal towns near Ninomiya in Sagami Province in 1720.[81] On his rounds of Awa Province in 1791, Kusayanagi Gendayū distributed boat amulets along with large- or medium-sized amulets and special gifts (chopsticks and ladles) to select villagers, including village heads and his hosts.[82] In 1807, Utsumi Shikibu, whose parishes included coastal villages in Sagami's Miura district and especially Awa Province, distributed 150 boat amulets in the winter and 35 sea-related amulets, probably to owners of boats.[83] In 1830, Utsumi Shikibu handed out four boat amulets and seven large amulets in each of two coastal villages in Awa, where he had 30 and 71 parishioners respectively, and three boat amulets and five large amulets in a village with 75 parishioners.[84]

On his parish rounds, Hachidayū relied on the good will of village officials to lodge him, to handle his luggage and to collect first-fruit donations. Therefore, he usually gave them special gifts and amulets. All amulets and gifts were light and could be easily carried to nearby villages on short parish rounds. However, when *oshi* visited more distant parishes, careful planning was necessary due to the sheer amount of luggage. In 1837, Hachidayū took careful notes describing his round of southwestern Shimōsa Province. The day before his departure, he prepared his luggage, wrapping everything in waterproof paper and shipping it by boat to Gyōtoku on the border between Edo and Shimōsa Province. The following day, he set out carrying only a box with money and traveled by boat from Musashi Province to Gyōtoku. After having lunch at an inn, he collected his belongings, rented packhorses, and went to spend the night at an inn in Funabashi. The next day he arranged for a porter to carry his luggage. After he finished in the Funabashi area, he set out for the next village, leaving behind all his luggage except what he needed during the day, and instructed the innkeeper to accept deliveries of first-fruit donations from 55 villages on his behalf. During the rest of his trip, he made overnight stops at the houses of village officials.[85]

In both 1837 and 1865, his routes were nearly identical (see Fig. 4.1). They circled clockwise from Funabashi around 58 villages, at nine of which he spent the night before returning to Funabashi. On this loop, he forwarded part of his luggage to his next overnight quarters. After his return to Funabashi, he set out on a northeastern route of 36 villages, shipping his luggage from village to village as he visited them. He spent his nights at seven different villages. On his way back, he returned to two earlier overnight stops to pick up luggage and first-fruit donations held for him there. After spending one more night in Koganechō, he went along the Mito Highway to Edo.[86]

On his trip, Hachidayū not only distributed amulets, gifts, and medicines but also collected first-fruit donations. Apart from the right to hand out amulets, the right to collect first-fruit donations was one of the most important privileges of the *oshi*. Since first-fruit donations were paid at least partially in kind, they were too heavy for him to carry along. Therefore, he relied on a system of hubs or entrepôts, where first-fruit donations from several villages were gathered (see Fig. 4.2). Murayama Hachidayū had first-fruit donations forwarded to contacts in central villages—often identical with those at whose houses he had

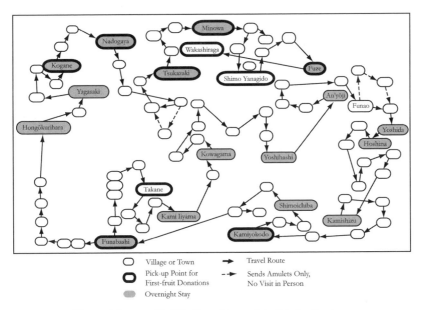

Village or Town

Pick-up Point for
First-fruit Donations

Overnight Stay

Travel Route

Sends Amulets Only,
No Visit in Person

Fig. 4.1 Murayama Hachidayū's parish rounds in Shimōsa Province.

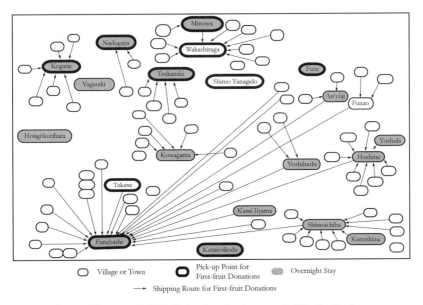

Village or Town

Pick-up Point for
First-fruit Donations

Overnight Stay

Shipping Route for First-fruit Donations

Fig. 4.2 Murayama Hachidayū's *hatsuho* collection routes in Shimōsa Province.

spent the night—and then on to larger depots where he would pick them up later. Villages near Funabashi forwarded their first-fruit donations directly to the inn in Funabashi where Hachidayū was staying, whereas more distant villages sent their first-fruit donations to smaller depots in villages that had served as overnight stops and then on to Hachidayū's inn in Funabashi, where the *oshi* picked them up on his return. On the northeastern route, villages where he made overnight stops served as depots for first-fruit donations. The *oshi* would either collect the donations on his way through or upon his return on the way back to Edo. When first-fruit donations from a village did not arrive at an entrepôt in time for him to collect them, he had them forwarded to his last stop.[87] Thus, Hachidayū relied on a highly efficient system that involved the cooperation of village officials.

However, Japanese scholars have debated whether, despite the efficiency of the system, parish rounds to distribute amulets and collect first fruits generated sufficient income for *oshi*. In 1865, Hachidayū collected about 19.1 *ryō* on rounds on which about twenty villages failed to contribute first-fruit donations. His own costs on the road amounted to about 7.8 *ryō* (40.8 percent)—excluding costs for amulets and gifts—with a profit of less than 11.3 *ryō*. Tanaka Sen'ichi concludes that Hachidayū's income from such rounds therefore was not very high.[88] In contrast, Tamamuro Fumio is more optimistic. On parish rounds in eastern Musashi in 1866, Hachidayū collected about 8.1 *ryō* from 3,450 households. Tamamuro suggest that income from first-fruit donations must have totalled about 28.9 *ryō*, assuming that the entire parish comprised 12,316 households, as documented in 1883. Tamamuro admits, however, that some parishes—especially distant ones—failed to contribute first fruits. In 1845, for instance, 21 villages in Shimōsa Province withheld their donations and three villages in Kazusa Province had not contributed first fruits for three years. Tamamuro calculates Hachidayū's financial loss as 7 percent (two *ryō*), leaving Hachidayū with a sizeable income of 26.9 *ryō*. However, assuming that Hachidayū's expenses for travel amounted to 40.8 percent (11 *ryō*) of his revenue, as suggested by Tanaka's research, his income would actually have been 15.9 *ryō*, minus his costs for amulets and gifts.[89] In comparison, the income from parish rounds was about twice the cost of a *tenaga* rite (which mostly profited Ōyama's Shingon clergy) but involved many times the labor.

Even if their rounds to distribute amulets and collect first-fruit donations were not the most effective means to make money, they served to help *oshi* maintain close contact with their parishioners. After all, *oshi* parishioners were likely to be affiliated simultaneously with Ōyama's competitors—other sacred sites in the Kantō region—or they might choose to shift their affiliation to another *oshi*.[90] In 1809, the head of the Ōba family, a *bakufu* intendant living in Kamimachi, Musashi Province, compiled a list of the yearly ceremonies celebrated by his family. He also made a list of regular donations his family gave to representatives from sacred mountains and famous shrines that were located mostly in the Kantō region but also as far away as Mt. Kōya and the Ise Shrines. The family spent nearly 2,000 *mon* per year on biannual donations to nearby Ōyama, Mt. Haruna, Enoshima, and Mt. Mitake, and on annual donations to the more distant Kashima Shrine, Taga Shrine, Tsushima Shrine, Mt. Atago, Mt. Fuji, Mt. Kōya, Mt. Akiba, and the Ise Shrines.[91] Given this stiff competition it was fortunate that the *oshi* did not have to rely only on first-fruit donations for income but also took in income from pilgrims staying at their inns at Ōyama. In comparison, the pilgrimage season yielded about four times the amount earned from first-fruit donations in the case of Hachidayū.

Conclusion

During the early modern period, Ōyama developed into a popular pilgrimage destination, which allowed it to flourish by relying on small-scale donations by ordinary pilgrims rather than on state patronage alone. Through a distinct division of labor and the mediation system, the clergy and the *oshi* formed a symbiotic relationship of mutual dependence. The Shingon clerics controlled Ōyama's major cultic sites but relied on the *oshi* to bring pilgrims to their doors for rituals. The *oshi* maintained close personal contact with their parishioners through their inns and their parish rounds. Their activities as innkeepers and proselytizers, along with their distribution of amulets and gifts and the collection of yearly donations, went hand in hand. The *oshi* flourished under the system as much as the Shingon clergy even though the new system initially took away their access to Ōyama's main cultic sites.

However, the Shingon Buddhist takeover of Ōyama's ritual life at a time when funeral rituals became the mainstay of most temples in Japan did not mean that mortuary rites took precedence at Ōyama. On the contrary, there was a strict separation between the Shingon temples on the mountain, which provided *goma* and *tenaga* rituals, and the Shingon ancestral temples at the foot of the mountain. This division harkened back to taboos against the ritual pollution of death, a prevalent concept in Shingon Buddhism in the medieval period. For *goma* and *tenaga* rituals to be efficacious, Shingon clerics needed to remain unstained by the pollution accrued in mortuary rites. The same reasoning continued into the modern period. When Ōyama Fudō was moved to Ōyama's lower slopes near the Raigōin—one of the Shingon ancestral temples—as a result of the disassociation of *kami* and Buddhas in the early Meiji period, Raigōin's cemetery was moved away from the temple lest the graves impede Fudō's efficacy.[92]

Since mortuary rites did not provide the mountain with a significant source of income, the religious institutions had to look to other dependable means of income: a yearly festival featuring a *kaichō*-like rite and *oshi*-maintained parishes. This proved to be a successful strategy pursued by many popular pilgrimage destinations such as Mt. Fuji, Mt. Haguro, and Zenkōji in the early modern period. Even after the disassociation of *kami* and Buddhas, Ōyama's new Shinto institutions retained the summer festival and a system that resembled the *oshi* parish system. Through the ingenious inception of the summer festival and the *oshi* parish system, Ōyama's religious specialists succeeded in turning the Ōyama cult from a temple complex dependent on state patronage into a popular pilgrimage destination.

FIVE

The Emergence of a Regional Pilgrimage

In this chapter, the Ōyama cult serves as an example of a pilgrimage that was not considered subversive by the authorities or society at large and that was strongly embedded in regional culture. As the center of a regional pilgrimage, the Ōyama cult strengthened the regional economy and was tightly bound into local social networks. The pilgrimage to Ōyama during the Sekison's summer festival in the Sixth and Seventh Months stimulated the regional transportation system, including both overland and sea routes. In Musashi and Sagami, the pilgrimage to Ōyama had such an impact on the local transportation infrastructure that a whole network of regional overland routes was known as Ōyama-michi (roads to Ōyama). From the late seventeenth century, Ōyama was such a magnet for pilgrims from urban, rural, and coastal areas that it left a strong cultural imprint on the entire Kantō region and even became a popular seasonal motif in woodblock prints and literary works by the early nineteenth century.

Pilgrims to Ōyama usually traveled in pilgrimage confraternities, organized by neighborhoods, villages, or particular professions. Communities would pool their financial resources to provide comfort and security for these spiritual travelers, making pilgrimages affordable and ensuring that they would cause only minimal social disruption to the village or neighborhood routine. These confraternities dispatched representatives to visit Ōyama during the summer festival, the only time of the year when the summit was open to pilgrims. Through the confraternities, the pilgrimage to Ōyama became an event that reinforced social relations and hierarchies rather than disrupted them.

Pilgrimage in Early Modern Japan

The early modern period has often been portrayed as the golden age of pilgrimage in Japan. Pilgrims increased numerically and included those from every profession and social class. Pilgrimages flourished due to favorable economic and sociopolitical conditions: the continued peace and improvements of the communications system, which allowed people to travel more easily; the growth of Edo and other cities into major urban centers, which provided the surrounding regions with a sizeable source of potential pilgrims; the widespread organization of populations into villages or urban neighborhoods, which provided the basis for village- and neighborhood-based confraternities; and the growing wealth across different social classes in an economy increasingly dependent on cash, which made the journey financially feasible.[1] Well-known transregional pilgrimage destinations such as the Ise Shrines, Mt. Kōya, Mt. Fuji, Zenkōji, the Eighty-Eight Stations of Shikoku, and the Thirty-Three Stations of Kannon circuits, in different regions throughout Japan as well as regional pilgrimage destinations such as Ōyama all flourished in this environment. Some of these pilgrimage destinations were already well-known destinations during the medieval period but became more widely popular in the early modern period, and many were incorporated into pilgrimage circuits. Other sites emerged as new pilgrimage destinations in this period. Many did so through careful management of access to the sacred and creating institutional structures that assured the continued flow of pilgrims. Some established pilgrimage seasons by opening a restricted area of the site—as did Ōyama, Mt. Fuji, and Mt. Haguro. Others periodically displayed a secret sacred image for brief periods—as did temples like Zenkōji. Paradoxically, limiting access to the site or main image of worship heightened the attraction and drew more pilgrims during the brief periods when access was granted.

While scholars generally agree that pilgrimage activity increased from the late seventeenth century onward, the pattern of the growth is open for debate. Natalie Kouamé argues that the Shikoku pilgrimage flourished particularly in the late seventeenth and the early nineteenth centuries. In contrast, Mark MacWilliams has stressed the continuous growth of the Bandō Kannon pilgrimage circuit in eastern Japan during the eighteenth century. Then again, the pilgrimage to Ise went through waves of exceptional popularity, which roughly followed a sexagenary cycle.[2] The growth pattern appears to have depended on the site and the region in which it was located. A peripheral pilgrimage circuit, like the one in Shikoku, perhaps experienced greater fluctuations than a circuit in the vicinity of a large urban center, like the Bandō pilgrimage in Edo's hinterland. Sites that featured routinized structures such as pilgrimage confraternities and *oshi* systems could probably count on a more steady flow of pilgrims than those lacking comparable structures. A site like Ōyama, then, had all the advantages that guaranteed a fairly stable influx of pilgrims: the vicinity of Edo, pilgrimage confraternities, and the *oshi* system.

Scholars have also disagreed about the social impact and meaning of pilgrimage practices. Was pilgrimage a means to escape from the constraints of one's daily routine? Did pilgrimage undermine the authority of *bakufu*? The images of periodic *nukemairi* (absconding pilgrimages) to the Ise Shrines or solitary, mendicant pilgrims traveling around the island of Shikoku are partially responsible for the pervasive view of pilgrimage in the early modern period as a disorganized and even subversive activity. Carmen Blacker, for example, argues that the archetypal pilgrim is the mendicant (*yugyōsha*), a wandering ascetic, who often appeared in art and literature throughout Japanese history. Blacker holds that temporary pilgrims who absconded to the Ise Shrines or traveled along the long circuit in Shikoku emulated the ideal of the solitary mendicant and turned to pilgrimage as a means of escape from the confines of the ordinary world, forsaking their community for an individualistic spiritual journey. During the early modern period, such mendicancy was regarded as antisocial and disruptive by *bakufu* and domainal authorities. Indeed, domainal authorities in Shikoku limited the number of days that pilgrims were allowed to stay in their domain and required them to follow the shortest route. Other authorities limited the number of days that pilgrims were allowed to complete their journeys or prohibited them from leaving their home domain outright.[3] In these cases, the authorities perceived religious travel as a burden on the communities that hosted pilgrims as well as on the home communities left behind.

The underlying assumptions about pilgrimage here are similar to those of Victor Turner, who discussed pilgrimage in terms of anti-structure and liminality. For Turner, the mobility of pilgrimage facilitated a radical departure from everyday norms and fostered a sense of *communitas*, which negated ordinary structures of social hierarchy.[4] Turner acknowledged the existence of more structured elements such as pil-grimage confraternities, annual festivals, licensing systems, and pilgrim-age infrastructure but linked them to "progressive routinization and institutionalization of the sacred journey."[5] Turner's ideal pilgrim was "one who divests himself of the mundane concomitants of religion—which become entangled with its practice in the local situation—to confront the special 'far' milieu, the basic elements and structures of his faith in their unshielded, virgin radiance."[6] As Paul Tremlett has noted, Turner's view of pilgrimage (and religion) could be characterized as a romanticist attempt to single out practices that seem to critique the values of modernity.[7]

Pilgrimages are always linked to a locale; hence, they cannot but be "entangled with its practice in the local situation"—despite Turner's claims to the contrary. Along with Michael Sallnow, Simon Coleman and John Eade have argued that pilgrimage does not need to be an excep-tional practice divorced from everyday life. Pilgrimage is not just about the process of a journey that opposes habitual structures.[8] Eade and Sallnow have pointed out that large, highly popular pilgrimage destina-tions often "develop more permanent economic infrastructures for deal-ing with the continual influx of pilgrims." Unlike Turner, they conclude that "distasteful as such commercialism might appear . . . it is neverthe-less a piece with the religious dealings taking place within the cult itself."[9]

Similarly, in the Japanese context, the mendicant was an important figure in religious lore and has often been revered as the founder of temples or pilgrimage circuits, but he should be recognized as a cultural ideal that is not representative of *all* religious travel in the early modern period.[10] Recently, Natalie Kouamé and Laura Nenzi have demonstrated that even in the case of the Shikoku pilgrimage and *nukemairi*, begging became a routinized practice that pilgrims used as a means to demon-strate their status as pilgrims. In fact, many were not socially marginal and had sufficient funds to travel in comfort and even to provide a source of income for those living along the pilgrimage routes.[11]

Furthermore, though some pilgrimages had anti-structural, socially subversive aspects, there were also forms of pilgrimage and mobility that were compatible with and were embedded within the social structures. This applies particularly to regional pilgrimages, such as the one to Ōyama, which usually did not imply lengthy journeys and often did not require the crossing of domainal boundaries. Even pilgrimages to the Ise Shrines, apart from years of mass pilgrimages, occurred largely in a very orderly fashion that did not reject but built on social ties: pilgrims traveled in village- or neighborhood-based pilgrimage associations and were housed by innkeepers at their destination with whom they and their villages had cultivated ties for generations. In addition to Ise confraternities, villages and urban neighborhoods also formed confraternities associated with sacred sites such as Zenkōji, Mt. Fuji, and Ōyama. Most of these sites, as discussed in Chapter 3, developed *oshi* systems or systems of comparable nature to house pilgrims and distribute amulets in villages in the region.

Pilgrimage Routes to Ōyama

Often represented in literature and art, the pilgrimage during the summer festival made Ōyama famous and affected the local economy and transportation systems. The pilgrimage routes to Ōyama (Ōyamamichi) made up an entire network that connected Ōyama with the Kantō provinces. Based on regional histories—primarily the *Shinpen Sagami no kuni fudoki kō* (1840) and the *Shinpen Musashi no kuni fudoki kō* (1830)—and physical evidence such as stone markers, Japanese local historians have reconstructed the extent of this network. By the first half of the nineteenth century, the Ōyamamichi network comprised a complex system of secondary and tertiary roads in Sagami and Musashi provinces that were linked to major highways such as the Tōkaidō, the Kōshū Kaidō, Nakasendō, and the Nikkō Kaidō, as well as sea routes from Awa and Kazusa across Edo Bay and from Izu to Sagami (see Fig. 5.1).[12] The name Ōyamamichi applied primarily to the direction pointing toward Ōyama, and the opposite direction might have been known by different names such as Edomichi, Fujimichi, or Odawaramichi. In some cases, Ōyamamichi was simply the common name of a major thoroughfare. In the *Shinpen Sagami no kuni fudoki kō*, though, the name Ōyamamichi was used to denote several roads in Sagami Province leading to Ōyama.[13]

On stone markers along routes as far away as Edo, the term Ōyamamichi was used as an alternate name for the Yagurazawa Highway. Overland routes to Ōyama tended to fork off from larger routes such as the Tōkaidō, the Kōshū Kaidō, and the Yagurazawa Highway. Most Ōyama-michi were secondary and tertiary routes and were narrower than the Tōkaidō, the major thoroughfare through the Kantō. The distribution of these routes corresponds to the spread of *oshi* parishes, which were found throughout Sagami, Musashi, Edo, Kazusa, Shimōsa, Awa, Kō-zuke, Shimotsuke, Kai, Shinano, and Izu by the nineteenth century. Pilgrims in these regions used this network of routes on their way to Ōyama. Since Ōyama drew more pilgrims from Edo and its environs than from regions to the north and west, Ōyamamichi in southeastern Sagami Province were most highly developed.[14]

Even though most routes predated the popularity of pilgrimage to Ōyama, increased pilgrimage traffic enhanced the infrastructure along these routes during the eighteenth century. The earliest concrete evidence of the increasing popularity of pilgrimages to Ōyama dates from the late seventeenth century when Ōyama appeared as a standard motif in illustrated travelogues and travel maps of Sagami Province. Ōyama was already featured as a site off the Tōkaidō in *Nan'yō no michi no ki* (1687),[15] the illustrated record of Hoshina Masanobu's journey along the Tōkaidō. Several views of Ōyama are also featured in Hishikawa Moronobu's *Tōkaidō bunken ezu* (1690)[16] in which Ōyama is shown as a background view for most stations and major landmarks in Musashi and eastern Sagami: Kawasaki, the border between Sagami and Musashi, Totsuka, the crossing of the Sagami River, and Hiratsuka.

Other historical evidence, such as *oshi* records and stone markers, clearly indicates Ōyama's sustained importance for the local economy and transportation infrastructure throughout the eighteenth century. Beginning around 1700, the *oshi* developed large parishes outside Sagami Province and nearby rural areas of Musashi, first in Edo and then in the remaining Kantō provinces. Large parishes from distant regions created an influx of pilgrims who were unfamiliar with the territory and needed food, lodging, and other services on the road in Sagami and Musashi. This created the need for an expanded infrastructure such as inns, ferries, rental of palanquins and horses, and clearly marked pilgrimage

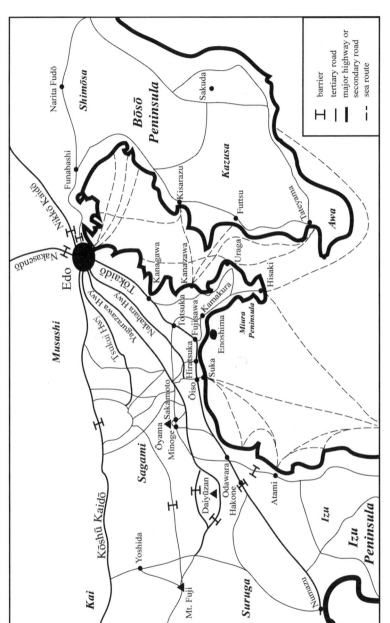

Fig. 5.1 Pilgrimage routes to Ōyama.

routes. Beginning in the Kyōhō era (1716–1735), villages on pilgrimage routes and pilgrimage confraternities began to set up stone markers identifying the way to Ōyama at points where secondary roads forked off from major highways such as the Tōkaidō and Kōshū Kaidō, or at intersections with other secondary roads. Ferrymen at crossing points along the Tama and Sagami rivers came to rely on pilgrims for income. Villagers set up small inns providing meals and lodging for weary travelers, especially during the summer festival at Ōyama.

Just as the road system used by pilgrims on their way to Ōyama expanded by radiating gradually from Ōyama across Sagami, Musashi, and Edo, villages along the route began to provide services to the pilgrims in the form of inns, rest facilities, ferries, and pack horses (see Figs. 5.2 and 5.3). The proliferation of unofficial and seasonal inns eventually led to another lawsuit by Sakamoto Village against its neighbors Koyasu Village and Kamikasuya Village in 1752. The 20 official inns operating in Koyasu around the year 1700 had increased to 43 small inns, whereas none of the 29 inns operating in Kamikasuya was officially sanctioned. These inns were established solely to accommodate pilgrims during the summer festival because there was no other substantial traffic through the villages. Many of these establishments were seasonal, operating only during the summer festival and providing temporary by-work for peasants hired from nearby villages.[17]

By the latter half of the eighteenth century, towns in Sagami and Musashi had come to rely financially on the pilgrimage traffic to Ōyama. The *Ōyama Fudō reigenki* often portrays peasants in Sagami who lodged or catered to pilgrims. In one story, set in 1766, a man from Naganuma Village in Sagami rents out his horse to pilgrims on the way to Ōyama during the pilgrimage season in the summer.[18] In another story, set in 1771, a married couple from Edo designates a peasant's house on a back road near the town of Totsuka as their customary overnight stop on pilgrimages to Ōyama.[19]

Evidence found in other sources, such as records of disputes and accidents involving station towns and river crossings, also suggests that the regional economy relied on pilgrimage travel to Ōyama. Many pilgrims from Edo and the Bōsō Peninsula traveled along the Tōkaidō, crossing the Tama River at the town of Kawasaki, the official crossing on the highway. But not all pilgrims took the official ferry at Kawasaki.

Fig. 5.2 Pilgrims at the river crossing at Tamura, Andō Hiroshige,
Sōshū Ōyamamichi Tamura watashi no kei. Courtesy of Kanagawa kenritsu reshikishi hakubutsukan.

Fig. 5.3 Pilgrims with a votive sword at the river crossing at Toda, Andō Hiroshige,
Sōshū Ōyama dōchū Todagawa no watashi. Courtesy of Kanagawa kenritsu reshikishi hakubutsukan.

During the summer festival in 1787, village officials and business representatives from Kawasaki on the Tōkaidō claimed to the authorities
that, despite earlier prohibitions, several villages along the southern
Tama River provided unauthorized ferry services via fishing boats to
pilgrims during the pilgrimage season to Ōyama. The authorities acted
promptly, issuing a prohibition against unauthorized ferrying that was
acknowledged by 34 communities in the area. Again, however, these
prohibitions were not universally effective. During the 1788 pilgrimage
season, the residents of Kawasaki settled a dispute about a man who
had used his fishing boat as an unauthorized ferry to transport pilgrims
to and from Ōyama but had escaped arrest. The station town renewed
its resolve to put an end to such violations of the law.[20]

The station town of Kawasaki was not the only one in the area to feel
the competition from nearby villages providing pilgrimage services at
more affordable prices. In 1820, villages near Fujisawa were prohibited
from serving lunch or overnight accommodations to pilgrims except for
five days during the beginning of Sekison's summer festival. On those
days, the number of pilgrims was particularly high, so that businesses
in Fujisawa, an official station of the Tōkaidō, would not suffer losses
even if the pilgrims lodged elsewhere.[21] The situation was no different
along other routes apart from the Tōkaidō as pilgrims tried to minimize
expenses along the way to Ōyama. By 1840, local communities along the
major routes from Kai and Musashi had come to charge Ōyama pilgrims
tolls to finance the repairs of roads and bridges, and overcharged them
for ferry services, horses, palanquins, meals, and lodging. Consequently,
pilgrims avoided these routes. This prompted local village heads and
representatives of innkeepers from eleven villages in Tama District in
Musashi and Aikō and Ōsumi Districts in Sagami to issue an agreement
to cease collecting tolls for roads, cut the fees for ferries and bridges
in half, and keep prices for horses, carriages, meals, and lodging within
reasonable limits.[22]

By the late eighteenth and early nineteenth centuries, the pervasive
regional importance of the seasonal pilgrimage to Ōyama could be seen
in the work of woodblock artists, who produced images in the newly
emerging genre of landscape prints, and by writers of popular fiction,
travel guides, and gazetteers. The Tōkaidō and Yagurazawa routes from
Edo inspired travel literature by Jippensha Ikku (1765–1831), Ryūtei Rijō

(early 1800s), Saitō Gesshin (1804–1878), and Dontei Robun (mid-1800s, known later as Kanagaki Robun)[23] and woodblock prints by Katsushika Hokusai (1760–1849), Andō Hiroshige (1797–1858), Utagawa Kuniyoshi (1798–1861), and Utagawa Sadahide (1807–1871).[24]

The *Tōkaidō meisho zue* (1797), a popular travel guide, urged pilgrims from the west to take the road forking off at Odawara and ascend Ōyama via Minoge. Pilgrims from Edo were encouraged to travel to Fujisawa on the Tōkaidō, take the tertiary roads forking off at Yotsuya or Hiratsuka, and ascend the mountain from the southeast via Sakamoto. The guide showed a network of roads leading to other famous sites, such as Mt. Hakone, Mt. Fuji, Kamakura, and Enoshima; identified the major sacred sites at Ōyama on the way to the summit; gave information about local specialties such as lathe work; listed the dates of the summer festival; and gave an idiosyncratic abridged version of the *Ōyamadera engi*—in other words, all the details a pilgrim might want to know.[25]

Such travel guides and prints clearly served to advertise the pilgrimage and famous travel destinations on the way. For example, Hokusai designed the *Kamakura Enoshima Ōyama shinpan ōrai sugoroku* (around 1833), a print used for a popular board game that allowed the players to advance around a circuit of popular travel destinations. The print showed a round trip circling these three famous places and providing travelers with not only a route and distances but also vital information about local specialties and famous sites (Fig. 5.4). The seven-day circuit started at Nihonbashi, continued along the Tōkaidō to Totsuka and Kamakura, and followed a coastal road to Enoshima. From there, the route turned north to Fujisawa along the Tōkaidō to Yotsuya Village, where the road forked off to Ōyama. On the return to Edo, pilgrims would take the route along the Yagurazawa Highway back to Nihonbashi.[26]

Another good example is a triptych entitled *Ōyama dōchū chōkō ezu* (1858) by Andō Hiroshige, who also designed several prints of the Tōkaidō that included references to Ōyama. The triptych shows the road from Edo to Ōyama via the Tōkaidō (see Fig. 5.5). Travelers on this route were advised to set out from Nihonbashi, pick up local specialties at Shinagawa, savor pears at Kawasaki, and travel via Kanagawa to Hodogaya, where they were advised to beware of women ushering travelers into inns.

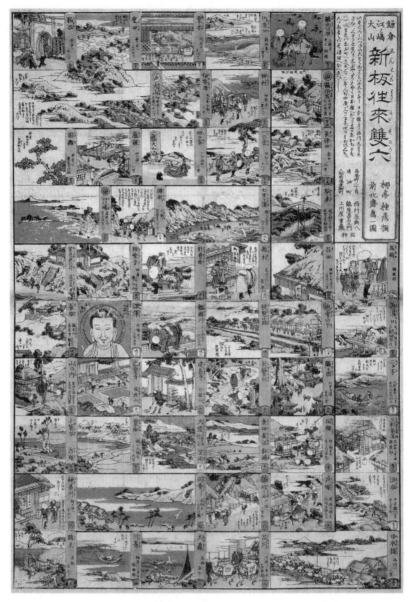

Fig. 5.4 Katsushika Hokusai, *Kamakura Enoshima Ōyama shinpan ōrai sugoroku*. Courtesy of Kanagawa kenritsu reshikishi hakubutsukan. A schematic of the *sugoroku* appears on the facing page.

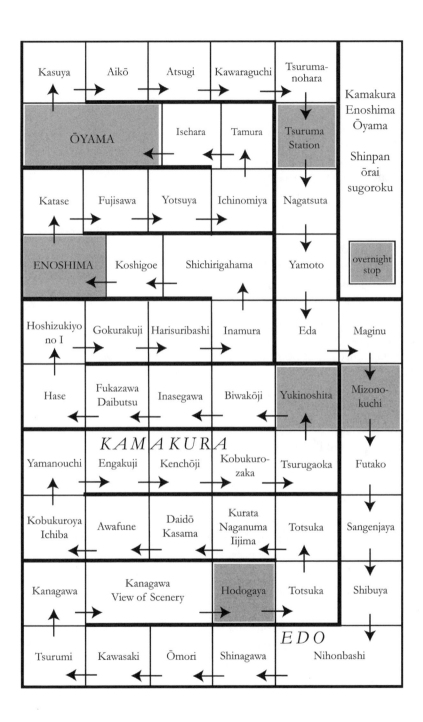

From there, they were to make another stop at Fujisawa, pick up local rice cakes at Totsuka, take a rest at Yotsuya, and cross the Sagami River at Tamura. On the southeastern foot of Ōyama, they could pick up pieces of lathe work as souvenirs and perform ablutions at Ōtaki or Rōbendaki. The next day, they were to ascend the mountain early in the morning, savoring the morning mist at the Maefudō Hall and, on a clear day, the view of Mt. Fuji at Raigōdani near the summit.[27]

Similarly, Jippensha Ikku, famous for his picaresque travelogues, included a visit to Ōyama in his *Hakone Enoshima Kamakura dōchūki*. The journey begins in Shinagawa in Edo and continues along the Tōkaidō to Hakone—a section published in 1813. In the following section, published in 1833, the route swings back via Mishima and Daiyūzan to Minoge on the southwestern foot of Ōyama. Having ascended the mountain, the traveler journeys from the southeastern foot via tertiary roads to the Tōkaidō, visits Enoshima and Kamakura to tour the temples at leisure, and returns to Edo along the Tōkaidō.[28] The consistency with which Ōyama appears in prints of Sagami Province indicates that by the nineteenth century it had become an important element in the region's local flavor. Still, we must remember that the prints were intended to depict famous places in the area. Therefore, they hardly convey the complexity of the Ōyamamichi system in its totality. This network included not only overland routes, which we have examined above, but also sea routes from the Izu and Bōsō peninsulas.

Pilgrims from the Izu and Bōsō peninsulas had a choice between overland and sea routes on their journey to Ōyama (see Fig. 5.1). In Izu, several inland routes connected with the Tōkaidō and from there to Ōyama. Yet many pilgrims found it far more convenient and faster to cut across the coastal seas by boat than to cope with a long overland detour, which would involve passing through official checkpoints; various expenses (e.g., tolls, ferries across rivers, pack horses, palanquins, overnight accommodations, and rest facilities); and the inconvenient re-packing of pack horses at post stations. Those who preferred to travel by boat had two possibilities. They could ease their trip to Ōyama by traveling from the port of Shimoda on the southern tip of the Izu Peninsula to the town of Atami in the northeast region of the province. Shimoda lay on an important sea route connecting western Japan and Edo via the port of Uraga (Miura, Sagami), and Atami was a transition point to

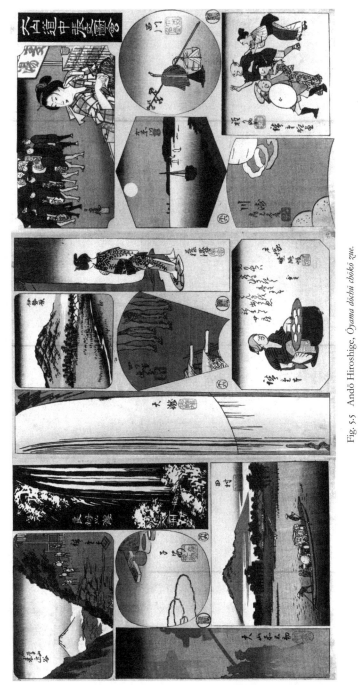

Fig. 5.5 Andō Hiroshige, *Ōyama dōchū chōkō zue*.
Courtesy of Kanagawa kenritsu reshikishi hakubutsukan.

overland routes to Odawara. Pilgrims could also travel from Shimoda to the port at Suka in Sagami and from there via the southeastern approach to Ōyama.[29]

Similarly, pilgrims from the northern Bōsō Peninsula could use either overland routes or sea routes across Edo Bay. Overland travel took pilgrims, especially those from the northern and central parts of the peninsula, via Edo across Musashi and Sagami to Ōyama. As discussed later in this chapter, a confraternity from a Sakuda Village in Kazusa made eleven pilgrimages to Ōyama between 1822 and 1862 and traveled overland via Edo on each of their trips.[30] Pilgrims from the southern parts of the peninsula, however, often traveled by boat. The routes across Edo Bay were appealing to pilgrims to Ōyama not only for their convenience but also because they enabled visits to Kamakura and Enoshima on the way, a practice followed by many pilgrims to Ōyama.

Sea routes from the Bōsō Peninsula across Edo Bay to Sagami or Musashi existed since the medieval period. One possible route was from Kisarazu in Kazusa, a convenient point for pilgrims from both Kazusa and southern Shimōsa, to Kanazawa and on to Kamakura. Even though the route is not directly linked to Ōyama but to Kamamura, it is likely that pilgrims to Ōyama also frequented it because many such pilgrims visited both Kamakura and Ōyama at the same time.[31] Another possible route was from Tateyamaura in Awa Province to Uraga in Miura, Sagami Province.[32] In 1861, for example, the village head of Nagasu Village requested that officials at the Uraga checkpoint supply a boat for pilgrims to Ōyama.[33]

The best-known route for pilgrims from the Bōsō Peninsula to Ōyama took them from the port of Futtsu in Kazusa to the port of Nojima in Susaki Village near the town of Kanazawa in Musashi, a route that minimized overland travel. By the late seventeenth century, this course was already familiar to *bakufu* officials as a way for women to avoid the official checkpoint in Musashi, which was meant to monitor the mobility of women as a means to control the activities of potential political opponents of the *bakufu*. Around 1720 or 1730, when the pilgrimage to Ōyama first flourished, the *bakufu* ordered the village headman of Nojima to inspect male and female pilgrims on their way from the Bōsō Peninsula to Ōyama.[34] The mention of female pilgrims is significant because confraternities from the Bōsō Peninsula appear also in other documents as being accompanied by women. In contrast, most Ōyama confraternities from other areas consisted only of male pilgrims.

Eventually, the sea routes across Edo Bay became so popular that inns and merchants along overland routes were losing business. For decades, official station towns along the Tōkaidō filed complaints about the use of sea routes. The frequency of the disputes indicates how common it was for travelers to rely on ferries across Edo Bay. This also applied to pilgrims. The cases from 1775 and 1805 clearly dated from the Sixth Month, the start of the busiest pilgrimage season for Ōyama.[35]

Despite these complaints about unauthorized travel across Edo Bay from station towns along the overland routes, the sea routes from the Bōsō Peninsula to Musashi Province became established as common routes for pilgrims to Ōyama. Since the port of Nojima functioned as a checkpoint, pilgrims using this route traveled with passports issued by village headmen in the Bōsō Peninsula to grant them easy passage. Examples of such travel permits from 1824 and 1860 attest to this, as they were both issued during Ōyama's pilgrimage season. Travel along the route became more formalized in other ways as well. In the Seventh Month of 1828, village leaders from Susaki, with the backing of other village heads in southern Musashi and southeastern Sagami, submitted a contract to the port of Nojima: the port was to handle pilgrims from Kazusa whereas the port of Susaki would handle pilgrims from Awa in order to avoid conflict and competition between the two villages over the large number of pilgrims to Ōyama.[36]

As in the case of overland routes, travel on sea routes stimulated by-work opportunities for those who were not officially allowed to engage in commerce with pilgrims. In addition to the authorized ferry services available for passage across Edo Bay, pilgrims could take private fishing boats. By 1852, the cost of the latter was about 25 to 50 percent cheaper depending on the route. In the last decades of the early modern period, the *bakufu*, hoping to contain local revolts and the mobility of masterless samurai, prohibited travel by unofficial ferry across Edo Bay on three separate occasions, but such closures were only temporary and not directed specifically at pilgrims.[37]

The pilgrimage to Ōyama also began to have a tangible impact on the regional communications system—both for overland and sea routes. The strongest impact of the pilgrimage was witnessed during the summer festival of Sekison between 6/28 and 7/17, when even villagers who normally did not cater to travelers operated inns, ferries, and other services along the roads to Ōyama. Even though the local transportation system was not created for and did not serve exclusively the pilgrimage to Ōyama, the pilgrimage contributed greatly to the expansion of the existing system, which, by the late eighteenth century, became almost synonymous with Ōyamamichi in the Kantō region.

Pilgrimage Confraternities

The summer pilgrimage to Ōyama had such a strong influence on the region because of the *oshi* system and the confraternities, both of which provided social stability to facilitate the cyclical flow of pilgrims. The *oshi* system ensured that pilgrims were looked after at their destination and that they maintained the parishioners' ties with the pilgrimage site through the *oshi*'s parish rounds. Confraternities allowed even those pilgrims without much expendable income to travel in comfort and safety. They enabled rural villages and urban neighborhoods to combine their financial resources so that several representatives could make the pilgrimage on their community's behalf. Summer pilgrimages were usually not perceived as anti-social but rather were sanctioned and fully supported by local confraternities enabling pilgrims to pay for their journeys but still making them accountable for their spending. Because of this, pilgrims did not burden the villages they visited on their way to Ōyama. Since these were journeys to a regional pilgrimage destination, they were brief, lasting only one or two weeks. A round trip from Edo took six to seven days to complete, even if the pilgrims took a detour via Kamakura and Enoshima. The overland route from northern Kazusa Province only took about twice as long, even including visits to other places along the way. In contrast, a round trip from Edo to the Ise Shrines would take at least one month, and the completion of the Shikoku circuit twice as long.[38] Most pilgrimages to Ōyama took place during a distinct season before the harvest and involved only a few members of the community, allowing the rest to maintain their daily routine as usual so that village or neighborhood life was hardly disrupted. Moreover, the pilgrimages were primarily undertaken for the good of the entire community rather than for personal reasons. Upon their return, pilgrims brought everyone amulets for protection from harm and illness. Therefore, pilgrims were not perceived as escapees from their home communities but rather as emissaries traveling on the community's behalf. Usually, neither the local communities nor *bakufu* authorities sought to prevent such journeys, unless pilgrims either were behaving in wasteful ways or extended their journeys to too many sacred sites.

Ōyama confraternities appear in documents on Ōyama beginning in the late seventeenth century. The mountain code from 1674 regulated pilgrimages of confraternities that comprised parishioners of several *oshi* and referred to confraternities as *mujinkō* or mutual loan associations, formed to collect and save money for a specific purpose. When such confraternities came on pilgrimage to Ōyama, any *oshi* with at least one parishioner among the confraternity members could provide room and board for the entire group. Other *oshi* or innkeepers were excluded from handling these confraternities, even if asked by the confraternity leader.[39] The mountain code from 1721 further specified that votive offerings were to be handled by the *oshi* of the confraternity leader.[40]

Stories of groups traveling to visit Ōyama during the summer festival were common in the *Ōyama Fudō reigenki*. In Story II.3, for example, Kajiya Giemon climbed Ōyama in a group of eleven pilgrims during the summer festival in 1745. In Story XII.5, a young man from Musashi Province traveled to Ōyama with five or six companions to make a pilgrimage to Sekison during the summer festival, when the mountain bustled with pilgrims. One of his companions must have been a parishioner of the *oshi* Zōzenbō because the group stayed at Zōzenbō's inn even though the young man's family had been associated with the *oshi* Okamoto Kinai for generations. When the young man disappeared in the mountains, his companions left it to Zōzenbō to look out for him. The young man finally reappeared one month later and found Sakamoto Village deserted by pilgrims because the festival was over. He lodged with Zōzenbō before finally returning home. Out of gratitude, the young man's family henceforth became Zōzenbō's parishioners. Traveling in a group or staying with an *oshi* did not protect the young man from getting lost, but it ensured that somebody would look for him. Traveling in confraternities and staying with *oshi* thus increased travel safety for pilgrims.

Confraternities usually made their pilgrimages during the summer festival and spent one or two nights at the inn of their *oshi*, who recorded their names in ledgers. Data from visitors at the *oshi* Murayama Hachidayū in 1831 give us a glimpse of pilgrimage patterns during the summer festival of Sekison. According to Hachidayū's register, nearly half the pilgrims who climbed Ōyama traveled in small village-based or neighborhood-based groups of two to four, probably consisting of representatives of Ōyama confraternities.[41] With an average of four members per group, few groups were larger than six members.

Most of these groups were so closely identified with their place of origin—their village, neighborhood, or business—that they were not marked specifically as confraternities unless they were dedicated to a specific ritual activity. This applies particularly to groups from rural areas. Nevertheless, despite the lack of identification as confraternities these unmarked groups were very likely sponsored by their home communities. Only about ten percent of the groups in the register are marked as confraternities, especially *omikikō*, confraternities dedicated to offering sacred rice wine (*omiki*). The majority of these confraternities came from Edo and the Funabashi area of Shimōsa Province. The number of pilgrims in these confraternities ranged from one to nineteen, averaging about seven pilgrims per confraternity.

Even though 90 percent of the pilgrims traveled in groups that were not specifically identified as confraternities, it is likely that these groups were in fact confraternities. In the register, two-thirds of the large groups with over eight pilgrims are unmarked. These unidentified groups were usually from single or two neighboring agricultural villages, which suggests that they were confraternities. Even smaller groups were probably sponsored by village, neighborhood, or business confraternities. A few single travelers and one group of four were specifically identified as representatives for merchant houses or neighborhoods in Edo even though they were not identified as confraternities.[42] Other small groups from agricultural villages were probably also representatives of local confraternities. Evidence from another *oshi* household indicates that such rural village-based confraternities were supported by 25 to 50 households, but they often dispatched only small groups between one and five pilgrims to the Ōyama summer festival to collect amulets for the other members.[43]

Pilgrims generally preferred the first and last days of the festival for their pilgrimages. The number of pilgrims at Hachidayū's inn peaked at the beginning of the summer festival during *hatsuyama* (6/28–6/30), *nanokadō* (7/1–7/7), and at the end of the festival during *bon'yama* (7/15–7/16). The highest number of visitors came on 7/15, the beginning of *bon'yama*, which fell on *obon*. The second highest number of pilgrims came on 6/28 and the third highest on 7/2, the day after the end of the summer retreat of the monks. The number of visitors, however, was low during *ainoyama* (7/8–7/14), remaining well below the average of 37.3 visitors per day.

The regional make-up of the pilgrims reflects the overall distribution of Hachidayū's parishes, which were concentrated in southeastern Musashi, Edo, and Shimōsa; therefore, the highest number of visitors (about 85 percent) came from these regions.[44] The number of pilgrims from Sagami was low, not only because the province was so saturated with Ōyama *oshi* parishes that each individual *oshi* had only small parishes here but also because pilgrims from nearby villages might not have spent the night at an *oshi*'s inn, leaving their villages early in the morning and returning at night. In the register, there is one example of a group of four pilgrims from Sagami who did not spend the night at the *oshi*'s but simply visited his inn on their pilgrimage during the day. Some of the pilgrims may also have bypassed the *oshi* completely and would not be recorded in the logbook. This happened so often that the mountain code from 1752 addressed this problem by requiring Shingon clerics to send word to the pilgrims' *oshi* if they came directly to their temples for rituals so that the *oshi* could collect their share of the donations.[45] It is therefore likely that the number of actual pilgrims from Sagami Province was higher than indicated by the record.

Evidence from Hachidayū's register also suggests that about 5 percent of the groups actually ended up staying at an inn other than that of their customary *oshi*. One group of pilgrims stayed in Koyasu Village and paid the *oshi* a visit to have a meal and give their dues for rituals. Moreover, several pilgrims traveling in associations, who actually belonged to other *oshi*, stayed at Hachidayū's inn and *vice versa*.[46] Cases like these, which might have become the source of conflict, were all regulated in the mountain codes in the late seventeenth and early eighteenth centuries. The codes allowed *oshi* to host each other's parishioners, as long as one of the fellow travelers was one of their parishioners, and required that notice about pilgrims who bypassed the *oshi* and proceeded straight up the mountain be conveyed to the *oshi* by the Shingon priests.[47]

Usually, the closer their villages were located to Ōyama, the more likely pilgrims were to travel in a larger group because more of its members could afford to make a pilgrimage. Conversely, pilgrims from more distant regions were likely to travel in smaller groups since their journeys were more expensive and took longer to complete. Two visitors from the most distant region, Etchū Province, for example, traveled as a pair whereas the average number of pilgrims per group from Edo, Musashi, Kazusa, and Shimōsa was around four. A few groups from Shimōsa exceeded this number because they often comprised members from two villages. In the case of Sagami, Edo, and Kazusa, several groups were large (six to eight members) while others consisted of only one or two, yielding an average of around four members per group. The distance from those sites to Ōyama was short or medium range, so the size of the group seems to have depended on established local community preferences. As we will see below, one village in Kazusa did not organize annual pilgrimages to Ōyama, but only every three to four years, saving money for the next trip in the interim. However, when they did go on pilgrimages, their groups consisted of eight to ten members.[48]

According to Hachidayū's register, several groups from Edo and Shimōsa visited Ōyama on their way back from Mt. Fuji. The pilgrimage to Mt. Fuji had become particularly popular after 1733 after the death of the ascetic Jikigyō Miroku (1671–1733) and the subsequent proselytization by his followers throughout the Kantō region.[49] This development coincided with the growing popularity of the pilgrimage to Ōyama. A joint pilgrimage to Ōyama and Mt. Fuji was such a common practice that the *bakufu* issued a prohibition against pilgrimages to Mt. Fuji that included a visit to Ōyama.[50] The authorities frowned upon the practice not because it opposed pilgrimages to Ōyama but because a dual pilgrimage extended the length of the journey unduly in the *bakufu*'s eyes. Nevertheless, many pilgrims ignored the prohibition and were readily accommodated by innkeepers at the foot of Ōyama, handling pilgrims' luggage on their way to and from Mt. Fuji.[51] A visit to Ōyama could easily be incorporated into a pilgrimage to Mt. Fuji because pilgrims from Edo and the eastern Kantō provinces would usually pass through the area on their journey to or from Mt. Fuji. Since pilgrims ascended Mt. Fuji via a different route than during their descent, they would climb Mt. Fuji via Yoshida, descend via Subashiri, and continue their journey home by taking the Yagurazawa Highway via Minoge to Ōyama or *vice versa*. Moreover, Mt. Fuji was open for pilgrimage between 6/1 and 7/26 and Ōyama between 6/28 and 7/17, making it convenient for pilgrims to visit both around the same time.[52]

Mt. Fuji was not the only destination often combined with a visit to Ōyama. As noted above, travel guides and woodblock prints of the Tōkaidō often encouraged travelers to visit Kamakura and Enoshima on the way to Ōyama. Some pilgrims also chose to visit these sites after seeing Ōyama. A group of six travelers from Kai Province, who recorded their journey in the *Fuji Ōyama dōchū zakki* (1839), for example, traveled from Mt. Fuji to Ōyama via Minoge Village. A teahouse there sent their luggage ahead to a rice wine shop in Koyasu Village while the pilgrims climbed to the summit. On their way down via Sakamoto Village, they collected their luggage and traveled on via Fujisawa to Enoshima and Kamakura. It was in Fujisawa and Enoshima, as well as in Hiratsuka, that many pilgrims to Ōyama broke their fast (*shōjin ochi*), allowing businesses from prostitution to seafood to prosper.[53] The connection among these famous sacred places is also clear from stone markers along the pilgrimage routes, which often indicate the way to Mt. Fuji, Ōyama, and Enoshima on the same marker. At a crossing between the ascent from Sakamoto and a route via Minoge, a tall stone marker from 1799 still indicates the path to Mt. Fuji and to Daiyūzan.[54]

A Village Confraternity from Kazusa Province

A pilgrimage association from Sakuda Village in Kazusa illustrates the activities of a village confraternity in Edo's rural hinterland. Sakuda was a small village with 126 households in central Kazusa that had had an Ōyama confraternity since the late eighteenth century. Individual villagers from Sakuda had made pilgrimages to Ōyama as early as the Seventh Month in 1722 and the Second Month in 1724. The confraternity collected rice and money from villagers to fund pilgrimages to Ōyama during the summer festival every three to four years.[55] Sugane Yukihiro notes that such rural confraternities sometimes also supported themselves by cultivating a communal plot of land, the yield of which was entirely dedicated to the confraternity.[56] Natalie Kouamé mentions similar practices among Konpira confraternities in her study of early modern pilgrimage in Shikoku.[57]

Even though the port of Kisarazu was not too far from Sakuda Village, the confraternity preferred to take overland routes to Ōyama, which allowed them to visit other sacred sites on their way. The group usually traveled across to the eastern coast of the Bōsō Peninsula and followed a coastal route via Edo to the Tōkaidō. Once near the Miura Peninsula, the confraternity often visited Kamakura and/or Enoshima before reaching Ōyama. At Ōyama, the confraternity lodged with the *oshi* Ogasawara Sakei, who had parishioners in Sakuda Village. On their return, the Sakuda confraternity often took an inland route along the Yagurazawa Highway to Edo, which allowed them to visit famous temples on the eastern outskirts of Edo such as Yūtenji and Meguro Fudō. Once back on the Bōsō Peninsula, the group usually followed an inland route as well, which led them to another famous temple, Narita Fudō.[58]

Despite Ōyama's proximity, pilgrimages could be expensive; therefore, confraternities were convenient for dividing the financial burden among the whole village. The Sakuda confraternity spent an average of about 19 *ryō*[59] on each pilgrimage (about 2 *ryō* per pilgrim). This included 7.5 *ryō*—or 39 percent of the cost—for *tenaga* services, which remained constant on all their pilgrimages, and a small sum for other donations, such as first-fruit donations, amulets, and fund-raising for a new bell or reconstruction of the Buddhist precinct after the earthquake in 1855. Accommodations at the *oshi*'s inn cost 0.25 *ryō* per pilgrim, an amount that also remained constant between 1838 and 1862. In addition, the group would spend about 0.5 *ryō* on tips for the *oshi*, his family, and servants.[60] The Sakuda confraternity perhaps spent money more generously than other confraternities. A confraternity from Edo, for example, came to Ōyama in 1857, stayed with the *oshi* Daitō Genban, and commissioned *kagura* and *tenaga* services for 20 percent of the costs incurred by the Sakuda confraternity. Their entire pilgrimage amounted to about 20 *ryō* for 26 members, or about 40 percent of the costs of the Sakuda confraternity.[61] Comparable data are also available from Murayama Hachidayū's inn in 1831 when pilgrims were charged only 33 percent of what the Sakuda confraternity paid for room and board. Perhaps the Sakuda confraternity opted for more expensive meals and rooms and commissioned their own *tenaga* rite instead of sharing the costs for the *tenaga* rites with other confraternities.

Two other aspects are striking about the data of the Sakuda confraternity: the group's size and the fact that the group often included women. The average size of the group was about ten members, rather large for a confraternity. Among the participants, several names appear repeatedly and may be names of members with special standing, such as confraternity leaders or officers. The group often included a significant number of women, who were represented at a ratio of one woman to two men. Between 1822 and 1862, the confraternity visited Ōyama eleven times. The gender breakdown is recorded for eight of these pilgrimages and shows that women accompanied the group six times. In 1844, four of the five women are listed as non-members of the confraternity and merely accompanied the group on the pilgrimage. From 1844 on, however, the women confraternity members are identified as mothers, wives, or daughters of villagers; their sons, husbands, or fathers are not necessarily listed among the other pilgrims. In 1857, four wives are listed as representatives, which may mean that these women made the pilgrimage on behalf of their husbands.[62]

In the early modern period, pilgrimage confraternities associated with some other sacred site, such as the Ise Shrines, tended to be limited to men, but women could sometimes join the pilgrimages as non-members.[63] Among Ōyama pilgrims from the Bōsō Peninsula, the practice of women accompanying confraternities appears to have been so common that the *bakufu* noted it as early as 1695. The *bakufu* did not oppose female pilgrims but was concerned that they were bypassing official checkpoints near Edo by ferrying from the Bōsō Peninsula to Musashi Province across Edo Bay.[64] A travel passport issued by the headman of Nashizawa Village in Kazusa provides another example. The passport was issued for a group of 80 men and women on pilgrimage to Ōyama so they could travel from Kazusa to Kanazawa in Musashi in the Seventh Month of 1824.[65] Likewise, Murayama Hachidayū's register of pilgrims during the summer festival in 1831 indicates that one group of eight from Kazusa included several women. The register also lists one example of a group of three from Endō Village in Sagami that included a villager's mother and another example of a husband and wife from Kazusa.[66] Clearly, confraternities from Bōsō Peninsula occasionally included village women in their journeys to Ōyama, but evidence from other provinces is scarce.

Urban Confraternities from Edo

The example of the confraternity from Sakuda Village illustrates the activities of a rural, village-based confraternity. In contrast, confraternities from Edo, with its high population density and professional diversity, provided fertile ground for many different kinds of confraternities. The diversity and pervasiveness of confraternities in Edo and its outskirts is illustrated in the handbook *Edo shokōchū chōtō kōchū fuda hikaechō*, which catalogues the inscriptions of lanterns and signs of different types of Edo-based confraternities during the early nineteenth century. The handbook was likely a valuable guide for an innkeeper in the Ōyama area who wanted to identify confraternities passing through. When confraternities went on pilgrimages they often carried lanterns that identified the confraternity's origin and type. Similarly, when the confraternity stayed at an inn or a teahouse on their journey or at pilgrimage sites, wooden signs (*fuda* or *kōkanban*) or cloth banners (*maneki*) identifying the confraternity were hung outside the inn.[67] Such lanterns, signs, and banners frequently appear in woodblock prints of the pilgrimage to Ōyama (see Fig. 5.6).[68] The handbook of confraternity signs allows us to compare Ōyama's confraternities to those of other sacred places near Edo and to gain of a sense of the types of confraternities associated with Ōyama.

Many but not all of the confraternity signs catalogued in the *Edo shokōchū chōtō kōchū fuda hikaechō* contained large, visible symbols of the confraternities identifying their origin or type. In many cases, some confraternities chose several large characters as their mark, but many signs also bore crests containing black letters in a red circle. The letters often indicated the sacred site, the origin of the confraternity, and the occupation of the members or, in the case of firefighters, the name of the unit. In some cases, symbols indicating the type of confraternity would be chosen (e.g., a tray with two rice-wine bottles for *omikikō*). Confraternities formed by businesses could simply use the house crest.[69]

When charting the sacred places to which these groups were dedicated, the number of signs and lanterns of Ōyama confraternities is the

Fig. 5.6 "Totsuka" from Andō Hiroshige, *Tōkaidō gojūsantsugi.*
Courtesy of Kanagawa kenritsu reshikishi hakubutsukan.

highest, followed by Enoshima and Mt. Fuji in distant second and third positions, respectively. This suggests that the handbook was intended as a reference tool for an innkeeper—or perhaps an *oshi*—at Ōyama, who would have to be able to identify both Ōyama confraternities and those of other sacred places passing through Ōyama on their pilgrimages. In addition to Ōyama, the most frequently represented sacred sites were located west of Edo in Musashi, Sagami, and Suruga, especially in the region between Edo and Ōyama. The list thus contained the most popular sacred sites of the western Kantō region. Yet despite its focus on Ōyama, the manual indicates how pervasive confraternities associated with sacred places in the Kantō region were in the city of Edo.[70]

Among the different types of Ōyama confraternities several can be distinguished based on the religious activity on which they focused. The manual contains 45 such Ōyama confraternities, of which the vast majority was dedicated to the offering of sake.[71] *Omikikō* would carry small shoulder boxes containing a jar of rice wine (*omikiwaku*) on their pilgrimage to Ōyama as depicted by Hiroshige in his prints of groups of pilgrims at Fujisawa (*Tōkaidō gojūsantsugi*) and Hodogaya (*Tōkaidō*

Fig. 5.7   "Fujisawa" from Andō Hiroshige, *Tōkaidō gojūsantsugi.*
Courtesy of Kanagawa kenritsu reshikishi hakubutsukan.

gojūsantsugi saiken zue) on their way to Ōyama from Edo via the Tōkaidō
(see Figs. 5.7 and 5.8, respectively). The prints also depict pilgrims carrying wooden talismanic swords, the offering of which was the purpose
of *odachikō*, represented in the manual in small numbers. A few confraternities were identified as *gomakō*, those dedicated to offering *goma*
rituals to Ōyama Fudō, and others as *tenagakō*, those dedicated to offering *kagura* and sets of 75 trays of different types of food to Ōyama
Fudō.[72] According to the *Ōyama Fudō reigenki*, such confraternities were
sometimes founded by zealous believers who had experienced a miracle,
such as the anonymous man from the leaven shop in Hongō Daikon-
batake who performed fervent prayers and ablutions until he had a
vision of a wooden sword of Sekison and who founded a *tenaga* confraternity out of gratitude for his wife's recovery from illness.[73] Other
unidentified confraternities, though their names did not indicate it, came
to Ōyama to commission similar rituals.[74]

Confraternities were also differentiated by the occupations of their
members. Edo parishes consisted primarily of merchant and artisan
houses. Similarly, confraternities often comprised members of specific
businesses. The handbook contains five examples of such merchant

Fig. 5.8   "Hodogaya" from Andō Hiroshige, *Tōkaidō gojūsantsugi saiken zue*.
Courtesy of Kanagawa kenritsu reshikishi hakubutsukan.

confraternities, including large establishments that had their own con-fraternity (using their house emblem for the confraternity) and small shops of the same type (such as rice shops, cereal shops, sweet shops, and fishmongers) that formed a joint confraternity.[75] Other confraterni-ties were based on occupational groups dealing with travel and trans-portation such as boat owners, post-horse operators, and innkeepers.[76] Firefighters represented the most common profession among occupa-tional Ōyama confraternities with a total of nine different confraternities listed in the handbook—about one-fifth of Edo's 48 firefighter units. Two additional confraternities consisted of construction workers (*tobi*) and carpenters, professions closely related to firefighters. Ōyama's ties with firefighter confraternities already existed in the late eighteenth cen-tury. For example, in 1778, the year that the shrines on Ōyama's summit were reconstructed after the fire in 1771, *tobi* as well as carpenters from Edo donated a pair of stone lions that remain on Ōyama's summit. In 1798, a firefighter confraternity from Edo erected a stone *torii* on Ōyama's summit, where there are also several stone lanterns donated by firemen's teams from Edo.[77]

The most colorful and notorious confraternities were those of *nō* and *kabuki* actors, whose pilgrimages were frequently portrayed in wood-block prints.[78] The handbook contains one example of an Ōyama con-fraternity of *nō* actors, but confraternities associated with *kabuki* theaters appear more frequently in the handbook. Generic confraternities asso-ciated with the Morita and Ichimura theaters do not identify a specific association with any particular sacred site but are known to have had confraternities directly associated with Enoshima. Nevertheless, actors at the Nakamura and Ichimura theaters, and teashops associated with the *kabuki* theater, appear as parishioners of Murayama Hachidayū's parish register of Edo (1847), and an actor from the Ichimura Theater donated a stone pillar at Ōyama.[79]

The variety of occupational Ōyama confraternities from Edo was determined by the specific demographics of Edo with its concentration of diverse professional groups, which did not exist in rural areas. Of course, fishing villages or villages engaged in sericulture might have had occupational confraternities, but it is unlikely that a similar diversity and concentration of merchant and artisan confraternities would have existed in agricultural areas. However, regardless of whether they were

based in an urban or rural environment, confraternities reinforced communal ties—be it within the village, neighborhood, or business world.
Therefore, they were not perceived as antisocial or subversive. Instead,
they fostered local community cohesion, cooperation, and stability.

Of course, pilgrims to Ōyama occasionally stirred up trouble. The
1753 mountain code reminded pilgrims not to quarrel, an indication that
this happened frequently. As Saitō Gesshin recounts in his *Bukō nenpyō*
(1849–1850), there were fewer pilgrims traveling from Edo to Ōyama in
1858 because confraternities from Edo had gotten into a fight with locals
at the Tōkaidō station town of Hodogaya in the previous year.[80] During
the summer festival in 1788, a group of eight men from Kazusa Province
were on their way back from Ōyama. They traveled via the Tōkaidō and
took a ferry across the Tama River at Rokugō, Kawasaki, where two of
the men fell into the river and drowned, leaving the villagers along the
river with the task of having to find a way to dispose of the bodies.[81] On
the whole, however, the pilgrimage caused very little social disruption.

Conclusion

The establishment of the *oshi* system and the development of Ōyama
confraternities in villages across the Kantō region gave the pilgrimage to
Ōyama stability. The steady, community-building aspects of the pilgrimage to Ōyama reinforced values of social harmony; hence, the *bakufu*
placed few obstacles in its way. The few regulations that pertained to
it were not so much meant to limit the pilgrimage to Ōyama but more
to ensure that pilgrims did not extend their pilgrimages unduly and maintained order on their journeys. They were either issued to prevent pilgrims to Mt. Fuji from continuing their already lengthy journey to
Ōyama, or to curb the competition faced by station towns from other
villages near the Tōkaidō, or to deal with times of crisis, such as in the
1860s when sea routes near Edo could have brought not only harmless
pilgrims but also insurgents from the north.[82] In contrast to the negative
attitude of some domains toward the pilgrimages to the Ise Shrines
and to Shikoku, neither the *bakufu* nor the pilgrims' home communities
considered the journey to Ōyama subversive. Ōyama was a regional
pilgrimage that was relatively short and did not require travel to distant
provinces. Pilgrims from Sagami, Musashi, and Edo did not have to
cross any checkpoints and could travel freely.

The pilgrimage to Ōyama is emblematic of early modern society. Confraternities enabled villagers and townspeople to participate in activities such as pilgrimage and travel that they would have been unable to afford on their own. Through their pilgrimages, they contributed to the regional infrastructure and the communications network. However, the confraternities were merely bound into their local contexts. Inns along the pilgrimage routes profited during the pilgrimage season but were not affiliated directly with Ōyama's religious institutions. As discussed in the final chapter, in the Meiji period, confraternities and inns along the pilgrimage routes were reorganized into a central network based at the Afuri Shrine, the primary religious institution at the time. In contrast to the Afuri Shrine's attempts to systematize and regulate the Ōyama cult during the early Meiji period, the pilgrimage to Ōyama and the Ōyama cult in general consisted of highly diverse groups in the early modern period. In essence, it was a localized and fragmented phenomenon.

SIX

Reconfiguring the Pantheon

As Chapter 1 has shown, institutional and political changes led to radical transfigurations of Ōyama's topography. The changes in spatial practices were closely linked to changes in the spiritual landscape. The capacity to accommodate the needs of different constituencies supporting and maintaining the cult was what made the Ōyama cult so successful during the early modern period. Foucault argues that heterotopias often have multiple meanings that change over time or are present concurrently depending on their social contexts.[1] This is a quality shared by many pilgrimage centers in the world. As John Eade and Michael Sallnow have noted: "The power of a shrine, therefore, derives in large part from its character almost as a religious void, a ritual space capable of accommodating diverse meanings and practices. . . ."[2] What is different about the early modern Ōyama—even perhaps early modern Japanese pilgrimage sites in general—and the kind of Christian pilgrimage center that Eade and Sallnow have in mind is that diversity of "theological currencies" extends beyond the juxtaposition of pilgrims and officialdom that controls the cultic site. It was not until the Meiji period that one could identify a dynamic similar to that noted by Eade and Coleman about Lourdes, "where the pragmatic miracle discourse of pilgrims confronts the transcendent, sacrificial discourse of officialdom."[3] In the case of early modern Ōyama, the cult was managed by multiple types of religious specialists. It is therefore impossible to identify a single official discourse. Instead, there is what Karen Smyers refers to in Bakhtinian terms as a "nonmonologic unity" in her study of the contemporary Inari cult in Japan: a cult with multiple ritualists affiliated with various religious institutions and a large popular following is bound to be diverse and filled with creative tensions.⁴ The multiplicity of meanings and shifting identifications illustrate how premodern and early modern Japanese approached their spiritual universe. As Allan Grapard has pointed out in discussing the medieval Kasuga cult: "What is found in Japanese cultic centers is not a hopeless incoherence but an extremely concrete combinatory phenomenon in which the various elements of combination retained some of their pristine identity, their fundamental characteristics, but also gained by accretion and interplay (it is tempting to say, by dialectic), a mass of meaning that they did not have as independent entities."⁵ Grapard is primarily referring to the medieval Japanese religious landscape, but as the case of Ōyama illustrates this medieval worldview continued into the early modern period, although it eventually was contested with the rise of Nativism.

The process of the accretion of multiple discourses by Ōyama's officialdom is amply illustrated by the various texts that discuss the principal deities of Ōyama's pantheon. These texts served two main functions to varying degrees: proselytization of the cult and genealogical legitimization of sacerdotal roles. Ōyama's deities appear in their earliest extant manifestation in the *Ōyamadera engi*, the founding legends of Ōyama. Taking this text as a starting point, this chapter traces the transformation of Ōyama's deities through a variety of different legends that were composed or compiled by Ōyama's Shingon clerics and *oshi*: the *Ōyama jiki* (1713), the *Myōōtarō raiyu* (n.d.), the *Sōyō Ōyama fu* (1792), the *Ōyama Fudō reigenki* (1792), and the *Afurijinja kodenkō* (1849). Some of the texts—the *Myōōtarō raiyu* and the *Sōyō Ōyama fu*—were intended for transmission within the household of a specific hereditary religious specialist rather than for proselytization, while others—the *Ōyamadera engi*, the *Ōyama jiki*, the *Ōyama Fudō reigenki*, and the *Afurijinja kodenkō*—were intended for open proselytization rather than secret transmission. Of these, the *Ōyamadera engi* and the *Ōyama Fudō reigenki* were most widely used for proselytization and hence had the most immediate impact on how pilgrims conceptualized Ōyama's deities. Regardless of their intended use, however, all the texts reflect how different religious specialists, Shingon clerics, and *oshi* represented Ōyama's deities. The various legends and divine genealogies from the late medieval period to the mid-nineteenth century show that, for most of the early modern period, Ōyama's deities were largely thought of in Buddhist terms. Once Shirakawa Shinto and Nativism made inroads among the *oshi* in this predominantly Buddhist environment, crucial changes occurred that set the stage for the disassociation of *kami* and Buddhas during the early Meiji period.

For most of the early modern period, the perceptions of Ōyama's deities were not static but constantly in flux as *kami* and Buddhas were redefined through different systems of association. The identification of *kami* and Buddhas goes back to the Heian period and the development of *honji suijaku* theory, which interpreted *kami* as localized manifestations of universal Buddhist divinities in highly complex systems of association. Grapard notes that the association between *kami* and Buddhas was linguistically based and highly localized: "Consequently, the associations between divinities of a given cult obeyed linguistically grounded modes of combination such as association, metaphor, palindrome, anagram, and anagogy. No single theory elucidates the nature of choices made in associating a given divinity to another one, and therefore research on these phenomena must be conducted cultic site by cultic site."[6] To the list of linguistic principles we can also add metonymy as iconographic attributes of one divinity were linked to other divine symbols, a common form of association in esoteric Buddhism. Furthermore, Mark Teeuwen and Fabio Rambelli stress that the associations between *kami* and Buddhas were not limited to a one-to-one correspondence but took the form of multiple identifications "that employed all strategies of correlation and combination developed by exoteric-esoteric Buddhist hermeneutics. As a result, it construed macrosemiotic entities in which Japanese, Chinese, and Indian elements were clustered on the basis of similarities of signifiers (linguistic and/or iconographic) and of the signifieds (functions, religious meanings, etc.)."[7]

The *honji suijaku* pantheon in the *Ōyamadera engi* originated in the medieval period when the tradition of mountain asceticism was prevalent on the mountain. In the early modern period, the deities evolved in a process of accretion as Shingon clerics and *oshi* added on to the medieval *honji suijaku* pantheon centered on Fudō Myōō without denying the veracity of earlier narratives. Compiled by Shingon clerics in the eighteenth century, the *Ōyama jiki* and the *Ōyama Fudō reigenki* stressed the centrality of Fudō Myōō, the focus of the Ōyama cult in the early modern period, but also created a new identity for Sekison Daigongen, a deity that had been identified with Fudō Myōō in the medieval legends but had become the focus of Ōyama's popular summer festival. Ōyama's deities were associated with divinities in Japan's ancient mythical histories through linguistic association by singling out deities that were connected to rocks (Tori no Iwakusufune no Mikoto) or contained the name Ōyama (Ōyamazumi no Mikoto). Along with institutional transformations on the mountain, Ōyama's deities expanded from a pantheon inspired by mountain asceticism to one that included the Shingon clergy's Ryōbu Shinto paradigms, which identified Sekison with the cosmic Buddha Dainichi and with Amaterasu. Later in the period, the pantheon shifted again to one composed of agricultural deities lifted from different pages of Japan's ancient mythical histories. Even though Ōyama had no exclusively Shinto deities during this period, and remained inherently combinatory until the formal disassociation of *kami* and Buddhas in the early Meiji period, the consciousness of coexisting Buddhist and Shinto universes on the mountain began to emerge gradually during this period. Inspired by the introduction of Shirakawa Shinto and Nativist thought, the *Sōyō Ōyama fu* and the *Afurijinja kodenkō* recreated identities for Ōyama's deities that dissociated them from a Buddhist context and created purely native genealogies for them. Composed by a fervent local Nativist, the *Afurijinja kodenkō* was the first text with an explicit normative agenda that denied all previous accretions and became the basis for the modern recreation of Ōyama's deities in the Meiji period.

Similar trends occurred at other sites as well. The cult of Mt. Fuji, for example, which had centered on the cult of the Buddha Dainichi in the medieval period, transformed into a Miroku cult due to the popularity of Jikigyō Miroku (1671–1733) in the Kantō region, whereas the deity at Mt. Fuji's Sengen Shrine became associated with Konohanasakuya Hime, a deity borrowed from the pages of the ancient chronicles. Like Ōyama, Mt. Fuji, which had been the training ground of *yamabushi*, suddenly attracted large numbers of pilgrims who climbed to the summit beginning around 1700.[8] Toward the end of the period, several Fuji *oshi* also became affiliated with the Shirakawa.[9] At Mt. Konpira, a major pilgrimage site in Shikoku, the cult of the *honji suijaku* deity Konpira Daigongen displaced the previous Kannon cult. Eventually, Konpira Gongen, sometimes identified as the protector of Yakushi Nyorai, the medicine Buddha, became identified with the native deity Ōmononushi, the mythical founder of Japanese medicine, whereas Nativists associated the deities with native legendary heroes and other deities including Yamato Takeru no Mikoto, Susanoo no Mikoto, and Kanayamabiko, and Emperor Sutoku.[10]

The Principal Deities in the Ōyamadera engi

The *Ōyamadera engi* linked the cult of Fudō at Ōyama to the cult of Maitreya by identifying Ōyama's Fudō, Ōyama's founder Rōben, and Ōyama itself with Mahākāśyapa, Maitreya, and Tuṣita Heaven respectively. In addition to identifying the mountain as a this-worldly representation of Tuṣita Heaven, the *Ōyamadera engi* depicted a typical pantheon associated with mountain asceticism. *Yamabushi* typically worshiped wrathful, ambivalent deities. According to Carmen Blacker, deities venerated by *yamabushi* are usually ambivalent protective deities of two types: one, wrathful *gongen* deities and wisdom kings (*myōō*)—particularly Fudō Myōō—and, two, ferocious animal spirits such as dragons. Dragons or serpents can be dangerous because they are said to control wind, rain, and thunder, but the mountain ascetic is able to subdue them with his esoteric spells and formulas.[11]

First and foremost, the medieval Ōyama cult centered on Fudō Myōō, the fierce Buddhist Wisdom King, who appears in various forms such as a powerful golden rock deity on the summit and is also known as Sekison Gongen (Venerable Rock Emanation) and Sekison Myōō (Venerable Rock Myōō);[12] Myōō Gongen, purportedly a living wooden image sculpted and enshrined by Rōben on the mountain slope; and the main image of worship at the Main Hall attributed to a disciple of the monk Gyōki (668–749).[13] Fudō's most common acolyte attendants, Kongara and Seitaka, were said to have manifested themselves as protective deities at the Tokuichi Shrine on the summit and the Hachidai Shrine dedicated to Hachidai Kongō Dōji (eight great *vajra*-wielding acolytes) on the mountain slope, respectively.[14] To this day, Taisanji, the present Shingon temple at Ōyama, enshrines a wooden statue of Fudō dating from the late Heian period and an iron triad of Fudō and his two attendants, Kongara and Seitaka, dating from the late Kamakura period and attributed to the Shingon monk Gangyō, as well as an early modern statue of Fudō.[15]

Furthermore, according to the *Ōyamadera engi*, a number of ambivalent deities that inhabited the mountain were said to have been malevolent in the past but had later been subdued to act as protective deities able to control precipitation. A ferocious dragon deity that inhabited Nijū no Taki, a waterfall on Ōyama's slopes, was said to have control over water. For example, he made a spring appear miraculously upon Rōben's request. The *kanbun* variant of the *Ōyamadera engi* also linked a thunder deity residing in the Ikazuchidaki waterfall on Ikazuchidake near Nijū no Taki, with another dragon who was said to control droughts and rainfall. These elements point to a rainmaking and fertility cult associated with Ōyama's dragons, a common element of dragon cults in East Asia.[16] According to the *Oyamadera engi*, the dragon was subdued by the Buddhist monk Rōben and had vowed to act as a protective deity for Ōyama as a Buddhist site from then on.[17] The theme of subduing and converting to Buddhism a thunder deity in the form of a dragon or snake is a common one in Japan. Scholars have understood these legends as accounts of how preexisting local cults were incorporated into the Buddhist fold.[18] Irene Lin sees this process of transformation as the Buddhist propitiation and harnessing of violent and threatening thunder gods and converting them into benevolent guardians of the Buddhist teachings.[19] Max Moerman suggests a less benign power dynamic in the process of appropriation. He notes in his study of the medieval Kumano cult that these narratives of peaceful submission probably veil violent interactions between prior local cults and Buddhist newcomers.[20] Whatever the nature of the process, through Buddhist assimilation, as Teeuwen notes, "the kami ceased to be wild, untamed powers that would arbitrarily lash out at those around them and instead became the executors of karmic retribution."[21] As Teeuwen and Rambelli explain, this Buddhist appropriation imposed a hierarchy on the local gods that placed them below the *honji suijaku* deities worshiped at these religious institutions. Since the Kamakura period, such local "real deities" were said to have no Buddhist original and to be malevolent, irascible beings in need of Buddhist salvation for the greater good of society.[22]

Ōyama also featured a *tengu* cult. In the concluding paragraphs of the *kanbun Ōyamadera engi*, we learn that Daitenma, originally an evil, demonic deity bent on preventing people from following Buddhism and sometimes associated with *tengu* as his attendants, came to Ōyama as

Fudō's attendant together with a powerful host of about 64,000 deities, including two deities of wind and fog, Kazesaburō and Kiri Ōji, enshrined in a Rain Shrine (Ugū). These deities were venerated in three of the five shrines on the summit: two *tengu* deities (Shōtengu and Daitengu) and the deities of the Fūu Shrine, dedicated to rain and wind. The vernacular version of the *Ōyamadera engi* is less specific about identifying the names of the deities and merely mentions that Tenma's host controls wind, rain, water, and fire.[23]

As ambivalent as dragons, *tengu* were animal-like figures associated with mountain ascetics. A *tengu* (literally: celestial dog/fox) is usually depicted as a half-human and half-birdlike demon with a red face, long nose or beak, wings, and claws. *Tengu* were thought to dress like mountain ascetics and to share their mountainous habitat and their supernatural gift of working magic. They could represent both evil tricksters who obstruct the pursuit of the Buddhist path and helpful assistants who could pass on valuable knowledge about magical practices.[24] In the early modern period, *tengu* were worshiped at two of Ōyama's shrines on the summit and appeared in the various narratives about the Ōyama's divinities from the *Ōyamadera engi* to the *Sōyō Ōyama fu*. In these texts, they were usually cast as minor divinities that control rain, wind, and thunder but also have the ability to cause mischief. However, compared to the cults of Fudō and Sekison, the *tengu* cult remained marginal. Therefore, in order to simplify the already cacophonous discourse about Ōyama's deities, this chapter omits a detailed discussion of the *tengu* cult.

The worldview presented in the *Ōyamadera engi* was clearly of medieval origin, but the text remained important for the proselytization of the Ōyama cult throughout the early modern period. The text—which existed as a *kanbun* version, an illustrated vernacular version, and abridged vernacular variant—was transmitted both within Ōyama's Shingon Buddhist institutions and among Ōyama's *yamabushi* and the *oshi*, until both the *kanbun* and abridged vernacular versions became more widely available in print in the late eighteenth and early nineteenth centuries. The most widely available version was an abridged version that appeared in the *Tōkaidō meisho zue*.[25] This was in turn copied in 1852 by the Ōyama *oshi* Inomata Gidayū,[26] who entitled it *Afurisan ryaku engi* and noted its inaccuracies but praised its potential for proselytization: "This abridged *engi* was excerpted from the original text and printed without authoriza-

tion. Therefore, it differs from the original in many points. Yet, it is
reproduced here in order to popularize the *engi* of this mountain among
the common people."[27] Inomata's observation was astute. The *Ōyamadera engi* remained a useful tool for proselytization even if Ōyama had
changed considerably since the early seventeenth century.

Tapping into Ancient Mythology: The Ōyama jiki

The *Ōyamadera engi* did not remain the only authoritative source on
Ōyama's deities. In the early eighteenth century, Ōyama's Shingon clergy
began to compile a new mythical history that traced the origins of the
deities back to antiquity. They were not alone in the endeavor to create
prestigious genealogies. According to Hiromi Maeda, in addition to issuing prestigious licenses and ranks to shrines, "Yoshida officials under-
took legend compositions for local shrines. In general, early modern
society stressed pedigree and genealogy in justifying a household's status.
Fabricating genealogies was commonly practiced among the samurai
class. Many daimyo manipulated their genealogies so that they appeared
to have descended from the Minamoto House—the quintessential ideal
of the Japanese warrior. By the eighteenth century, the forging of the
household's pedigree had also spread to elder peasants."[28] Maeda also
notes that once *bakufu* legislation made a firm distinction between temples and shrines founded before 1692 and those founded after, those
founded before 1692 assumed a higher standing. As a consequence,
status-conscious villagers began to compose fictitious founding legends
to prove the antiquity of their village shrines in the late seventeenth
and early eighteenth centuries.[29] By the end of the eighteenth century,
these legends increasingly linked local *honji suijaku* deities with famous
emperors and imperial heroes from Japanese antiquity.[30] Simultaneously,
Confucian interpretations of *kami* matters by scholars such as Hayashi
Razan (1583–1657), who stipulated the unity of Confucianism and Shinto,
and Yamazaki Ansai (1618–1682), who developed Suika Shinto, recon-
figured the ways in which the *kami* were conceptualized. Parallel to the
rise in interest in antiquity within Confucian circles in the late seventeenth and early eighteenth centuries—as exemplified by Yamaga Sokō
(1622–1685), Itō Jinsai (1627–1705), and Ogyū Sorai (1666–1728)—the
national learning movement developed, in part influenced by Itō Jinsai's
Kogidō academy.[31]

Around this time, as discourse about Japan's indigenous roots was becoming increasingly important both in Confucian and Nativist circles, Ōyama's Shingon clerics began to stress Ōyama's mythical origins in the age of the gods. In 1713, the Shingon monk Kaizō, who served as Hachidaibō's abbot at the time, compiled the *Ōyama jiki* (A Record of Matters Concerning Ōyama), a work pieced together from various myths and legends. Kaizō was one of Ōyama's most powerful abbots who reshaped Ōyama physically, institutionally, and ritually in the first three decades of the eighteenth century. Earlier in 1713, he decided to extend the summer festival of Sekison Daigongen by two days in order to accommodate the increasing numbers of pilgrims. In the winter of the same year, he finished his version of the *Ōyama jiki*. The text was initially transmitted among Ōyama's Shingon clerics. In 1730, the Shingon monk Tsūga, a monk at one of Ōyama's Shingon subtemples, made a copy of the text.[32] In 1792, it was reproduced in printed form by Shinzō, another cleric at Ōyama, in his *Ōyama Fudō reigenki*, through which it became accessible to a wider audience.[33] This version was cited by the *oshi* Sudō Shigeo in his *Afurijinja kodenkō* (1847) and was copied in 1858 by the Ōyama *oshi* Inomata Gidayū, who had also made copies of the abridged version of the *Ōyamadera engi* in 1852 and the *kanbun* version of the *Ōyamadera engi* in 1855.[34]

Kaizō probably did not invent most of the legends in the *Ōyama jiki* but appears to have compiled them from several sources, which he interpreted through a Shingon lens. In his colophon, Kaizō stated that he compiled popular tales and legends concerning Ōyama's Buddhist deities and *kami* in an effort to systematize previously unrelated accounts. It is difficult to identify his sources with certainty. The text contains obvious echoes of the *Nihongi* (720) and the *Sendai kuji hongi* (early Heian period), but the compiler was not concerned about discrepancies with the ancient chronicles and transplanted the myths freely into a local context. The text initially follows the genealogy provided by the *Sendai kuji hongi* but adds its own details. Later readers and critics of the *Ōyama jiki* recognized the similarities with the *Sendai kuji hongi taiseikyō* and the *Jinnō hongi*, but they also criticized the obvious discrepancies.[35]

The *Ōyama jiki* linked Fudō Myōō with deities and legendary imperial ancestors borrowed from the myths of the *Nihongi* and the *Sendai kuji hongi* through *onmyōdō* and *honji suijaku* theory. Since it is impossible to recover all of Kaizō's original sources, it is difficult to determine to what extent the *Ōyama jiki* contained original material. However, based on the compiler's material taken from the *Ōyamadera engi*, it appears that the *Ōyama jiki*'s compiler's creative contribution consisted of synthesizing and reinterpreting extant legends, some of which were already linked to Ōyama, whereas others were imaginatively transplanted into the local context.

The section on Rōben, which is obviously based on the *Ōyamadera engi*, is a transparent example of the compiler's editorial method. The text consists of a highly abridged summary of the source text. The summary is in fact so abbreviated, changed, and rearranged that it is difficult to follow unless the reader is familiar with the source text. For instance, the compiler notes that the sacred sword Tsurugi, which appears in Japan's early mythical histories, was the source of a miraculous light on the summit rather than a golden statue of Fudō.[36] The substitution is convenient because the sword is one of Fudō's attributes; hence, the author implies the identity of Fudō and the sword while he creates an elegant link to Japan's imperial genealogies. The underlying logic of association here is iconographic metonymy. In addition, the order of Rōben's stops during his ascent is reversed so that he first visits the area around the Main Hall on the slope, has a vision of Fudō, sculpts a statue from the sacred tree, and then climbs to the summit where he discovers a sacred rock in the shape of a seated statue rather than climbing to the summit first and descending to the central slope next.[37] Through this revision, the area around the Main Hall is given primacy, a reflection of the fact that the Main Hall of Fudō was the main cultic center of the Shingon-controlled complex in the early modern period. The *Ōyama jiki* also omits any reference to Rōben as an incarnation of Maitreya but places primacy with Fudō. This seems to indicate that the cult of Maitreya and the urgency of *mappō* were not as important to the early modern compiler. This section is a concrete illustration of Allan Grapard's argument that the *honji suijaku* paradigm was not just a theory but actually a practice that reflected administrative, economic, and ritual realities.[38]

To briefly sum up the contents of the text, the *Ōyama jiki* consists of an introduction that expounds the principle of immovability (i.e., Fudō, the Immovable), a section outlining the origins of Ōyama's deities during the age of the gods, a section on Ōyama in antiquity between 630 BC and

755 AD, and a conclusion that explains Fudō as the underlying essence of all the deities at Ōyama.[39] The most ancient deity is Fudō, who, according to the compiler, existed even before the beginning of the universe when all else was primordial chaos. Through linguistic associations, the compiler traces the origins of Ōyama's local deities back to Ōyamazumi no Mikoto, whose name the compiler seems to have interpreted as Lord Local Deity Who Resides on Ōyama. According to the compiler, Ōyamazumi no Mikoto was the offspring of Izanagi and Izanami in the Age of the Gods, descended on Ōyama, and fathered Tori no Iwakusufune no Mikoto (Lord Bird Rock Camphor Boat) with his consort Ame no Hanasakuya Hime. Renowned among the heavenly gods for his valor, Ōyamazumi no Mikoto became the guardian spirit of the land. Tori no Iwakusufune no Mikoto, who later became known as the rock deity Sekison on Ōyama's summit, took the shape of a sacred rock in order to give the people his protection.

The genealogy served political and sectarian purposes. The identification was sanctioned by the *bakufu* so that Tori no Iwakusufune no Mikoto (rather than Fudō as in the *Ōyamadera engi*) became the official deity of the Sekison Shrine, and Ōyamazumi no Mikoto was identified with Tokuichi (rather than Fudō's acolyte Kongara as in the *Ōyamadera engi*), who was enshrined next to Sekison on the summit.[40] The genealogy also conveniently placed Ōyama into the sectarian network of the Kogi Shingon School. As the text points out, Ame no Hanasakuya Hime was enshrined at Hakone, which was managed by Kongōōin, another important Kogi Shingon temple ranked above Ōyama.[41]

Yet the identification was by no means universally accepted. According to Shinzō, the compiler of the *Ōyama Fudō reigenki*, Tori no Iwakusufune no Mikoto's connection with Ōyama was contested.[42] In contrast, Ōyamazumi no Mikoto seems to have been popularly associated with the Ōyama and the Afuri Shrine since the *Tōkaidō meisho zue* identified him with Sekison.[43] Another mid-eighteenth century text identified Sekison with the so-called wayside deities (*dōsojin*)—and thus aligned him with Sarutahiko, Kōshin, and the blue-faced Vajrasattva.[44] This suggests that the exact contents of the *Ōyama jiki* were not widely known or at least were not commonly accepted.

The compiler of the *Ōyama jiki* regarded Fudō as the ultimate underlying deity of all the deities on the mountain. The introduction begins with a discussion of the mysterious powers of Fudō Myōō and the meaning of the universal potential for enlightenment. According to the compiler, the mind of enlightenment was called Fudō—immovable—to express its omnipresence and permanence. Furthermore, before the beginning of Heaven and Earth, the Fudō at Ōyama in Sagami was called Tokoyo Ugokazu no Mikoto (Eternally Unmoving Lord), giving Ōyama Fudō unlimited universality and linking him to the utopian realm of immortals, *tokoyo*.[45]

The *Ōyama jiki* included the major deities of Ōyama mentioned in the *Ōyamadera engi*: Fudō both as Sekison and the living wooden statue, the dragon at Nijū no Taki, and the thunder deity at Ikazuchidake. Yet in contrast to the *Ōyamadera engi* that only linked Fudō and Sekison Daigongen, the compiler of the *Ōyama jiki* identified most of the deities—Ōyamazumi no Mikoto, Iwakusufune no Mikoto (i.e., Sekison), the dragon Kurikara, and the thunder deity Byakuryaku Raidenjin—as manifestations of Fudō. He even argued that Ōyama's sacred spots—the summit, Nijū no Taki, Ikazuchiyama, and the entire mountain Ōyama—contained traces or were manifestations of Fudō.[46] Thus, unlike the medieval *Ōyamadera engi*, which depicted some of these deities as demonic "real deities" tamed by Buddhist conversion, the *Ōyama jiki* treated all of them as *honji suijaku* deities.

The *Ōyama jiki* provided a native genealogy that did not turn for the origins of the deities to foreign India but rather to the mythical past of Japan. The text may have had a different function than the *Ōyamadera engi*: it was probably intended less for proselytization and inspiring faith in Ōyama's deities than for establishing their pedigree. The *Ōyama jiki* does not prove the miraculous powers of Ōyama's deities, which the compiler seems to take for granted, but demonstrates their ancient, mythical native roots. Conversely, the *Ōyamadera engi* is less focused on the ancient roots of Ōyama's deities than on their miraculous, awesome powers. As a result, the two texts were seen to complement rather than contradict each other.

Devotion to Fudō and Sekison in the Ōyama Fudō reigenki

Over half a century after the compilation of the *Ōyama jiki*, another Shingon cleric, the monk Shinzō from Hachidaibō's subtemple Yōchi-in, compiled a comprehensive work focused on Fudō as Ōyama's central deity: the *Ōyama Fudō reigenki*. Despite sharing his sense of devotion toward Fudō with Kaizō, and even including Kaizō's *Ōyama jiki* in his compilation, Shinzō's approach differed radically. Kaizō sought to inspire awe for Ōyama's deities by tracing their most distant origins—in other words, by proving their pedigree (whereas Shinzō was concerned not only with their pedigree but also with chronicling their efficacy) not just in the distant past but also in the most recent past—to prove that Ōyama Fudō still worked his miracles. Moreover, whereas Kaizō's text was probably initially not intended for proselytization, Shinzō's was clearly designed for this very purpose.

Shinzō may have been motivated to compile a collection of recent miracles to encourage faith in Fudō and Sekison because of a sequence of disasters and, as he perceived them, miraculous omens. In the winter of 1773, Shinzō and his fellow monk Gyōjitsu from Daikakubō were called to the Main Hall by the guard on duty, who had discovered that Fudō was shedding tears. The two monks climbed up the altar and wiped away the tears with a piece of paper, but the tears continued to fall. Both took this to be an ominous sign and, to allay natural disasters, carried out Buddhist rituals before the main image of worship for one week. Two and a half months later, a fire broke out in Sakamoto Village. The wind spread the fire through the village, burning half the town to the ground. Shinzō interpreted Fudō's tears as a warning that had foretold the fire just as, he reasoned, the time during Kaizō's tenure when Fudō's eyes had turned red before an earthquake in 1703 that destroyed the entire mountain. Shinzō also pointed out that whenever branches mysteriously broke off trees on the mountain and in the village, these were divine omens that foreshadowed disasters.[47]

In 1792, soon after this series of apparent omens and disasters, Shinzō published the *Ōyama Fudō reigenki*, the 15-volume, 125-story collection of miracle tales featuring Ōyama Fudō and Sekison Daigongen. Shinzō appears to have begun his collection around 1777, right after the reconstruction of the shrines on the summit.[48] As Matsuoka Takashi has argued, Shinzō may have intended his work for proselytization to help Ōyama's religious institutions overcome this difficult time by spreading the faith in Ōyama's deities.[49] Conversely, Hakoyama Kitarō holds that Ōyama's deities, especially Sekison Daigongen, were able to gain tremendous popularity in the second half of the eighteenth century because the Kantō region was plagued by repeated natural disasters and famine, which led people to seek divine assistance against such catastrophes at a sacred mountain that overlooked the entire region.[50] Whether Shinzō was driven by economic hardship or spurred on by a popular trend, he explained his motivations in the preface to the first volume as his wish to encourage and spread faith in Ōyama Fudō and Sekison Daigongen. The motifs of miracles inspiring faith in the hearts of devotees as well as sincere faith as a precondition for a miracle are repeated throughout the entire collection.

Whereas other legends promoted Ōyama's efficacy by turning to the distant past, Shinzō emphasized more recent times. Yet despite this focus, Shinzō did not discount the ancient legends and opted to be comprehensive. The first volume documented Ōyama's pedigree through a survey of its history from antiquity (through the inclusion of the *Ōyama jiki* and a summary of the *Ōyamadera engi* to the Kamakura-period restorer Gangyō). The first volume ends with Ōyama's history under the Tokugawa *bakufu* and the current ritual calendar. Already his inclusion of legends concerning Gangyō, Ōyama's thirteenth-century revitalizer, and Ōyama's early modern history indicate that Shinzō was willing to rely on more recent material than that set in antiquity. The focus on recent history is particularly strong in the remaining fourteen volumes, which contain 125 miracle tales that Shinzō compiled from accounts he apparently heard from pilgrims, *oshi*, and Buddhist clerics at Ōyama about ordinary devotees rather than particularly famous patrons. Most stories are set after 1740—particularly in the 1770s and 1780s—whereas only three are set before 1600.[51]

Shinzō made a clear effort to be inclusive, but he was a Shingon monk at one of Ōyama's subtemples, and therefore, his work represented the view of the Shingon priesthood at Ōyama. This is reflected not only by Shinzō's tendency to minimize the role of Ōyama's *oshi* and to question the powers of self-proclaimed healers operating in the name of Ōyama but also in the content of the opening and the makeup of his sponsors. The first volume concentrated on Ōyama's Buddhist history: the history of the Buddhist institutions and famous monks at Ōyama. The colophon in the final volume, which lists the work's sponsors, indicates that the compilation was funded primarily by Buddhist clerics. Eighteen of the 34 contributors were monks, of whom 16 were from Ōyama. Together the clerics contributed about 60 percent of the printing costs. Only four sponsors were from Sakamoto Village, two of whom can be identified as *oshi*. Together, they contributed less than 10 percent of the costs. The remaining donors were laymen, mostly from Edo, who contributed about 35 percent.

Given the tension between Shinzō's wide range of sources and his sectarian bias, his view of Ōyama's deities emerge in three different ways: one, his attitude toward earlier legends of Ōyama; two, how frequently he selects miracle tales that deal with particular deities; and, three, his direct commentary on the deities and their miracles. To begin with the first point, Shinzō had a critical attitude toward earlier legends of Ōyama such as the *Ōyamadera engi* and the *Ōyama jiki*. Even though he reproduced the texts of both, he raised doubts about their veracity by pointing out disparities between them and other standard versions of Rōben's life, Japanese mythology, and history. His version of Rōben's life and his connection with Ōyama is described in a brief summary of the *Ōyamadera engi*. This is supplemented with alternate versions of Rōben's life from two standard collections of the lives of eminent monks in Japan, the *Genkō shakusho* and the *Honchō kōsōden*. Similarly, Shinzō appended his own commentary to his copy of the *Ōyama jiki*, in which he explained that the origins of the *Ōyama jiki* were unknown but that it had been transmitted for a long time at Ōyama. According to Shinzō, the *Ōyama jiki* was not just a text of unknown (and thus dubious) origins but some people had come to doubt the *jiki*'s authenticity because of its obvious disparities with commonly accepted versions of Japan's ancient past, the *Sendai kuji hongi taiseikyō* and the *Jinnō hongi*. Apparently, the text was especially questioned in regard to Tori no Iwakusufune no Mikoto's actual connections with Ōyama.[52]

Shinzō made no attempt to argue for the veracity of the *Ōyama jiki* or to deny the existence of disparities with earlier texts. As a Shingon monk well-versed in *dharma-kāya*, *honji suijaku*, and Ryōbu Shinto theory, he had another solution. He explained that it was of no consequence whether the *Ōyama jiki* was true. Differing identifications could be explained as skillful means used by the Buddha. All phenomena and beings were manifestations of the *dharma-kāya*, Mahāvairocana (Dainichi). Similarly, the Buddhas and bodhisattvas of India and China took on new forms when they manifested themselves in Japan in order to spread the

Buddhist teachings. To exorcise evil and inspire faith, they manifested themselves in the forms of poisonous snakes and fierce animals. Here Shinzō probably had the deities of Ōyama in mind, such as the dragon deity at Nijū no taki. Ultimately, he argued, all Buddhas, *kami*, and bodhisattvas consisted of the six elements, that is, of the same universal principles. Therefore, devotion to any deity would lead one onto the path of faith. All *kami* and Buddhas were manifestations of Dainichi. The idea of an underlying Buddhist principle or ultimate reality was already present in the *Ōyama jiki*. Whereas the *Ōyama jiki* linked all the deities with Fudō, Shinzō took the orthodox Shingon view that all phenomena were emanations of the cosmic Buddha Dainichi. If all deities could in fact be traced to Dainichi—the central Buddha of both the Womb World and the Diamond World mandalas—the exact identification of Sekison Daigongen's *honji* did not matter. If worship of any deity could inspire faith, then worship of Fudō, Sekison, or any other deity was equally efficacious.

What is of special interest here is not just that Shinzō tried to explain the ultimate reality behind Ōyama's deities but also that he questioned the relative truth of earlier legends and then explained away discrepancies through the Buddhist concept of skillful means. In a work that is devoted to proving the deities' miraculous efficacy, it may appear counterproductive to challenge the accepted provenance of the gods. On the one hand, his critical analysis may be a narrative device to present himself as a trustworthy chronicler—someone who does not accept fanciful stories blindly. On the other hand, he may have been raising common challenges that he could not avoid answering.

Shinzō even identifies a potential source of the criticism. When he points out that the identification of Ōyama's deities with Dainichi was based on *honji suijaku* and Ryōbu Shinto theories, he also stresses that this is not to be confused with the theories of Yuiitsu Shinto, i.e., Yoshida Shinto. Shinzō's argument hints at the fact that Shingon's Ryōbu Shinto explained *kami* as manifestations of the Buddhist deities in the Womb World and the Diamond World mandalas, whereas Yuiitsu Shinto reversed the relationship treating the *kami* as universal deities and the Buddhist deities as relative manifestations. His aversion to Yoshida Shinto is noteworthy since one or two *oshi* had been licensed by the Yoshida earlier in the period. It is not clear why he singled out Yoshida

Shinto because it was never a serious challenge to the Shingon clergy in contrast to Shirakawa, which was first gaining ground at Ōyama around Shinzō's time even though its full impact was not felt until the mid-nineteenth century. Still, his willingness to question and acknowledge criticism of earlier traditions indicates that some were beginning to challenge earlier legends and mytho-histories of the mountain.

While Shinzō held that all deities ultimately came down to the same substance, he gave their relative manifestations different attributes and degrees of relevance. This is apparent in the numeric distribution of the miracle tales in regard to which deity is at the center of each tale. Fudō and Sekison were the main focus of fourteen of the *Ōyama Fudō reigenki*'s fifteen volumes, which contain 125 miracle tales. About 75 percent of the stories deal with miracles of Fudō, whereas nearly 40 percent include miracles worked by Sekison. Ōyama's other deities only appear in about 7 percent of the stories. Fudō clearly predominates in the category of healing. However, Sekison resembles Fudō in the case of protection from the elements (thunder, flood, drought, harm at sea, and so on). Shinzō explains in his commentary on a story in which Fudō warns a faithful believer of being struck by lightning that Ōyama's deities are so efficacious at protecting from and warning people of thunder and lightning because one of the deities under Sekison— namely the deity on Kaminariyama (i.e., Ikazuchidake, Thunder Peak), a cloud-veiled peak on Ōyama's mountain side permanently closed off to pilgrims—was a thunder deity.[53] Shinzō usually casts Fudō as a protective, benevolent, and compassionate deity, whereas Sekison emerges as a deity who might grant protection but whose wrath one should be careful not to incur: the deity rewards the faithful but punishes the unfaithful. This distinction is not unusual in a *honji suijaku* context. According to Satō Hiroo, medieval local *kami* were more likely to be cast as vengeful than as abstract Buddhist-saving deities.[54]

It is significant that Sekison Daigongen occupies nearly 40 percent of the stories in the *Ōyama Fudō reigenki*, a collection that is dedicated in name to Fudō. If the *Ōyama Fudō reigenki* had been compiled with the same understanding as in the *Ōyamadera engi* and the *Ōyama jiki* that Fudō and Sekison were one and the same, this fact would not have been so surprising; but by Shinzō's time, Sekison seems to have developed a distinct identity independent of Fudō, not just as his emanation.

In his commentary on a story[55] in which a Nichirenshū follower fails to show the golden seal of Sekison proper respect and is quickly punished, Shinzō launches into a discourse on the nature of Sekison. Failing to show respect would lead to severe divine punishment since Sekison was a mighty deity. He agreed that Sekison was a *honji suijaku* deity but explained that Sekison was Ōhirume no Muchiwake Mitama no Kami, another name for Amaterasu Ōmikami,[56] but which also suggested a connection with the cosmic Buddha Dainichi because the first two characters are identical to the name of the cosmic Buddha. The identification is interesting because it subtly implies a shift of Sekison's gender from male to female. However, this does not seem to have been the main concern of Shinzō, who does not discuss this shift any further. As mentioned above, Shinzō considered all Buddhas and *kami* ultimately as emanations of Dainichi, no matter what they were called. The link between Amaterasu and Dainichi had been common in medieval *honji suijaku* thought associated with Ise. According to the *Bikisho* (1394), a text of the Shingon Ono lineage, for example, Amaterasu was associated with the Buddhist deities Dainichi, Fudō Myōō and Aizen Myōō, Daibonten, King Enma, and Kōbō Daishi. Amaterasu identified with Dainichi (and other Buddhist deities) who figured in medieval esoteric Buddhist rituals associated with the Ise Shrines.[57] Although Shinzō does not explicitly refer to these teachings, his Ryōbu Shinto–inspired identification of Sekison with Amaterasu (rather than Tori no Iwakusu-fune no Mikoto) gives Sekison a more prestigious pedigree.

At the same time, Shinzō identified the Eleven-Faced Kannon as Sekison's direct *honji*.[58] Kannon was enshrined as Sekison's *honji* at Kannonji, a Shingon temple founded at the foot of the mountain in the early 1600s.[59] The tendency for people to identify Sekison Daigongen with Kannon may have been based on practical considerations. Ōyama was en route between Iiyama and Iizumi Kannon, two stations on the Bandō Thirty-Three Places of Kannon pilgrimage, which was flourishing during the early modern period. By forging a connection with Kannon, the Shingon clergy at Ōyama could hope to attract more pilgrims.[60]

The *Ōyama Fudō reigenki* thus displayed a wide range of notions of the divine that drew on sacred scriptures, myths, and medieval lore as well as the latest eyewitness accounts by pilgrims. Its inclusiveness reflects the attitude of the Shingon clergy who were steeped in textual knowledge and also well versed in—even dependent on—the beliefs held by ordinary pilgrims and who were willing to incorporate both aspects into an integrated whole. After all, as Shinzō pointed out in his commentary on the *Ōyama jiki*, what did it really matter when all was simply an expression of the Buddha's skillful means to save all beings?

The Impact of Shirakawa Shinto in the Myōōtarō raiyu and Sōyō Ōyama fu

Despite their many differences, the *Ōyamadera engi*, the *Ōyama jiki*, and the *Ōyama Fudō reigenki* shared a focus on Fudō. In the case of the latter two, the focus on Fudō reflected the interests of the Shingon clergy because Fudō was the central deity in the Main Hall over which they had exclusive ritual control. From the late eighteenth century, however, the Shingon clergy's ritual monopoly began to crumble with the arrival of Shirakawa Shinto. As noted in Chapter 3, Shirakawa Shinto made its way into Ōyama first through sacerdotal licenses issued to Ōyama's shrine carpenter, Tenaka Myōōtarō Kagenao. Two texts that originated in the same Tenaka household represent a view of Ōyama's deities distinct from the Shingon clergy's views: the *Myōōtarō raiyu* and *Sōyō Ōyama fu*. These texts also illustrate how the connection with the Shirakawa household affected discourse about Ōyama's deities. Both texts were probably intimately related with Kagenao's efforts to have his ancestor deified and establish his family in a sacerdotal position through Shirakawa licenses, but whereas the first of these harkened back to the *Ōyamadera engi*, the second was more similar to the *Ōyama jiki*. Both texts were intended to prove the pedigree of the Tenaka lineage as the shrine carpenter, and both stressed the Tenakas' purportedly long-standing connection with the imperial court through their descent from the Inbe, but only the *Sōyō Ōyama fu* made the effort to link Ōyama's deities with the imperial ancestors.

According to Fabio Rambelli, many craftsmen and tradesmen in "premodern Japan used to trace their history back to mythological space and time by producing narratives that were heavily influenced by *honji suijaku* discourse."[61] Texts documenting the sacralized discourse on labor peaked in the late medieval and early modern periods. Many of these accounts were related to the genre of *engi* literature. Among craftsmen, carpenters in particular often incorporated genealogies that traced their lineage back to deities that appeared in ancient myths set in the age of the gods. Carpenters ritualized their labor because their work was thought to disrupt the cosmic harmony, which needed to be restored through the performance of rites. This process guaranteed that the carpenters could perform their work in safety. Even though contemporary carpenterial rites are usually cast in a Shinto format, they relied heavily on esoteric Buddhist symbolism in the premodern period.[62]

Both the *Myōōtarō raiyu* and the *Sōyō Ōyama fu* of the Tenaka household belong to this body of texts sacralizing the carpentry profession. Even though there are no dated versions extant before 1792, variants of the *Myōōtarō raiyu*, which tells the story of the Tenakas' legendary eighth-century ancestor Kanamaru Monkan, probably existed earlier in the early modern period. Like three shrine-priest/*oshi* households in Minoge and Sakamoto, the Tenaka traced their history at Ōyama back to the eighth century, when Rōben founded Ōyamadera. A link with Rōben and the legends surrounding him was a means to grant religious authority. Through the liberal adaptation of the *Ōyamadera engi*, the Tenaka were able to reaffirm their special status as carpenters and their hereditary name as artisans. It is likely that Tenaka Myōōtarō Kagenao relied on the *Myōōtarō raiyu* in the 1770s in order to demonstrate the special status of the Tenaka carpenter at Ōyama and to have his legendary ancestor deified by the Shirakawa.[63] Kagenao's acquisition of a Shirakawa license, his interest in his legendary family history, and the deification of his ancestor coincided with the rebuilding of the shrines on the summit in the 1770s, for which he acted as headman.

The Tenaka not only linked their first ancestor to Rōben but also claimed that this ancestor had been granted the name Myōōtarō by the protective tree deity of Ōyama, Myōō Gongen, while he constructed Ōyamadera with imperial patronage. Even though the legend echoes elements from the *Ōyamadera engi*, it creates a completely different identity for Myōō Gongen that dissociates Myōō Gongen from Fudō Myōō. In the *kanbun engi*, Rōben intended to make a replica of the sacred stone image of Fudō on Ōyama's summit from the wood of a sacred zelkova tree growing on Ōyama's slope. He received divine protection when the sky became ominously dark with clouds after he felled the tree, and before he finished carving, the statue began to bleed. The story of Myōōtarō echoes the theme of the bleeding zelkova tree but transforms the legendary ancestor of the Tenaka into the protagonist. It is *through* his labor and the use of his carpentry tools that Kanamaru Monkan establishes contact with the deities of Ōyama: Kanamaru Monkan accompanied Rōben to Ōyama, where he became the head carpenter. During the construction of Ōyamadera, he dropped his hammer. When he called for assistance, he was addressed as "Myōōtarō" by a mysterious old man who was leaning on the root of a zelkova tree and was listening to Kanamaru's hammering. The old man handed Kanamaru the hammer and ordered him to revere Myōō Gongen. Mounting a cloud, the old man disappeared accompanied by a host of several thousand dogs. When Rōben learned about the incident, he decided to cut down the zelkova tree and build a shrine from it, but before the tree was completely felled, it began to bleed. Rōben practiced Buddhist rituals for 21 days. Mysteriously, the zelkova tree changed into a statue of the old man. Rōben fell down in awe and prostrated himself while the sun clouded over.[64] According to this version then, Myōō Gongen is not just a copy of Fudō but a local deity. The central role given Kanamaru Monkan's hammer as a symbol of his work and object that mediates between the carpenter and the divinity hints at the fact that carpenters and other premodern craftsmen tended to sacralize their professional tools as ritual and symbolic instruments in esoteric Buddhist terms.[65]

When he compiled the *Sōyō Ōyama fu*, Kagenao's interests had expanded from Myōō Gongen, enshrined on the central slope, to the deities on Ōyama's summit. Unlike the *Myōōtarō raiyu*, which is reminiscent of the *Ōyamadera engi*, the *Sōyō Ōyama fu* resembles the *Ōyama jiki* in its concern with Ōyama's pre-Buddhist history. Like the *Ōyama jiki*, the *Sōyō Ōyama fu* draws on Japan's mythical history to explain the ancient origins of Ōyama and freely transplants the ancient myths and legends into the Kantō region. Like Kaizō, Kagenao claimed that he compiled the text from old records rather than authored it. Although this might apply to sections of the text, Kagenao's assertion may well have been a deliberate strategy to claim authenticity for his text.[66] Despite many instances of creative misreading, the text proved Kagenao to be erudite. He identified various sources that he used to substantiate his own account: the *Nihon sōkoku fudoki*, the *Nihon kokumei fudoki*, Hayashi Razan's *Honchō jinjakō*, the *Taiseikyō*, the *Kokuzō hongi*, the *Nihongi*, and the *Sendai kuji hongi*.[67] Like the *Ōyama jiki*, the *Sōyō Ōyama fu* also displays a similar concern with genealogy and chronology: it begins with the formation of the universe and then traces Ōyama's deities through the age of the gods down to the reign of Emperor Yūryaku (456–479). However, the *Ōyama jiki*'s emphasis on Fudō is completely absent from the *Sōyō Ōyama fu*, as is the Buddhist history of Ōyama.

The influence of the Shirakawa connection on Kagenao's thinking about Ōyama's deities is evident in the *Sōyō Ōyama fu*, which Kagenao compiled under the name Carpenter Inbe Kagenao. Through his choice of the surname Inbe, which he also used when he acted in a shrine-priestly function, Kagenao harkened back to his legendary ancestor Kanamaru Monkan, who bore the imperially sanctioned surname Inbe.[68] The connection with the Inbe was not accidental. Carpenters at other religious institutions, such as the Miwa Shrines, also traced their lineage back to the Inbe and their divine ancestors.[69] In the *Sōyō Ōyama fu*, Kagenao emphasized the Inbe's ancient sacerdotal duties under imperial patronage. Since Shirakawa licensees supposedly had a connection with the imperial court—however tenuous—Kagenao seems to have been keen on proving that his distant ancestors, the Inbe, served at Ōyama as the emperor's ritual representatives. With the compilation, Kagenao may have wanted to draw attention to the fact that he, a descendant of Kanamaru Monkan, an Inbe, had also served the rulers of Japan and to imply that their connection with the sacred mountain preceded the arrival of the Buddhist clergy. After all, the Inbe had served as carpenters and sacerdotal intermediaries for the court and received rewards for their services. Kagenao fabricated the history of the Inbe's connection with Ōyama because he considered himself a descendent of the Inbe and claimed special ritual privileges on the basis of tradition and his Shirakawa license.

In addition to constructing an imperial connection for his purported ancestors, the *Sōyō Ōyama fu* provides an insight into Kagenao's idiosyncratic views about Ōyama's deities, which he viewed primarily as rain-making deities. Even though rainmaking had always been one aspect of their powers, Kagenao was the first to limit their efficacies to this category. Like the compiler of the *Ōyama jiki*, Kagenao traced Ōyama's deities back to the age of the gods. He claimed that after Izanagi and Izanami created the land, they descended onto Ōyama. Izanami changed into a rock that appeared on Afurisan (written as Ame-furi-san "Rain

Falling Mountain"), the summit of Ōyama, where she was venerated as Kikuri Hime. Izanagi changed into a tree known as Amefuriki ("Rain Falling Tree") on Ōyama's slope. To explain the presence of the many small chapels and shrines on the mountain slope and around the Main Hall, Kagenao points out that Izanagi was accompanied by a host of deities that manifested themselves as Buddhas and bodhisattvas, in other words, *honji suijaku* deities.[70]

Kagenao's identification of Sekison with Izanami and the zelkova tree with Izanagi is highly idiosyncratic. Kagenao may have associated Izanami and Izanagi with Ōyama because the deities commonly associated with the shrines on the summit were said to be the descendents of Izanami and Izanagi. Kagenao's identification of the zelkova tree with Izanagi indirectly implies a connection with the sacred zelkova tree that later provided the wood for the statue of Myōō Gongen and had a special legendary connection with the Tenaka. By chosing Izanagi, a deity linked closely to the imperial line, Kagenao created yet another link between his ancestor Kanamaru and the imperial house. Yet Sekison's identification with Izanami is curious. Not only had Kagenao (like Shinzō) changed the commonly accepted gender of the deity, he had also chosen a divinity that is usually said to have died during Japan's age of the gods and therefore is associated with the realm of the dead. As noted in Chapter 1, the taboo against the pollution of death was strictly observed around the shrine dedicated to Sekison. It is likely that Kagenao was not interested in Izanami's association with the underworld but in the male-female pairing of the deities. The yin-yang theme is echoed through other sections of the text that also associate Ōyama's minor deities, such as *tengu*, with male-female pairs.

Kagenao composed a genealogy for Ōyama's deities that was quite different from the accepted identification of Ōyamazumi no Mikoto and Tori no Iwakusufune no Mikoto with the deities on Ōyama's summit. Yet Kagenao never directly questioned the presence and authority of the Shingon Buddhist clergy at Ōyama even though he highlighted his presumed ancestors' sacramental role as shrine priests. In the *Myōōtarō raiyu*, the monk Rōben is relegated to a minor role, whereas the carpenter is at the center of the story. It is he who is credited with being the first to encounter the Myōō Gongen deity and having received his artisan name from the deity. In the *Sōyō Ōyama fu*, Kagenao related the deities of Ōyama to the imperial lineage, which he then linked to his own by association. Still, Kagenao merely gave an alternative account and had no intention of purging Buddhist influences from Ōyama.

Ultimately, Kagenao's descendents would have to choose between their dual lineages as the carpenterial associates of Rōben and as Shinto ritualists in the Meiji period during the disassociation of *kami* and Buddhas. In 1870, the incumbent carpenter, Kagemoto, chose to remain Buddhist and retain his carpenterial name Tenaka Myōōtarō, claiming that his ancestors had a long-standing special relationship with Ōyama Fudō, whereas his adolescent son was to establish a new household as a Shinto priest and consequently renounced the name Tenaka Myōōtarō.[71] In effect, Kagemoto chose the lineage established by the *Myōōtarō raiyu* over his identity as a Shinto priest described in the *Sōyō Ōyama fu*. This proved that the *Myōōtarō raiyu*, like the *Ōyamadera engi*, did not lose its importance for the Tenaka carpenters despite the increasing Shinto-ization of Ōyama. Yet whereas Ōyama flourished for most of the early modern period as a combinatory multiplex, once Nativism arrived at the mountain, tensions developed that ultimately gave rise to distinct Buddhist and Shinto mental universes.

Nativism and the Afurijinja kodenkō

The earliest and clearest indication of this development is embodied by the *Afurijinja kodenkō*, authored by the local Nativist and *oshi* Sudō Shigeo. In 1847, Sudō had joined the Hirata School of national learning. Only about two years later, he composed the *Afurijinja kodenkō*, which aimed to recover the true and original deities, rituals, sacred sites, and name of Ōyama through the study of three ancient texts—the *Kojiki*, the *Nihongi*, and the *Engi shiki*—and with commentaries by Nativist scholars such as Motoori Norinaga's *Kojikiden*. Shigeo not only sought to uncover the true roots of Ōyama but also wanted to expose the Buddhist clerics at Ōyama as frauds and evil sorcerers who managed to falsify Ōyama's deities and rituals and set up oppressive institutions that usurped the role of the original shrine priests. For Sudō, the *oshi*— whom he called *shishoku* (using the characters 祠職 [shrine priest] instead of 師職, the more common alternative term for *oshi*)—were the descendants of these original shrine priests and therefore the rightful heirs of the original tradition. Sudō claimed to have composed his text for those "shrine priests" and pilgrims, but his text also addressed fellow members of the Hirata school, including as it did a short preface for the text by Hirata Kanetane (1799–1880), Hirata Atsutane's adoptive son and successor.[72]

In his treatise, Sudō wanted to prove that prior traditions that contradicted his theories were fraudulent inventions and to find deities that he could identify as Ōyama's original deities. These he determined to be Ōyamazumi no Kami, Okami no Kami, and Ōikazuchi no Kami.[73] His strategy resembled that of Hirata Atsutane, who had similarly studied and reevaluated legends and historical records, and had claimed in his *Gozu Tennō rekijinben* that the traditional identification of Susano'o with Gozu Tennō as the *honji suijaku* deity of the Konpira Shrine was a fraudulent fabrication by diviners at the Gion Shrine. Instead, Hirata argued, the deity should be identified with Ōkuninushi and the spirit of Emperor Sutoku.[74] Even earlier, Motoori Norinaga had attempted in his *Ise nikū sakitake no ben* (1798) to define the authentic identity and nature of the principal deity enshrined at the outer Ise Shrine and depose any identifications that he considered unorthodox; for example, those of Confucians and *onmyōdō* specialists. Motoori Norinaga argued that Miketsukami, that is, Toyouke Hime, was the principal deity and not Ame no Minakanushi no Kami, Kuni no Tokotachi no Mikoto, or Sumemima no Mikoto. He also disputed a theory that accepted Toyouke Hime as a deity of low rank and questioned several variant genealogies of the deity.[75]

In similar fashion, Sudō radically denied all prior identifications of Ōyama's deities because they diverged from the ancient chronicles, the *Kojiki* and the *Nihongi*. Given the proliferation of theories by 1848, this was no small task. Sudō chose to focus on the *Ōyama jiki* and the *Ōyamadera engi*, which he perceived as central texts, adding commentaries on several minor traditions originating at Ōyama and elsewhere as well as on the *Ōyama Fudō reigenki*. He dealt with the *Ōyama jiki* first because it treated Ōyama's deities dating back to the age of the gods. His primary objection was with the identification of Sekison with Tori no Iwakusufune and of Tokuichi with Ōyamazumi no Kami probably because he rejected the authority of the Shingon Buddhist clergy, who promoted this identification. Sudō disputed the veracity of the identification even though it had found official backing by the *bakufu*. He pointed out that in the *Kojiki* and the *Nihongi*, Tori no Iwakusufune, a boat, was created by Izanagi and Izanami and used to set afloat the leech child, their deformed first born. First of all, this proved that the deity was not the offspring of Ōyamazumi as the *Ōyama jiki* claimed. Second, Motoori Norinaga had shown that the name Tori no Iwakusufune (Bird Rock Camphor Boat) was a textual corruption: the boat was not made from camphor (*kusu*) but from reeds (*ashi*). Therefore, Tori no Iwakusufune did not actually exist but was merely a name that the Buddhist monks had lifted from the pages of the ancient records and had falsely identified as a *gongen* through their *honji suijaku* theories. The deity was also not Ame no Torifune (Heavenly Bird Boat), who was a completely different deity, or Iwa Ubason, according to popular tradition, because this deity did not appear in the ancient records and therefore did not exist. Similarly, Sudō asserted that Tokuichi could not be identified with Ōyamazumi no Kami because the latter was actually identical with Sekison. The belief that Tokuichi was the protective deity of the land was false, as was the popular belief identifying him with Nagare no Ōmoto no Mikoto, a deity who—Sudō claimed—did not exist because he did not appear in the ancient records.[76]

Sudō also took a swipe at the *Ōyamadera engi*. Sudō considered both the *kanbun* and the vernacular versions of the *engi* to be a text highly colored by fabrications by the Shingon clergy. Since he argued that Sekison was really Ōyamazumi no Kami, he could not allow the deity to be identified with Fudō as the *engi* suggested. He portrayed Rōben as a conniving sorcerer who used his magic to conjure up a mysterious light from the summit, apparitions of Buddhist deities, and Buddhist temples, when in fact he had unearthed on the summit the seat of the deity (*shintai*) of Ōyamazumi no Kami, who meted out his divine wrath on those who had defiled him. Likewise, the serpent deity that appeared to Rōben at Nijū no taki was Okami no Kami, who was later falsely identified with Kurikara. Sudō's most ingenious argument against the identification of Sekison with Fudō is that Buddhist scriptures describing Fudō were not introduced to Japan until after Kūkai's return from China, which was long after Rōben supposedly discovered Fudō on the summit and long after Kōzō—Gyōki's disciple—was said to have enshrined a statue of Fudō at Ōyama. Therefore, Fudō could not have existed at Ōyama at this early point. Sudō gained further ammunition against the claim that Sekison was Fudō from the revised identification of Sekison as a manifestation of Kannon. To Sudō, this proved not only that Sekison was not Fudō but also that the identification with Kannon was a desperate attempt by the clergy to renew people's faith when people failed to believe the earlier association with Fudō.[77]

Sudō felt the need to address legends of Ōyama's medieval history. He critically dissected the story about Gangyō's restoration of Ōyama in the Kamakura period, which is contained in the *Ōyama Fudō reigenki*. According to Sudō, Gangyō was as conniving a sorcerer as Rōben was and was driven by vanity to produce a large statue of Fudō with the help of Enoshima Benten. Not only were the stories about his sculpting a large statue from a small amount of gold unbelievable (since it was actually not made from gold but from iron), but also he used his magic to conjure up a vision of Benten as a great serpent at the installation ceremony. If that serpent had really been a deity from Ōyama, it would have devoured everyone without fear of Gangyō's meaningless magic powers.[78] Sudō's denial of Gangyō's legitimacy is important because the Shingon clergy claimed Ōyama for the Shingon School based on its association with Gangyō, who was a Shingon Ritsu monk.

Sudō turned to the *Kojiki*, *Nihongi*, and *Kojikiden* to reconstruct what he claimed were the ancient true deities of Ōyama. He chose three deities—Ōyamazumi, Okami, and Ōikazuchi—created by Izanagi when he cut the fire deity Kagutsuchi into three pieces. Sudō argued that they resided on Ōyama's summit, on Ōyama's slope at Nijū no Taki, and on Ikazuchidake, respectively. These were deities that appeared in the ancient chronicles, which gave them the seal of orthodoxy. Sudō probably chose these three deities because two local place names (Ōyama and Ikazuchidake) resembled those of two deities. Sudō cited other Nativists, such as Motoori Norinaga and Hirata Kanetane, in his explanation of the nature of these deities. He argued that Ōyamazumi no Kami was the deity after whom the mountain was named. According to the ancient texts, he was a rock deity and father of Konohanasakuya Hime, the wife of Ninigi no Mikoto. The deity's popular name was Sekison. Okami no Kami was a serpent deity residing at Nijū no Taki. The deity had later been called Kurikara Ryūō by the Buddhist clergy, but this was not its original name. Ōikazuchi no Kami resided at Ikazuchidake, a sacred peak near Nijū no Taki. Sudō believed that all three deities could produce rain and were to be ritualized through the ancient *toshigoi no matsuri* rite, just as Ōyama's deities had been in the days of the *Engi shiki*. According to Sudō's analysis, this rite carried out in the Second Month was initially supposed to ensure the pacification of the realm and unruly deities. Since it was celebrated at the beginning of the rice-planting cycle in the New Year, it later served to petition the gods for sufficient rainfall and a good harvest for the rest of the year.[79]

Sudō wanted a return to an Ōyama that, he envisioned, existed in a mythical past before the arrival of Buddhism and before the Shingon clergy's takeover of the mountain. Yet, in the end, the texts he chose to reconstruct this utopian ideal were either unrelated to Ōyama (the *Kojiki* and the *Nihongi*) or contained very few details (the *Engi shiki*), which, ironically, forced him to deduce the pre-Buddhist nature of Ōyama's deities from a text whose veracity he fiercely denied (the *Ōyamadera engi*). He stated: "Because [the *kanbun Ōyamadera engi*] is an old record, if one separates out what is false and takes only what is true, one can reconstruct what really happened."[80] His selection is therefore based on the local deities that Rōben was said to have encountered on his first visit to Ōyama. Yet, though he borrowed the themes of dragons and rainmaking from earlier sources, he nevertheless invented a new pantheon in his attempts to recover Ōyama's orthodox deities.

Conclusion

The debate about Ōyama's pantheon illustrates how deeply intertwined the *kami* worship was with Buddhism in early modern Japan. It also illustrates the growing importance of genealogy and pedigree. Ōyama's pantheon was one of ever-increasing complexity in the early modern period as the mountain changed from a *shugendō* site to one controlled by Shingon clerics and, toward the end of the period, was shaped by strong Shirakawa Shinto and Nativist influences. Originating in the late Kamakura period and maintaining its appeal through the early modern period, the *Ōyamadera engi* defined the Ōyama cult as combination of a Maitreya and Fudō cult with a dragon-centered rainmaking cult. Ōyama and its deities were given foreign origins to heighten their prestige. The *Ōyama jiki* and *Ōyama Fudō reigenki*, both the works of Shingon clerics, maintained the focus on the Fudō cult but omitted any reference to the Maitreya cult. Rather than identifying Ōyama and its deities as foreign, the texts indigenized them by depicting Ōyama's deities as local emanations of more abstract esoteric Buddhist deities—Fudō in the case of the *Ōyama jiki*, and Kannon and ultimately Dainichi Nyorai in the case of the *Ōyama Fudō reigenki*. Despite their tendencies to seek an underlying principle, the two texts by Shingon clerics easily incorporated earlier legends about Ōyama into a loose composite by explaining discrepancies through theories of emanation and skillful means used by the Buddha to save human beings. Under the influences of Shirakawa Shinto and Nativism, the focus on Fudō disappeared. Instead, the *Sōyō Ōyama fu* and the *Afurijinja kodenkō* lifted deities from the pages of historical chronicles depicting the mythical age of the gods and transformed Ōyama into a self-contained sacred territory chosen by indigenous gods as their residence. Unlike the more universally efficacious Buddhist deities, who also provided healing powers and promised prosperity, protection, and salvation, these gods were pure agricultural deities that controlled the elements of nature. However, there was an essential difference between the Shirakawa-inspired *Sōyō Ōyama fu* and the Nativist-aligned *Afurijinja kodenkō*. Whereas the former merely minimized earlier local traditions but still embraced a *honji suijaku* model, the latter actively rejected them and set up a normative model. This model left no room for multiple explanations but sought a single, cohesive truth that valued "veracity" over expediency.

What motivated the changing conceptions of the divine at Ōyama? All these texts were affected by Ōyama's institutional structures, and through them, ritual, which in turn served as a means to control Ōyama's economic assets. The connection is perhaps most obvious in Kagenao's *Sōyō Ōyama fu* and Sudō's *Afurijinja kodenkō*. Kagenao, who was a carpenter and an *oshi*, sought to establish his family as descendents of the Inbe, a sacerdotal family associated with the imperial court in antiquity, whereas Sudō, also an *oshi*, aimed to recover Ōyama's authentic deities and rituals based on the *Engi shiki*. Both turned away from focusing on Fudō, whose cult was under the exclusive control of the Shingon Buddhist clergy. In contrast, Kaizō and Shinzō, the compilers of the *Ōyama jiki* and the *Ōyama Fudō reigenki*, placed Fudō at the center of their pantheons. Even though he may have been truly motivated to inspire faith leading to prosperity, good health, and salvation, Shinzō clearly wanted to encourage believers to make a pilgrimage to Ōyama to visit

Sekison Daigongen during the summer festival or Ōyama Fudō at any time of the year to hold a *goma* fire ritual for Fudō through one of the Shingon clerics, and to purchase amulets and talismans consecrated by the Shingon clergy. Despite challenges to the Fudō cult from around 1800, Ōyama's ritual life continued to revolve around Fudō under the auspices of the Shingon clergy, even though the pilgrimage to Sekison's shrine on the summit was the primary attraction of the summer festival. It was only after the Meiji restoration that Fudō would lose his central position and the deities selected by Sudō Shigeo would take his place.

Ultimately, which of the identifications was actually more widely accepted among early modern devotees of the Ōyama cult? The *Ōyama-dera engi* remained an important tool for proselytization throughout the period, but ritual practice indicates that the Maitreya cult lost its significance in the early modern period. Fudō remained at the center of the Ōyama cult, but with the growing popularity of the summer festival, Sekison also played an important role and acquired a distinct identity from Fudō. By the eighteenth century, Sekison's *honji* was identified with Kannon rather than Fudō. The deities mentioned in the *Ōyama jiki* were perhaps not widely known or commonly accepted, but they were officially recognized by the *bakufu*. In contrast, the identifications in Kagenao's *Sōyō Ōyama fu* had no currency beyond his household. The *Myōōtarō raiyu* was known at least on the village level and eventually more widely circulated because it was mentioned in the *Ōyama Fudō reigenki* and later in the 1840 gazetteer of Sagami, the *Shinpen Sagami no kuni fudokikō*. There is no indication, however, that it had any impact on the ritual practices of the pilgrims. The *Ōyama Fudō reigenki* reflects the concerns of pilgrims to Ōyama most closely, but it also contains the theories of Shinzō, its compiler. There is no indication that his identification of Sekison with Amaterasu was widely accepted among devotees. Finally, Sudō's *Afurijinja kodenkō* gave a critical assessment of Ōyama's pantheon and was supposedly authored for the benefit of pilgrims. It did not promote actual beliefs held by pilgrims; on the contrary, Sudō dismissed any beliefs held by devotees that he considered unorthodox. Instead, the text established a new, normative Shinto pantheon based on Nativist scholarship. This pantheon was eventually adopted after the disassociation of *kami* and Buddhas in the Meiji period, but even then it was not accepted completely by devotees. As discussed in Chapter 7, the planned removal of Fudō from the mountain was met with resistance from nearby villages that depended on pilgrimage travel because the villagers realized that the shrines on the summit would not attract a sustained flow of pilgrims throughout the year. Despite efforts to redefine the deities on the summit in Shinto terms in the early 1870s, in the 1890s the deity of the Afuri Shrine was still widely referred to as Sekison, its combinatory name throughout the early modern period.[81] In the end, the early modern deities had tremendous staying power. It was the deities' powers to accommodate a wide range of concerns that made Ōyama an attractive pilgrimage site. Even the normative efforts of the shrine's officialdom during the early Meiji period did not diminish this wide appeal.

SEVEN

A New Order, 1868–1885

In 1868, the newly established Meiji regime issued orders to disassociate *kami* and Buddhas. At Ōyama, the disassociation eventually led to the cult's transformation into a Sect Shinto organization during the subsequent Great Teaching Campaign (*taikyō senpu undō*; 1870–84). Even though it is tempting to assign responsibility for the far-reaching changes to the Meiji regime, the concrete forces behind the implementation of the transition were of local origin. As Gaynor Sekimori notes in her study of the disassociation at Mt. Haguro, the Meiji regime needed the support of local communities for the implementation of its policies. Local elites often served as power brokers and mediated between the central government and the local populace.[1] As in the case of Mt. Haguro, Ōyama's disassociation was highly dependent on local and regional contexts, which were complicated by the presence of four interest groups with conflicting agendas: the Shingon clergy, a Nativist *oshi* faction that wanted change, an *oshi* faction that supported the status quo, and other innkeepers and artisans in villages at the foot of the mountain who stood to lose business if changes at Ōyama were too drastic and affected the pilgrimage trade negatively. Each of these groups used governmental orders to safeguard its own interests or found ways to resist the full implementation of these orders.

At many religious institutions, reliable historical documents about the concrete circumstances during this time of upheaval are scarce. Fortunately, in Ōyama's case, we can rely on several important historical sources covering the transition from the early modern to the Meiji periods, including several detailed diaries kept by *oshi* involved in this transition. These documents reveal the tensions between local economic, political, and ideological interests underlying Ōyama's modern transformation. They also illustrate that the disassociation of *kami* and Buddhas was a slow process that involved much negotiation among the various interest groups. In the course of this decade-long transformation, Ōyama's primary religious institution changed from a combinatory Shingon multiplex into a Shinto shrine: the Afuri Shrine, which later unified its *oshi* parishes into a centralized Sect Shinto organization, Ōyama Keishin Kōsha, under the leadership of the Nativist and doctor Gonda Naosuke (1809–1887).

The Disassociation of Kami *and Buddhas*

During the Meiji restoration in 1868, the *kami* and Buddhas were disassociated by a government decree in an attempt to sever the state's ties with a Buddhist system that had supported the Tokugawa regime. In its stead the new regime attempted to establish a Shinto system, which promoted the unity of rites and politics (*saisei itchi*). In some instances the disassociation of *kami* and Buddhas turned into the suppression of Buddhism, *haibutsu kishaku*, the willful destruction, dismantling, and even burning of Buddhist temples, hermitages, chapels, statuaries, and scriptures and the forced laicization and banishment of Buddhist clerics. In a more moderate form, the disassociation of *kami* and Buddhas deprived many clerics of necessary sources of income, forcing them to move to other temples or return to lay life to continue their priestly function as Shinto priests. Some Buddhist clerics lost parishioners who chose to hold Shinto rather than Buddhist funerals. This accelerated the closure or merging of temples no longer economically viable through either a chronic lack of funds or more recent losses.[2]

Specifically, in the spring of 1868, the new Meiji regime opted to raise Shinto above Buddhism in order to reverse the reliance on Buddhist temple registration by the previous regime. In the intercalary Fourth Month of 1868, the Jingikan was established as one of the highest organs of state and raised in rank even above the Dajōkan (Great Council of State) as an expression of the policy of the unity of rites and politics the following year. The Jingikan held this exalted position until August 1871, when it was demoted to the Jingishō (Ministry of Divinity).

In March 1872, it was dissolved and incorporated into the Kyōbushō (Ministry of Doctrine).[3] However, during the height of its power, the Jingikan gave Nativist Shinto proponents the opportunity to influence national policy. The new regime issued orders for the disassociation of *kami* and Buddhas and sought to establish Shinto as the national faith. While doing so, it destroyed the economic basis of Buddhist institutions by confiscating temple lands and undermining the temples' bonds with their parishes by instituting shrine parishes (*ujiko*) to replace temple registration. Between the Third and Fifth Months of 1868, the government issued orders that forced Buddhist clerics serving at shrines either to become laicized if they wished to continue as shrine priests (*kannushi* and *shajin*) or to leave their shrines. Moreover, shrine priests and their families were required to hold Shinto funerals instead of Buddhist ones. The new legislation also demanded the removal of Buddhist images, Buddhist implements such as bells and gongs, and *honji suijaku* titles or names for deities at Shinto shrines (such as *gongen*, *gozu tennō*, and *bosatsu*). These had to be replaced by more orthodox Shinto names and objects of worship.[4]

These orders were not implemented unilaterally as soon as they were promulgated. Even though the orders were issued in swift succession in 1868, it took over one year to relay and employ them in some regions, including areas in the Kantō region, such as parts of Musashi Province. Even within one single province, there were tremendous differences depending on the local context.[5] In other words, both the disassociation of *kami* and Buddhas and the suppression of Buddhism were highly regionalized and localized processes. The manner in which these orders were implemented varied from region to region, depending on whether the regional authorities were highly anti-Buddhist or had no particular anti-Buddhist agenda. Thus, local or regional manifestations of the disassociation ranged from fierce attempts to eradicate Buddhism, to moderate adaptations of the old system to the new system in name only, or even to open resistance against the orders.

Moreover, the aim of the implementation differed depending on the regional and local contexts. In some cases, local authorities pursued the implementation as a means to enforce their power. In other cases, the implementation of the policy was a way to demonstrate opposition and resistance to previous local authorities.[6] In isolated incidents, shrine officials used the opportunity to banish Buddhist temples from shrine land or enforced a violent purge destroying innumerable Buddhist statues, scriptures, and implements in shrine precincts. At some institutions, clerics were forced to revert to lay status while at others the Buddhist clergy panicked and became laicized voluntarily. The Meiji regime soon acknowledged that its attempts to separate Buddhism and Shinto had led to violent excesses against Buddhist institutions by low-ranking shrine priests who sought retribution for their low status in the old system. In the Ninth Month of 1868, the Meiji regime issued an admonition that its orders did not justify indiscriminate violence against Buddhist institutions or the random laicization of Buddhist clerics. Nevertheless, as a result of the disassociation of *kami* and Buddhas, large numbers of Buddhist temples were merged, closed, or dismantled in the early 1870s. On the opposite end of the scale, Jōdoshin clerics and their parishioners in Mikawa Province (modern Aichi Prefecture) engaged in resistance against the anti-Buddhist/pro-Shinto policies and were severely punished in sentences ranging from death penalties to several years of incarceration and corporal punishment.[7]

In other regions, the disassociation of *kami* and Buddhas was much more moderate. The old system was preserved in some measure. Often the transformation lasted several years and was merely observed in name rather than in substance. Pre-Meiji shrines and their deities received new, "orthodox" Shinto names to replace *honji suijaku* ones. In many instances, combinatory institutions were turned into Shinto institutions by removing Buddhist clerics from shrines and replacing them with full-time shrine priests who, in fact, were laicized Buddhist clerics who had been managing the shrine all along. Similarly, the Buddhist cleric's residence became the shrine priest's residence. Even Buddhist statuary, chapels, and implements were often preserved by removing and sending them to other Buddhist temples rather than destroying them. In some cases, shrines and temples became mutually independent institutions. When the resident Buddhist cleric refused to become laicized, a shrine priest was appointed from another shrine nearby to take over the residency.[8] In regions where the disassociation of *kami* and Buddhas was less than fervent, such as in Musashi Province, the transformation was often only partial. At many shrines, physical evidence of the Buddhist connection remained in the form of pagodas, Buddhist or *honji suijaku* statues, mandalas, Buddhist scriptures, gongs, and bells decorated with Sanskrit letters.[9]

Many Buddhist temples survived these changes because they had parishes that provided them with a steady economic basis through the performance of funerary rites. The primary victims were not functioning Buddhist temples with large parishes but prayer temples (*kitōdera*) and small Buddhist chapels or hermitages without parishes that were no longer economically viable.[10] Yet even powerful Buddhist temples were not entirely immune from economic pressure as their temple land was confiscated and they lost parishioners who henceforth chose to hold Shinto or independent funerals. In many regions, temples of the Shingon and Tendai schools bore the brunt of the economic losses since many of their temples relied on the administration of shrines and the performance of prayer rites (*kitō*). However, the Zen schools also faced large numbers of temple closures. Many Rinzai and Sōtō temples had been former Tendai or Shingon temples before the sixteenth century and practiced prayer rites for *honji suijaku* deities akin to those at esoteric temples. In contrast, Jōdoshin temples were not affected as much because most had parishes.[11]

Shugendō temples disappeared completely. These temples had no funeral parishes but relied on combinatory prayer rites and the administration of shrines for their income, and were therefore indirectly forced into bankruptcy. In the Ninth Month of 1872, *shugenja* were ordered to either become Shinto priests or Buddhist clerics, officially abolishing the tradition of *shugendō*. Many, especially those who opted to become Buddhist clerics, did not survive the change and had to give up their profession as religious specialists.[12] Those who chose to become Shinto priests fared better during the transition. For example, Kichijōji, a former *shugendō* temple in Shibusawa Village at the foot of Ōyama, had become a Shingon temple but was forced to close its doors in 1873 because it had no parishioners. In contrast, the resident *shugenja* at Sennōin in nearby Yokono Village, who had served as the *bettō* for a local shrine, chose to become its head shrine priest in 1869 and survived the transition.[13] At Ōyama, we witness a similar development. While Ōyama's *shugendō* tradition had largely been eradicated in the 1660s, six *shugenja* remained in Minoge Village. Of those six, four chose to obtain Shirakawa licenses in 1868. These four ultimately survived the

Meiji transition whereas the other two who had not been as quick to adapt did not.[14]

In cases of large combinatory institutions that were the focus of pilgrimage cults, such as Ōyama and Enoshima in Sagami Province, the presence of *oshi* complicated the situation. Since *oshi* were not Buddhist clerics, they were not covered by the early Meiji legislation, but their association with Buddhist institutions or their *shugendō* heritage placed them in a heterodox category. Initially, the *oshi* were incorporated into the new order as low-ranking Shinto priests, but their profession was ultimately banned in 1872, forcing them to regroup as ministers in the Great Teaching Campaign.[15]

Ōyama, a combinatory institution with a major Shingon prayer temple and a large number of *oshi*, underwent dramatic changes during this period. A Shingon academy with thriving cults of the Buddhist deity Fudō and the *honji suijaku* deity Sekison Daigongen in the early modern period, it became a dual site at which a new form of "pure" Shinto dominated the mountain, and its Buddhist component was marginalized. A comparison of a print from the 1880s of the new Shinto inner sanctum and worship hall with a print from the 1830s of its combinatory predecessor, the Main Hall dedicated to Fudō, illustrates the complete transformation of Ōyama (see Figs. 1.10 and 7.1). The print from the Meiji period showing the new Shinto structures bears no direct sign of the former Buddhist structures, but the basic layout had been preserved: many of the central Buddhist buildings had simply been replaced by Shinto ones that served similar purposes. The Tower Gate and a basin for ritual cleansing had been replaced by a Shinto *torii* gate and Shinto-style purification basin. The Main Hall had become a Shinto-style worship hall and surrounded by a Shinto-style fence. The three *honji suijaku* shrines behind the main hall—a joint shrine of Sannō Gongen, Shinmyō, and Kumano Gongen; a joint shrine of Myōō Gongen, Sekison, and Kashima; and a joint shrine of Sengen, Zaō Gongen, and Bishamon-ten—had been Shintoized to become a Hie Shrine, the inner sanctuary (*hon-den*), and a Sengen Shrine surrounded by a Shinto-style fence. A residential building had been added to the right of the worship hall in place of the monastic residential complex (see Fig. 7.1). The treasure hall had been turned into a storehouse, and the bell tower had been moved and replaced by a drum tower. There were few significant changes to the way the space was organized except for the new fence surrounding the worship hall and the shrines behind it, a sign that the divine had been symbolically become more remote—or, as Basil Chamberlain and William Benjamin Mason had it, more "obscure."[16] There was one other structural alteration to indicate changes in access to the divine: the votive picture hall had been moved from the summit entrance to the open space in front of the worship hall. During the early modern period, the summit was closed to women and others considered ritually impure; therefore, the votive picture hall beside the entrance to the path to the summit doubled as a place to worship Ōyama's shrines on the summit from afar. During the Meiji transformation, the summit was made accessible to all pilgrims regardless of their gender. Thus a hall to worship the deities from afar was no longer needed.

How did this transformation take place? During the first six years of the Meiji period, Ōyama witnessed a disassociation of *kami* and Buddhas under the leadership of the head shrine priest Ōyama Isamu, a former Shingon cleric at Hachidaibō, the most important Buddhist temple on Ōyama during the early modern period. The disassociation at Ōyama was severe but did not lead to wanton destruction. It established distinct Shinto and Buddhist spheres, despite initial plans to remove Buddhism completely from the site. Ultimately a new system emerged, modeled indirectly on the old system by maintaining the spatial and ritual frameworks. What occurred at Ōyama demonstrates not only the changes brought by the disassociation of *kami* and Buddhas, which created a fundamentally new basis for Japanese religions, but also the shrine's considerable continuity with its premodern roots. Ōyama's institutional structures developed under Tokugawa rule were tenacious and beneficial to its various components. While some radicals may have resented the old system, it ultimately created a stable balance. When this balance was dislodged, multiple conflicts occurred that eventually led to the reincorporation of crucial elements of the earlier system.

The Oshi *during the* Bakumatsu *Era and the Restoration*

To understand the context of the disassociation of *kami* and Buddhas at Ōyama, we have to recall the conditions at Ōyama during the *bakumatsu* period. Many *oshi* had profited from the status quo and had enjoyed a

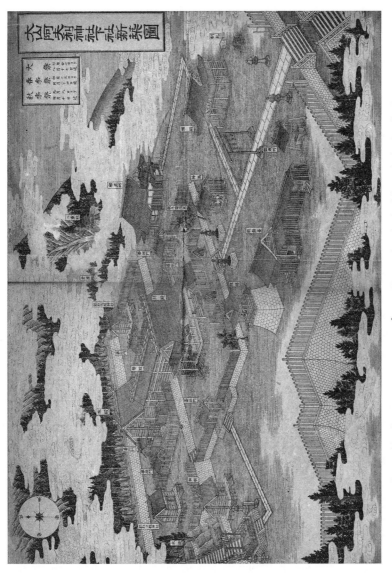

Fig. 7.1 Tenaka Myōtarō Kagemoto, *Ōyama Afurijinja shimosha shinchiku zu*. Author's collection.

good relationship with the Shingon clergy, some even serving as clergy-appointed village officials or managing parishes in the clerics' stead. Yet the financial, institutional, and political tensions on local and national levels during the last decade of the early modern period led to social ferment among a segment of wealthy *oshi*. They had sought to gain official recognition for their Shirakawa licenses from the Shingon clergy in the early 1850s but failed to do so until 1865. Exacerbating the situation was the discontent voiced by Nativist *oshi*, who demanded the re-institution of an orthodox Shinto priesthood, of orthodox Shinto ritual based on the *Engi shiki*, and of orthodox Shinto deities lifted from the pages of the *Kojiki* (i.e., Ōyamazumi no Kami, Takaokami no Kami, and Ōikazuchi no Kami).

The most outspoken member of the Nativist *oshi*, Sudō Shigeo, fiercely criticized the Buddhist monopoly over the rites held at Ōyama and envisioned a different ritual cycle in his *Afurijinja kodenkō*. Sudō had no interest in dividing the rituals of the Shingon clergy and the *oshi* into complementary spheres. He pointed out that the Afuri Shrine appeared in the *Engi shiki* among the list of shrines worshiped by the ancient imperial court during the *toshigoi* festival on 2/4. According to the scholarship of Kamo no Mabuchi (1697–1769) and Motoori Norinaga (1730–1801), he explained, this rite was a festival to mark the beginning of the rice-planting season each year. Citing the *Engi shiki*, he discussed at length the seating arrangement of the officials of the Department of Divinity, the prayers recited by the shrine priests, and the cloth offerings made by the provincial governors. This kind of ritual, he pointed out, was of utmost antiquity, dating back to Emperor Sujin (r. 97–30 BC) under whom the provincial shrines began to be worshipped by the imperial court, whereas the *toshigoi* festival itself originated under Emperor Tenmu (r. 673–686). In the medieval period, Sudō argued, some of the original shrine priests at Ōyama were co-opted by Buddhism through their worship of Fudō (installed by the conniving Buddhist clergy) and became *yamabushi* but still maintained the authentic ritual calendar, celebrating the primary festival during the Second Month. The Shingon clergy eventually displaced them, took over the site under the Tokugawa, and wasted their time performing *kitō* rituals for good harvests instead of for funerals, as they were supposed to. A sacred-tree rite practiced by the *yamabushi* during the Second Month was gradually replaced by a tamer rite that consisted of offerings of rice and rice wine, a *mikoshi* parade, and Buddhist rites performed by the Shingon clergy. The clergy also changed the date of the festival from the fourth to the 28th of the Second Month, i.e., Fudō's *ennichi*. This led Sudō to lament: "Why do they not long to reestablish the old shrine rituals, which have declined? . . . Will there be a time when the ancient ritual prayers and the true festival will be reinstated? What a shame!" He believed that only the great festival during the Seventh Month, even though the Shingon clergy had also altered its original dates, had preserved some of the authentic rituals, such as a divination ritual performed for pilgrims by a peasant in the employ of the Shingon clergy.[17]

In this situation, Sudō proposed to restore the original rituals by turning to observances held by other shrines in the region. He pointed to the festival celebrated in Kokufu Village (Yurugi District, Sagami Province), which involved a gathering of the *mikoshi* of the Ichinomiya (Kōza), Ninomiya (Yurugi), Sannomiya (Ōsumi), Yonnomiya (Ōsumi), and Tsurumine Hachiman Shrine (Ōsumi) at the Rokusho Shrine on the fifth day of the Fifth Month.[18] Sudō emphasized that these were shrines of great antiquity since four of them appeared among the thirteen official provincial shrines of Sagami Province mentioned in the *Engi shiki*. Sudō assumed that another nine official shrines, including the Afuri Shrine, originally participated in the festival but were eventually excluded. He urged his readers: "One ought to study the festival of Kokufu Village with great care."[19] His strong anti-Buddhist critique clearly foreshadowed efforts after the Meiji Restoration to separate Buddhism and Shinto in order to recover a pure form of Shinto.

What made the situation at Ōyama particularly volatile during the Meiji restoration was that a Nativist group of *oshi* was militantly supportive of the new regime even though, presumably, many *oshi* were content with and profited from the old early modern system. Comparable strong support for the new regime was found at other important sacred sites in Japan such as Mt. Hiko and the Suwa Shrine where some religionists spurred by Hirata Nativism supplied military assistance during the Boshin War (1868–1869).[20] Similarly, Ōyama's *oshi* established contact with the imperial forces, provided financial support, and even formed a small military unit, which they called *jingitai* (Divinity Corps). The corps' name reflected its composition of members with priestly backgrounds, many of whom were connected with the Shirakawa house or the Hirata school of Nativism.[21] For four months, it served on guard duty in Edo and to rout hidden *bakufu* forces in the Kantō region owing to its members' detailed knowledge of the terrain gained through their parish rounds. The strong Shirakawa-Hirata background and military ambitions of these politically active *oshi* created an effective force that was to play an important role during the process of restructuring Ōyama over the next few years.[22] Unlike Ōyama's Shingon clergy, who did not endorse the new regime, these radical *oshi* displayed enthusiastic support for the imperial restoration and were rewarded when the new regime initially backed them in their attempts to transform Ōyama into a Shinto institution. From 1869, once decisions were no longer approved by the central government in Tōkyō but by regional judicial courts in Yokohama, the radicals would find less sympathy from the regional administration, which was more concerned with maintaining public order than with purging Buddhism from a newly established Shinto site.

Dismantling the Buddhist Institutions

The decree to disassociate *kami* and Buddhas in 1868 had complex implications for the Ōyama cult. Although Ōyama did not suffer the most violent kind of disassociation but a moderate one, the site and its cult changed dramatically. Its Shingon Buddhist temples lost control over the shrines on the summit and the primary cultic site on the mountain slope. The loss in income previously derived from the management of the site—in the case of Hachidaibō and its subtemples, on the mountain, and from local parishes; and in the case of the small parish temples, at the foot of the mountain—forced the Shingon temples to close or merge into a single temple. Simultaneously, a new Shinto priesthood emerged that was independent from its Buddhist predecessors and took on the task of site management. Despite Ōyama's firm place in the Shingon establishment as a regional academy during the early modern period, the new Meiji regime never considered the possibility that Ōyama should remain a Buddhist institution. Other equally combinatory sites with Buddhist ties such as Daiyūzan, a sacred mountain in western Sagami Province, were able to maintain their Buddhist affiliation. In contrast, Ōyama was ordered to become a Shinto institution. To justify the decision for this conversion, the authorities cited the *Engi shiki*. Since the *Engi shiki* listed the Afuri Shrine, another name for the Sekison Shrine on Ōyama's summit, as a provincial shrine, and since there was no reliable historical evidence indicating that Ōyama's Buddhist temples existed before the tenth century, it was easy to argue that the site had originally been Shinto—even though the *Engi shiki* did not explicitly state this.

Although it was never questioned whether Ōyama should become Shinto, the unclear terms of the disassociation left a number of important questions unsolved. First, after the Shingon clergy had relinquished their control over Ōyama's shrines, what was to happen to the cult of Fudō and to the Buddhist clerics who had trained on the mountain? Second, once all 150 *oshi* became Shinto priests, who was to determine a hierarchy among them? Third, what rituals were to be celebrated and what deities were to be worshipped at the new shrine once all traces of Buddhism were removed? These questions presented difficult challenges and caused much conflict during the first six years of the Meiji period.

Ultimately, the early reforms were still limited. Although significant changes took place in this early period, they were often superficial, consisting of symbolic renaming rather than profound structural changes in religious institutions. There was, in fact, equally strong opposition to far-reaching reforms from many former *oshi*. Moreover, in the years immediately after the imperial restoration and the disassociation of *kami* and Buddhas, the reforms at Ōyama focused on the primary sacred site—its rituals, deities, institutions, and finances—and the ranking of former *oshi* who had suddenly become shrine priests (*negi*). There were few changes to the regional manifestations of the Ōyama cult in *oshi* parishes and confraternities in the Kantō region.

Changing a combinatory site into a predominantly Shinto site was a complex process of transformation that took several years to implement. The first six months after the restoration were marked by continued unrest and anxiety during which an organized transformation of Ōyama was impossible. The power of the Hachidaibō abbot was at a nadir at the time of the Meiji restoration. Yet another new abbot, Jitsujō, had been appointed in the Third Month of 1868.[23] As a youth, Jitsujō had been ordained at another Shingon academy in Sagami Province, where he remained until he was a young man, but had spent eighteen years on Mt. Kōya before returning to Sagami Province as Ōyama's new abbot.[24] A newcomer to Ōyama, he was unable to mount effective resistance against the disassociation of *kami* and Buddhas when the new Meiji regime issued its orders in the month of his appointment. At the end of the intercalary Fourth Month of 1868, the abbot and four other senior clerics were summoned to Edo and received orders to relinquish control of the Sekison Shrine. The authorities argued that it was one of 2,861 shrines that appeared in the *Engi shiki* and therefore ought to be administered by a head shrine priest (*kannushi*) rather than a Buddhist cleric. Furthermore, the clerics were told to evacuate their temples on the mountainside, remove images of Fudō, and move to the foot of the mountain. They also lost control over the shrines on Ōyama's slope and most of Ōyama's temple land—100 *koku* on the mountain and in Sakamoto Village—but were allowed to keep 57 *koku* that had once been granted to the Hachidaibō abbot as a personal stipend. The clerics were much alarmed by the news.[25] Immediately after the clerics' return to Ōyama, in the beginning of the Fifth Month, village officials appointed by Hachidaibō turned in their seals, indicating that the Buddhist temples had lost their power to confer authority. Simultaneously, the clerics began to send Buddhist statues as well as their belongings to small temples in the region to which they had some connection.[26]

However, when the clerics attempted to transfer Ōyama Fudō away from the mountain, several hundred residents from Sakamoto Village and neighboring villages mounted physical resistance and petitioned the authorities to have Fudō stay at Ōyama or move the image to another village at the foot of Ōyama on Hachidaibō's remaining temple land. This land had not been confiscated by the restoration authorities because it had originally been awarded to the Hachidaibō abbot as a personal stipend rather than to Ōyama's Shingon temples as a whole.[27] In the meantime, the image was temporarily housed on the border between Sakamoto Village and neighboring Koyasu Village, while Ōyama's Shingon temples were merged into one single temple named Myōōji in honor of Fudō Myōō.[28] Unlike at other sites, such as Mt. Haguro and Suwa, there are no references that the Ōyama resistance was based on fears of divine retribution or that there was any resistance against the dismantling of the Buddhist precinct.[29] Instead, any form of resistance was based on economic motivations: the villagers did not want to lose pilgrimage business through the months outside the summer festival.[30]

The following three months brought little relief for the anxieties of the clergy and villagers as the fighting continued between the imperial forces and pockets of masterless samurai, who, on occasion, also strayed into Sakamoto Village and were confronted by armed village leaders.[31] In this volatile climate, anything seemed possible. Before long, an *oshi* started a rumor in the Fifth Month that the village leadership, with ties to the militarized unit supporting the imperial forces, was planning to assassinate the abbot and another cleric. The rumor proved to be unfounded two months later, but at the time it was deemed credible enough to send Ōyama's clerics scurrying to neighboring Hinata Village to escape harm.[32] It was not until the end of the Ninth Month that order was reestablished at Ōyama when the Hachidaibō abbot returned from Tokyo, the new name of Edo. There he had arranged for the merging of Ōyama's Shingon temples and for the appointment of a laicized disciple as head shrine priest. The Shingon clergy greeted the news with displeasure, but, eventually, the Hachidaibō abbot and five former *oshi* who claimed to represent the Afuri Shrine reached an agreement in the Tenth Month of 1868:

1) Ōyamadera was to be renamed Afurijinja because that was the name that appeared in the *Engi shiki*.

2) Seijun, a disciple of the Hachidaibō abbot, was to be laicized and take the new name Ōyama Isamu so that he could serve as head shrine priest.

3) The *oshi* were to be renamed shrine priests.

4) Ōyama Isamu and the shrine priests should hold Shinto funerals for their families.

5) The shrine priests should collect donations from the main shrine, adjacent shrines, and branch shrines.

6) Only Shinto rituals were to be celebrated.

7) All Buddhist statues and implements, including Ōyama Fudō, were to be removed.[33]

These resolutions were the first steps of an arrangement that went beyond the dismantling of Buddhist institutions to envision the formation of Ōyama as a Shinto institution, but numerous issues complicated their implementation.

The location of Ōyama Fudō posed a lingering problem. Early in 1869, nearby villages petitioned the newly established prefectural authorities in Yokohama to have Fudō enshrined on Ōyama proper and so ensure a continuous flow of pilgrims throughout the year, not just during the summer festival. As a result, Fudō and the Buddhist temple Myōōji were moved to the lower slopes of Ōyama in the early summer of 1869.[34] In return for allowing the Buddhist clergy back onto the mountain, the clerics and shrine priests reached an agreement whereby the Buddhist temples fully recognized that their place on the mountain was limited to the area around the former Hachidaibō branch temple Raigōin and that the former location of the Fudō's Main Hall was shrine land.[35] By the end of the 1869, lumber from the former Buddhist temple complex had been sold off, but the cleanup lasted well into 1870.[36] The formal construction of a permanent hall for Fudō would take many years, lasting from 1876 to 1884.[37]

The Creation of New Shinto Institutions

As Ōyama's Buddhist institutions were demolished during the disassociation of *kami* and Buddhas, Ōyama's *oshi* became the priests of the Afuri Shrine. During the first stages of the disassociation, while the Hachidaibō abbot was still in Edo in the intercalary Fourth Month of 1868, rumors of the laicization of Buddhist clerics in charge of small shrines in nearby villages and even of Kōya *hijiri* drifted into Sakamoto Village. To assure the bewildered *oshi* of the veracity of the news, the holders of Shirakawa licenses convened a meeting. The organizers included six *oshi*, three of whom had ties to the *jingitai*, the military unit supporting the imperial forces. Around the same time, five *oshi* decided to renounce their Buddhist-inspired *oshi* names and adopt lay names, beginning the process of the *oshi*'s clear disassociation from the Buddhist institutions at Ōyama.[38] During the chaotic summer months, the *oshi* had little opportunity to form a full-fledged Shinto priesthood. They did, however, maintain contact with the Shirakawa in Kyoto.[39] The architects of the disassociation of the *kami* and Buddhas, Kamei Koremi (1824–1885) and Fukuba Bisei (1831–1907), who were influenced by the teachings of the Nativist Ōkuni Takamasa (1792–1871), were at odds with the Yoshida and Shirakawa Shinto leadership as well as with the leaders of the Hirata school.[40] On the local level, however, their policies were supported and even implemented by Hirata adherents and, at least initially, by shrine priests licensed by the Shirakawa as well.

As mentioned above, the first concrete steps to establish a Shinto priesthood were taken in the Ninth and Tenth Months of 1868 when all former *oshi* became shrine priests (*negi*) following negotiations involving the new regime in Edo, Ōyama's Buddhist establishment, and pro-Shinto Nativists and Shinto priests at Ōyama.[41] The Hachidaibō abbot's disciple, Seijun, who took the name Ōyama Isamu, occupied the office of the head shrine priest (*kannushi*). Ōyama Isamu, who knew little about Shinto rites, apparently proceeded to study rituals with an outsider called Ōki Gen'ichirō. He also married the daughter of Fukuhara Jōjirō, a former Tokugawa vassal from Edo who had come to Ōyama with Jitsujō, and made him his deputy.[42] Led by the head shrine priest and by holders of Shirakawa licenses, the priests determined how the income of the Afuri Shrine was to be distributed and set its new ritual calendar. Even though the income was now divided among all shrine priests rather than being monopolized by the Shingon clergy, the head shrine priest received the largest individual share. A small sum from the donations at the shrines on the summit was set aside for repairs. The rest of the donations at the shrines on the mountain and the income from the summer festival were divided among the shrine priests, but again the head shrine priest took the largest portion.[43] The head shrine priest was also given an important role in central rituals, the calendar of which was essentially derived from Buddhist observances in the early modern period.[44]

According to the *Meiji ishin shinbutsu bunri shiryō*, there was considerable antipathy against Ōyama Isamu and Fukuhara Jōjirō amongst the *oshi*. However, documents from the early Meiji years contain no indication of much resistance existing against the two.[45] If there was discontent, it was spread among different groups of shrine priests—those who sought to gain advantage from their new status and those who feared losing their old rank. The new system recognized all former *oshi* as shrine priests. This created a new problem, namely how to resolve the hierarchical organization of the shrine priests. In the Eleventh Month of 1868, the leaders among the shrine priests established seven ranks for priests at the Afuri Shrine, creating a new system of ritual authority. This was vastly different from the three-tiered system of upper-, medium-, and lower-level *oshi* in the early modern period. Even though the system left room for advancement through the purchase of rank, it met with resistance from former *oshi* who suddenly saw them-

selves deprived of their rightful rank and believed that the new system
unfairly favored those with financial means.[46] Incidentally, the opposition was formed by the same former *oshi* who had accused several
other *oshi* of belonging to the Shirakawa faction, said to be planning
to murder the Hachidaibō abbot and another cleric soon in the summer
of 1868.[47] Eventually, the seven ranks were abolished by order of the
prefectural authorities in Yokohama in the summer of 1869 due to
pressure from shrine priests opposed to the new system. In their place,
the shrine priests adopted a three-tiered system that was derived from
the ranking system used by the Shingon clergy to distinguish among
oshi during the early modern period. Soon after, the shrine priests who
had held Shirakawa licenses severed their ties with the Shirakawa.[48]

Ōyama's shrine priests had to take one more step to become fully
independent of the Buddhist clergy. Even though shrine priests had
been ordered to hold Shinto funerals beginning in the Tenth Month
of 1868, this was not fully enacted at the Afuri Shrine until the spring
of 1870 when the Jōdo temple Saiganji, one of several parish temples in
Sakamoto Village, acknowledged that fourteen shrine priests who had
been former parishioners would hold Shinto funerals in compliance
with the order by the Department of Divinity and would henceforth
set up new tombstones with posthumous Shinto names.[49] Why did
Saiganji take this long to recognize Shinto funerals for its shrine-priest
parishioners? The reasons for this lay in the fluidity of the definition
of an *oshi*, the predecessor of the shrine priest (*negi*). Some villagers
in Sakamoto Village had been artisans and merchants who over the
years had acquired *oshi* licenses through purchase, adoption, or by
receiving them from the Shingon clergy, but they continued their prior
profession in addition to acting as *oshi*. Many of these artisan-*oshi*
or merchant-*oshi* appear to have been parishioners of two Jōdo temples
in Sakamoto Village, Saiganji and Saigōji, whereas full *oshi* tended to be
parishioners of the two Shingon village temples, Kannonji and Raigōin.
When all Ōyama's *oshi* became shrine priests, it was unclear whether
those acting in dual roles should be counted as ordinary townspeople
or as shrine priests, a decision that would determine which type of
funeral their families observed for them. The question remained unresolved until the spring of 1870 when these artisan-shrine/merchant-
shrine priest families were made to decide which of their two pro-

fessions they would choose. Some families decided to split into two branches: one categorized as townspeople and another registered as shrine priests. One such family was that of the Ōyama Shrine carpenter, who bore the hereditary name Tenaka Myōōtarō for carpenters and the hereditary name Ogawa Ranbutsu for *oshi*. In the Fifth Month of 1870, the head of the family, Kagemoto, retained the carpenterial name, Tenaka Myōōtarō, and remained affiliated with his Buddhist temple but gave up his duties as an innkeeper. His eldest son, Chiyotarō Kagechika, who had succeeded him as an *oshi*, turned shrine priest three months earlier, kept the former *oshi* parish and inn, took the name Ogawa Kiyoto, and severed his connection with his Jōdo parish temple, Saigōji.[50]

Ōyama's physical reconstruction as a Shinto shrine also took nearly half a decade to complete. In 1869, the precinct was redesigned spatially to reflect its new Shinto orientation. First, the shrines on the summit were given Shinto names. Henceforth, "orthodox" Shinto deities lifted from the pages of the *Kojiki* were worshipped at the shrines instead of the previous *honji suijaku gongen* and *tengu* deities.[51] In accordance with these physical changes, talismans were redesigned to bear the new Shinto names. Second, the temporary worship hall on the central slope was moved forward to a more central position. Third, *shintai*, objects in which Shinto divinities were said to reside, were placed in enclosed receptacles to conceal them from the view of ordinary humans. Finally, Rōbendaki, a waterfall named after the Buddhist founder of Ōyamadera, was renamed Suwa no Taki in reference to the Suwa Shrine in Nagano Prefecture, which had likewise undergone the process of disassociation to become a Shinto shrine. In this way, all major landmarks on Ōyama were given a new Shinto identity. The mountain itself was no longer a Buddhist precinct now that the Shingon Buddhist clergy was limited to only one temple in a small section on the lower slopes. Nor did this temple have the status of a Shingon academy.

In this new environment, the notion of barring women from having full access to Ōyama's deities became outmoded. During the early modern period, the ban on women was not maintained simply due to the belief that women were ritually impure, but it was also closely linked with Buddhist supremacy over the mountain and had served as a means to ensure moral behavior among the monks in training. Without the presence of a Buddhist academy, there was no need to keep women pilgrims out. Hence the new Shinto priesthood requested permission for women to climb to the summit from the prefecture. Whether the petition was granted at the time is unclear, but the general prohibition against women entering sacred ground was lifted—not just at Ōyama— by the Great Council of State in March 1872.[52] The Meiji regime issued orders to lift the ban against women on sacred mountains in conjunction with the 1872 Exhibition of Arts and Manufacturers in Kyoto so that foreign tourists who had come to Japan for the exposition could enjoy hiking in mountains around Kyoto.[53]

The final stage in the site's Shinto transformation concluded with the construction of the Afuri Shrine's cultic center. Between May 1873 and April 1874, a new inner sanctuary and worship hall were built in the former location of the Main Hall.[54] During this period, Ōyama Isamu, the former Shingon monk turned head shrine priest, was replaced by Gonda Naosuke, the physician and Nativist scholar in the Hirata school, in August 1873. Gonda would eventually transform the Ōyama cult into a Sect Shinto organization, Ōyama Keishin Kōsha, by centralizing the parishes of Ōyama's former *oshi*, who then served not just as Shinto priests (*negi*) but also first as state propagandists (*kyōdōshoku*) and then as ministers (*sendōshi*) for Ōyama Keishin Kōsha.[55] Similar developments occurred at other famous mountain sites throughout Japan, such as the Kotohira Shrine in Shikoku (formerly known as Mt. Konpira), the Ideha Shrine on Mt. Haguro in the northeast, and Mt. Hiko in Kyūshū, where new head shrine priests, often of Nativist stock, were appointed by the government to oversee the full removal of Buddhist remnants at the site and organize affiliated pilgrimage associations into patriotic movements in conjunction with the Great Teaching Campaign.[56]

The replacement of Ōyama Isamu by Gonda Naosuke was occasioned by changes in the ways shrine priests were selected for their posts and came at a time when the livelihood of the former *oshi* at Ōyama was threatened. In June 1871, the Dajōkan stripped shrine priests of their hereditary rights and made them subject to appointment by local governments. Even more alarming, in October 1871, the Dajōkan also officially prohibited the practice of collecting funds on parish rounds.[57] Extant records indicate that until the prohibition, Ōyama's innkeeper-proselytizers had continued this practice, which had become an integral

part of their yearly activities in the early modern period.[58] As the fore-
going chapters have demonstrated, parish rounds not only provided
a necessary source of income but also served as a means to maintain
bonds with parishioners who would stay at their *oshi*'s inn on their
pilgrimages to Ōyama. The abolition of the practice seriously undermined the ability of Ōyama's innkeepers to collect donations and ensure
the continued flow of pilgrims. The innkeepers indeed appear to have
observed the order because no references to parish rounds after 1871
exist. The marked decline in the number of *oshi*—and their successors
the *sendōshi*—is perhaps the most telling evidence for the impact of the
Great Council of State's policy.

In the early Meiji period, the number of innkeeper-proselytizers
declined dramatically. Even though a slight decline had already begun
in the 1830s, years that were marked by natural disasters such as the
Great Fire in 1855 and by political turmoil, the sharpest decline took
place between 1871 and 1877, after the prohibition of parish rounds and
before the reorganization of the former *oshi* system into a Sect Shinto
organization under Gonda, which eventually allowed the numbers to
stabilize between 1883 and 1904.[59] In this situation, the former *oshi*
were desperate to develop new strategies to maintain contact with their
former parishioners in the Kantō region. The Great Teaching Campaign of 1870 to 1884 presented an opportunity for legal proselytization.
However, the young head shrine priest of the Afuri Shrine, Ōyama
Isamu, lacked leadership skills and stature, whereas Gonda possessed
the learning and seniority necessary to assure Ōyama a prominent position in the campaign.

Gonda Naosuke and the Great Teaching Campaign

The ultimate transformation of Ōyama into a Sect Shinto organization
would fall to Gonda, appointed in 1873 to replace Ōyama Isamu and
spearhead the efforts of the Afuri Shrine in the Great Teaching Campaign. After a prolific career as a physician in Chinese and Japanese
medicine and having been a strong supporter of the imperial cause
in the *bakumatsu* period, Gonda gave up his medical practice in the early
1870s when Chinese and Japanese medicine were losing their popularity. Around the same time, he temporarily incurred disfavor with
the authorities because of his political activism. Gonda spent his last

years at Ōyama engaging in activities as a scholar of Japanese literature with a successful career in the Shinto establishments of Kanagawa and Shizuoka Prefectures. In 1858, Gonda first made contact with an Ōyama *oshi* who happened to be a fellow member of the Hirata school and was eventually recruited to serve as head shrine priest by two other *oshi* who were former members of the pro-imperialist military corps. One was also a Hirata school member.[60]

During his fourteen years at Ōyama, Gonda completed its transformation into a major regional Shinto site by establishing a center for Shinto learning and extended the restructuring process to Ōyama's parishes, *kō*, and pilgrimage routes across the Kantō. He advanced Ōyama's ritual life and institutional outreach to the larger Kantō region and remained a prolific writer, composing works on Japanese literature and linguistics, Shinto prayers, Shinto funerary and offertory rituals, Shinto posthumous names, and the nature of the soul. He became involved in the Great Teaching Campaign and the propagational efforts of its Shinto successor, the Shintō Jimukyoku (Office of Shinto Affairs), and eventually taught at a central institution for Shinto learning in Tokyo, the Kōten Kōkyūsho (Research Institute for the Imperial Classics), which later became Kokugakuin University.[61]

Immediately after Gonda's appointment, the Afuri Shrine was integrated into the new national hierarchy of Shinto shrines. It was named a prefectural shrine, the highest rank among civic shrines.[62] Ultimately, three other shrines in former Sagami Province gained the same rank.[63] The new Shinto hierarchy placed the Ise Shrines on the top of the pyramid and beneath it government shrines (including imperial shrines [*kanpeisha*] and national shrines [*kokuheisha*] funded by the central government), civic shrines (prefectural, district, town, village, and unranked shrines eligible for funding by prefectural, district, or municipal governments, respectively), and newly founded special shrines (*bekkakusha*). As a civic shrine on the prefectural level, the Afuri Shrine was to receive financial support from the prefectural government, which had to dispatch a representative to present offerings.[64] Yet Ōyama had a much better financial resource in its parishes throughout the Kantō-Tōkai region. Under Gonda's direction and through experience gained in the Great Teaching Campaign, the Afuri Shrine developed into the headquarters of a large Sect Shinto organization that comprised former *oshi* parishes.

Gonda became deeply involved the regional Great Teaching Campaign once he arrived at the Afuri Shrine in 1873. Between 1870 and 1875, the campaign was conducted by Shinto priests, Buddhist clerics from all sects, and a variety of performers. The goal of the campaign was to instill the Japanese with a trans-sectarian national faith based on emperor veneration, patriotism, and reverence for the gods. The campaign was initially begun under the Jingikan, but from 1872, after the dissolution of the Jingishō, it was headed by its own central organ in Tokyo, the Taikyōin, and carried out on regional and local levels by branch offices, the Chūkyōin and Shōkyōin.[65] The campaign gave the *oshi* an opportunity to continue their existence as religious professionals in the form of state propagandists (*kyōdōshoku*) after the official prohibition against parish rounds. Through Gonda and the vice chief priest of the Afuri Shrine, Sudō Shigeo, as well as the Myōōji abbot, Jitsujō, Ōyama emerged as an important force in the regional campaign. In August 1873, around the time he became chief priest (*gūji*) of the Afuri Shrine, Gonda was also appointed *daikōgi* (Great Lecturer).[66] In January 1874, he was selected as the Shinto leader of the regional campaign office at the Matsubara Shrine in Odawara, also a prefectural shrine.[67] Gonda continued to rise in the hierarchy of the campaign until it began to crumble in 1875 due to irreconcilable differences among its diverse participants. After the Buddhist clerics withdrew from the campaign in 1875, it became an effort to preach Shinto as the national faith.[68]

After 1875, Gonda furthered Ōyama's standing as a regional Shinto center. He was appointed *gonshō kyōshō* (vice junior doctrinal director) in 1875 by the Shintō Jimukyoku (Office of Shinto Affairs), a central Shinto organ derived from the Taikyōin after the latter's demise in 1875.[69] In December 1876, Ōyama became the regional branch of the Shintō Jimukyoku of Ashigara Prefecture, previously located in Odawara, and Gonda was appointed as its new head.[70] The selection of the Afuri Shrine over the Matsubara Shrine indicates its growing prominence as the foremost Shinto institution in the region at the time. Gonda also established a school for the regional branch of the Shintō Jimukyoku at the Afuri Shrine in April 1877, for which he acted as supervisor.[71] In November 1879, Gonda was also appointed chief priest of the Mishima Taisha in Izu, which was ranked as an imperial shrine and happened to be dedicated to Ōyamazumi no Kami, just like the Afuri Shrine. The arrangement forced Gonda to split his time between both shrines for the next two years until he left his post at the Mishima Taisha and settled down at Ōyama in 1881.[72] Once Ōyama had been recognized as a regional center for the dissemination of Shinto, Gonda rose quickly through the ranks, finally becoming Great Doctrinal Director (*daikyōshō*) and member of the Shintō Jimukyoku's advisory commission in 1883. After the dissolution of this body later in 1883, he became head of the editing division of the Shintō Honkyoku (Shinto Head Office), founded by Inaba Masakuni (1834–98) as an umbrella organization within Sect Shinto. Like Gonda, Inaba was a Hirata Nativist and hoped to continue the objectives of the campaign even after it had officially ended. He had been appointed the head priest of the Mishima Taisha in Shizuoka, where Gonda had also served in addition to his appointment at Ōyama.[73] In keeping with the Great Teaching Campaign, Gonda had an interest in the veneration of the Japanese emperor, nation, and deities along with Confucian ethics of filial piety and obedience. His *Kokoro no hashira* (1871), which advocated veneration of the emperor and the native gods in order to maintain peace and harmony for the family and the nation, became a textbook for the Shintō Jimukyoku and the Shintō Honkyoku.

Even though Gonda was highly active within new Shinto organizations, he also found the time to reshape Ōyama's ritual life. As a prolific writer, he made use of his literary background to complete this task. In his *Shinkyō kafu* (1881), he created Shinto ritual music devoid of Buddhist influences by selecting suitable Japanese poems (*waka*) on the teachings of the *kami* and adding a melody and percussion to them. His songs were intended for recitation at gatherings in Sakamoto Village and in Ōyama confraternities.[74] His *Saiten shūrei kogoto* (1886) and *Saiten shūrei shiki* (1886) contained concrete instructions for rituals to be held at the Afuri Shrine, such as regulations for priests regarding seating arrangements and their movements during rituals, ritual prayers during the summer festival, offerings to the deities, and *tenaga* rites. He also devised new festivals, such as the Fire Pacification Festival, Spirit Pacification Festival, and Rice Gruel Festival.[75] Through these means, Gonda attempted to create Shinto rituals for the Afuri Shrine that did not rely on Buddhist precedents.

Gonda sought to reform rituals held not only at the shrine but also in individual shrine-priest households. He advocated daily prayers to

Afuri Shrine's deities, Amaterasu; local tutelary deities; and the family ancestors in his *Maiasa shinpai norito*. Moreover, he authored works dealing with posthumous names and rituals for the memorialization of the deceased, including the *Shigōkō* (1873)—a collection of posthumous names based on the *Kojiki*, the *Nihongi*, and later records; a section of songs to be recited at funerals in the *Shinkyō kafu*; daily prayers to the ancestral spirits; and the *Sōgishiki* (1887), a two-volume work explaining the meaning behind funeral rituals and giving concrete instructions on how to perform a funeral, send off the spirit of the deceased, prepare the grave site, and bestow posthumous names.[76]

Burdened with multiple appointments and responsibilities, Gonda could hardly have managed the Afuri Shrine on his own and relied on other shrine priests and local followers to carry out his reforms. First, Gonda was supported by several high-ranking priests at the Afuri Shrine, such as Sudō Shigeo and Kanzaki Tomoe, who had obtained Shirakawa licenses and had become members of the Hirata school like Gonda. Second, Gonda developed a following of disciples at Ōyama soon after his appointment. In 1874, seventeen Ōyama shrine priests became his students.[77] Another twelve became Gonda's disciples in 1885 upon the introduction of an Ōyama disciple, Masuda Inamaro, who was a shrine priest with a Shirakawa license and had been active in the *jingitai* during the Meiji restoration.[78] Most of these disciples had large parishes, averaging nearly 10,000 parishioners each and having been ranked upper-level *oshi* in the early modern period.[79] Many of these disciples belonged to households that had obtained Shirakawa licenses or had ties to the Hirata school. Even though a few belonged to families who opposed the disputed seven-rank system in the first Meiji years, most came from families who had been in favor of it. They thus came from a privileged stratum within the village elite that had long maintained political power and wealth and had sought social change at the end of the early modern period. They gave Gonda an important power base in the village, without which he would have been unable to sustain his reforms.

Gonda's credentials and appointments resemble those of fellow Hirata Nativist Nishikawa Sugao (1838–1906), who was appointed as the head priest at the Ideha Shrine at Mt. Haguro in 1873. Like Gonda at Ōyama, Nishikawa fully implemented the transition of Haguro from a combinatory complex to a distinctly Shinto site. Before his arrival, many

of the early changes after the initial disassociation had been merely superficial. Like Gonda, he oversaw Haguro's integration into the Great
Teaching Campaign and the streamlining of former parishes of mountain ascetics into a network of confraternities.[80] In contrast to Nishikawa, however, Gonda had several advantages. First, he had the support
of local Hirata Nativists at Ōyama, who had initiated his appointment.
Second, the Shingon clergy was not a significant force of opposition
at the site by the time of his appointment. Finally, the former *oshi* turned
negi had already resolved issues of internal hierarchy and distribution of
income. Therefore, he was able to avoid the kind of opposition Nishikawa encountered at Haguro.

The Emergence of Ōyama Keishin Kōsha

Gonda and the administration of the Afuri Shrine deftly used the Great
Teaching Campaign as a means to reorganize the Ōyama cult into a
Sect Shinto organization called Ōyama Keishin Kōsha. In 1877, Gonda
began to restructure Ōyama parishes and confraternities by compiling
a comprehensive register, the *Kaidōki* (Record of Providing Guidance),
which listed the parishes of all former *oshi* for the first time in Ōyama's
history. He also issued regulations to standardize the religious activities
and the organization of Ōyama *kō* as well as the pilgrimage routes to
Ōyama and their rest stops.[81] Regulations to prescribe the duties of the
sendōshi, who were the descendants of the *oshi* and became the ministers
of the organization, followed in 1881 as did regulations aimed at standardizing pilgrimage routes.[82] Due to these changes, parishes were no
longer considered independent holdings by *oshi* but units in a larger,
integrated network. The reformation into a Sect Shinto organization
also gave the former *oshi* a means to circumvent the Great Council of
State's prohibition against parish rounds. Ultimately, as they did in the
case of the disassociation of *kami* and Buddhas, the former *oshi* were
able to adapt a governmental policy that could have had disastrous consequences for the Ōyama cult to suit their local needs .

   While the category of the shrine priest, created during the disassociation of *kami* and Buddhas, had given the *oshi* a new role as officiants at
the newly established Afuri Shrine, the category of the *sendōshi* recreated
virtually the same role as that of the *oshi* as innkeeper and fund-raiser,
and combined it with the former *oshi*'s role as state propagandist. Similar

to the early modern *oshi*, who were licensed by the Shingon clergy, the modern *sendōshi* were supervised by Ōyama's primary religious institution, the Afuri Shrine. The shrine granted each *sendōshi* the exclusive claim to his parishioners as listed in the *Kaidōki*. His duties and rights included a special *sendōshi* name (equivalent to the former *oshi* name), the distribution of amulets, fundraising and the collection of *naorai* (the modern equivalent of first-fruit donations, *hatsuho*), and the handling of pilgrims and rituals carried out on their behalf, now termed *kitō* (prayers) and *ōmikagura* (sacred dance) instead of *goma* and *tenaga* service, previously provided by the Shingon clergy.[83]

However, some of Gonda's reforms had no precedent in the early modern period. The mountain codes governing the *oshi* neither limited what teachings the *oshi* could pass on to their parishioners nor were based on the assumption that an *oshi* would act in the role of a preacher. In contrast, the code issued by Gonda Naosuke and the shrine establishment clearly gave the *sendōshi* the role of a preacher but prohibited him from harboring secret teachings, which again reflects a previously non-existent concern with orthodoxy. We can assume that this rule was especially directed at *sendōshi* who refused to accept the newly established "pure Shinto" Ōyama cult and continued to propagate Buddhist beliefs. It also served as a reassurance that the organization was not going to be used as a cover for a clandestine political organization.[84]

The *Kaidōki*, compiled as the central register of all former *oshi* parishes, constitutes a valuable record that allows us for the first time to gain a sense of the spread of the Ōyama cult across the Kantō region (see Fig. 3.1). Developed from holdings accumulated by the *sendōshi*'s predecessors, the *oshi*, the holdings reflect the spread of the Ōyama cult in the early nineteenth century. The *sendōshi* had an estimated total of 930,000 confraternity households, averaging about 7,860 households per *sendōshi*.[85] The size of the organization was immense if one takes into consideration that one of two very similar organizations at the Ise Shrines, Jingūkyō, was about one-third of its size.[86] The distribution of the Ōyama cult indicates that Sagami and Musashi comprised about 40 percent of the entire affiliated households, almost equaling the entire membership of Ise's Jingūkyō. As the spearhead of the Shinto hierarchy and the most important national shrine, Ise was not as dependent as Ōyama on income from such an organization.

The confraternities were found across the Kantō and eastern Tōkai regions with Sagami at the center. Even though the total number of confraternities in some provinces, such as Musashi, was larger than in Sagami, once the density of the population and the size of the provinces are taken into consideration, Sagami emerges as the province with the highest concentration of confraternities per village and district, the lowest average for the number of members per confraternity (because each village had several confraternities), and the highest number of *sendōshi*-holding parishes per district (because virtually all *sendōshi* had confraternities in Sagami), followed by Musashi and Kazusa. As noted in Chapter 3, the most densely covered areas (Sagami, Musashi, Kazusa, and Awa) were probably the regions through which the Ōyama cult spread most early, whereas distant areas explored later (such as Iwashiro, Shimotsuke, Kōzuke, Shinano, and Tōtōmi) were shared among fewer *sendōshi* and had larger confraternities and a lower concentration of confraternities. *Sendōshi* from Sakamoto Village had confraternities in all provinces, but the confraternities of *sendōshi* from Minoge Village were concentrated in Sagami, Musashi, Izu, and Suruga and also included holdings in Kai and Shinano, due to Minoge's geographic position on the western pilgrimage route to Ōyama.[87]

The *Kaidōki* also provides information about the economic circumstances of the *sendōshi*. The *sendōshi* in Sakamoto Village fell roughly into three equal groups: 31 percent with a small number of confraternity households (1–2,999), 34 percent with a medium number of confraternity households (3,000–6,999), and 35 percent with a large number of confraternity households (over 7,000). The latter included 22 percent with an especially large number of confraternity households (over 10,000). In contrast, 60 percent of Minoge Village's *sendōshi* had a small number of confraternity households, 30 percent had a medium number, and 10 percent had a large number; none had an especially large number of confraternity households.[88] This meant that about one-third of the *sendōshi* in Sakamoto Village and two-thirds of the *sendōshi* in Minoge had only a few confraternity households and must have relied on bywork as merchants, artisans, or peasants to survive.[89]

Just as the role of the *sendōshi* was based largely on that of the *oshi*, the reorganization of Ōyama confraternities was based on the older parish system of the early modern period. Gonda made efforts to centralize and standardize this diverse and highly localized network. During the early modern period, Ōyama parishes had been administered by *oshi* while Ōyama confraternities had been organized on a local level with a local confraternity head (*kōmoto*) and perhaps several officers (*sewa'nin*). Derived from mutual savings associations (*mujinkō*), confraternities usually required contributions from their members, which were channeled into a communal fund to be used for several purposes—as a bank, as a security fund during hard times, or to cover the cost of pilgrimages. Gonda recognized the generic nature of a confraternity but also imbued his instructions with a sense of morality, admonishing members to help each other during weddings and funerals; to assist the poor, widows, and orphans; to save emergency funds in the case of famines; and to counsel members of their community who were lazy. Likewise, the structure of confraternities was adapted from early modern structures but given new names, such as *sentō* for confraternity heads and *kanji* for confraternity officers. However, Gonda's reforms also contained an important new feature: previously independent confraternities became an interconnected network (*kōsha*) modeled on a guild. Gonda ranked confraternities according to their size—large (over 100 members), medium (between 50 and 100 members), and small (below 50 members). Correspondingly, confraternity leaders were ranked by three levels—*daisentō*, *chūsentō*, and *shōsentō*—depending on the size of their confraternity. Also, these confraternities were supervised by *sendōshi* just as the *oshi* had managed their parishes, in effect equating confraternities and parishes. Furthermore, only the terms confraternity (*kō*) and association (*kessha*) were used. The term parish (*danka*), with its Buddhist connotation, disappeared and was replaced with the neutral term *mochiba* (territory).

Gonda attempted to lift the groups from a merely local context not only by standardizing their organizational hierarchy, financial practices, and social function, but also by advocating specific rituals. While the Afuri Shrine provided special prayers for safety and a good harvest, groups were to perform regular rituals on the local level: one, the daily worship of Amaterasu, the deities at the Afuri Shrine (i.e., Ōyamazumi no Kami, Takaokami no Kami, and Ikazuchi no Kami), and the groups' local tutelary deity; two, reverence for the ancestors; and, three, in case of need, healing rituals. To prevent the organization from serving as a cover for subversive political or social activities, the confraternities were ordered to avoid heretical teachings or the discussion of political matters and to encourage industriousness and harmony among their members. For Gonda, the Ōyama cult was to exceed its previous local and regional limitations and include greater national concerns related to the emperor, patriotism, and the Japanese gods. Confraternities, rather than being independent local bodies that could foster dissidence, were to be streamlined into a central organization that promoted societal and familial harmony.[90]

In a similar vein, Gonda set up a system regulating the pilgrimage routes to Ōyama, which had already developed into customary routes in the early modern period but had never received official sanction from Ōyama's religious institutions. Gonda's system was similar to inn guilds (*kōsha*) that developed in the early nineteenth century to offer travelers safe and reliable service at member inns. Such inn guilds included Naniwakō, which was said to have been founded in 1804 by Matsuya Jinshirō, a merchant from Osaka. By early nineteenth century, even inns along the Ōyama pilgrimage routes that forked off the Tōkaidō at the town of Fujisawa (via Sakamoto Village) and at Odawara (via Minoge) belonged to Naniwakō. This also included one *oshi* in Sakamoto Village, whose inn was near Ōdaki, a waterfall used by pilgrims for purification rituals.[91] Using such guilds as a model, Gonda designated specific rest and overnight stops for Ōyama Keishin confraternity members on pilgrimage to Ōyama to ensure safety and convenience during their journey along the routes that had developed during the early modern period. The inns had standardized signs to make them easy to identify. Upon producing papers identifying them as Ōyama Keishin confraternity members, pilgrims were to be provided with lodging and hospitality at reasonable rates regardless of their confraternity's ranking, but if a group had ten or more members staying at the inn, one of the confraternity's officers was to receive free lodging. The inns were to discourage confraternities from indulging in food and drink and were to report violators to their confraternity officers. The inns were to act as liaisons between the confraternity members and their *sendōshi* in case of emergencies, such as sudden illness. They were also to help recover lost items and to make arrangements with local providers of packhorses, palanquins, and *jinriki-sha* to ensure reasonable rates for transportation.[92] In addition, Gonda revised pilgrimage chants in an attempt to erase any Buddhist remnants from the Ōyama cult.[93]

To what extent were these efforts to standardize the roles of the *sendōshi* and confraternities and to integrate individual parishes and independent confraternities into a centralized organization actually implemented? The stabilization in the number of *sendōshi* after 1883 suggests that Gonda's Sect Shinto organization managed to provide a solid economic basis that sustained its ministers. Moreover, Gonda's *sendōshi* disciples occasionally introduced to Gonda new students that were teenage residents of villages where Ōyama *sendōshi* had parish holdings.[94] This indicates at least a limited appeal of Gonda and his teachings in Ōyama's Sect Shinto organization, but due to the relatively small number of students, we cannot conclude that Gonda and his teachings, which focused largely on the afterlife, were very popular with Ōyama confraternities. Despite his efforts to rid the shrine of its Buddhist influences, the summer festival originally established by the Shingon clergy remained the primary pilgrimage attraction.

This is supported by evidence from the Murayama, a former *oshi* family that became *sendōshi* under Gonda. The Murayamas' ritual calendar, *Nenjū gyōji* (1875–1892), indicates that new festivals, such as the New Year's festivities including the Hikime and Rice Gruel Festival in January, were important occasions but focused primarily on the *sendōshi*'s family. Other festivals, such as the spring festival (April 15–24) and the autumn festival (September 8–10), occupied several days, including preparations, while festivals such as the one on May 5 received about the same treatment as national holidays. By contrast, the preparations for the summer festival were much more elaborate, lasting over two weeks, longer than for any other festival during the year. The festival itself lasted three weeks and required the *sendōshi* to hire extra servants to help accommodate pilgrims. This suggests that the shrine's efforts to attract pilgrims all year round were only partially successful and that the Ōyama cult continued to revolve around its popular summer festival.[95]

Moreover, Ōyama's Shingon Buddhist institution, Myōōji, continued to exist, albeit on a smaller scale than its predecessors, with the support of pilgrims.[96] Many pilgrims continued to venerate Ōyama Fudō, which had, after all, been the focus of worship at Ōyama for several hundred years. They even continued to use the combinatory name for Ōyama's principal deity. As Basil Chamberlain and William Benjamin Mason remarked in their 1891 travel guide to Japan, pilgrims continued to be attracted to the shrine on the mountain, "although the old Buddhist objects of worship have here, as in so many other parts of the country, been replaced officially by comparatively obscure Shinto deities . . . the people of the neighboring countryside often call the mountain by the name of Sekison-san."[97] Gonda Naosuke managed to assure the survival of the Ōyama cult by adapting its old structures to a new environment but did not create the cult anew.

Conclusion

Despite the radical changes, Ōyama's early Meiji transformation demonstrates that Ōyama's early modern institutions were tenacious because they created a balance that benefited the Shingon clergy, the *oshi*, and merchants in nearby villages. Ultimately, the old structures could not be completely abolished but resurfaced on physical, institutional, and ritual levels. That it could be modified to such an extent had in itself roots in the early modern period: the development of a strong Shirakawa/Nativist faction, the weakened authority of the Hachidaibō abbot, and the unfortunate destruction of the Buddhist precinct and Sakamoto Village by an earthquake and fire in 1855, which minimized the physical need to separate Shinto and Buddhist institutions and objects of devotion. The removal of all the Buddhist chapels on the mountainside, many of which were probably donated by pilgrimage associations in the Kantō region, would have been a major task—and would probably have led to strong opposition by the descendents of the donors. Ultimately, the whole Ōyama cult was not restructured until the consolidation of former *oshi* parishes and the creation of a Sect Shinto organization in the late 1870s and 1880s. During the transformation, the central authorities provided the initial impetus and basic framework for the change much as the Tokugawa had in the early seventeenth century with the issuing of *hatto*, but the actual implementation was up to local forces who were guided less by abstract ideological ideals than by concrete socioeconomic interests. During the lengthy process of transformation after the initial phase of disassociation, they looked to regional authorities for adjudication of local disputes rather than receiving centrally organized orders. At the same time, the regional authorities in Yokohama were more concerned with maintaining order than creating a pure form of Shinto.

Ōyama had been recreated as a sacred site and given a new priesthood. The early reforms changed the face of Ōyama, but they remained limited in their effect because of their reliance on the old order. Even though the shrine priests may have been eager to take ritual duties from the Shingon clergy, they were far too diverse a group to reach a consensus to dispose of their traditional status distinctions. Hence, the new shrine-priest and *sendōshi* systems were based to a large extent on the previous *oshi* system. Likewise, the new Sect Shinto organization took as its basis *oshi* parishes and Ōyama confraternities and reorganized them into a centralized system. In addition, the residents of the villages at the foot of the mountain were not willing to part with the sacred image of Fudō that attracted so many pilgrims throughout the year. The persistent dual Buddhist and Shinto presence reflected Ōyama's heritage as a combinatory sacred site, as did its overall spatial layout. Despite such changes, modern Ōyama was not a completely modern invention but still reflected the early modern precedents of the reforms.

Yet it is undeniable that modern Ōyama was a very different institution than its predecessor in the early modern period. Early modern Ōyama, although it possessed clear boundaries of various kinds, was a completely combinatory multiplex. It was only after the disassociation of *kami* and Buddhas that there were clearly distinguishable Buddhist and Shinto spaces at Ōyama. Ōyama's slopes had become a new heterotopia that reflected the utopian ideals of the new regime, which determined what roles Shinto and Buddhism were supposed to play in society. In an expression of Shinto's presumed greater orthodoxy, the shrines occupied the summit down to the center slopes, whereas the Buddhist temple was marginalized on the lower slopes. Although both still existed at Ōyama, they had become distinct entities that constituted a dual rather than a combinatory site. The drastic change completely altered the underlying principles of the Ōyama cult and reflected profound changes in the larger religious landscape of Japan: not only did Shinto and Buddhism become such clearly separated entities for the first time in the Meiji period, but also early modern Ōyama had never been as centralized as the modern Ōyama that emerged as a Sect Shinto organization.

Epilogue

At the start of this study, I suggested that focus on a particular site or region rather than a specific religious tradition better illustrates the combinative nature of premodern religions than a study of a specific religious "tradition" and that Ōyama could serve as such a focal point. The multiple facets of this complex cult—its geographical setting, its institutional history, its pilgrimage cult, and its combinatory aspects— cut across the boundaries of religious traditions, incorporating what is currently often termed Buddhism, Shinto, and folk religion. As noted in the Introduction, Allan Grapard has made a forceful argument for the need of examining specific institutional complexes to gain a better understanding of the concrete workings of the Japanese religious land- scapes.[1] Similarly, Helen Hardacre states, "[I]n order to understand the religious life of the Edo period, it is crucial to have detailed knowl- edge of the religious institutions that provided the framework of reli- gious activity."[2] Unlike Grapard, however, this framework, she argues, should be regional rather than limited to a specific site in order to understand the "interplay of the variety of religious institutions."[3] This study has aimed to find a middle ground between these two approaches by placing a specific site, Ōyama, into regional sectarian, parishioner, and pilgrimage networks.

The case of the Ōyama cult reveals important characteristics of early modern Japanese religions. Ōyama's landscape was transformed as the mountain's role shifted from a remote retreat of anchorites to a popular pilgrimage site and sectarian academy controlled by Shingon Buddhist clerics. Regional academies became essential because of two new systems mandated by the Tokugawa regime: the head-branch temple system and the temple registration system, which made it necessary to train large numbers of clerics in the doctrines of their sects to staff the growing number of parish temples. Furthermore, the sudden centrality of Edo as the seat of the shogunate propelled Ōyama from a marginally important site into a significant regional center that attracted large numbers of pilgrims. The clergy was assisted in the management of the Ōyama's pilgrimage cult by a new type of religious professional that emerged at many pilgrimage centers during this period: the *oshi*. These *oshi* established large parishes in the Kantō region that became the economic basis for the Ōyama cult. Through the development of a parish system, Ōyama's institutions became less reliant on state patronage and land grants, which dwindled over the course of the period. This decline of state sponsorship has been interpreted by past scholars as an indicator of the decreasing importance of Buddhism during this period.

However, the vitality of the Ōyama cult demonstrates that early modern Buddhism was far from moribund or corrupt. It was not a mere instrument of the state, as has often been claimed in earlier scholarship that subscribed to the theory of the degeneration of Buddhism, first developed by Tsuji Zennosuke.[4] During the early modern period, the state did play a greater role in shaping religious institutions than in the medieval period, but the degree of the state's involvement in the affairs of religious institutions was not the same throughout the entire period. The state's involvement was greater as the new regime asserted its power during the seventeenth century and decreased once its control had been securely established. While some domains such as Mito and Okayama actively suppressed Buddhism, the *bakufu* did not pursue such a strict policy. With less money to spare as the period wore on, the *bakufu* merely ceased to provide as much financial support as it had during the seventeenth century. The early modern system was not unremittingly oppressive but gave many institutions opportunities to operate on their own terms by harnessing local and regional resources. Throughout early modern Japan there were many regional cultic sites like Ōyama, each with its unique context. Many experienced similar transformations as pilgrimage became popular everywhere in Japan, as religious institutions relied increasingly on a broad social base for their survival, and as Buddhism became a part of the daily lives of people from all walks of life for the first time in Japanese history. Since the cult relied increasingly on a broad social base for its income, Ōyama's religious institutions flourished even when the ruling elite's official patronage dwindled.

Ōyama's emergence as a popular pilgrimage destination had a profound impact on the Kantō region. As the flow of commerce and travel increased in early modern Japan through improved road and transportation networks, the pilgrimage to Ōyama also thrived, particularly because the mountain was a regional center easily accessible to pilgrims. Moreover, pilgrims traveled in confraternities, which gave villagers and townspeople an affordable means to engage in religious travel without disrupting village or neighborhood life. Hence the authorities did little to restrict the pilgrimage. Regional pilgrimages flourished throughout Japan in this period. In the Kantō region alone, other sites such as Narita Fudō, Mt. Haruna, Mt. Mitake, Mt. Takao, Mt. Akiba, Mt. Fuji, the Mishima Taisha, Enoshima, and the various temples in Kamakura attracted large numbers of pilgrims and shaped a distinct regional identity.

The case of Mt. Fuji is a particularly illustrative point of comparison. Like Ōyama, early modern Mt. Fuji was a site at which *yamabushi* and *oshi* coexisted and competed for control over pilgrims. At Mt. Fuji as at Ōyama, a number of political, geographical, and demographic factors worked in favor of the Fuji *oshi* rather than the *yamabushi*. From the medieval period to the late seventeenth century, Mt. Fuji was largely controlled by *yamabushi* who lived in Murayama on the western side of mountain. At that time, the Fuji cult was largely oriented toward the Tōkaidō and Kansai regions in the west. The *yamabushi* received the patronage of the Imagawa, who controlled Suruga Province and some of the provinces to west. However, after the defeat of Imagawa Yoshimoto (1519–1560) by Oda Nobunaga in 1560 and the takeover of the region by Takeda Shingen (1521–1573) in 1568, the Murayama *yamabushi* fell out of favor due to their close association with the defeated Imagawa. In 1679, the *yamabushi* lost control of the summit to the Sengen Shrine in Ōmiya, also located on the western side of the mountain. The westward orientation of the Fuji cult changed with the arrival of the independent ascetic Kakugyō Tōbutsu (1541–1646). Even though Kaku-

gyō secluded himself in a cave on the western slope, he remained independent of the *yamabushi* in Murayama. He soon turned his attention
toward Edo, where he gained a following due to his renown as a healer,
and his successors were of Edo merchant stock. With the growing importance of Edo, the eastern and northeastern ascents accessible from
the Kōshū Kaidō became increasingly popular. Jikigyō Miroku, Kakugyō's sixth generation successor, developed an affiliation with a Fuji
oshi in Yoshida on the northeastern side of the mountain and eventually
starved himself to death on the ascent from Yoshida in 1733. Subsequently, this route through the *oshi* settlement became particularly
popular among Fuji confraternities whereas the *yamabushi* settlement
on the western side of the mountain entered a gradual decline.[5]

However, several essential factors distinguished the Fuji *oshi* and Fuji
confraternities from their counterparts at Ōyama. They were much less
centrally organized and depended to a greater extent on self-appointed
charismatic figures, who lacked official recognition. The teachings of
Fuji confraternities had a strong egalitarian and millenial slant that emphasized world renewal, an aspect completely absent from the Ōyama
cult. Moreover, Fuji confraternities from the Edo area had to pass
through barriers along the Kōshū Kaidō and the Tōkaidō—including
the dreaded checkpoint at Hakone, which made the pilgrimage more
cumbersome and was a source of potential conflict with the authorities.
Therefore, the authorities outlawed the activities of Fuji confraternities
on ten occasions in the eighteenth and nineteenth centuries.[6] By contrast, in the case of the Ōyama cult, the symbiotic but hierarchical relationship between the Shingon clergy and the *oshi* legitimized the latter
in the eyes of the authorities and provided limits for the devotional
activities of the confraternities. Pilgrims from Edo, Musashi, and Sagami, where the Ōyama cult was particularly strong, did not have to
pass through any official barriers along the pilgrimage routes, whereas
pilgrims from Izu and the Bōsō peninsula could bypass the barriers
by opting for sea routes. Consequently, the authorities did nothing to
hinder the activities of Ōyama devotees.

Toward the end of the period, several *oshi* acquired Shirakawa Shinto
licenses, which gradually Shintoized the Ōyama cult. Ōyama was not
the only sacred site where this occurred. *Oshi* at Mt. Fuji, Mt. Mitake,
and Enoshima also received Shirakawa licenses, but only at Ōyama did

this development lead to conflict with the Shingon clergy. On the one hand, Mt. Mitake and Mt. Fuji *oshi* were not subordinate to the Buddhist clergy but formed independent guilds.[7] On the other hand, the Ōyama *oshi* who had become members of the Hirata school became fierce advocates of the Shintoization of the Ōyama cult, demanding the lessening of Shingon control over the site. This development also impacted the ways in which religious specialists represented Ōyama's deities, which had initially been identified as manifestations of Fudō but gradually gained a distinct identity as interest in Japanese antiquity and the Nativist movement grew during the early modern period.

Like any early modern mountain cult, the Ōyama cult remained combinatory until the Meiji restoration in 1868, which ushered in a fundamental change to the Japanese religious landscape: the disassociation of *kami* and Buddhas divided Buddhism and Shinto into distinct traditions. Already the site of a strong Nativist movement, Ōyama's highly combinatory cult was suddenly divided into Shinto and Buddhist spheres, both physically and institutionally. Parallel developments occurred at Mt. Konpira, the modern transformation of which was just as complex, even though it did not involve any Buddhist clergy.[8]

What finally unhinged the institutional stability of the Ōyama cult, beginning in the late eighteenth century, and what accelerated its demise during the last years of the early modern period was neither moral corruption nor a single event but several interrelated factors that reflected larger societal changes and upheaval, which eventually undermined the established hierarchies. During this period, foreign encroachment from the West, natural disasters, disease, and violent unrest weakened a political and religious system that had served its adherents well by maintaining peace and stability for about two hundred years. At Ōyama, many factors created fissures in an otherwise stable system: the physical destruction of Ōyama by an earthquake and a subsequent fire in 1855; friction among Ōyama's Shingon institutions; the Shingon institutions' gradual loss of financial support from the Tokugawa regime; the intellectual and social ferment among the *oshi* due to a new Shinto licensing system through the Shirakawa house and due to the introduction of Nativism, which questioned the orthodoxy of Ōyama's Buddhist rituals, deities, and institutions; and the loss of income from a decline in the number of pilgrims due to natural disasters and disease. All these factors gradually undermined the power balance between clerics and *oshi*. They set the stage for the eventual disassociation of *kami* and Buddhas in the early Meiji period. Yet the early modern structures governing Japanese religions proved to be more tenacious than first expected by the innovators, who were ultimately forced to reincorporate some aspects of the previous system to maintain institutional vitality and stability.

Ōyama's modern transformation illustrates the value of regional history in furthering our understanding of a crucial watershed such as the disassociation of *kami* and Buddhas. Although it is tempting to construct a narrative that focuses on the national implications of the early Meiji regime's religious policies and ideology, their actual implementation differed among localities. Heterotopic sites such as Ōyama were reshaped by the dynamic tension between a strong sense of place formed by regional networking and local politics with national trends and policies. By enforcing or resisting the reforms, various local groups vied for power and influence in order to further their interests, a process that is easily lost when writing history from a bird's-eye perspective. The cult's transformation from a combinatory to a dual cult with distinct Shinto and Buddhist spheres is emblematic of the transition of the Japanese religious landscape from the premodern to the modern periods. The case of the Ōyama cult demonstrates that distinct religious traditions are in fact relatively recent categories that do not adequately reflect the premodern Japanese religious landscape. The Ōyama cult is thus a useful reference point in the exploration of social change that occurred during the transition from the medieval to the modern periods. Ultimately, the larger religious landscape is emplaced in specific local and regional contexts.

Reference Matter

Notes

Introduction

1. Chamberlain and Mason, *A Handbook for Travellers in Japan*, 61–62; Note-helfer, *Japan Through American Eyes*, 278–87; Tenaka Myōōtarō Kagemoto, *Ōyama miyadaiku Myōōtarō nikki*, 758, 767.

2. Chamberlain and Mason, *A Handbook for Travellers in Japan*, 61.

3. See, for example, Hur, *Prayer and Play in Late Tokugawa Japan*; Williams, *The Other Side of Zen*; Vesey, "The Buddhist Clergy and Village Society in Early Modern Japan"; Maeda, "Imperial Authority and Local Shrines."

4. Ooms, *Tokugawa Ideology*, 13.

5. Ibid., 13.

6. Foucault, "Of Other Spaces," 22.

7. Soja, *Postmodern Geographies*, 10.

8. Hardacre, *Religion and Society in Nineteenth-Century Japan*; Hur, *Prayer and Play in Late Tokugawa Japan*; Thal, *Rearranging the Landscape of the God*.

9. Grapard, *The Protocol of the Gods*, 4.

10. Glare, ed., *Oxford Latin Dictionary*, 467.

11. For the sake of consistency, this study uses the standard modern reading "Afurisan." In the early modern period, however, the name was usually pronounced "Aburisan." Afurisan has been interpreted as a derivation of either Araburisan (Wild/Violent Mountain)—indicating the nature of its deities—or Amefurisan (Rain Falling Mountain)—reflecting its rain-making powers.

12. As estimated in Tamamuro Fumio, "Ōyama shinkō no kenkyū dōkō," 369.

13. Shinjō, *Shaji to kōtsū*, 37–38.

14. Shinjō, *Shinkō Shaji sankei no shakai*, 155–62. For the emergence of the village as a social unit in late medieval society, see Tonomura, *Community and Commerce in Late Medieval Japan*.

15. Kazuhiko Yoshida, "Religion in the Classical Period," 153–54.

16. Shinjō, *Shinkō Shaji sankei no shakai*, 153–89.

17. Ibid., 160–82, 758–59.

18. Ibid., 181–84.

19. For similar prejudice against outcasts and itinerant preachers during the medieval period, see Amino, "Chūsei zenki no 'sanjo' to kumenden," 39; Kaminishi, *Explaining Pictures*, 112–17.

20. Bodart-Bailey, ed. and trans., *Kaempfer's Japan*, 117, 119–20.

21. *STK*, 486.

22. These included ninth-century glazed urns, a Heian-period mirror, Song-dynasty coins, a *sūtra* container, a small bronze pagoda, several small Buddhist clay statues, and other clay artifacts from the medieval and early modern periods. Utsumi Benji, *Sōshū Ōyama*, 15, 37–58; Hiratsuka-shi hakubutsukan, ed., *Ōyama no shinkō to rekishi*, 1–2.

23. The *Ōyamadera engi* probably dates from the late thirteenth century, but the oldest extant manuscript of it is a vernacular version from 1532. The oldest extant manuscript of the *kanbun* version dates from 1637.

24. Vernacular *Ōyamadera engi* in Kojima, *Kanagawa-ken katarimono shiryō*, vol. 2, 55.

25. Kanbun *Ōyamadera engi* in Kojima, *Kanagawa-ken katarimono shiryō*, vol. 2, 23–24.

26. Bock, trans., *Engi-shiki*, 136.

27. *IHSS* 1991, 229, 378, 407–10; *IHSS* 1995, 247, 254.

28. *IHSS* 1991, 635–36; *IHSS* 1995, 277–79. For Kenjō's biography, see Itō, "Gangyō shōnin Kenjō no kenkyū (shō)," 29–37.

29. Goodwin, *Alms and Vagabonds*, 15–16.

30. *IHSS* 1995, 279; *IHSS* 1991, 105–7.

31. Teeuwen and van der Veere, *Nakatomi harae kunge*, 10; Teeuwen, "The Creation of a *honji suijaku* Deity," 119.

32. *SSKFK*, vol. 3, 111; *IHSS* 1991, 230–34; *IHSS* 1995, 302–3, 325, 333–34.

33. *SSKFK*, vol. 3, 111–12; *IHSS* 1991, 234–35, 240–1, 260–1; *IHSS* 1995, 378–79. On prayers for military success and Buddhist monks' campaigns during the military conflicts of the Warring States period, see Thornton, *Charisma and Community Formation in Medieval Japan*.

34. Kanagawa Prefectural Government, ed., *The History of Kanagawa*, 115.

35. *SSKFK*, vol. 3, 112–13. According to the *Afurijinja kodenkō, yamabushi* from Ōyama were involved in the final battle at Odawara but sustained only one

fatal casualty. After the battle, they were allowed to return to Ōyama, but the temple land was confiscated (*STK*, 486). Hideyoshi ordered the residents of Ōyama not to engage in military activities by not permitting them to raise troops or to create havoc, fell bamboo or trees, or set fires. Tōma, "Ōyama shi," 49–50; *SSKFK*, vol. 3, III–13, 134–35.

36. *IHSS* 1994, 94–95.

37. *STK*, 486.

38. Tamamuro Fumio, "Ōyama shinkō no kenkyū dōkō," 369, 377–78.

Chapter 1

1. Hori, "Mountains and Their Importance for the Idea of the Other World in Japanese Folk Religion," 1–23. In his study of sacred mountains around the world, Edwin Bernbaum provides a similar typology of sacred mountains that applies not only to Japan: mountains as *axis mundi*, mountains as lofty portals to other worlds, mountains as the abode of the divine and of spirits, mountains as places of refuge, and mountains as sources of water, material blessings, and spiritual powers. Bernbaum, *Sacred Mountains of the World*, 208–12.

2. *IHSS* 1994, 60.

3. Powell, "Literary Diversions on Mount Jiuhua," 23.

4. See Eliade, "Sacred Places: Temple, Palace, Centre of the World" in *Patterns in Comparative Religion*, 367–87 and "Sacred Space and Making the World Sacred" in *The Sacred and the Profane*, 20–67.

5. Foucault, "Of Other Spaces," 24.

6. Ibid., 25.

7. Lefebvre, *The Production of Space*, 33, 37.

8. Ibid., 48, 236–37.

9. Grapard, "Geosophia, Geognosis, and Geopiety," 374–75, 382–94.

10. Shinkei, *Oi no kurigoto*, 1075–83. For an English translation of Shinkei's description, see Ramirez-Christensen, *Heart's Flower*, 161–62. Shinkei's account follows Chinese literati models in its depiction of sacred mountains. For example, William Powell notes in his discussion of Tang-dynasty descriptions of Mt. Jiuhua that literati poets tended to portray grand vistas of the mountain as a whole rather than specific sacred spots on the mountain. Powell terms this view of the mountain as the "cult of site" and contrasts this with the notion of the mountain as a "site of cult." He argues that the latter would have applied to the Buddhist monks living on the actual mountain. See Powell, "Literary Diversions on Mount Jiuhua," 25.

11. Grapard, "Geotyping Sacred Space," 225.

12. Reader and Tanabe, *Practically Religious*, 61.

13. Moerman, *Localizing Paradise*, 59.

14. For a detailed study of various versions of the *Ōyamadera engi*, see Kojima, *Kanagawa-ken katarimono shiryō*, vol. 1, 3–30.

15. Kojima, *Kanagawa-ken katarimono shiryō*, vol. 2, 54.

16. Ibid., 7–8.

17. Goodwin, *Alms and Vagabonds*, 58–59, 61, 64, 144.

18. *SSKFK*, vol. 3: 109–12.

19. For a discussion of the iron statue of Ōyama Fudō, see *IHSS* 1995, 436–41. Iron statues, though rare in Japan, usually date from the early Kamakura period through the Muromachi period. Similar statues are found in the Kantō region—in Tochigi, Aichi, and Kanagawa Prefectures.

20. *SSKFK*, vol. 3, 110–11.

21. Kaminishi, *Explaining Pictures*, 11, 13, 90–93, 96–99, 103–10.

22. *IHSS* 1995, 104–6.

23. There are examples from 1307, 1637, and 1684 of such copies.

24. Kojima, *Kanagawa-ken katarimono shiryō*, vol. 2, 53–55.

25. Lefebvre, *The Production of Space*, 35.

26. Kojima, *Kanagawa-ken katarimono shiryō*, vol. 2, 49–51.

27. Lefebvre, *The Production of Space*, 35.

28. Kojima, *Kanagawa-ken katarimono shiryō*, vol. 2, 51–52.

29. Ibid., 22.

30. Other famous examples include the hunter that appeared to Kūkai when he first climbed Mt. Kōya. See Hakeda, *Kūkai*, 48. At Mt. Murō, a dragon king was said to reside on the mountain and to have promised to protect the site. See Fowler, "In Search of the Dragon," 147. The motif of the subjugation of a serpent by a Buddhist monk is a frequent one in *engi* literature. See MacWilliams, "Temple Myths and Popularization of Kannon Pilgrimage in Japan," 390–98.

31. Kojima, *Kanagawa-ken katarimono shiryō*, vol. 2, 52–53. A variant text of the *Ōyamadera engi* from 1637 identified both Ōyama and the smaller peaks near Nijū no Taki, the waterfall where the dragon deity appeared to Rōben, with the five Wisdom Kings. See Kojima, *Kanagawa-ken katarimono shiryō*, vol. 2, 21.

32. For the connection between dragons and water, see Fowler, "In Search of the Dragon," 147–51; Zhao, *Asian Thought and Culture*. For more on the relationship between esoteric Buddhism and rainmaking rites in Heian Japan, see Ruppert, "Buddhist Rainmaking in Early Japan," 143–74.

33. Kojima, *Kanagawa-ken katarimono shiryō*, vol. 2, 54.

34. The oldest Fudō statue at Ōyama actually dates from the Heian period. For a discussion of the wooden statue of Fudō, see *IHSS* 1995, 419–422.

35. Tōma, "Ōyama shi," 50–51; *IHSS* 1994, 94–95.

36. *SSKFK*, vol. 3, 107.

37. Depictions of Maitreya's descent onto earth, as well as more diagrammatic mandalas, usually show Maitreya at the center and Fudō in the bottom right-hand corner. See Okazaki, *Pure Land Buddhist Painting*, 135, 152–56; Shinbo, *Besson mandara*, plates 100–4; Ten Grotenhuis, *Japanese Mandalas*, 106, 112.

38. Kojima, *Kanagawa-ken katarimono shiryō*, vol. 2, 49.

39. Foucault, "Of Other Spaces," 25.

40. Kojima, *Kanagawa-ken katarimono shiryō*, vol. 2, 18–20, 51–52; *IHSS* 1994, 60.

41. There are several examples of 49 caves on a sacred mountain representing the 49 halls of Tuṣita Heaven such as Mt. Hiko in Kyūshū, Takakuradake on Sakakiyama in Izumi Province, Mt. Kasagi in Kyōto, the Kumano Mountain Range, and Iwayadera in Ehime Prefecture (Shikoku). Among these, the ones at Mt. Hiko, which date to the early Kamakura period, are the most famous. Kinpusen is another well-known example of a Maitreya cult. The mountain was regarded as a representation of Maitreya's Tuṣita Heaven. Furthermore, according to the *Shozan engi*, Ōmine is the inner and Kasagi the outer sanctuary of Tuṣita Heaven. See Miyake, *Shugendō jiten*, 4, 160, 178, 280, 371.

42. Lefebvre, *The Production of Space*, 251.

43. Kojima, *Kanagawa-ken katarimono shiryō*, vol. 2, 22.

44. This description applies mainly to the southwestern ascent via Sakamoto but was replicated in simplified form on the ascent from Minoge (*SSKFK*, vol. 3, 133–35). The ascent from Minoge was lined with fewer shrines, chapels, and statuary because it was Ōyama's secondary ascent and attracted fewer pilgrims than Sakamoto, the main ascent.

45. Ōmine-san, for example, near Yoshino also features four gates: Hosshinmon, Shugyōmon, Dōkakumon, and Myōkakumon. They represent a symbolic death and spiritual rebirth through the attainment of *nirvana* upon reaching the summit. A prohibition against entering the first gate is still in place. Blacker, *The Catalpa Bow*, 213–18.

46. Foucault, "Of Other Spaces," 26.

47. *SSKFK*, vol. 3, 117–18.

48. Ibid., 117; Utsumi Benji, *Sōshū Ōyama*, 226

49. *SSKFK*, vol. 3, 112, 116–17; Utsumi Benji, *Sōshū Ōyama*, 226.

50. *SSKFK*, vol. 3, 114, 118; *OCSK*, 121–27; Harada, *Sagami Ōyama*, 26–28.

51. *IHSS* 1994, 85; *OFRK* ix.3.

52. *STK*, 490.

53. *SSKFK*, vol. 3, 133.

54. Ibid., 105–6.

55. *IHSS* 1994, 26.

56. Beginning in the 1830s and 1840s, Rōbendaki, Ōdaki, and the Outer Fudō Hall appeared in prints by Hokusai, Andō Hiroshige, Utagawa Sadahide, Utagawa Kuniyoshi, and Utagawa Toyokuni II. The only place near the summit depicted in two woodblock prints by Andō Hiroshige is Raigōdani. Both prints, however, show very little of Ōyama but depict a view of Mt. Fuji. Full views of Ōyama—such as Utagawa Kuniyoshi's "Sagami no kuni Ōsumikōri Amefuri no Ōyama zenzu" from the Kaei era (1848–1853) and Utagawa Sadahide's "Sagami no kuni Ōsumigun Ōyamadera Afurijinja shinkei" (1858)—focus on the inns, temples, and waterfalls (Ōdaki and Rōbendaki) in zones one and two. In contrast to the lavish detail on the foot of the mountain, their depiction of zone three is truncated. This suggests that the actual climb was neither artistically appealing nor very familiar to the artists. One should also note that whereas Sadahide's depiction of the mountain is fairly accurate and realistic, Kuniyoshi's print is more stylized and contains several mistakes: it shows the Tower Gate in front of the Outer Fudō Hall and does not show the Fudō Hall at all. This seems to indicate that Kuniyoshi merely depicted famous places at Ōyama rather than attempted to copy the layout of the mountain realistically. In the same way, illustrations in the *Sōchū ryūon kiryaku* (1839) and the *Shinpen Sagami no kuni fudoki kō* (1840) depicted zones one and two in great detail and did not pay equal attention to zone three. For the most complete published collection of prints of Ōyama, see Atsugi-shi kyōiku iinkai shakai kyōiku ka, ed., *Kyōdo shiryō tenshishitsu tokubetsu ten—Sagami Ōyama*, 6–19; Kanagawa kinseishi kenkyūkai, *Edo jidai no Kanagawa*; Ōto and Yamaguchi, eds., *Edo jidai zushi 14*, plates 201, 247–48, 258–63; *IHSS* 1992, ii–iii.

57. Tōma, "Ōyama shi," 55–56. Until the end of the mid-nineteenth century, Ōyama's geography saw very few physical changes. Further reconstruction projects in 1638, 1676, 1694, and 1704 did not alter the basic layout of the site. The only significant changes that took place around 1700 were the addition of a cemetery of the Hachidaibō abbots on level one of zone two and six new Shingon subtemples in level three of zone two, reflecting the growing prosperity of the Shingon clergy. After 1704, Ōyama was struck by few natural disasters and fire so that it needed few repairs for the next one and a half centuries. Only the shrines on the mountain top were destroyed in 1719, 1731, and 1771, but the rest of the mountain remained virtually unchanged until the mid-nineteenth century, except for a pagoda near the Main Hall, which was added in 1795. *SSKFK*, vol. 3, 113–15, 119–20.

58. Grapard, "Geotyping Sacred Space," 226–27.

59. Ibid., 227.

60. Ushiyama, "'Nyonin kinsei' sairon," 1–2.

61. *SSKFK*, vol. 3, 119–20; *STK*, 471.

62. *KKS*, 671–74.

63. *STK*, 469.

64. Bowring, *The Religious Traditions of Japan*, 56.

65. *STK*, 471.

66. Miyazaki, "'Fuji no bi to shinkō' saikō," 124–31; Miyazaki, "Fujisan ni okeru nyonin kinsei to sono shūen," 277–80; Miyazaki, "Female Pilgrims and Mt. Fuji," 339–91.

67. *TMZ*, 226; *SSKFK*, vol. 3, 118; Ishida, *Reigaku Ōyama*, 77. A mid-nineteenth century woodblock print by Utagawa Sadahide, which illustrates the layout of Ōyama's mountainside, clearly shows that women were allowed to ascend to the area around the Main Hall and worship Sekison from there. In the print, Sadahide shows the entrance to the ascent to Sekison Shrine between the Votive Picture Hall and Main Hall. He labels the entrance as "Wooden Doors" and explains: "Open from the 27th of the Sixth Month to the 17th of the Seventh Month. Women do not ascend beyond the wooden gate but worship at this hall [i.e., the Votive Picture Hall]." See *IHSS* 1992, ii. The same layout is found in the illustrations of Ōyama in the *Sōchū ryūon kiryaku* and the *Shinpen Sagami no kuni fudoki kō*, which also mention that the summit was open for only three weeks during the summer festival. See *TMZ*, 226; *SSKFK*, vol. 3, 118; *STK*, 491; *IHSS* 1994, 25–26; Miyata, *Edo saijiki*, 148.

68. Sadahide's print labels another "wooden door on the path from Minoge Village," explaining "Open from the 27th of the Sixth Month to the 17th of the Seventh Month." Other sources also mention a wooden gate on the western ascent from Minoge Village via Mt. Harutake, which was ordinarily kept closed. *IHSS* 1992, ii; *SSKFK*, vol. 3, 133.

69. Suzuki Masataka, *Nyonin kinsei*, 6–7, 13.

70. Ibid.

71. Faure, *The Power of Denial*, 224–28. Kurumisawa points to the spiritual and reproductive powers traditionally associated with women, which might incur the wrath of the deity residing on the mountain should a woman enter its realm. At several mountains, such as Hakusan, Tateyama, Mt. Kōya, Togakushi, and Mt. Iwaki, stones marked the point beyond which women were not to advance. There are legends of women who promptly turned to stone or of old post-menopausal women who suddenly started menstruating when they violated this prohibition. According to Kurumisawa, this points to the paradoxical understanding of women's reproductive function as both powerful and impure. See Kurumisawa, "Nyonin kinsei o megutte," 20–25. In his discussion of the sacred geography of Tateyama, Suzuki Masataka focuses on the meaning of the pilgrimage for women in the face of taboos regarding menstrual and parturitive blood. The issue is, of course, particularly important in the case of

Tateyama, which features a "blood pool hell." See Suzuki Masataka, "Tateyama shinkō," 7–21.

72. *IHSS* 1992, ii; *TMZ*, 226; *SSKFK*, vol. 3, 118; *STK*, 491; *IHSS* 1994, 25–26; Miyata, *Edo saijiki*, 148.

73. *OFRK* XII.5.

74. *IHSS* 1994, 26.

75. Asakawa chōshi hensan iinkai, ed., *Asakawa chōshi 2: shiryōhen*, 960.

76. *IHSS* 1994, 25–26.

77. *OFRK* IV.11.

78. *OFRK* VI.8.

79. *OFRK* IV.7.

80. *OFRK* IV.10.

81. *OFRK* IV.11.

82. *OFRK* VI.6.

83. Grapard, "Geotyping Sacred Space," 227, 232–33. Quote on 233.

84. *OFRK* IX.3.

Chapter 2

1. According to the research of Duncan Williams, the Shingon school in Sagami Province lost 22 temples and the Tendai school 16 temples to other Buddhist schools; Williams, "Representations of Zen," 66. Satō Shunkō notes a similar phenomenon among *shugendō* temples in the Akita Domain; Satō Shunkō, "Seshū no shiten kara miru shugen jiin to Sōtōshū jiin," 263–68. In the case of Ōyama, Kōgakuji in Kominoge Village within Ōyama's temple land, for example, was a Sōtō temple by 1840 but had originally been established by Kenryū, a Shingon monk and Ōyama Hachidaibō's third abbot, in the early seventeenth century; *SSKFK*, vol. 3, 135. Shōrinbō, originally a Tendai temple on the slopes of the mountain until the early seventeenth century, moved to Sakamoto Village and later became a Jōdo village temple called Saigōji by the eighteenth century; *STK*, 470–71; *STK*, 92; *ONK*, 64.

2. Toyoda, *Nihon shūkyō seidoshi no kenkyū*, 147–48. Based on records from the 1830s, Toyoda compiled data regarding land grants given by the *bakufu* to temples of various Buddhist sects (excluding *monzeki* and Tōshōgū lands, which reached the level of daimyo domains, i.e., 10,000 *koku* or more), which yielded a total of 234,631.65 *koku*. According to records from the mid-seventeenth century, official temple and shrine land granted by the *bakufu* comprised about 263,000 *koku*, which equaled about one percent of the total land held by the *bakufu*, the imperial court, and the daimyo domains.

3. Jiin honmatsuchō kenkyūkai, ed., *Edo bakufu jiin honmatsuchō shūsei*, 37–58, 1009–99; Tamamuro Fumio, "Jiin honmatsuchō no seikaku to mondaiten," 16; Sakamoto, "Honmatsuchō ni mieru kinsei no Kogi Shingonshū," 27–35; Sakamoto, "Chūsei Kantō ni okeru Shingonshū kyōdan no tenkai," 31–32; Hardacre, "Sources for the Study of Religion and Society in the Late Edo Period," 247–51.

4. Hall, "The *Bakuhan* System," 138.

5. *STK*, 486.

6. Udaka, *Tokugawa Ieyasu to Kantō bukkyō kyōdan*, 150–51. For more on the *shimebarai* and death-related Shugendō rites, see Udaka, *Tokugawa Ieyasu to Kantō bukkyō kyōdan*, 81–93, 132–51.

7. See Hardacre, "Sources for the Study of Religion and Society," 251–53.

8. *SSKFK*, vol. 3, 113.

9. Ibid.

10. Tōma, "Ōyama shi," 54.

11. *SSKFK*, vol. 2, 262, 296–97.

12. Ibid., 249; *ONK*, 43; Sakamoto, "Chūseimatsu minami Kantō ni okeru Kogi Shingonshū no honmatsu kankei," 90–91, 98–99; Jiin honmatsuchō kenkyūkai, ed., *Edo bakufu jiin honmatsuchō shūsei*, 37–58, 1009–99.

13. *STK*, 37; Tōma, "Ōyama shi," 54–56.

14. *STK*, 23; *ONK*, 44, 58; Tōma, "Ōyama shi," 56.

15. Furushima, "The Village and Agriculture," 502–3.

16. Tōma, "Ōyama shi," 56. The Kogi Shingon delegation headed by the monk Raikei from Mt. Kōya's Henshōkōin, included three monks from the Kantō region, Jitsuō, Kaiun (Izu Hannyain), and Yūyō (Ōiso Chifukuji).

17. *ONK*, 45.

18. *IHSS* 1994, 21, 23; *ONK*, 44–45, 58; Tōma, "Ōyama shi," 57–58.

19. Jiin honmatsuchō kenkyūkai, ed., *Edo bakufu jiin honmatsuchō shūsei*, 37–58. Six percent of all Kogi and Shingi Shingon temples were landed. In the Kogi Shingon school, most landed temples were head temples whereas the largest number of landed temples in the Shingi Shingon school were branch temples. Sakamoto, "Honmatsuchō," 27–35.

20. Hall, "The *Bakuhan* System," 148.

21. This development is parallel to the other sects of Japanese Buddhism. For a discussion of these sects, see Williams, "Representations of Zen," 22–30; Katō, "Hakuhō Eryō to shie jiken," 391–435; Tamamuro Fumio, *Nihon bukkyō shi: kinsei*, 6–25; Tamamuro Fumio, *Nihonjin no kōdō to shisō 16: Edo bakufu no shūkyō tōsei*, 13–46; Nosco, "Keeping the Faith," 136–42.

22. Sakamoto, "*Shingonshū shohatto* to Shingon gokohonji no seiritsu ni tsuite," 285–96. Sakamoto uses the example of the *Shingonshū shohatto* (Regulations for the Shingon School). The generic regulations decreed by the *bakufu* were usually followed up in greater detail by regulations formulated by clerics from high-ranking Shingon institutions.

23. Williams, "Representations of Zen," 24.

24. Udaka, *Edo bakufu no bukkyō kyōdanshi tōsei*, 72.

25. *Daigoji hatto* and *Tōji hatto* from 1609 identify Kōyasan, Tōji, and Daigoji as sharing the responsibility for the scholarly training of Shingon monks. *Kōyasan hatto* from 1649 lists five temples as training academies: Kōyasan, Tōji, Daigoji, Ninnaji, and Takaosanji. *Tokugawa kinrei kō*, vol. 5, 75, 88.

26. Sakamoto, "Chūseimatsu minami Kantō," 85–87.

27. According to the head-branch-temple register from 1633, there were 29 *hōdanjo* (15 in Sagami, 6 in Musashi, 3 in Izu, 5 in Kōzuke) and 4 *jōhōdanjo* (2 in Sagami and 2 in Kōzuke). See Jiin honmatsuchō kenkyūkai, ed., *Edo bakufu jiin honmatsuchō shūsei*, 37–58.

28. *KKS*, 671–74.

29. *ONK*, 45, 58–59; *IHSS* 1994, 16; Tōma, "Ōyama shi," 57–60.

30. *STK*, 469; *ONK*, 59–61; Tōma, "Ōyama shi," 61–63; an incomplete version is found in *IHSS* 1994, 19–20.

31. *STK*, 470–471; *ONK*, 61–64; Tōma, "Ōyama shi," 63–65.

32. *ONK*, 63–64.

33. *STK*, 470–471; Tōma, "Ōyama shi," 63–65; *ONK*, 64/1–64/2.

34. Tōma, "Ōyama shi," 64.

35. Matsuoka, "Sagami Ōyama oshi no keisei to tenkai," 7.

36. Tōma, "Ōyama shi," 66–67.

37. Ibid., 67.

38. See Jiin honmatsuchō kenkyūkai, ed., *Edo bakufu jiin honmatsuchō shūsei*. For an analysis of the Jōdo, Tendai, and Shingon registers, see also Udaka, *Edo bakufu no bukkyō kyōdanshi tōsei*, 1–149.

39. Tōma, "Ōyama shi," 67; Jiin honmatsuchō kenkyūkai, ed., *Edo bakufu jiin honmatsuchō shūsei*, 37–58. Other Buddhist schools, such as the Tendai, Jōdo, and Shingi Shingon schools, had similar regional training facilities, which were also known under the name *danrin*. For more on the *danrin* system, see Vesey, "The Buddhist Clergy and Village Society in Early Modern Japan," 207–15; Tamayama, "Kantō jūhachi danrin no seiritsu," 207–16.

40. Although Ōyama did not hold the largest number of Kogi Shingon branch temples, it was the predominant institution in the Isehara area. Within the Isehara area, it was the temple with the largest temple land, since most other temples and shrines had only about 2 or 3 *koku*; *IHSS* 1999, 587–588. The second

largest temple was its Kogi Shingon neighbor, Mt. Hinata Ryōzenji Hōjōbō, which had 64 *koku* and was also a branch temple of Mt. Kōya's Muryōjuin. Like Ōyama, Mt. Hinata was a sacred complex that attracted pilgrims and was made up of multiple institutions. By 1791, it consisted of eight Shingon temples, nine *shugendō*, and three retainer hermitages but had only one branch temple. Jiin honmatsuchō kenkyūkai, ed., *Edo bakufu jiin honmatsuchō shūsei*, 1084.

41. This list included three of the five great Shingon temples in the Kantō region, but Ōyama, even though it ranked higher than some of these, was conspicuously absent.

42. Udaka, *Edo bakufu no bukkyō kyōdanshi tōsei*, 162–63, 168, 178–79, 195–96.

43. Kanagawa Prefectural Government, ed., *The History of Kanagawa*, 135.

44. Tōma, "Ōyama shi," 67–68.

45. *ONK*, 46; Tōma, "Ōyama shi," 68.

46. *SSKFK*, vol. 3, 112–113; *ONK*, 47–50; Tōma, "Ōyama shi," 68–70.

47. *STK*, 488.

48. *IHSS* 1994, 87, 92.

49. According to a document from 1786, the *bakufu* expelled many *yamabushi* or forced them to become *oshi* at this time (*IHSS* 1994, 86–87, 94–95). As Matsuoka has observed, the order from the magistrate of temples and shrines order in 1663 was the first instance in which Ōyama's lay ritualists were called *oshi*. This seems to indicate a transitional period in which the former *yamabushi* expelled from the mountain in the early seventeenth century slowly became *oshi*. Matsuoka, "Sagami Ōyama oshi no keisei to tenkai," 8–9.

50. *IHSS* 1994, 66.

51. Even though the mountain itself had become a Kogi Shingon institution, the institutions in Sakamoto remained of mixed affiliation. The coexistence of Shingon and non-Shingon institutions, however, was precarious. Many of the participants in the conflict were not affiliated with the Shingon School. The three Rinzai temples, whose monks were banished, were three of fourteen Rinzai temples in Sakamoto. Some of the parties expelled in 1663, e.g., Daigaku and Daiyōji, still had residences on the mountain in 1591. Daiyōji, in fact, had the third largest residence after Hachidaibō; *IHSS* 1994, 94–95; Matsuoka, "Sagami Ōyama oshi no keisei to tenkai," 13. The three *yamabushi* who were allowed to remain and perhaps even those *yamabushi* expelled were members of the Tendai-affiliated Honzan branch; *SSKFK*, vol. 3, 106.

52. *SSKFK*, vol. 3, 105.

53. Tōma, "Ōyama shi," 75–76, 79.

54. *IHSS* 1994, 43; Tōma, "Ōyama shi," 75–76.

55. Jiin honmatsuchō kenkyūkai, ed., *Edo bakufu jiin honmatsuchō shūsei*, 52, 1088–99; Tōma, "Ōyama shi," 75–94.

56. *IHSS* 1994, 43, 45, 52; "Jikakuchō," 476.

57. *IHSS* 1994, 43–52; Tōma, "Ōyama shi," 75–94.

58. *IHSS* 1999, 205–227. Ōyama became involved in a suit against ten lower-level Kogi Shingon, Nichiren, and Zen temples by Honzanha *shugendō* in Sagami over the right to carry out a purification rite called *shimeharai.*

59. Udaka, *Edo bakufu no bukkyō kyōdanshi tōsei,* 168, 196–97.

60. Not being part of the Ōyama's temple land and located on Ōyama's secondary ascent, Minoge was less affected by this process.

61. Kanagawa Prefectural Government, ed., *The History of Kanagawa,* 163.

62. Tōma, "Ōyama shi," 94–95.

63. Kanagawa Prefectural Government, ed., *The History of Kanagawa,* 163–65.

64. Ibid., 163–65.

65. Chiba, "Atogaki," 188–89.

66. *SSKFK,* vol. 3, 120; Tōma, "Ōyama shi," 95–96. For a detailed description of the events, see *OFRK* IX.3. The clergy took on a similar role after fires destroyed the shrines again in 1731 and 1771.

67. His role in regulating the *oshi* would later lead the Nativist *oshi* Sudō Shigeo to describe Kaizō as an oppressor; *STK,* 491.

68. *IHSS* 1994, 23–24.

69. The word *toritsugi* first appeared in Raikei's code in 1609. A reference to the system appears again in 1702. Matsuoka, "Sagami Ōyamadera no 'toritsugi' seido no kōzō," 24–25.

70. Matsuoka, "Sagami Ōyamadera no 'toritsugi' seido," 31.

71. Ibid., 23–35. The system continued in nearly identical form until the end of the early modern period with few changes, such as shifting affiliations or shifts in status, by 1824.

72. *OFRK* IX.3; Tōma, "Ōyama shi," 96–97.

73. Tōma, "Ōyama shi," 98–99.

74. Matsushita, ed., *Kantō Kogi Shingonshū honmatsuchō,* 93–101.

75. "Shoshū kaikyū," 476.

76. The Sagami section of the *Kogi Shingonshū homatsuchō* in Kansei 3 (1791) was officially compiled under the name of the *furegashira* of Mt. Kōya rather than a coalition of powerful academies from the Kantō region. Jiin honmatsu-chō kenkyūkai, ed., *Edo bakufu jiin honmatsuchō shūsei,* 1009–99. According to the register, Ōyama comprised twelve subtemples but now also had five branch temples, four of which were located in the immediate vicinity and functioned as small village temples. The fifth was located on the outskirts of Edo; Jiin honmatsuchō kenkyūkai, ed., *Edo bakufu jiin honmatsuchō shūsei,* 1079.

77. Evidence pertaining to the background of individual clerics other than the Hachidaibō abbots is scattered and anecdotal, but there are a few examples

including the monks Chōō, Tsūga, and Shinzō. For instance, according to the *Ōyama Fudō reigenki*, the monk Chōō once resided at the Ōyama subtemple Jutokuin and later transferred to the academy Enzōji in Chigasaki Village as its abbot by 1740. He died in the Hōreki era (1751–63); *OFRK* IX.5. Tsūga was a native of Suruga Province and a monk at a small academy called Seisuiji. As a young monk, he served as the subabbot at Ōyama's subtemple Jutokuin approximately between 1713 and 1715, later returned to Seisuiji as its abbot, had three disciples, and passed away in 1778. His disciple Shinkyō later visited Ōyama's Hachidaibō, where he met the monk Shinzō, who had heard about Tsūga from his teacher Sandō, the subabbot monk at Yōchiin. Shinzō himself was a native from Itado Village in Sagami Province and moved from Enzōji, an academy in Chigasaki Village, to the Ōyama subtemple Yochiin, where he served as resident monk from 1773 to at least 1792; *OFRK* III.8; *IHSS* 1994, 262. The monk Kōen was originally from Izumo and had come to Edo in service but absconded and became ordained at Ōyama. He resided at Daikanjin, a temple on Ōyama's slopes that had traditionally been charged with maintaining the lamps in the Main Hall, then transferred to Hinata and Kawakami Village for three or four years before returning to Daikanjin at Ōyama. In 1773, his former wife found him at Ōyama and persuaded him to return to Izumo with her until their young daughter had found a husband; *OFRK* IV.3. The network included not only monks but also nuns who were ordained by the abbots of local temples. For example, the nun Kōjun from Itado Village had resolved to become a nun in old age in the spring of 1771 and was ordained by the monk Kōgen at Hōjūin, her local bodaiji. In her religious pursuit, she was assisted by Kōgen and Zen priests at Jōgenji in Hori Village and Anyōji in Koinaba Village. She later raised funds for a bell at the local Bishamondō. Her endeavor was reported to Ōyama Fudō by Kōgen, who told her story to Shinzō; *OFRK* X.5. Similarly, the nun Myōgen, who worked as an itinerant blind shamisen player, was ordained by the monk Ryōjitsu at Shinpukuji and became a faithful Kōmyō Mantra devotee. Ryōjitsu later moved to Nakanoin at Ōyama, where Myōgen continued to visit him periodically; *OFRK* IX.2.

78. Matsushita, *Kantō Kogi Shingonshū honmatsuchō*, 93–101.

79. Ibid., 199–200.

80. *OFRK* IX.5.

81. *OFRK* VIII.1.

82. *OFRK* XII.1.

83. *OFRK* V.7.

84. According to a document from 1786, six of the twelve subtemples had developed parishioners, some apparently through purchase from an *oshi* in the 1780s; *IHSS* 1994, 85–97; Tōma, "Ōyama shi," 104–118.

85. *IHSS* 1992, 114–119; *IHSS* 1994, 299–301.

86. Matsuoka, "Sagami Ōyama oshi no danka shūseki katei no kōzō," 55–58.

87. *ONK*, 64.

88. *SSKFK*, vol. 3, 120.

89. Matsushita, *Kantō Kogi Shingonshū honmatsuchō*, 94–95.

90. Tōma, "Ōyama shi," 119.

91. Even in the Heian period, the construction of gateways as an expression of high court rank was covered by sumptuary laws. In the early modern period in particular, gateways became an important status symbol because their lavishness represented the power of the *daimyō*—or the temple—to the outside world. See Coaldrake, *Architecture and Authority in Japan*, 87–88, 193–207.

92. Tōma, "Ōyama shi," 99.

93. Ibid., 100–104, 118; *OFRK* xv.3.

94. *IHSS* 1994, 144–45; Matsuoka, "Sagami Ōyama oshi no keisei to tenkai," 3.

95. Tōma, "Ōyama shi," 120–21.

96. *IHSS* 1994, 416–24.

97. Tōma, "Ōyama shi," 118–24.

98. On the control that Buddhist temples had over adjunct shrines in parts of Sagami and Musashi Provinces, see Hardacre, "Sources for the Study of Religion and Society," 251–53; Hardacre, *Religion and Society in Nineteenth-Century Japan*, 76–82.

Chapter 3

1. Shinjō, *Shinkō Shaji sankei no shakai-keizai shiteki kenkyū*, 187, 758–75, 853–996.

2. Nobuyuki Yoshida, "Osaka's Brotherhood of Mendicant Monks," 158–79; Groemer, "A Short History of Gannin," 43–72. Incidentally, even though they had no official connection with the mountain, *gannin bōzu* in Edo peddled popular objects associated with the pilgrimage to Ōyama and offered their services to perform proxy pilgrimages during the Ōyama pilgrimage season; Groemer, "The Arts of the Gannin," 275–320.

3. Hagiwara, *Miko to bukkyōshi*, 221–22. Barbara Ruch discusses the various images of the *Kumano bikuni* that associated the nuns with various activities ranging from *etoki*, fundraising for temples, and the distribution of talismans, to the performance of songs and even prostitution. Ruch, "Woman to Woman," 241–49, 556–57, 560–62. See also Ruch, "Medieval Jongleurs and the Making of a National Literature," 279–309; Akai, "The Common People and Painting," 167–88; Formanek, "*Etoki*," 11–43; Moerman, *Localizing Paradise*, 181–232; Kaminishi, *Explaining Pictures*, 103–18, 137–64.

4. Miyake Hitoshi, "Oshi," 826; Shinjō, *Shinkō Shaji sankei no shakai*, 152.

5. *SSKFK*, vol. 3, 226–27; Suzuki Masataka, *Yama to kami to hito*, 177–81; Miyake and Itoga, "Hasugesan no shugendō," 495–502.

6. *STK*, 470–71.

7. *IHSS* 1999, 440.

8. Ibid., 225–26, 440–41, 446–48. Matsuoka Takashi identifies Enzōbō as a *shugendō* temple at Ōyama, but a temple by that name appears in no other document related to Ōyama. It is more likely that Enzōbō refers to a temple by that name at nearby Mt. Hasuge. From the late Muromachi period to 1622, Mt. Hasuge was affiliated with Gyokurōbō in Odawara but later became directly affiliated with Shōgoin in Kyoto; Miyake and Itoga, "Hasugesan no shugendō," 487, *SSKFK*, vol. 3, 225–27.

9. *IHSS* 1999, 442–46, 455; *IHSS* 1994, 66, 69, 87; *STK*, 490.

10. Tamamuro Fumio, ed., *Zusetsu Nihon bukkyō no rekishi Edo jidai*, 97–98.

11. Groemer, "A Short History of Gannin," 50–51, 56–58.

12. Tōkyō-to kōmonjokan, ed., *Tōkyō shishi kō sangyōhen*, vol. 6, 90–91; Tōkyō-to kōmonjokan, ed., *Tōkyō shishi kō sangyōhen*, vol. 7, 132–35. See also Tōkyō Daigaku shiryō hensanjo, ed., *Dainihon Kinsei shiryō*, vol. 16, 10–31, 61–69 (for information on how urban authorities tried to curb itinerant preachers in Edo, Kyoto, and other towns).

13. Kuroita et al., eds., *Kokushi taikei 41, Tokugawa jikki 4*, 549, 552–53. Tōkyō-to kōmonjokan, *Tōkyō shishi kō sangyōhen*, vol. 7, 838–39.

14. Groemer, "A Short History of Gannin," 56–63.

15. Tamamuro Fumio, *Nihon bukkyō shi: kinsei*, 166–21.

16. Groemer, "A Short History of Gannin," 49.

17. *Satō Ryōjike shozō monjo*, vol. 2, doc. 9.

18. The ten that had gone out of business were listed as closed in a head-branch temple register in the late eighteenth century, but they appear in no other documents from the late seventeenth century, which suggests that they disappeared much earlier. *IHSS* 1999, 607.

19. *OCSK*, 72–75; *SSKFK*, vol. 3, 106, 127, 134; *IHSS* 1994, 87.

20. *IHSS* 1999, 205–27.

21. Mase, "Bakuhan kokka ni okeru jinja sōron to chōbaku kankei," 65–67.

22. Before that year, the *bakufu* had issued individual law codes for a few large shrines, namely the Ise Shrines (1603, 1633, 1635, 1644), the Tsurugaoka Hachiman Shrine (1628), Nikkō Tōshōgū (1634, 1655), and the Sannō Shrine in Edo (1659); *Tokugawa kinrei kō*, 1–10, 52–59. See also Hardacre, *Religion and Society in Nineteenth-Century Japan*, 47–48; Hagiwara, "Yoshida shintō to gōson kannushisō," 1–8; Kiyohara, *Shintōshi*, 506–44.

23. Hardacre, *Religion and Society in Nineteenth-Century Japan*, 49; Takano, "Idō suru mibun," 348.

24. Maeda, "Court Rank for Village Shrines," 335–38, 340–41.

25. Hardacre, *Religion and Society in Nineteenth-Century Japan*, 51; Toki, "Kinsei no shinshoki soshiki," 232–33.

26. *SSKFK*, vol. 3, 106–7; *IHSS* 1994, 91–92; *SMC*, 184.

27. *IHSS* 1994, 86–92; *SSKFK*, vol. 3, 106–7, 120.

28. *STK*, 490.

29. Ooms, *Tokugawa Village Practice*, 86.

30. *SSKFK*, vol. 3, 133; *IHSS* 1994, 92.

31. *IHSS* 1994, 84–85.

32. Ibid., 92, 111.

33. Ibid., 67–80.

34. Ibid., 24–25.

35. Ibid., 183–93.

36. Ibid., 805–20.

37. 3,173 *tsubo* of land with a yield of about ten *koku* were transferred from Koyasu Village to become Sakamoto Village's Shinchō to replace approximately 3,175 *tsubo* of land yielding about seven and a half *koku* that had been washed away in a flood from Sakamoto Village to Koyasu Village; *STK*, 490.

38. In a survey taken during the Genroku era, Sakamoto Village's yield was officially still calculated as 72 *koku*, but it appears to have been 100 *koku*, according to temple records. Later, that figure indeed rose to 100 *koku* in official records, indicating Ōyama's temple land was limited to Sakamoto Village and no longer included a section of Koyasu Village. By the mid-nineteenth century, the yield of Sakamoto Village was 100 *koku* (exactly the amount of Ōyama's temple land) with a ratio of 0.32 *koku* per household. Kamikoyasu and Shimokoyasu Villages combined had 483 *koku* with 122 households, a much higher ratio of *koku* per household (3.96); *SSKFK*, vol. 3, 103–5.

39. *IHSS* 1994, 69–71.

40. The remaining articles also stipulated that donations for *kitō* by pilgrims traveling in mixed *kō* should henceforth be housed by the *oshi* of the *kō* leader; *IHSS* 1994, 25–27.

41. *IHSS* 1994, 24.

42. Documents with lists of *oshi* in Sakamoto yield numbers for 1718, 1730, 1735, 1786, 1824, and 1835. See *IHSS* 1994, 105–12; Samukawa chōshi henshū iinkai, ed., *Samukawa chōshi chōsa hōkokusho 1*, 84–87, 90–91; Samukawa chōshi henshū iinkai, ed., *Samukawa chōshi chōsa hōkokusho 2*, 93, 101–3; *IHSS* 1994, 86–97; *OCSK*, 11–21. Ariga Mitsuo and Matsuoka Takashi have compiled similar data about the numerical distribution in the eighteenth and nineteenth centuries, reaching contradictory conclusions. Ariga argues that the number of *oshi* rose from 158 in 1786 to 166 in 1840 for Sakamoto and Minoge Villages com-

bined. He continues his calculation until 1985 showing that there was a drastic decline in *oshi* in the modern period leaving only 30 percent of the *oshi* in business, which he attributed to the aftermath of the disassociation of *kami* and Buddhas. See Ariga, *Ōyama monzenmachi no chiriteki kenkyū*, 54. However, Ariga's figures for 1797, 1835, and 1840 are not reliable. The first is only an estimate in the *TMZ*. The other two numbers do not reflect that several *oshi* families had ceased to exist. Matsuoka argues that number of *oshi* declined in the latter half of the eighteenth century. He surveys a larger number of documents, including temple and *oshi* registers and village surveys that predate Ariga's material and are more reliable. Matsuoka argues that the number of *oshi* declined from 189 in the early eighteenth century to 133 in the late eighteenth and early nineteenth centuries for Sakamoto and Minoge Villages combined. He sees the most significant decline between 1730 and 1786 affecting especially *oshi* of middle or lower rank in the mediation system between inns and Shingon temples. Matsuoka attributes the decline to the impact of natural disasters and famine between 1765 and 1790, which led to a decrease in pilgrims—a period in which wealthy *oshi* were more likely to survive; see Matsuoka, "Sagami Ōyama oshi no keisei to tenkai," 25. However, Matsuoka probably overcounts the number for 1730 because he includes villagers who may have run seasonal inns without *oshi* licenses and hence had no distinctive *oshi* names. Furthermore, his count for 1835 is too low. Therefore, the decline seems to be drastic between 1730 and 1835, but, in fact, there was no significant decline in the number of *oshi*.

43. *IHSS* 1994, 26.

44. Toyoda, *Myōji no rekishi*, 139; Ōtō, *Kinsei nōmin to ie, mura, kokka*, 227–32.

45. Bodart-Bailey, *Kaempfer's Japan*, 117.

46. There is no documented use of this kind of name before 1695. Compare with Matsuoka Takashi's chart listing the historical development of different types of *oshi* in *IHSS* 1999, 606–16. For relevant documents of parish sales, see *IHSS* 1994, 182–93.

47. Ibid., 91.

48. Ibid., 97.

49. Ibid., 90–91.

50. Ibid., 71–80. According to Matsuoka, the magistrate of temples and shrines ultimately supported Sakamoto's charges and prohibited the residents of Koyasu from acting as *oshi*, but I have found no evidence for this in the Hōreki documents. Matsuoka, "Sagami Ōyama oshi no keisei to tenkai," 11.

51. *IHSS* 1994, 71–80.

52. *IHSS* 1992, 805–20; *IHSS* 1994, 183–239. From 1665 to 1698, the *oshi* Utsumi Jirōemon—who later adopted the *oshi* name Utsumi Yūkei—acquired about 4,800 *danna* for a total of nearly 200 *ryō* at an average price of about

25 houses per *ryō* in Sagami, Musashi, and Kazusa. Parishioners in Kazusa and Musashi were about the same average price, but parishioners in Sagami were slightly more expensive. He acquired the parishioners primarily from other residents of Sakamoto but also from a few residents of Koyasu. *IHSS* 1994, 183–93.

53. The *oshi* Murayama Hachidayū has been studied in detail by Kimura Motoi, Tanaka Sen'ichi, Tamamuro Fumio, and Matsuoka Takashi. Tamamuro focuses on nearby parishes in Sagami, whereas Tanaka and Matsuoka focus on more distant parishes in Shimōsa and Kazusa. The studies are based on material from the 1830s to the 1880s. As Matsuoka had shown, much of the material was compiled by Hachidayū upon his retirement from a Hachidaibō office. See Kimura, "Jisha to shomin no shinkō," 764–74; Tamamuro Fumio, *Nihon bukkyō shi: kinsei*, 278–91; Tanaka, "Sagami Ōyamakō no oshi to danka," 157–91; Matsuoka, "Sagami Ōyama oshi no danka shūseki katei no kōzō," 49–65.

54. *IHSS* 1994, 182–93.

55. Tamamuro Fumio, *Nihon bukkyō shi: kinsei*, 288–90.

56. *IHSS* 1994, 195.

57. For a list of all documents pertaining to *danka* sales, pawning, and leasing, see *ISSM*. For examples of specific documents, see *IHSS* 1994, 183–239.

58. Ariga, *Ōyama monzenmachi*, 65–96; Tanaka, "Meiji shoki ni okeru Ōyamakō no bunpu," 193–204.

59. *IHSS* 1994, 105–12; Matsuoka, "Sagami Ōyamadera no 'toritsugi' seido no kōzō," 30–35.

60. *IHSS* 1994, 85–92, 111. For a slightly different categorization, see Matsuoka, "Sagami Ōyama oshi no keisei to tenkai," 12–25.

61. *IHSS* 1994, 86–92.

62. Samukawa chōshi henshū iinkai, ed., *Samukawa chōshi chōsa hōkokusho 2*, 101–3.

63. *IHSS* 1994, 87.

64. Tōma, "Ōyama shi," 100–103.

65. *IHSS* 1994, 144–45; Matsuoka, "Sagami Ōyama oshi no keisei to tenkai," 3.

66. Toki, "Shirakawa, Yoshida no shinshoku shihai," 66.

67. *Tokugawa kinrei kō*, 17–20.

68. Toki, "Shirakawa, Yoshida no shinshoku shihai," 57–66. See also Mase, "Bakuhan kokka," 63–93; Matsuoka, "Bakumatsu Meiji shoki," 151–74; Shinno Junko, "Shozan shosha sankei senadatsushoku o meguru yamabushi to shake," 105–31; Endō, "Bakumatsu shakai to shūkyōteki fukko undō," 135–78; Inoue Tomokatsu, "Chiiki shakai ni okeru Yoshida shintō no juyō," 48–66.

69. See sections on Suruga, Kai, Sagami, and Musashi Provinces in *SMC*. For more on Yoshida and Shirakawa Shinto at Mt. Mitake, see Saitō 1970: 257–69.

For a brief synopsis of the Mt. Mitake in the early modern period, see Hardacre, *Religion and Society in Nineteenth-Century Japan*, 95–104.

70. *SSKFK*, vol. 3, 106–7; *IHSS* 1994, 91–92; *SMC*, 184.

71. *SMC*, 175–79; *ONK*, 56–57.

72. Samukawa chōshi henshū iinkai, ed., *Samukawa chōshi chōsa hōkokusho 2*, 101–3.

73. *IHSS* 1994, 43–52; Tōma, "Ōyama shi," 86–90.

74. *IHSS* 1994, 156–68, 173–80.

75. Matsuoka, "Bakumatsu Meiji shoki," 153; *SMC*, 175–77, 185.

76. Matsuoka, "Bakumatsu Meiji shoki," 152–55.

77. Ibid., 152–55. The Yoshida license of the latter did not prevent him from seeking an additional license from the Shirakawa. These, however, were exceptions as all the other *oshi* had not held positions as shrine priests prior to their affiliation with the Shirakawa. *Oshi* from Minoge Village, who were fewer in number and less affected by the tensions existing in Sakamoto Village, did not seek Shirakawa licenses until 1868.

78. Matsuoka, "Bakumatsu Meiji shoki," 155.

79. *SMC*, 173–74.

80. Matsuoka, "Bakumatsu Meiji shoki," 155–59.

81. Tenaka Tadashi, "Ōyama no shinbutsu bunri."

82. *Satō Ryōjike shozō monjo*, vol. 2, docs. 8–10. Only the remaining Tendai-affiliated *yamabushi* were allowed to perform their own funerals.

83. Matsuoka, "Bakumatsu Meiji shoki," 155–59.

84. Ketelaar, *Of Heretics and Martyrs in Meiji Japan*, 3–4.

85. Walthall, "Nativism as a Social Movement," 205.

86. Yamamoto, "Kinsei ni okeru Edowan kōtsū ni tsuite," 297.

87. *STK*, 491.

88. Ibid., 472–73, 490–91.

89. In her study on Nativism in the Ina Valley, Anne Walthall also points out the connections between the Shirakawa House and the Hirata school; Walthall, "Nativism as a Social Movement," 217, 222.

90. Matsuoka, "Bakumatsu Meiji shoki," 160.

91. Ibid., 153, 159–61. Making a distinction between the *oshi*'s reasons to join the Shirakawa and Hirata schools, Matsuoka argues that the former was related to sacerdotal rights whereas the latter was motivated by an interest in literature. Although this may be the case, it is difficult to separate the two as most Nativists were also licensed by the Shirakawa, and little is known about what motivated these Shinto ritualists to enter the Hirata school.

92. This calculation is based on a classification of *oshi* in Matsuoka, "Sagami Ōyama oshi no keisei to tenkai," 12–23.

Chapter 4

1. *SSKFK*, vol. 3, 111–13; *IHSS* 1995: 247–49, 254, 277–80, 302–3, 334, 379.
2. *IHSS* 1994, 41.
3. Ibid., 53.
4. *OFRK* I.
5. *IHSS* 1994, 42–43.
6. Ibid., 46; *OFRK* I; Tōma, "Ōyama shi," 123.
7. *OFRK* I; Tōma, "Ōyama shi," 123.
8. Vaporis, *Breaking Barriers*, 206.
9. Tamamuro Fumio, *Nihon bukkyō shi: kinsei*, 291–96; Tamamuro Fumio, "Ōyama Fudō no mokudachi no rieki ni tsuite," 86–93.
10. Rotermund, *Hōsōgami ou la petit vérole aisément*, 54–56.
11. Suzuki Shōsei, "Sagami Ōyama shinkō no seiritsu to hatten," 82–83.
12. Kojima, *Kanagawa-ken katarimono shiryō*, 51–53, 55–56.
13. *OFRK* V.1, V.2, IV.8, VII.2, VI.6, IX.3. In the Hiratsuka area, a collection of old amulets from Ōyama and other sacred sites was found stashed in the eaves of a historic building in order to protect the house from fire. Hiratsuka-shi hakubutsukan shishi hensangakari, ed., *Hiratsuka shishi 12*, 774–76. For an analysis of the practice, see Tamamuro Fumio, "Ōyama Fudō no mokudachi no rieki ni tsuite," 86–93.
14. *OFRK* II.3, XII.9, II.6, II.7, XII.1, XII.2, VI.5, IV.9.
15. Tamamuro Fumio, *Nihon bukkyō shi: kinsei*, 295–98; *OFRK* III.1, II.5, III.10, III.11, V.6.
16. Evidence from sources other than the *Ōyama Fudō reigenki* supports this diversity as well as the growth of the Sekison Daigongen cult. See Shinno, *Seinaru tabi*, 40–45; Kodama and Kawamura, eds., *Kinsei nōsei shiryō shū 3*, 184–85; Nakazawa, "Yamanashi-shi Esohara buraku no Sekisonkō," 18–21; Hakoyama, "Nakayoshida no Sekisonkō hoka," 7–12.
17. Agrarian villages turned to Ōyama during times of disaster regardless of the season. See Suzuki Heikurō, *Kōshi nikki*, vol. 4, 82; Suzuki Heikurō, *Kōshi nikki*, vol. 6, 46.
18. Eade and Sallnow, *Contesting the Sacred*, 24.
19. Tōma, "Ōyama shi," 69, 72–73; *SSKFK*, vol. 3, 113–15; Utsumi, *Sōshū Ōyama*, 230–31; *OFRK* I.
20. *OFRK* IV.9.
21. Tenaka Myōōtarō Kagemoto, *Ōyama miyadaiku Myōōtarō nikki*, vol 2, 516–17, 603, 639, 645, 646–64; Tenaka Tadashi, "Ōyama no shinbutsu bunri."
22. The text as quoted by Miyata states that people took ablutions on 6/17. This may be a mistake for 6/27 because the summer festival did not begin until 6/28.

23. Cited in Miyata, *Edo saijiki*, 148–51.

24. Kojima, *Kanagawa-ken katarimono shiryō*, 46–53.

25. *IHSS* 1994, 25–26.

26. *OFRK* 1; *IHSS* 1994, 53; *STK*, 491; *SSKFK*, vol. 3, 118; *TMZ*, 226. The practice of opening the summit to pilgrims was, of course, also seen at other mountains in Japan such as Mt. Fuji or Mt. Haguro. In his study of the annual ritual cycle of the Haguro cult, Earhart mentions practices conducted during *natsu no mine* (summer peak) that are very similar to Ōyama's summer festival. However, Earhart does not explore the historical origins of these rites but only distinguishes between the rituals practiced before and after the Meiji restoration. We do not know, therefore, whether these rituals are indeed of medieval origin or developed during the early modern period, when pilgrimages to Mt. Haguro became increasingly popular. Earhart, *A Religious Study of the Mount Haguro Sect of Shugendō*, 103–10.

27. *OFRK* 1; *IHSS* 1994, 53; *STK*, 491; *SSKFK*, vol. 3, 118; *TMZ*, 226.

28. H. Byron Earhart provides a concise description of the *gōō* amulets and their consecration in his study of the Haguro cult. He points out that Haguro amulets were consecrated by *yamabushi* upon their delivery to their parishioners—a marked difference from Ōyama, where the *oshi* did not have this privilege. Similar to Ōyama, however, Buddhist temples usually own the printing blocks for such amulets. See Earhart, *A Religious Study of the Mount Haguro Sect of Shugendō*, 78–81.

29. For rituals conducted during the summer festival, see *OFRK* 1; *IHSS* 1994, 53. For more on the summer retreat, see *KKS*, 672–73; *STK*, 469–70; Yamasaki, *Shingon*, 168–69.

30. See Sugane, "Kinsei no Ōyamakō to Ōyama oshi," 35–38; *IHSS* 1994, 367–72.

31. Teiser, *The Ghost Festival in Medieval China*, 27–28.

32. Ibid., 34–35. Earhart notes a similar connection between the summer retreat of the *yamabushi* at Mt. Haguro and the opening of the mountain for pilgrims during *natsu no mine* (summer mountain); see Earhart, *A Religious Study of the Mount Haguro Sect of Shugendō*, 103.

33. Tamamuro Taijō, "Kaichō," 508–9; Kitamura Satoshi, "Kaichō," 75–76. For detailed studies of *kaichō* in Edo, see Hiruma, "Edo no kaichō," 273–472; Hiruma, *Edo no kaichō*; Kitamura Gyōon, *Kinsei kaichō no kenkyū*; and Ambros, "The Display of Hidden Treasures."

34. Hur, *Prayer and Play in Late Tokugawa Japan*, 212–13.

35. *STK*, 469–70; Tōma, "Ōyama shi," 65.

36. *IHSS* 1994, 320.

37. Sugane, "Kinsei no Ōyamakō to Ōyama oshi," 35–38.

38. *IHSS* 1994, 42–43.

39. *OFRK* XIII.5.

40. See Yamasaki, *Shingon*, 173–75; Payne, *The Tantric Ritual of Japan*; Saso, *Tantric Art and Meditation*, 1–31; Saso, *Homa Rites and Mandala Meditations in Tendai Buddhism*, 24–102.

41. *SSKFK*, vol. 3, III; *IHSS* 1995, 325.

42. *IHSS* 1994, 43.

43. The subtemples that provided *goma* services for parishioners of *oshi* even had special rooms for this purpose. One subtemple, Daikakubō, had a room for mediation (*toritsugi no ma*) near its entrance. The room was used to receive parishioners, give them brief instruction, discuss the miracle efficacy of Ōyama's deities, and perform rituals in the alcove. Matsuoka, "Sagami Ōyamadera no 'toritsugi' seido no kōzō," 28–30; *IHSS* 1994, 112–23.

44. *IHSS* 1994, 310–11.

45. *OFRK* II.6.

46. *SSKFK*, vol. 3, 120; Suzuki Yoshiaki, "Ōyama shinkō no keimō katsudō," 21–22. Although he does not give a reason for the development, Tanaka Sen'ichi has argued that the practice of pilgrimage to Chatōjidera did not start until the nineteenth century. After Raigōin and Kōenbō were disestablished in the Meiji period, the services were taken over by a Jōdo temple at the foot of the mountain. Tanaka, "Sagami Ōyama no Chatōji mairi ni tsuite," 21–41.

47. The other shrine priests were: the head shrine priest (*kannushi*), Satō Chūmu, and the three shrine priests (*shinke*) Utsumi Keibutayū, Utsumi Hyōbutayū, and Utsumi Shikibutayū. In addition, there were five shrine priests—or mediums (*kannagi*)—in charge of performing *kagura*: Jakumanbō, Akaibō, Daimanbō, Jōmanbō, and Hondaibō. *IHSS* 1994, 92; *STK*, 470–71.

48. *STK*, 470–71.

49. *IHSS* 1994, 84.

50. Ibid., 92.

51. *SSKFK*, vol. 3, 105–6; Asaka, "Ōyama shinkō tōzan shūraku keisei no kiban," 19.

52. *IHSS* 1994, 334.

53. Ibid., 72.

54. Ibid., 24, 26.

55. Minamiashigara-shi, ed., *Minamiashigara shishi 6, tsūshihen 1*, 701–2.

56. *IHSS* 1994, 391–94.

57. Ibid., 410–13. For example, it explained how to assess the suitability of husband and wife by the shape of the woman's eyes or how to deduce the shape of a man's penis by the shape of his jaw, nose, or neck and the size

of a woman's breasts by the shape of her nose. People's temper, filial piety, and depth of faith could be predicted by the size and shape of their eyes.

58. Ibid., 403–9.

59. Makoto Hayashi, "Tokugawa-Period Disputes between Shugen Organizations and *Onmyōji* over Rights to Practice Divination," 168–72.

60. For an example of an *oshi*'s handling of pilgrims, see *OFRK* xii.5, and of an *oshi* as an intermediary, see *OFRK* v.4.

61. *IHSS* 1994, 23–27.

62. Ibid., 325–67.

63. Ibid., 23–27, 67–80.

64. Ibid., 14. Inomata's version of the abridged version of the *Ōyamadera engi* was based on the *Tōkaidō meisho zue*. In this passage, Inomata edited the text to be more specific about the months in which the *oshi* made their rounds. The original text in the *Tōkaidō meisho zue* reads: "Among the houses that are lined up tightly on both sides of the road at the foot of this mountain, there are many *oshi*. They have parishioners in many provinces to whom they distribute amulets annually." *TMZ*, 228.

65. *STK*, 469; *KKS*, 672.

66. *OFRK* i; *IHSS* 1994, 52–53.

67. Tamamuro Fumio, *Nihon bukkyō shi: kinsei*, 282–85.

68. Ibid., 285–87.

69. See Ibid., 287–88; *IHSS* 1994, 254–62, 271–93. Tamamuro distinguishes between 87 packages of medicine and 4,284 bags of tea. This may a misreading due to the similarity between the characters *kusuri* (medicine) and *cha* (tea). In his chart for 1845, Tamamuro also lists bags of tea, but the document actually says medicine. Comparable Murayama documents from other years all have medicine. Similar documents of other *oshi* also list medicine and tea, but medicine is the more common item. Therefore, the document from 1837 probably listed medicine rather than tea. See Tamamuro Fumio, *Nihon bukkyō shi: kinsei*, 287–88; *IHSS* 1994, 254–62.

70. Tamamuro Fumio, *Nihon bukkyō shi: kinsei*, 287–88; Tamamuro Fumio, "Ōyama shinkō," 370–71.

71. *IHSS* 1994, 263–70. The *Ōyama Fudō reigenki* contains three stories about boils healed by ointments after prayer to Fudō and the miraculous discovery of the medicine. These ointments were produced in nearby villages but bore no direct link to the *oshi*. See *OFRK* iii.8; x.6; xii.8. In addition to handing out medicines, Takao distributed smallpox amulets on occasion, such as in 1854; see *IHSS* 1994, 270. For more on folk remedies to ward off smallpox, see Rotermund, *Hōsōgami ou la petit vérole aisément* and Rotermund, "Demonic Affliction or Contagious Disease," 373–98.

72. *IHSS* 1994, 320–21. It is of interest that Mt. Kōya, Ōyama Hachidaibō's head temple, was also associated with the distribution of *ōbaku*-based medicine, e.g., *daranisuke*. For the role of sect-specific medicines such as *gedokuan* in the Sōtō School, see Williams, *The Other Side of Zen*, 86–102. More research is needed to determine if Ōyama *oshi* received their medicines or recipes from Mt. Kōya through a Kogi Shingon–based distribution system akin to the system used by the Sōtō School to distribute their medicine, *gedokuan*.

73. Shinjō, *Shinkō Shaji sankei no shakai-keizai shiteki kenkyū*, 181–85.

74. Tamamuro Fumio, "Ōyama shinkō," 372. Tamamuro shows that, on his tour of seven nearby villages in Sagami Province in 1828, Hachidayū tended to distribute large amulets, rice crackers, kelp, dried persimmons, and paper to his hosts; gave important village residents large amulets, rice crackers, and kelp; and handed out small amulets and rice crackers to the rest. On average, he distributed 6 or 7 large amulets and about 41 small amulets per village. Tanaka Sen'ichi has similar evidence from 89 villages in Shimōsa, which Hachidayū visited in the 1837. Hachidayū gave large amulets to important villagers and small amulets to the rest, handing out an average of 5 large amulets and 34 small amulets per village. Tanaka, "Sagami Ōyamakō no oshi to danka," 163–66. Matsuoka Takashi's figures for the same 89 villages are slightly lower but yield about the same average (5 large and 33 small amulets). He adds evidence from 66 villages in Musashi and Kazusa, yielding around 4 or 5 large amulets and 57 small amulets per village. Matsuoka, "Sagami Ōyama oshi no danka shūseki katei no kōzō," 62–63.

75. Matsuoka, "Sagami Ōyama oshi no danka shūseki katei no kōzō," 62–64; Tanaka, "Sagami Ōyamakō no oshi to danka," 186.

76. Registers in Edo, perhaps due to the high concentration of parishioners with similar status—mostly merchants and artisans—were even marked with a special code that identified specific sets of gifts and amulets. See *IHSS* 1992, 232, 228–61, 286.

77. Special paper amulets were made from mulberry paper containing rice starch.

78. *IHSS* 1992, 353–77; *IHSS* 1994, 272.

79. *IHSS* 1992, 391–421; *IHSS* 1994, 267.

80. *IHSS* 1992, 218, 222.

81. Ibid., 519–20.

82. Ibid., 157–59.

83. *IHSS* 1994, 246.

84. *IHSS* 1992, 163–64.

85. Tanaka, "Sagami Ōyamakō no oshi to danka," 168–71.

86. Ibid., 168–73, map A.

87. Ibid., 174–75, map B. Based on evidence from the Taishō and Shōwa period, Tanaka suggests that the *oshi* probably exchanged the grain for money, which they could transport more easily to Ōyama.

88. Tanaka, "Sagami Ōyamakō no oshi to danka," 174–75.

89. Tamamuro Fumio, *Nihon bukkyō shi: kinsei*, 290–92.

90. *OFRK* xii. 5 provides an example of how parishioners might shift their affiliation due to personal contact with another *oshi*.

91. Tōkyō-to Setagaya-ku kyōiku iinkai, ed., *Karei nenjū gyōji: kōyaku Kami-machi Ōba-ke*, 109–13.

92. Chiba, "Atogaki," 196–97.

Chapter 5

1. Blacker, "Religious Travellers in the Edo Period," 593; Hoshino, "The Historical Significance of Pilgrimages in Japan," 8–10.

2. Vaporis, *Breaking Barriers*, 198–216, 236–54; Foard, "The Boundaries of Compassion," 231–52; Kouamé, *Initiation à la Paléographie Japonaise*, 5–6; Kouamé, "Shikoku's Local Authorities and *henro* during the Golden Age of Pilgrimage," 413–25; MacWilliams, "Temple Myths and Popularization of Kannon Pilgrimage in Japan," 378–81; Davis, *Japanese Religion and Society*, 45–80; Nenzi, "To Ise at All Costs," 75–114.

3. Blacker, "Religious Travellers in the Edo Period," 593–608. Blacker is relying on the scholarship of Hoshino Eiki, Shinjō Tsunezō, and Gorai Shigeru. Of the three, only Shinjō covers all aspects of pilgrimage throughout Japanese history. Much of Gorai's scholarship focuses on *yamabushi* and mendicancy, and Hoshino's scholarship on pilgrimage deals primarily with Shikoku.

4. Turner, *Image and Pilgrimage in Christian Culture*, 1–39.

5. Ibid., 25.

6. Ibid., 15.

7. Tremlett, "The Problem of Belief," 24.

8. Sallnow, *Pilgrims in the Andes*, 9; Coleman and Eade, eds., *Reframing Pilgrimage*, 3.

9. Eade and Sallnow, *Contesting the Sacred*, 26.

10. Hoshino Eiki has linked the beggar-type pilgrim particularly to the Shikoku circuit, which had fewer facilities than the pilgrimage routes to Ise or the Saikoku Thirty-Three Kannon circuit. Hoshino, "The Historical Significance of Pilgrimages in Japan," 10–13.

11. Kouamé, "Shikoku's Local Authorities and *henro*," Kouamé, *Pèlerinage et Société dans le Japon des Tokugawa*; Nenzi, "To Ise at All Costs." Natalie Kouamé argues that the subversive image of pilgrims created by Japanese scholars such as Shinjō Tsunezō and Maeda Takashi is an exaggeration. She points out that the

Shikoku pilgrimage was not as "turbulent and socially disruptive" as the pilgrimage to Ise because individual pilgrims rarely created any public disturbances. Kouamé, "Shikoku's Local Authorities and *henro*," 419–20; Kouamé, *Initiation à la Paléographie Japonaise*, 5–6. Yet the poverty and solitary nature of the pilgrims in itself may have been suspicious to the authorities, who also saw them as a drain on the local economy. In terms of the pilgrimage to Ise, large-scale pilgrimage waves occurred only four times during the early modern period: 1650, 1705, 1771, and 1830. Davis has emphasized that even the pilgrimage waves to Ise ultimately helped preserve the social order. See Davis, *Japanese Religion and Society.* Nenzi shows that while the term *nukemairi* initially designated unauthorized mendicancy on the journey to Ise, eventually in the late early modern period, the term was also applied to wealthy pilgrims who were not destitute social marginals but essentially engaged in leisurely travel. Nenzi, "To Ise at All Costs."

12. For a list of the various routes, see Ōyama Afurijinja, ed., *Sagami Ōyama kaidō*, 143–44; Asaka, "Ōyama shinkō tōzan shūraku keisei no kiban," 27.

13. *SSKFK*, vol. 1, 133–36, 284–87; *SSKFK*, vol. 2, 278–81, 331–35; *SSKFK*, vol. 3, 159–62, 253–56; *SSKFK*, vol. 4, 5–9. The name appears particularly in the districts of Ōsumi, Kōza, Aikō, Kamakura, Yurugi, Ashigara Kami, and Ashigara Shimo—those closest to Ōyama—but not in Miura and Tsukui, which were more remote.

14. *SSKFK*, vol. 1, 133–36, 284–87; *SSKFK*, vol. 2, 278–81, 331–35; *SSKFK*, vol. 3, 159–62, 253–56; *SSKFK*, vol. 4, 5–9. Ōyamamichi in southeastern Sagami usually ranged between nine to twelve feet, whereas some of those in western Sagami were as narrow as six feet. In comparison, the Tōkaidō was about eighteen to thirty feet wide in Sagami Province.

15. Kanagawa kinseishi kenkyūkai, ed., *Edo jidai no Kanagawa*, 42–43, plate 7.

16. Ōto and Yamaguchi, eds., *Edo jidai zushi 14*, vol. 1, plates 13, 430, 431. Panoramic views of the area continued to include Ōyama. Distant scenic views of Ōyama from Hirano (Sagami) to the southeast and from the Matsuru Peninsula in the southwest were also included in the *Netsukai meishōzu* (1800). See Kanagawa kinseishi kenkyūkai, ed., *Edo jidai no Kanagawa*, 74–75, plate 1.

17. *IHSS* 1994, 71–80.

18. *OFRK* iii.5.

19. *OFRK* iv.5.

20. See Kawasaki-shi shimin myūjiamu, ed., *Kawasaki shiryō sōsho 3*, vol. 1, 163–64, 167–68, 184–85.

21. Kawasaki-shi shimin myūjiamu, ed., *Kawasaki shiryō sōsho 3*, 184–85.

22. Sagamihara-shi, ed., *Sagamihara shishi*, vol. 6, 469.

23. From the mid-eighteenth century, the pilgrimage to Ōyama along these two routes from Edo appeared in travel literature about the Kantō-Tōkai

region, such as the *Zoku Edo sunago onmei sekishi* (1735), the *Edo sōganoko meisho taizen* (1747), the *Tōsei zamochi banashi* (1766), and the *Tōto saijiki* (1838). In works of pure fiction, Ōyama appeared first in a puppet play and then in a number of *kokkeibon*. Comic travelogues on the pilgrimage to Ōyama depicted the entertaining, sometimes even rowdy and raunchy, aspects. The journey to Ōyama and Sekison's wooden swords were the topics of *Ōyama Sekison osamedachi homekagami* (1779), a puppet play by Ki Jōtarō, Hirawaraya Tōsaku, and Matsu Kanshichi. The pilgrimage to Ōyama appeared again as the subject of Ryūtei Rijō's *Ōyama dōchū kurige shiriuma* (6 vols.; published 1817–1822), republished as *Ōyama dōchū hizakurige* (6 vols.; published 1832), both of which were illustrated by Utagawa Kuniyoshi. Ryūtei Rijō's *Ōyama dōchū hizakurige* contains the picaresque adventures of Tokurobei, from Hyakufukuya in Edo's Asakusa district, who decides to make a second pilgrimage to Ōyama toward the end of the Sixth Month accompanied by his young employee Fukushichi. A few decades later, Dontei Robun published his *Ōyama dōchū hizakurige* in 1857, borrowing the title of Ryūtei Rijō's earlier *Ōyama dōchū hizakurige* and the two main characters in Jippensha Ikku's *Tōkaidōchū hizakurige* (1802–1809). Dontei Robun's borrowing of Jippensha Ikku's two characters for pilgrimages to Ōyama was based on a textual reference in Jippensha Ikku's work: in *Tōkaidōchū hizakurige*, when Kita and Yaji give an elderly pilgrim to Enoshima directions from Fujisawa, Yaji mentions that he traveled to Ōyama in the previous year. See Jippensha, *Tōkaidōchū hizakurige*, vol. 1, 92–93.

24. The woodblock prints often included images of Ōyama in their portrayal of Tōkaidō stations where Ōyamamichi forked off, such as Hodogaya, Totsuka, Yotsuya, Hiratsuka, and river crossings on the way to Ōyama, such as Tamura and Toda. Hokusai, Hiroshige, Toyokuni, Kuniyoshi, and Sadahide also produced several prints of Ōyama itself. One favorite motif was Ōyama's waterfalls, especially Rōbendaki and Ōdaki. Although Hokusai and Hiroshige were familiar with the landmarks along the road to Ōyama, neither appears to have had very detailed knowledge of Ōyama itself because their representations are geographically inaccurate.

25. *TMZ*, 225–28.

26. Kanagawa kinseishi kenkyūkai, ed., *Edo jidai no Kanagawa*, 75, plate 4.

27. Ōto and Yamaguchi, *Edo jidai zushi 14*, plate 248.

28. The section on Ōyama contains the story of a pilgrim who offered a tree instead of the customary wooden votive sword and subsequently had a dream of a *tengu* who chided him for the unusual offering. See Jippensha, *Jippensha Ikku Hakone Enoshima Kamakura dōchūki*, 34–35.

29. Ōyama Afurijinja, *Sagami Ōyama kaidō*, 143–44; Asaka, "Ōyama shinkō tōzan shūraku keisei no kiban," 27.

30. Sugane, "Kinsei no Ōyamakō to Ōyama oshi," 35–39.

31. Ōyama Afurijinja, *Sagami Ōyama kaidō*, 134–35, 172–73.

32. *SSKFK*, vol. 5, 294–95.

33. Ōyama Afurijinja, *Sagami Ōyama kaidō*, 174.

34. Abe, "Kaikokuzen, Edowan no funatabi o megutte," 337–38.

35. Ibid., 337–38.

36. Ōyama Afurijinja, *Sagami Ōyama kaidō*, 172; Abe, "Kaikokuzen, Edowan no funatabi o megutte," 314–16.

37. Yasuike, "Chūsei, kinsei ni okeru Edo naikai watashifune no tenkai," 255–62; Yamamoto, "Kinsei ni okeru Edowan kōtsū ni tsuite," 286–303.

38. Kanagawa kinseishi kenkyūkai, ed., *Edo jidai no Kanagawa*, 75; Sugane, "Kinsei no Ōyamakō to Ōyama oshi," 35–38; Tōkyō-to Setagaya-ku kyōiku iinkai, ed., *Ise dōchūki shiryō*; Setagaya kuritsu kyōdo shiryōkan, ed., *Shaji sankei to daisankō*.

39. *IHSS* 1994, 24–25.

40. Ibid., 23–24.

41. Ibid., 323–67; Asaka, "Ōyama shinkō tōzan shūraku keisei no kiban," 23–26.

42. *IHSS* 1994, 323–64.

43. Ibid., 367–72.

44. Asaka Yukio has slightly different numbers. The difference is primarily caused by whether one counts pilgrims from a district on the border toward Shimōsa or Musashi Provinces. See Asaka, "Ōyama shinkō tōzan shūraku keisei no kiban," 23–26.

45. *IHSS* 1994, 27.

46. Tanaka, "Sōshū Ōyamakō no oshi to danka," 79–80; *IHSS* 1994, 323–64.

47. *IHSS* 1994, 23–27.

48. Sugane, "Kinsei no Ōyamakō to Ōyama oshi," 30–41.

49. Hirano, "Fujikō, Ōyamakōno junpai to yūzan," 29. For development of the cult of Jikigyō Miroku, see Tyler, "The Tokugawa Peace and Popular Religion," 109–17.

50. Hara, "Ōyama, Fuji, Enoshima," 25.

51. During the dispute between villages of Sakamoto and Koyasu in 1752, evidence indicates that even small inns in Koyasu offered a service to handle the luggage of pilgrims. See *IHSS* 1994, 72.

52. Hirano, "Fujikō, Ōyamakōno junpai to yūzan," 29–31.

53. Hara, "Ōyama, Fuji, Enoshima," 27; Hirano, "Fujikō, Ōyamakō no junpai to yūzan," 31.

54. Harada, *Sagami Ōyama*, 25.

55. The confraternity visited Ōyama eleven times between 1822 and 1862, yielding an average of one pilgrimage every 3.7 years. However, between 1822 and 1844, pilgrimages were eight or six years apart and became more frequent between 1844 and 1862, when the confraternity went to Ōyama every two to three years. Sugane, "Kinsei no Ōyamakō to Ōyama oshi," 35–38.

56. Unpublished research by Sugane Yukihiro.

57. Kouamé, *Initiation à la Paléographie Japonaise*, xxxix–xl, 23. A Konpira confraternity from Kamiagawa Village in Iyo Province that was dedicated to making monthly pilgrimages farmed a communal field to support itself.

58. Sugane, "Kinsei no Ōyamakō to Ōyama oshi," 35–38. For Ogasawara's connection with Sakuda Village, see the *Kaidōki* in *IHSS* 1999: 709.

59. The confraternity calculated its costs in gold and copper currencies. The various expenses have been converted into gold currency to facilitate comparisons between them.

60. Sugane, "Kinsei no Ōyamakō to Ōyama oshi," 35–38.

61. Matsuoka, "Sagami Ōyamadera no 'toritsugi' seido no kōzō," 37–38.

62. Sugane, "Kinsei no Ōyamakō to Ōyama oshi," 35–38.

63. Vaporis, *Breaking Barriers*, 243.

64. Yasuike, "Chūsei kinsei ni okeru Edo naikai watashifune no tenkai," 259–60. Women, especially *samurai* women, were subjected to strict inspections at these checkpoints to prevent them from being smuggled out of Edo in preparation for a planned uprising against the *bakufu*. See Vaporis, *Breaking Barriers*, 159–74.

65. Yasuike, "Chūsei kinsei ni okeru Edo naikai watashifune no tenkai," 256–60.

66. *IHSS* 1994, 343, 356.

67. Hiratsuka kikakushitsu shishi hensanshitsu, ed., *Hiratsuka to Ōyama*, 38.

68. See Ōto and Yamaguchi, *Edo jidai zushi 14*, plates 248, 262; Gotō, *Ukiyoe taikei 14*, 99, plate 6; cover of Matsuoka, *Edo no sankeikō*; Itabashi kuritsu kyōdo shiryōkan, ed., *Tokubetsuten tabi to shinkō*, 31, plate 2.

69. Matsuoka, *Edo no sankeikō*, 219–20.

70. Ibid., 196–200.

71. Ibid., 197.

72. *Gomakō, omikikō*, and *hyakumikō*—confraternities resembling *otenagakō*—were also found at Enoshima, but in contrast to Ōyama, *omikikō* made up a much smaller percentage. See Matsuoka, *Edo no sankeikō*, 197–99.

73. *OFRK* XIII.5.

74. Matsuoka, "Sagami Ōyamadera no 'toritsugi' seido no kōzō," 37–38; Sugane, "Kinsei no Ōyamakō to Ōyama oshi," 35–38.

75. Matsuoka, *Edo no sankeikō*, plates 34, 70, 127, 142, 152, 201–2, 211.

76. Ibid., 204–6, 208–9, plates 7, 16, 64.

77. Harada, *Sagami Ōyama*, 27–28.

78. See, for example, Atsugi-shi kyōiku iinkai shakai kyōikuka, ed., *Kyōdo shiryō tenshishitsu tokubetsu ten*, 15–19.

79. Matsuoka, *Edo no sankeikō*, 215–19, plates 47, 91, 130, 172.

80. *IHSS* 1994, 27; Saitō, *Bukō nenpyō*, 166.

81. Kawasaki-shi shimin myūjiamu, ed., *Kawasaki shiryō sōsho 3*, vol. 1, 167–68.

82. Hara, "Ōyama, Fuji, Enoshima," 25; Sugane, "Kinsei no Ōyamakō to Ōyama oshi," 16–17; Yasuike, "Chūsei kinsei ni okeru Edo naikai watashifune no tenkai," 255–62; Yamamoto, "Kinsei ni okeru Edowan kōtsū ni tsuite," 286–303.

Chapter 6

1. Foucault, "Of Other Spaces," 25.

2. Coleman and Eade, eds., *Reframing Pilgrimage*, 15.

3. Eade and Sallnow, *Contesting the Sacred*, 15.

4. Smyers, *The Fox and the Jewel*, 11.

5. Grapard, *The Protocol of the Gods*, 75.

6. Ibid., 82.

7. Teeuwen and Rambelli, "Introduction," 48.

8. Tyler, "The Tokugawa Peace and Popular Religion," 109–17. Miyazaki Fumiko suggested in a conversation with the author that a shift similar to the one at Ōyama occurred at Mt. Fuji.

9. *SMC* 40–47, 254, 451–64, 560.

10. Thal, "Rearranging the Landscape of the Gods," 32–41, 70–86; Thal, *Rearranging the Landscape of the Gods*, 115–26.

11. Blacker, *The Catalpa Bow*, 174–77. Rotermund uses a slightly different typology distinguishing (1) Shinto deities (e.g., Inari, Hie Sannō, Gion, deities of the road [*dōsōjin*], etc.); (2) Buddhist deities (e.g., the five wisdom kings, including Fudō, acolytes and attendant hosts, dragons, heavenly deities, *yasha*, Kannon, Daikoku); (3) *Ryōbu* deities (e.g., *gongen* deities); and (4) Daoist deities (North Star, Konjin ["Metal Spirit"], and Kōshin). Hartmut O. Rotermund, *Die Yamabushi* (Hamburg: Kommissionsverlag, Cram, de Gyuter & Co., 1967), 62–76. However, this typology is difficult to uphold because most of these deities tend to be combinatory, which makes it virtually impossible to draw a line between Shinto, Buddhist, *Ryōbu*, and Daoist deities.

12. According to Hisasaki, the *shintai* of Sekison Daigongon was a small, blue-green rock shaped like a lingam. Lingam-shaped stones are often the focus of fertility cults. Hisasaki saw the rock when climbing to the summit in

1950 and also cites historical sources from the early eighteenth century. Hisa-saki, "Sagami Ōyama reiseki," 20–21.

13. According to the *kanbun engi*, Kōzō enshrined a statue of Fudō at Ōyama to fulfill the wish of his master, Gyōki, in 761. However, Gyōki died in 749, six years before Rōben supposedly opened up Ōyama. The attribution is thus probably fictitious.

14. Kojima, *Kanagawa-ken katarimono shiryō*, vol. 2, 22–23, 55.

15. *IHSS* 1995, 419–22, 436–40. The Heian-period statue is surrounded by statues of the other four wisdom kings, which date from 1855, the year of the great earthquake that destroyed Ōyama completely.

16. Brian Ruppert shows that Buddhist monks had already been involved in rainmaking rites and dragon cults in early Chinese Buddhism. With the intro-duction of Shingon Buddhism in the Heian period, rainmaking rites became an important part of the Shingon repertoire. Ruppert, "Buddhist Rainmaking in Early Japan," 143–74.

17. Kojima, *Kanagawa-ken katarimono shiryō*, vol. 2, 20–21, 52–53.

18. See, for example, Fowler, "In Search of the Dragon," 147–51; Moerman, *Localizing Paradise*, 52–53. For more on thunder gods in Japanese culture, see Lin, "From Thunder Child to Dharma Protector," 54–76, and Ouwehand, *Namazu-e and Their Themes*, 141–43.

19. Lin, "From Thunder Child to Dharma Protector," 66–73.

20. Moerman, *Localizing Paradise*, 52–53.

21. Teeuwen, "The Creation of a *honji suijaku* Deity," 117.

22. Teeuwen and Rambelli, "Introduction," 31–33.

23. Kojima, *Kanagawa-ken katarimono shiryō*, vol. 2, 22–23, 55.

24. Rotermund, *Die Yamabushi*, 190–206; Blacker, *The Catalpa Bow*, 182–85; Wakabayashi, "Tengu,"; Miyamoto, *Tengu to shugenja*. For more on *tengu* at Ōyama, see Chigiri, *Tengu no kenkyū*, and Chigiri, *Zushū tengu retsuden*.

25. *TMZ*, 226–28.

26. *Inomata Saburō ke shozō monjo*, vol. 1, document 3, 151–64.

27. *IHSS* 1994, 10.

28. Maeda, "Court Rank for Village Shrines," 341.

29. Ibid., 339–41.

30. Thal, "Redefining the Gods," 386; Inoue Tomokatsu, "Kanseiki ni okeru ujigami, hayarigami to shōtei ken'i," 1–26.

31. Ooms, *Tokugawa Ideology*.

32. *IHSS* 1994, 58; According to the *Ōyama Fudō reigenki*, the monk Shōgenbō Tsūga was originally from Otowasan Seisuiji in Sunpu and served as the resident monk of Jutokuin in Kyōhō 13 (1728). That year, he was miraculously cured from a painful abscess by Ōyama Fudō. Even after he returned to Seisuiji as its abbot,

he remained a faithful believer in Fudō, reciting scriptures dedicated to Fudō 10,000 times and holding *goma* rituals 1,000 times each year until the end of his life. He passed away on An'ei 7 (1778)/10/15. See *OFRK* III.8.

33. *OFRK* I.

34. *Inomata Saburō ke shozō monjo*, vol. 1, 151–64, 205–29, 235–45.

35. *OFRK* I.

36. A sacred sword shining with an unusual light resembles a passage in the *Owari no kuni fudoki* where Yamato Takeru's sword Kusanagi gives off a mysterious light, which Yamato Takeru regards as proof of the divinity of the sword. See Isomae, "Myth in Metamorphosis," 365.

37. *IHSS* 1994, 57–58.

38. Grapard, *The Protocol of the Gods*, 82.

39. *IHSS* 1994, 55–59.

40. According to the *Afurijinja kodenkō* (1849), the Shingon priesthood obtained official recognition by the *bakufu* to identify Sekison with Tori no Iwakusufune no Mikoto and Tokuichi with Ōyamazumi no Mikoto at some point in the early modern period. *STK*, 476. Indeed, the *Sagami no kuni fudoki kō* (1840) identified Tori no Iwakusufune as the deity venerated at Afurijinja as Sekison Daigongen and Ōyamazumi as the deity at the Tokuichi. *SSKFK*, vol. 3, 118.

41. *SSKFK*, vol.2, 79–80, 97. Modern scholars have argued that the connection between Konohanasakuya Hime and Ōyamazumi no Mikoto linked Ōyama and Mt. Fuji. Asaka Yukio points out that in popular belief Ōyama represented the male principle (*yang*) whereas Mt. Fuji presented the female principle (*yin*). This, Asaka argues, was why pilgrims visited both sites on one journey. Hara Junchirō expands this theory, explaining that Ōyama was considered *yang* because its deity was the male deity Ōyamazumi no Mikoto, and Mt. Fuji was considered female because it was associated with the female deity Konohanasakuya Hime, enshrined at Sengensha. See Asaka, "Ōyama shinkō tōzan shūraku keisei no kiban," 28–29; Hara, "Ōyama, Fuji, Enoshima," 25.

42. *OFRK* I.

43. *TMZ*, 226, 228.

44. *STK*, 491.

45. *IHSS* 1994, 55.

46. Ibid., 58.

47. *OFRK* XV.3. The motif of the crying Fudō appears frequently in *setsuwa* literature, from the late Heian period on. Fudō's tears are usually seen as a sign that he will take the place of a person who is suffering, especially from an illness, and thereby cure the patient. See Nakamae, "Fudō no namida naki-Fudō setsuwa bikō," 29–48.

48. In *OFRK* VIII.4, he uses 1777 as the reference.

49. Matsuoka, "Sagami Ōyama oshi no keisei to tenkai," 3.

50. Hakoyama, "Nakayoshida no Sekisonkō hoka," 12–13.

51. For a detailed analysis of the distribution of the stories, see Tamamuro Fumio, *Nihon bukkyō shi: kinsei*, 293; Tamamuro Fumio, "*Ōyama Fudō reigenki* ni miru Ōyama shinkō," 127–47.

52. *OFRK* I.

53. *OFRK* XIII.5.

54. Satō explains that if Buddhas took a vengeful role, they were usually not understood as abstract deities but as the Buddhas of specific temples and hence served in a similar capacity as local *kami*. See Hiroo Satō, "Wrathful Deities and Saving Deities," 96–101.

55. *OFRK* IV.9.

56. *Shinmei jiten* (Tokyo: Makotonodō shoten, 1912), 93.

57. Teeuwen and Rambelli, "Introduction," 34–35, 48.

58. *OFRK* IV.9.

59. *SSKFK*, vol. 3, 117–18.

60. The *Tōkaidō meisho zue* mentions that pilgrims on the Bandō Kannon pilgrimage, who had visited Iizumi Kannon, also visited Ōyama via Minoge. See *TMZ*, 228. *Bakumatsu*-period maps of the Bandō Kannon pilgrimage show Ōyama as a stop between Iiyama and Iizumi Kannon. See Kanagawa kinseishi kenkyūkai, *Edo jidai no Kanagawa*, 76; Yamashita, *Chizu de yomu Edo jidai*, 195. Several stories in the *Ōyama Fudō. reigenki* give examples of faithful believers in Ōyama Fudō and Bandō Kannon. See *OFRK* VIII.3, IX.2, X.3.

61. Rambelli, "*Honji suijaku* at Work," 257.

62. Ibid., 257, 259–60, 268–69, 275.

63. The actual origins of the legend are difficult to determine and may lie somewhere in the eighteenth century, when forging genealogies became a preoccupation among the peasantry. For more on forged genealogies, see Maeda, "Court Rank for Village Shrines," 339–41. One undated manuscript appears to have been sent by a carpenter, bearing the name Tenaka Myōōtarō, to the magistrate of temples and shrines. It is difficult to link the text with Kagenao with absolute certainty. See Chiba, ed. "Myōōtarō raiyu," 138. The earliest extant variant of the text appears in *OFRK* XIII.1. The *Sagami no kuni fudoki kō* (1840) references the story of the first ancestor of the Tenaka carpenters and identifies its source twice as a "record from the An'ei era," which may in fact have been the *Myōōtarō raiyu*. See *SSKFK*, vol. 3, 107. If the *SSKFK*, indeed relied on the *Myōōtarō raiyu*, and it dated from the 1770s period, that would place it right around the time of the deification of Kanamaru Monkan in 1773.

64. Chiba, "Myōōtarō raiyu," 135–36.

65. See Rambelli, "*Honji suijaku* at Work," 261–67, 269–72.

66. There is no extant indication that any of Kagenao's theories were shared by other *oshi* or ever became well known among the *oshi*. For example, Sudō Shigeo's *Afurijinja kodenkō*, which was written only 60 years later by another *oshi* and refers to virtually every legend about Ōyama, excludes the *Sōyō Ōyama fu*. Written in *kanbun* and full of archaic expressions, Kagenao's text was probably intended not for a broad audience but only his descendents. There is no indication that it was ever passed on to anyone outside the family.

67. Although Kagenao occasionally documents certain sources to back up his points, extant versions of these sources do not contain the information he claims they do. Barring a purposeful falsification of the contents of his sources, Kagenao either had a variant text available or cited the text incorrectly from memory.

68. *IHSS* 1994, 59, 175–79. He used the name Inbe Kagenao or Myōōtarō Inbe Kagenao when he received instructions on ritual prayers from a Shirakawa-affiliated shrine priest at the Hibita Shrine in Koyasu and in prayers carried out during the reconstruction of the shrines on the summit. Kanamaru Monkan's imperially sanctioned surname Inbe appears in the *Myōōtarō raiyu*. Chiba, "Myōōtarō raiyu," 135.

69. Rambelli, "*Honji suijaku* at Work," 259.

70. *IHSS* 1994, 59–60.

71. Tenaka Myōōtarō Kagemoto, *Ōyama miyadaiku Myōōtarō nikki*, vol. 2, 716–20, 790, 792. The Ōyama Shrine carpenter bore the hereditary name Tenaka Myōōtarō as carpenters and the hereditary name Ogawa Ranbutsu as *oshi*. In the Fifth Month of 1870, the head of the family, Kagemoto, chose to keep the carpenterial name Tenaka Myōōtarō and to remain affiliated with his Buddhist temple, but he gave up his duties as an innkeeper and shrine priest. His eldest son, Chiyotarō Kagechika, who had succeeded him as an *oshi*, turned shrine priest three months earlier, retained the former *oshi* parish and inn, and became a *negi*, taking the name Ogawa Kiyoto and severing his connection with his Jōdo parish temple, Saigōji.

72. The divine genealogy Sudō sought to establish at Ōyama agreed with that of the Hirata School and was known to other Nativists at Ōyama. In 1865, for example, Hirata Kanetane printed a genealogy chart entitled "Jindai ryaku keizu" ("An Abridged Genealogy of the Age of the Gods"), originally compiled by his father Hirata Atsutane in 1815 on the basis of the *Kojiki* and the *Nihongi*. The chart identified Ōyamazumi as a mountain and a sea god. The same chart found its way into the possession of Kanzaki Futayū, an *oshi* turned Nativist since 1859. *Kanzaki Shigeru ke monjo*, vol. 4, document 13, 38–43.

73. These deities were indeed adopted as Ōyama's official Shinto deities after the disassociation of *kami* and Buddhas.

74. Thal, "Redefining the Gods," 387.

75. Teeuwen, trans., *Motoori Norinaga's The Two Shrines of Ise.*

76. *STK*, 475–77.

77. Ibid., 483–85.

78. Ibid., 483–85.

79. Ibid., 472–77.

80. Ibid., 478.

81. Chamberlain and Mason, *A Handbook for Travellers in Japan*, 61.

Chapter 7

1. Sekimori, "The Separation of Kami and Buddha Worship," 199–200.

2. Tamamuro Fumio, "Shinbutsu bunri rei," 920; Murata, *Shinbutsu bunri no chihōteki hatten*, 1. Murata almost equates the terms *shinbutsu bunri* and *haibutsu kishaku*. This is because his study focuses on the impact of disassociaton among Buddhist rather than Shinto institutions. From a Buddhist point of view, the policy of disassociation was certainly destructive. Yet to focus on the destruction alone easily translates into a tale of victims, martyrs, and heroes of resistance colored by sectarian myths. This view discounts the fact that quite a number of Buddhist clerics disrobed voluntarily to participate as Shinto priests in the new system. Ketelaar provides a detailed account of the impact of the policy of disassociation on Meiji Buddhism.

3. Hardacre, *Shintō and the State*, 29–30.

4. Tamamuro Fumio, *Shinbutsu bunri*, 120–25.

5. Murata, *Shinbutsu bunri no chihōteki hatten*, 21.

6. Ibid., 14–15.

7. Tamamuro Fumio, *Shinbutsu bunri*, 133–75, 199–205.

8. Ibid., 175–99.

9. Murata, *Shinbutsu bunri no chihōteki hatten*, 21.

10. Tamamuro Fumio, *Shinbutsu bunri*, 175–99.

11. Nagano, "Meiji ishin to Hikosan yamabushi," 910–11; Tamamuro Fumio, "Shūshō: shinbutsu bunri," 352; Togawa, ed., *Yamagataken bunkazai chōsa hōkokusho* 16, 9; Murata, *Shinbutsu bunri no chihōteki hatten*, 29–30, 102, 140–41, 184–85, 198–99, 202; Hardacre, *Religion and Society in Nineteenth-Century Japan*, 154; Thal, "Redefining the Gods," 379–404, 398–99. For a detailed analysis of the impact of Shinto funerals, see Murata, *Shinbutsu bunri no chihōteki hatten*, 210–72.

12. Date, *Nihon shūkyō seido shiryō ruiju kō*, 622; Earhart, *A Religious Study of the Mount Haguro Sect of Shugendō*, 36; Renondeau, *Le Shugendō*, 86.

13. Hadano shishi hensanshūbi iinkai, ed., *Hadano shishi tsūshi 3 kindai*, 14, 34.

14. Matsuoka, "Bakumatsu Meiji shoki," 154; Ariga, *Ōyama monzenmachi no chiriteki kenkyū*, 55–57, 90–96.

15. Date, *Nihon shūkyō seido shiryō ruiju kō*, 620.

16. Chamberlain and Mason, *A Handbook for Travellers in Japan*, 61.

17. *STK*, 472–73, 487–91. Quote appears on 490.

18. The festival is described in *SSKFK*, vol. 2, 301.

19. *STK*, 476.

20. Sekimori, "The Separation of Kami and Buddha Worship," 210; Takami Inoue, "The Interaction between Buddhist and Shinto Traditions at Suwa Shrine," 303–4. As Sekimori notes, not all sacred sites supported the new regime. Mt. Haguro, for example, continued its support for the Tokugawa regime.

21. Once the unit reached Edo, it was renamed *chōgotai* ("Chastize the Barbarians" Corps).

22. Matsuoka, "Bakumatsu Meiji shoki," 161–63; Tenaka Myōōtarō Kagemoto, *Ōyama miyadaiku Myōōtarō nikki 2*, 499–500, 543. Matsuoka mentions that *oshi* from Mt. Fuji had a similar role in the *chōgotai* during the restoration. As Matsuoka admits, it is not clear to what extent the *oshi* used their stay in Edo to form connections with the newly established Jingi Jimukyoku, which had issued orders for s*hinbutsu bunri*.

23. Tōma, "Ōyama shi," 127; Tenaka Myōōtarō Kagemoto, *Ōyama miyadaiku Myōōtarō nikki 2*, 583.

24. Matsushita Takahiro, ed., *Kantō Kogi Shingonshū honmatsuchō*, 93–94.

25. Tenaka Myōōtarō Kagemoto, *Ōyama miyadaiku Myōōtarō nikki 2*, 504–5, 509–10.

26. Ibid., 516. While the cleric at Jutokuin sent his belongings to Kōmyōin, a Hachidaibō branch temple in nearby Ōtake Village, the clerics at Daikakubō and Hōjuin sent theirs to Chionji in Atsugi, a small branch temple of Sōjiin. The Hachidaibō abbot sent his belongings to Kōzu Village (Ashigarashimo District, Sagami Province), presumably to the temple where he had trained during his youth. This temple was either Anrakuin, one of Kōkongōji's branch temples, or Hōkongōji, a powerful Shingon academy with 31 branch temples, which could offer the high-ranking Hachidaibō abbot a prestigious sanctuary after his transfer from Ōyama. Ibid., 516; *SSKFK*, vol. 3, p.177; *SSKFK*, vol. 2, 248–49.

27. Tenaka Myōōtarō Kagemoto, *Ōyama miyadaiku Myōōtarō nikki 2*, 516–17, 524–25. Of Hachidaibō's temple land comprising 157 koku, 100 *koku* in Sakamoto became shrine land while 57 *koku* in Kominoge remained temple land and were later transferred to Myōōji, a merger that comprised all former subtemples at Ōyama. *IHSS* 1994, 753.

28. Tenaka Myōōtarō Kagemoto, *Ōyama miyadaiku Myōōtarō nikki 2*, 521.

29. Sekimori, "The Separation of Kami and Buddha Worship," 212–13; Takami Inoue, "The Interaction between Buddhist and Shinto Traditions at Suwa Shrine," 307–9.

30. Tenaka Tadashi, "Ōyama no shinbutsu bunri," 4; Tenaka Myōōtarō Kagemoto, *Ōyama miyadaiku Myōōtarō nikki* 2, 603, 639, 645, 646–49.

31. Tenaka Myōōtarō Kagemoto, *Ōyama miyadaiku Myōōtarō nikki* 2, 531–43.

32. Ibid., 551, 589–91.

33. *IHSS* 1994, 693.

34. Tenaka Tadashi, "Ōyama no shinbutsu bunri"; Tenaka Myōōtarō Kagemoto, *Ōyama miyadaiku Myōōtarō nikki* 2, 603, 639, 645, 646–49.

35. *IHSS* 1994, 696.

36. Tenaka Myōōtarō Kagemoto, *Ōyama miyadaiku Myōōtarō nikki* 2, 781–82.

37. Chiba, "Atogaki," 199–200.

38. Tenaka Myōōtarō Kagemoto, *Ōyama miyadaiku Myōōtarō nikki* 2, 507–9.

39. Ibid., 544.

40. Breen, "Ideologues, Bureaucrats, and Priests," 232; Thal, *Rearranging the Landscape of the Gods*, 131.

41. *IHSS* 1994, 693.

42. Washio, "Sagami Ōyama Afurijinja chōsa hōkoku," 581. Washio has the monk's name as Kyōjun, but early Meiji-period documents from Ōyama give the name Seijun. *IHSS* 1994, 693; *Kanzaki Eiichi ke shozō monjo*, vol. 5, doc. 35, 214.

43. *IHSS* 1994, 680; Matsuoka, "Bakumatsu Meiji shoki," 164

44. *IHSS* 1994, 680.

45. Washio, "Sagami Ōyama Afurijinja chōsa hōkoku," 581. Washio also claims that Ōyama Isamu was replaced in 1869 by Gonda Noasuke. However, Gonda did not take his place until 1873. Ōyama Isamu appears in documents as the head shrine priest of the Afuri Shrine until 1872.

46. Matsuoka, "Bakumatsu Meiji shoki," 164–68, *IHSS* 1994, 682–93.

47. Tenaka Myōōtarō Kagemoto, *Ōyama miyadaiku Myōōtarō nikki* 2, 551, 589–91.

48. Matsuoka, "Bakumatsu Meiji shoki," 166–70; *IHSS* 1994, 684–85.

49. *IHSS* 1994, 702–3. This evidence is consistent with extant remains of Saiganji's, Raigōin's, and Kannonji's *ninbetsu shūmon aratamechō*. See *Satō Ryōji ke shozō monjo*, vol. 2, docs. 8–9. Most of the remaining 130-odd *negi* in Ōyamachō would have been parishioners at Raigōin and Kannonji, two Shingon temples, which suddenly lost their primary source of income. Raigōin was dismantled during the physical disassociation of *kami* and Buddhas. Its former precinct had become the location of the merged Buddhism temple Myōōji. Kannonji also did not survive the transition.

50. Tenaka Myōōtarō Kagemoto, *Ōyama miyadaiku Myōōtarō nikki* 2, 716–20, 790, 792.

51. Ōyamazumi no Mikoto was worshipped at the Afuri Shrine, whereas his brothers, Ikazuchikami and Takaokami, were enshrined at the former shrines

to Daitengu and Shōtengu. In this, the *negi* took their cue from Sudō Shigeo, who as we recall had argued that the true deities of Ōyama were the three brothers Ōyamazumi no Mikoto, Ikazuchikami, and Takaokami but identified the latter two with the deities at Ikazuchiyama and Nijūnotaki, respectively, in his *Afurijinja kodenkō*. Sudō was one of the senior shrine priests at the time and had therefore a strong influence on the changes put in place.

52. Matsuoka, "Bakumatsu Meiji shoki," 168; *Inomata Saburō ke shozō monjo*, vol. 2, 328; *IHSS* 1994, 754; Date, *Nihon shūkyō seido shiryō ruiju kō*, 620.

53. Suzuki Masataka, *Nyonin kinsei*, 9.

54. Tenaka Tadashi, "Ōyama no shinbutsu bunri," doc. 4.

55. Matsuoka, "Bakumatsu Meiji shoki," 171.

56. Thal, "Redefining the Gods," 397–98; Sekimori, "The Separation of Kami and Buddha Worship," 214–29.

57. Breen, "Ideologues, Bureaucrats, and Priests," 236; Date, *Nihon shūkyō seido shiryō ruiju kō*, 616.

58. According to Suzuki Michirō, Murayama Hachidayū left records of his parish rounds in Sagami and Tōkyō in 1870 and 1871. Suzuki Michirō, "Meiji shoki ni okeru Sagami Ōyama oshi no keizai seikatsu," 178. Records from other former *oshi* households suggest that they continued to go on parish rounds until 1871 and occasionally sold small portions of their parishes to other households (but not to a greater extent than in the early modern period). See *Inomata Saburō ke shozō monjo*, *Utsumi Teruo (Shikibu) ke shozō monjo*, *Kanzaki Eiichi ke shozō monjo*, *Daitō Naoe ke shozō monjo*, *Takao Isao ke shozō monjo*, and *Wada Mitsuko ke shozō monjo*.

59. Ariga, *Ōyama monzenmachi no chiriteki kenkyū*, 54. See lists of *oshi*, *negi*, and *sendoshi* in *IHSS* 1994, 86–92, 105–11, 681–82, and *IHSS* 1999, 621–804. Although the decline was closely linked to the prohibition of parish rounds, the Shinto establishment at the Afuri Shrine probably had a hand in the demise of certain *oshi/sendōshi* households. The Shinto establishment probably used the occasion to rid itself of anti-Shinto / pro-Buddhist households. This is suggested by the fact that many who did not survive the transition were highly ranked *oshi* during the early modern period. Highly ranked *oshi* with large parish holdings would have been less likely to be affected by economic adversity than their poorer peers. Moreover, several of those who went out of business belonged to the group of shrine priests who had successfully opposed the establishment of the seven-rank system in 1868 and 1869.

60. Kanzaki Shirō, *Yuishintō no kyūkōsha*, 13–15, 20–21, 45–53, 94–95, 97–104, 124. In 1858, Gonda, a Hirata school member with ties to the Shirakawa, established his first contact with an Ōyama *oshi*, Hirata Gitayū, who visited him in his native village in Musashi Province. Kanzaki Shirō, *Yuishintō no kyūkōsha*, 13–15,

20–21. Hirata Gitayū, who had no family relations with Hirata Atsutane, had obtained a Shirakawa license in 1856 and joined the Hirata school in 1858 (Matsuoka, "Bakumatsu Meiji shoki," 160). In 1873, Gonda was appointed as head shrine priest (*shikan*) of the Afuri Shrine, replacing the head shrine priest Ōyama Isamu. Gonda was apparently invited by two former members of the military corps and holders of Shirakawa licenses, Yamada Tariho and Masuda Inamaro, who had both played active roles in the early Meiji restructuring of Ōyama. Washio, "Sagami Ōyama Afurijinja chōsa hōkoku," 591. Yamada had been a member of the Hirata School since 1857. Matsuoka, "Bakumatsu Meiji shoki," 160. Masuda had been elected as one of the highest-ranking priests at the Afuri Shrine in 1870. *IHSS* 1994, 706. The two were among the first at Ōyama to become Gonda's students in 1874. Kanzaki Shirō, *Yuishintō no kyūkōsha*, 216–17.

61. Kanzaki Shirō, *Yuishintō no kyūkōsha*, 196–98. Founded in 1882, the Kōten Kōkyūsho became Kokugakuin in 1890 and was renamed Kokugakuin Daigaku in 1920. Today, the institute is referred to as the Research Institute for Japanese Classics or the Research Center for Japanese Classics by Kokugakuin University, but this seems to imply an ideological statement, namely that "imperial classics" and "Japanese classics" are naturally the same. Hence, I have chosen to translate the name literally as Research Institute for Imperial Classics here.

62. Matsuoka, "Bakumatsu Meiji shoki," 171.

63. Other than the Afuri Shrine, three other shrines in Sagami gained the same rank: Matsubara Shrine in Odawara, Hakone Shrine, and Enoshima Shrine. See "Fuken shahyō."

64. Hardacre, *Shintō and the State*, 84–86, 96–97.

65. Ibid., 42–48.

66. Kanzaki Shirō, *Yuishintō no kyūkōsha*, 197.

67. Gonda's Buddhist counterpart was Kaizen, a *chūkōgi* (middle lecturer) and the abbot of the Kogi Shingon temple Kongōchōji, which had functioned as a Shingon academy in the early modern period. He and Kaizen had been appointed by an assembly of Shinto priests, which comprised Sudō Shigeo, vice head shrine priest and most senior *negi* at Afurijinja; a Vice Junior Lecturer (*gonshōkōgi*) as a regional Shinto representative; and Buddhist monks from seven different schools. The Buddhist representatives included Jitsujō, the abbot of Ōyama's Myōōji, as the Kogi Shingon representative. The Matsubara Shrine in Odawara—whose head priest often acted as the Shinto representative—was chosen as the site of the Chūkyōin and Gyokurōbō, a Tendai-affiliated former Honzanha *shugendō* temple, as temporary administrative headquarters. Under the two heads of the regional office were five departments—proceedings and reception, general affairs, research, accounting, and record keeping—which were manned by Shinto priests and Buddhist monks at a ratio

of two to three, giving the Buddhist priesthood a greater representation. The costs of the regional campaign were to be borne by about 21.6 to 25 percent by shrines and 75 to 78.4 percent by Buddhist temples. Once Gonda and Kaizen had been appointed, they issued regulations defining the duties of the Shinto and Buddhist head and the five departments of the regional campaign as well as admonitions to regional proselytizers to control and ensure the smooth progression of the campaign. See Kokugakuin daigaku Nihon bunka kenkyūjo, ed., *Shaji tori shirabe ruisan, Shintō, kyōka hen*, 142–49.

68. Kanzaki Shirō, *Yuishintō no kyūkōsha*, 197; Hardacre, *Shintō and the State*, 48–51.

69. For more on the transformation of the Taikyōin into the Office of Shinto Affairs, see Nitta, "Shinto as a 'Non-religion,'" 258–63.

70. Since he simultaneously held a position as a priest at the Afuri Shrine and Mishima Taisha, he became the head of the prefectural Shintō Jimukyoku in Shizuoka and Kanagawa in 1880. He maintained this joint appointment for about three years until he resigned from the Shizuoka branch in 1883. Kanzaki Shirō, *Yuishintō no kyūkōsha*, 197–98.

71. Ibid., *Yuishintō no kyūkōsha*, p.146. One of his students from Hitachi, Oyama Tadayuki, was an instructor, and Masuda Kōzō, another disciple and the son of former Nativist *oshi*, acted as principal. Kanzaki Shirō, ed., *Kokushi taikei 20*, 77. Occasionally, the date for the founding is given as February 1875.

72. Kanzaki Shirō, *Yuishintō no kyūkōsha*, 129.

73. Ibid., *Yuishintō no kyūkōsha*, 197–98; Hardacre, *Shintō and the State*, 69; Inoue Nobutaka, "The Formation of Sect Shinto in Modernizing Japan," 422.

74. Kanzaki Shirō, *Yuishintō no kyūkōsha*, 133–34; Gonda, *Shinkyōkafu*.

75. Kanzaki Shirō, *Yuishintō no kyūkōsha*, 131–33, 184.

76. Ibid., *Yuishintō no kyūkōsha*, 185–87; Gonda, *Shigōkō*; Gonda, *Shinkyōkafu*, 14–26; Gonda, *Sōgishiki*.

77. Gonda Naosuke had taken disciples since 1843. Once Gonda was appointed at Afuri Shrine and later at Mishima Taisha in Shizuoka Prefecture, his new disciples came from Sagami, Izu, Suruga, and Musashi, the majority being residents at Ōyama. Gonda's disciples at Ōyama were primarily young. Those that became his disciples in 1874 included only four over the age of 40. In the case of his disciples at Ōyama, this implied that many were Shinto priests in training. Kanzaki Shirō, *Yuishintō no kyūkōsha*, 199–224.

78. Matsuoka, "Bakumatsu Meiji shoki," 160, 163.

79. Ariga, *Ōyama monzenmachi*, 65–96.

80. Sekimori, "The Separation of Kami and Buddha Worship," 214–29.

81. Both documents, the *Ōyama keishin kōsha kisoku* (a set of regulations that prescribed the structure and activities of Ōyama *kō*) and the *Kaidōki*, were

probably compiled in 1877, though it is difficult to date them with certainty. See Ariga, *Ōyama monzenmachi*, 62. As the title of the *Kaidōki* suggests, the register was meant to assist the *sendōshi* in their task of providing guidance to the confraternities. This register listed the holdings of each *sendōshi* in various villages across the Kantō and Tōkai regions by province and district, and was updated several times between 1883 and 1920. This register served as a parish register for the Keishin Kōsha headquarters at the Afuri Shrine. Reproduced in *IHSS* 1994, 769–71; *IHSS* 1999, 621–804.

82. The regulations of the pilgrimage routes were entitled *Ōyama keishin kō-sha teikyūhaku kisoku*. The regulations affecting the *sendōshi* were entitled *Ōyama keishin kōsha chōkai kiyaku*. Reproduced in *IHSS* 1994, 772–76.

83. *IHSS* 1994, 772–76.

84. Ibid., 23–27, 772–74.

85. Tanaka, "Meiji shoki ni okeru Ōyamakō no bunpu," 202–4. The estimate is based on the average number of confraternities per village in the province.

86. In 1872, Tanaka Yoritsune, the chief priest of the Ise Shrines, formed a similar confraternity-based organization, Jingūkyō, in the context of the *taikyō senpu undō*. Its ministers were mostly former *oshi*, who often also acted as preachers in the campaign. In 1875, Jingūkyō had 304,704 members organized into *kōsha*, which were largely based on former Ise confraternities led by *oshi*. See Hardacre, *Shintō and the State*, 47–48.

87. Ariga, *Ōyama monzenmachi*, 65–96.

88. Ibid., 65–96.

89. Ibid., 65–96; Suzuki Michirō, "Meiji shoki ni okeru Sagami Ōyama oshi no keizai seikatsu," 175–91; Tanba, "Sendōshi no machi," 205–40.

90. *IHSS* 1994, 770–71.

91. Yamashita, *Chizu de yomu Edo jidai*, 208–11.

92. *IHSS* 1994, 775–76.

93. Kanzaki Shirō, *Yuishintō no kyūkōsha*, 130–31; *IHSS* 1994, 820–21.

94. Kanzaki Shirō, *Yuishintō no kyūkōsha*, 217–24.

95. *IHSS* 1994, 815–25; Tamamuro Fumio, *Nihon bukkyō shi: kinsei*, 278–81.

96. Municipal and prefectural taxation records from 1887 indicate that Myōō-ji was ranked among the 24 households with the highest incomes. The Afuri Shrine was ranked among the five highest. Tanba, "Sendōshi no machi," 211–12.

97. Chamberlain and Mason, *A Handbook for Travellers in Japan*, 61.

Epilogue

1. Grapard, *The Protocol of the Gods*, 4.

2. Hardacre, *Religion and Society in Nineteenth-Century Japan*, 209.

3. Ibid., xvi.

4. See Tsuji, *Nihon bukkyō shi*.

5. Tyler, "A Glimpse of Mt. Fuji in Legend and Cult," 152, 157; Tyler, "The Tokugawa Peace and Popular Religion," 103–4, 111–13; Earhart, "Mt. Fuji and Shugendō," 213–15; Collcutt, "Mt. Fuji as the Realm of Miroku," 254; Miyazaki, "The Formation of Emperor Worship," 284–90.

6. Miyazaki, "The Formation of Emperor Worship," 284–90; Tyler, "A Glimpse of Mt. Fuji," 157.

7. *SMC* 40–47, 57–59, 254, 451–64, 560.

8. Thal, "Rearranging the Landscape of the Gods," 86–178.

Works Cited

Abbreviations

IHSS 1991   *Isehara shishi 1: shiryōhen—kodai, chūsei*
IHSS 1992   *Isehara shishi 2: shiryōhen—Ōyama*
IHSS 1994   *Isehara shishi 5: shiryōhen—zoku Ōyama*
IHSS 1995   *Isehara shishi 6: tsūshihen—senshi, kodai, chūsei*
IHSS 1999   *Isehara shishi 9: betsuhen—shaji*
KKS   *Kanagawa kenshi, shiryō hen 8—kinsei*, vol. 5, no. 2.
OCSK   "Ōyama chishi onshirabe kakiage."
ONK   *Ōyamadera engi narabi kiroku.*
OFRK   *Ōyama Fudō reigenki.*
SMC   *Shirakawa-ke monjin chō.*
SSKFK   *Shinpen Sagami no kuni fudoki kō*, vols. 1–5
STK   *Shintō taikei: jinjahen*, vol. 16.
TMZ   *Nihon meisho zue fūzoku zue 17, shokoku no maki 2: Tōkaidō meisho zue.*

References

Abe Yukihiro 阿部征寛. "Kaikokuzen, Edowannai no funatabi o megutte" 開国前、江戸湾内の船旅を巡って. In *Ōyama shinkō* 大山信仰, ed. Tamamuro Fumio 圭室文雄, 307–40. Tokyo: Yūzankaku, 1992.

Afurijinja monjo 阿夫利神社文書. Tōkyō daigaku shiryō hensanjo, 1921. Handwritten copy.

Akai, Tasurō. "The Common People and Painting." In *Tokugawa Japan: The Social and Economic Antecedents of Modern Japan*, ed. Nakane Chie, Ōishi Shinzaburō, and Conrad Totman, 167–88. Tokyo: Tokyo University Press, 1990.

Akisato Ritō 秋里籬島. *Nihon meisho zue fūzoku zue 17—shokoku no maki 2: Tōkaidō meisho zue* 日本名所風俗図会 17—諸国の巻 2: 東海道名所図会. Edited by Hayashi Hideo 林英夫. Tokyo: Kadokawa shoten, 1981.

Ambros, Barbara. "The Display of Hidden Treasures: Zenkōji's Kaichō at Ekō-in in Edo." *Asian Cultural Studies* 30 (Spring 2004): 1–26.

Amino Yoshihiko 網野善彦. "Chūsei zenki no 'sanjo' to kumenden: meshi-tsugi, zōshiki, kagochō o chūshin ni" 中世前期の「散所」と給免田: 召次・雑色・駕輿丁を中心に. *Shirin* 史林 59, no. 1 (1976): 1–40.

Ariga Mitsuo 有賀密夫. *Ōyama monzenmachi no chiriteki kenkyū* 大山門前町の地理的研究. Fujisawa: Fujisawa-shi bunkazai hōgoiin, 1989.

Asaka Yukio 浅香幸雄. "Ōyama shinkō tozan shūraku keisei no kiban" 大山信仰登山集落形成の基盤. In *Ōyama shinkō* 大山信仰, ed. Tamamuro Fumio 圭室文雄, 17–40. Tokyo: Yūzankaku, 1992.

Asakawa chōshi hensan iinkai 浅川町史編纂委員会, ed. *Asakawa chōshi 2: shiryōhen* 浅川町史 2: 資料編. Asakawa: Kyōsei, 1997.

Atsugi-shi kyōiku iinkai shakai kyōikuka 厚木市教育委員会社会教育課, ed. *Kyōdo shiryō tenjishitsu tokubetsu ten—Sagami Ōyama* 郷土資料展示室特別展—相模大山. Atsugi-shi: Atsugi-shi kyōiku iinkai, 1992.

Bernbaum, Edwin. *Sacred Mountains of the World*. Berkeley, CA, Los Angeles, and London: University California Press, 1997.

Blacker, Carmen. *The Catalpa Bow*. London: George Allen & Unwin, 1986.

———. "Religious Travellers in the Edo Period." *Modern Asian Studies* 18, no. 4 (1984): 593–608.

Bock, Felicia Gressit, trans. *Engi-shiki: Procedures of the Engi Era, Books VI–X*. Tokyo: Monumenta Nipponica Monographs, Sophia University Press, 1972.

Bodart-Bailey, Beatrice, ed. and trans. *Kaempfer's Japan: Tokugawa Culture Observed*. Honolulu, HI: University of Hawai'i Press, 1999.

Bowring, Richard. *The Religious Traditions of Japan: 500–1600*. Cambridge, UK: Cambridge University Press, 2005.

Breen, John. "Ideologues, Bureaucrats, and Priests: On 'Shinto' and 'Buddhism' in Early Meiji Japan." In *Shinto in History: Ways of the Kami*, ed. John Breen and Mark Teeuwen, 230–51. London: Curzon Press, 2000.

Chamberlain, Basil Hall and W. B. Mason. *A Handbook for Travellers in Japan*. London: John Murray, 1891.

Chiba Kōzen 千葉興全. "Atogaki" 後書. In *Ōyamadera engi* 大山寺縁起, 140–215. Isehara: Taisanji, 1984.

———, ed. "Myōōtarō raiyu" 明王太郎来由. In *Ōyamadera engi* 大山寺縁起, 135–38. Isehara: Taisanji, 1984.

Chigiri Kōsai 知切光歳. *Tengu no kenkyū* 天狗の研究. Tokyo: Tairiku shobō, 1975.

————. *Zushū tengu retsuden: Nishi Nihon hen* 図聚天狗列伝:西日本編. Tokyo: Miki shobō, 1977.

Coaldrake, William. *Architecture and Authority in Japan*. London and New York: Routledge, 1996.

Coleman, Simon and John Eade, eds. *Reframing Pilgrimage: Cultures in Motion*. London and New York: Routledge, 2004.

Collcutt, Martin. "Mt. Fuji as the Realm of Miroku: The Transformation of Maitreya in the Cult of Mt. Fuji in Early Modern Japan." In *Maitreya*, ed. Helen Hardacre and Alan Sponberg, 248–69. Cambridge, UK: Cambridge University Press, 1988.

Daitō Naoe-ke monjo 大藤直兄文書. Isehara shishi hensanshitsu, Kanagawa Prefecture. Microfilm.

Date Mitsuyoshi 伊達光美. *Nihon shūkyō seido shiryō ruiju kō* 日本宗教制度史料類聚考. Tokyo: Ganshōdō shoten, 1931.

Davis, Winston. *Japanese Religion and Society*. Albany, NY: State University of New York Press, 1992.

Eade, John and Michael Sallnow. *Contesting the Sacred: The Anthropology of Christian Pilgrimage*. London and New York: Routledge, 1991.

Earhart, H. Byron. *A Religious Study of the Mount Haguro Sect of Shugendō*. Tokyo: Sophia University Press, 1970.

————. "Mt. Fuji and Shugendō." *Japanese Journal of Religious Studies* 16, nos. 2–3 (1989): 205–26.

Eliade, Mircea. *Patterns in Comparative Religion*. Lincoln, NE and London: University of Nebraska Press, 1996.

————. *The Sacred and the Profane: The Nature of Religion*. San Diego, New York, and London: Harcourt Brace Jovanovich, 1959.

Endō Jun 遠藤潤. "Bakumatsu shakai to shūkyōteki fukko undō: Shirakawa-ke to Hirata kokugaku Furukawa Mitsura o shōten to shite" 幕末社会と宗教的復古運動—白川家と平田国学·古川躬行を焦点として. *Kokugakuin daigaku Nihon bunka kenkyūjo kiyō* 國學院大學日本文化研究所紀要 83 (1999): 135–78.

Faure, Bernard. *The Power of Denial: Buddhism, Purity, and Gender*. Princeton, NJ, and Oxford, UK: Princeton University Press, 2003.

Foard, James H. "The Boundaries of Compassion: Buddhism and the National Tradition in Japanese Pilgrimage." *Journal of Asian Studies* 41, no. 2 (1982): 231–52.

Formanek, Susanne. "*Etoki*: Mittelalterliche Religiöse Welten Ertklärt in Bildern." In *Buch und Bild als Gesellschaftliche Kommunikationsmittel in Japan Einst und Jetzt*, ed. Susanne Formanek and Sepp Linhart, 11–43. Vienna: Literas, 1995.

Foucault, Michel. "Of Other Spaces." *Diacritics* 16, no. 1 (1986): 22–27.

Fowler, Sherry. "In Search of the Dragon: Mt. Murō's Sacred Topography." *Japanese Journal of Religious Studies* 24, nos. 1–2 (1997): 145–62.

"Fuken shahyō" 府縣社表. *Shaji torishirabe ruisan* 社寺取調類纂. Sophia University, 1887. Microfilm.

Furushima, Toshio. "The Village and Agriculture." In *The Cambridge History of Japan*, vol. 4, ed. John W. Hall and James L. McClain, 478–518. Cambridge, UK: Cambridge University Press, 1991.

Glare, P. G. W., ed. *Oxford Latin Dictionary*. Oxford, UK: Clarendon Press, 1990.

Gonda Naosuke 権田直助. *Shigōkō* 諡号考. Tokyo: Okabeke, 1873.

———. *Shinkyōkafu* 神教歌譜. Ōyama: Ōyama Afurijinja jimusho, 1881.

———. *Sōgishiki* 葬儀式. 3 vols. Ōyama: Ōyama Afurijinja jimusho, 1887.

Goodwin, Janet. *Alms and Vagabonds: Buddhist Temples and Popular Patronage in Medieval Japan*. Honolulu, HI: University of Hawai'i Press, 1994.

Gotō Shigeki 後藤茂樹, ed. *Ukiyoe taikei 14: Tōkaidō gojūsanji* 浮世絵大系 14: 東海道五拾三次. Tokyo: Shūeisha, 1976.

Grapard, Allan. *The Protocol of the Gods: A Study of the Kasuga Cult in Japanese History*. Berkeley, CA: University of California Press, 1992.

———. "Geosophia, Geognosis, and Geopiety: Orders of Significance in Japanese Representations of Space." In *NowHere: Space, Time, and Modernity*, ed. Roger Friedland and Deirdre Boden, 372–401. Berkeley, CA: University of California Press, 1994.

———. "Geotyping Sacred Space: The Case of Mount Hiko in Japan." In *Sacred Space: Land, City, Shrine*, ed. Benjamin Z. Kedar and R. J. Zwi Werblowsky, 215–49. New York: New York University Press, 1998.

Groemer, Gerald. "The Arts of the Gannin." *Asian Folklore Studies* 58 (1999): 275–320.

———. "A Short History of Gannin: Popular Religious Performers in Tokugawa Japan." *Japanese Journal of Religious Studies* 27, no. 2 (2000): 41–72.

Hadano shishi hensan iinkai 秦野市史編纂委員会, ed. *Hadano shishi tsūshi 3 kindai* 秦野市史通史 3: 近代. Hadano: Hadano-shi, 1992.

Hagiwara Tatsuo 萩原龍夫. *Miko to bukkyōshi: Kumano bikuni no shimei to tenkai* 巫女と仏教史:熊野比丘尼の使命と展開. Tokyo: Yoshikawa kōbunkan, 1983.

———. "Yoshida shintō to gōson kannushisō" 吉田神道と郷村神主層. *Shintō shūkyō* 神道宗教 4 (1952): 1–8.

Hakeda, Yoshito. *Kūkai*. New York: Columbia University Press, 1972.

Hakoyama Kitarō 箱山貴太郎. "Nakayoshida no Sekisonkō hoka" 中吉田の石尊講ほか. *Ueda bonchi* 上田盆地 16 (1973): 7–21.

Hall, John W. "The *Bakuhan* System." In *The Cambridge History of Japan*, vol. 4, ed. John W. Hall and James L. McClain, 128–82. Cambridge, UK: Cambridge University Press, 1991.

Hara Jun'ichirō 原淳一郎. "Ōyama, Fuji, Enoshima" 大山、富士、江ノ島. *Chihōshi kenkyū* 地方史研究 48, no. 4 (1998): 24–28.

Harada Tetsuo 原田哲夫. *Sagami Ōyama* 相模大山. Tokyo: Kindai bungeisha, 1995.

Hardacre, Helen. *Religion and Society in Nineteenth-Century Japan: A Study of the Southern Kantō Region, Using Late Edo and Early Meiji Gazeteers*. Ann Arbor, MI: Center for Japanese Studies, University of Michigan, 2002.

———. *Shintō and the State*. Princeton, NJ: Princeton University Press, 1989.

———. "Sources for the Study of Religion and Society in the Late Edo Period." *Japanese Journal of Religious Studies* 28, nos. 3–4 (2001): 227–60.

Hayashi Jussai 林述斎 et al., eds. *Dainihon chishi taikei 21: shinpen Sagami no kuni fudoki kō* 大日本地誌大系 21: 新編相模国風土記稿. 5 vols. Tokyo: Yūzankaku, 1972.

Hayashi, Makoto. "Tokugawa-period Disputes between Shugen Organizations and *Onmyōji* over Rights to Practice Divination." *Japanese Journal of Religious Studies* 21, nos. 2–3 (1994): 167–89.

Hirano Eiji 平野栄次. "Fujikō, Ōyamakō no junpai to yūzan" 富士講、大山講の巡拝と遊山. *Chihōshi kenkyū* 48, no. 4 (1998): 29–32.

Hiratsuka-shi hakubutsukan shishi hensangakari 平塚市博物館市史編纂係, ed. *Hiratsuka-shi minzoku chōsa hōkoku 2—Toyota, Okazaki* 平塚市史民俗調査報告—豊田、岡崎. Hiratsuka: Hiratsuka-shi, 1982.

———, ed. *Hiratsuka shishi 12: betsuhen—minzoku* 平塚市史 12: 別編—民族. Hiratsuka: Hiratsuka-shi, 1993.

Hiratsuka-shi hakubutsukan 平塚市博物館, ed. *Ōyama no shinkō to rekishi* 大山の信仰と歴史. Hiratsuka: Hiratsuka-shi hakubutsukan, 1987.

Hiratsuka kikakushitsu shishi hensanshitsu 平塚市企画部市史編纂室, ed. *Hiratsuka to Ōyama* 平塚と大山. Hiratsuka: Hiratsuka-shi kankō kyōkai, 1977.

Hiruma Hisashi 比留間尚. *Edo no kaichō* 江戸の開帳. Tokyo: Yoshikawa kōbunkan, 1980.

———. "Edo no kaichō" 江戸の開帳. In *Edo chōnin no kenkyū* 江戸町人の研究. Vol. 2, ed. Nishiyama Matsunosuke 西山松之助, 273–472. Tokyo: Yoshikawa kōbunkan, 1973.

Hisasaki Mitsuo 久崎光生. "Sagami Ōyama no reiseki" 相州大山の霊石. *Ashinaka* あしなか 41 (1954): 20–21.

Hori, Ichirō. "Mountains and Their Importance for the Idea of the Other World in Japanese Folk Religion." *History of Religions* 6, no. 1 (1966): 1–23.

Hoshino, Eiki. "The Historical Significance of Pilgrimages in Japan, with Special Reference to the Shikoku Pilgrimage." *Young East* 9, no. 3 (1983): 3–14.

Hur, Nam-lin. *Prayer and Play in Late Tokugawa Japan: Asakusa Sensōji and Edo Society.* Cambridge, MA: Harvard University Asia Center, 2000.

Inomata Saburō-ke shozō monjo 猪股三郎家所蔵文書. Isehara shishi hensan-shitsu, Kanagawa Prefecture. Microfilm.

Inoue, Nobutaka. "The Formation of Sect Shinto in Modernizing Japan." *Japanese Journal of Religious Studies* 29, nos. 3–4 (2002): 405–27.

Inoue, Takami. "The Interaction between Buddhist and Shinto Traditions at Suwa Shrine." In *Buddhas and Kami in Japan: Honji Suijaku as a Combinatory Paradigm*, ed. Mark Teeuwen and Fabio Rambelli, 287–312. London and New York: RoutledgeCurzon, 2003.

Inoue Tomokatsu. "Chiiki shakai ni okeru Yoshida shintō no juyō: sōgen senji no juju o chūshin ni" 地域社会における吉田神道の受容: 宗源宣旨の授受を中心に. *Nihonshi kenkyū* 日本史研究 416 (1997): 48–66.

———. "Kanseiki ni okeru ujigami, hayarigami to chōtei ken'i" 寛政期における氏神・流行神と朝廷権威. *Nihonshi kenkyū* 日本史研究 365 (1993): 1–26.

Isehara shishi henshū iinkai 伊勢原市史編集委員会, ed. *Isehara shishi 1: shiryō hen—kodai, chūsei* 伊勢原市史 1: 資料編—古代・中世. Isehara: Isehara-shi, 1991.

———, ed. *Isehara shishi 2: shiryō hen—Ōyama* 伊勢原市史 2: 資料編—大山. Isehara: Isehara-shi, 1992.

———, ed. *Isehara shishi 5: shiryō hen—zoku Ōyama* 伊勢原市史 5: 資料編—続大山. Isehara: Isehara-shi, 1994.

———, ed. *Isehara shishi 6: tsūshi hen—senshi, kodai, chūsei* 伊勢原市史 6: 通史編—先史・古代・中世. Isehara: Isehara-shi, 1995.

———, ed. *Isehara shishi 9: betsuhen shaji* 伊勢原市史 9: 別編—社寺. Isehara: Isehara-shi, 1999.

Ishida Kōjirō 石田光治郎. *Reigaku Ōyama* 霊岳大山. Tokyo: Futaba shoten, 1917.

Isomae, Jun'ichi. "Myth in Metamorphosis: Ancient and Medieval Versions of the Yamato Takeru Legends." *Monumenta Nipponica* 54, no. 3 (1999): 361–85.

Itabashi kuritsu kyōdo shiryōkan 板橋区立郷土資料館, ed. *Tokubetsuten: tabi to shinkō—Fuji, Ōyama, Haruna e no sankei* 特別展:旅と信仰—富士、大山、榛名への参詣. Tokyo: Itabashi kuritsu kyōdo shiryōkan, 1996.

Itō Kōken 伊藤宏見. "Gangyō shōnin Kenjō no kenkyū (jō)" 願行上人憲静の研究 (上). *Mikkyō bunka* 密教文化 117 (1977): 29–37.

Jiin honmatsuchō kenkyūkai 寺院本末帳研究会, ed. *Edo bakufu jiin honmatsu-chō shūsei* 江戸幕府寺院本末帳集成. 3 vols. Tokyo: Yūzankaku, 1981.

"Jikakuchō" 寺格帳. In *Zokuzoku gunsho ruijū* 続々群書類従, vol. 10, 447–530. Tokyo: Kokusho kankōkai, 1907.

Jippensha Ikku 十返舎一九. *Jippensha Ikku no Hakone Enoshima Kamakura dōchūki* 十返舎一九の箱根江の島鎌倉道中記. Edited by Tsuruoka Tokio 鶴岡節雄. Tokyo: Senshūsha, 1982.

———. *Tōkaidōchū hizakurige* 東海道中膝栗毛. Vol. 1. Edited by Asou Isoji 麻生磯次. Tokyo: Iwanami bunko, 1998.

Kaminishi, Ikumi. *Explaining Pictures: Buddhist Propaganda and Etoki Storytelling in Japan*. Honolulu, HI: University of Hawai'i Press, 2006.

Kanagawa-ken kikaku chōsabu kenshi hensanshitsu 神奈川県企画調査部県史編集室, ed. *Kanagawa kenshi: shiryōhen 8—kinsei 5* 神奈川県史: 資料編 8—近世 5, vol. 2. Yokohama: Kanagawa-ken, 1979.

Kanagawa kinseishi kenkyūkai 神奈川近世史研究会, ed. *Edo jidai no Kanagawa: koezu de miru fūkei* 江戸時代の神奈川:古絵図でみる風景. Yokohama: Yūrindō, 1994.

Kanagawa Prefectural Government, ed. *The History of Kanagawa*. Yokohama: Kanagawa Prefectural Government, 1985.

Kanzaki Eiichi-ke shozō monjo 神崎栄一家所蔵文書. Isehara shishi hensanshitsu, Kanagawa Prefecture. Microfilm.

Kanzaki Kaoru-ke shozō monjo 神崎薫家所蔵文書. Isehara shishi hensanshitsu, Kanagawa Prefecture. Microfilm.

Kanzaki Shirō 神崎四郎. *Yuishintō no kyūkōsha: Gonda Naosuke ō* 惟神道の躬行者: 権田直助翁. Ōyama: Afurijinja jimusho, 1937.

———, ed. *Kokushi taikei 20: Gonda Naosuke shū* 国史大系 20:権田直助集. Tokyo: Chihei shuppan, 1944.

Katō Shōshun 加藤正俊. "Hakuho Eryō to shie jiken" 伯蒲恵稜と紫衣事件. *Zen bunka kenkyūjo kiyō* 禅文化研究所紀要 9 (1977): 391–435.

Kawasaki-shi shimin myūjiamu 川崎市市民ミュージアム, ed. *Kawasaki-shi shiryō sōsho 3: Kawasakishuku kankei shiryō* 川崎市資料叢書 3:川崎宿関係資料, vol. 1. Kawasaki: Kawasaki-shi shimin myūjiamu, 1990.

Ketelaar, James Edward. *Of Heretics and Martyrs in Meiji Japan*. Princeton, NJ: Princeton University Press, 1990.

Kimura Motoi 木村礎. "Jisha to shomin no shinkō" 寺社と庶民の信仰. In *Kanagawa kenshi: tsūshihen 2—kinsei 1* 神奈川県史:通史編 2—近世 1, 633–825. Yokohama: Kanagawa-ken, 1981.

Kitamura Gyōon (Satoshi) 北村行遠 (聡), *Kinsei kaichō no kenkyū* 近世開帳の研究. Tokyo: Meisho shuppan, 1989.

Kitamura Satoshi 北村聡. "Kaichō" 開帳. In *Kokushi daijiten* 国史大辞典, vol. 3, ed. Kokushi daijiten henshū iinkai 国史大辞典編集委員会, 75–76. Tokyo: Yoshikawa kōbunkan, 1983.

Kiyohara Sadao 清原貞雄. *Shintōshi* 神道史. Tokyo: Kōseikaku, 1932.

Kodama Kōta 児玉幸多 and Kawamura Yū 川村優, eds. *Kinsei nōsei shiryō shū 3, hatamotoryō nanushi nikki* 近世農政史料集 3: 旗本領名主日記. Tokyo: Yoshikawa kōbunkan, 1972.

Kojima Yōrai 小島瓔禮. *Kanagawa-ken katarimono shiryō—Sagami Ōyama engi* 神奈川県語り物資料—相模大山縁起. 2 vols. Yokohama: Kanagawa-ken kyōiku-chō shidō-bu, 1970–1971.

Kokugakuin daigaku Nihon bunka kenkyūjo 國學院大學日本文化研究所, ed. *Shaji torishirabe ruisan: Shintō, kyōka hen* 社寺取調類纂: 神道・教化篇. Tokyo: Kokugakuin daigaku Nihon bunka kenkyūjo, 1989.

Kondō Yoshihiro 近藤喜博. *Shirakawa-ke monjin chō* 白川家門人帳. Osaka: Shirakawa-ke monjin chō kankōkai, 1972.

Kouamé, Natalie. *Initiation à la Paléographie Japonaise à travers les manuscrits du pèlerinage de Shikoku.* Paris: Langues & Mondes—L'Asiathèque, 2000.

———. *Pèlerinage et Société dans le Japon des Tokugawa: Le Pèlerinage de Shikoku entre 1598 et 1868.* Paris: École Française d'Etrême-Orient, 2001.

———. "Shikoku's Local Authorities and Henro during the Golden Age of Pilgrimage." *Japanese Journal of Religious Studies* 24, nos. 3–4 (1997): 413–25.

Kuroita Katsumi 黒板勝美 et al., eds. *Kokushi taikei 41: Tokugawa jikki 4* 国史大系 41: 徳川実紀 4. Tokyo: Chihei shuppan, 1965.

Kurumisawa Tomoo 胡桃沢友男. "Nyonin kinsei o megutte" 女人禁制をめぐって. *Ashinaka* あしなか 53 (1956): 20–25.

Lefebvre, Henri. *The Production of Space.* Malden, MA, and Oxford, UK: Blackwell Publishing, 2005.

Lin, Irene H. "From Thunder Child to Dharma Protector: Dōjō hōshi and the Buddhist Appropriation of Japanese Local Deities." In *Buddhas and Kami in Japan: Honji Suijaku as a Combinatory Paradigm*, ed. Mark Teeuwen and Fabio Rambelli, 54–76. London and New York: RoutledgeCurzon, 2003.

MacWilliams, Mark Wheeler. "Temple Myths and Popularization of Kannon Pilgrimage in Japan: A Case Study of Ōya-ji on the Bandō Route." *Japanese Journal of Religious Studies,* 24, nos. 3–4 (1997): 375–412.

Maeda, Hiromi. "Court Rank for Village Shrines: The Yoshida House's Interactions with Local Shrines during the Mid-Tokugawa Period." *Japanese Journal of Religious Studies,* 29, nos. 3–4 (2002): 325–58.

———. "Imperial Authority and Local Shrines: The Yoshida House and the Creation of a Countrywide Shinto Institution in Early Modern Japan." Ph.D. diss., Harvard University, 2004.

Mase Kumiko 間瀬久美子. "Bakuhan kokka ni okeru jinja sōron to chōbaku kankei" 幕藩制国家における神社争論と朝幕関係. *Nihonshi kenkyū* 日本史研究 277 (1985): 63–93.

Matsuoka Takashi 松岡俊. *Edo no sankeikō: chōtō to kōchūfuda ni miru reijō shinkō* 江戸の参詣講: 挑灯と講中札にみる霊場信仰. Hadano: Hadano-shi, 1995.

———. "Bakumatsu Meiji shoki ni okeru Sagami Ōyama oshi no shisō to kōdō" 幕末明治初期における相模大山御師の思想と行動. In *Ōyama shinkō* 大山信仰, ed. Tamamuro Fumio 圭室文雄, 151–74. Tokyo: Yūzankaku, 1992.

———. "Sagami Ōyamadera no 'toritsugi' seido no kōzō" 相模大山寺の 「取次」制度の構造. *Hadano shishi kenkyū* 秦野市史研究 16 (1996): 23–42.

———. "Sagami Ōyama oshi no danka shūseki katei no kōzō" 相模大山御師の檀家集積過程の構造. *Isehara no rekishi* 伊勢原の歴史 11 (1996): 49–65.

———. "Sagami Ōyama oshi no keisei to tenkai" 相模大山御師の形成と展開. *Isehara no rekishi* 伊勢原の歴史 7 (1992): 1–27.

Matsushita Takahiro 松下隆洪, ed. *Kantō Kogi Shingonshū honmatsuchō* 関東古義真言宗本末帳. 2 vols. Hiratsuka: Fukuseisan Hōzen'in Goenkinen Jigyōiinkai, 1984.

Minamiashigara-shi 南足柄市, ed. *Minamiashigara shishi 6: tsūshihen 1* 南足柄市史 6: 通史編 1. Tokyo: Kyōsei, 1999.

Miyake Hitoshi 宮家準. *Shugendō jiten* 修験道辞典. Tokyo: Tōkyōdō shuppan, 1986.

———. "Oshi" 御師. In *Kokushi daijiten* 国史大辞典, vol. 2, ed. Kokushi daijiten henshū iinkai 国史大辞典編集委員会, 826. Tokyo: Yoshikawa kōbunkan, 1980.

Miyake Hitoshi and Itoga Shigeo 糸賀茂男. "Hasugesan no shugendō" 八菅山の修験道. In *Nikkōsan to Kantō no shugendō* 日光山と関東の修験道, ed. Miyata Noboru 宮田登 and Miyamoto Kesao 宮本袈裟雄, 481–504. Tokyo: Meicho shuppan, 1979.

Miyamoto Kesao 宮本袈裟雄. *Tengu to shugenja: sangaku shinkō to sono shūhen* 天狗と修験者: 山岳信仰とその周辺. Tokyo: Jinbun shoin, 1989.

Miyata Noboru 宮田登. *Edo saijiki* 江戸歳時記. Tokyo: Yoshikawa kōbunkan, 1981.

Miyazaki, Fumiko. "Female Pilgrims and Mt. Fuji: Changing Perspectives on the Exclusion of Women." *Monumenta Nipponica* 60, no. 3 (2005): 339–91.

———. "The Formation of Emperor Worship in the New Religions: The Case of Fujidō." *Japanese Journal of Religious Studies* 17, nos. 2–3 (1990): 281–314.

——— 宮崎ふみ子. "'Fuji no bi to shinkō' saikō" 「富士の美と信仰」再考. *Kan* 環 2 (2000): 124–31.

————. "Fujisan ni okeru nyonin kinsei to sono shūen" 富士山における
女人禁制とその終焉. *Kan* 環 12 (2003): 271–83.

Moerman, D. Max. *Localizing Paradise: Kumano Pilgrimage and the Religious Landscape
of Premodern Japan.* Cambridge,MA: Harvard University Asia Center, 2005.

Murata Yasuo 村田安穂. *Shinbutsu bunri no chihōteki tenkai* 神仏分離の地方的
展開. Tokyo: Yoshikawa kōbunkan, 1999.

Nagahata Kyōsuke 永畑恭典, ed. *Meikai bukkyō jiten* 明解仏教事典. Tokyo:
Hon no tomosha, 1988.

Nagano Tadashi 長野覚. "Meiji ishin to Hikosan yamabushi" 明治維新と
英彦山山伏. In *Zōho Hikosan* 増補英彦山, ed. Tagawa kyōdo kenkyūkai
田川郷土研究会, 889–924. Fukuoka: Hisamoto Mita, 1978.

Nakamae Masashi. "Fudō no namida: naki-Fudō setsuwa bikō" 不動の涙:
泣不動説話微考. *Kokugo kokubun* 国語国文 65, no. 4 (1996): 29–48.

Nakane Chie. "Tokugawa Society." In *Tokugawa Japan: The Social and Economic
Antecedents of Modern Japan*, ed. Chie Nakane and Shinzaburō Ōishi, 213–31.
Tokyo: University of Tokyo Press, 1990.

Nakazawa Shigetaka 中沢茂隆. "Yamanashi-shi Esohara buraku no Sekisonkō" 山梨市江曽原部落の石尊講. *Kaiji* 甲斐路 28 (1976): 18–21.

Nenzi, Laura. "To Ise at All Costs: Religious and Economic Implications of
Early Modern *Nukemairi.*" *Japanese Journal of Religious Studies* 33, no. 1 (2006):
75–114.

Nitta, Hitoshi. "Shinto as a 'Non-religion': The Origins and Development of
an Idea." In *Shinto in History: Ways of the Kami*, ed. John Breen and Mark
Teeuwen, 252–71. Honolulu, HI: University of Hawai'i Press, 2000.

Nosco, Peter. "Keeping the Faith: *Bakuhan* Policy towards Religion in Seven-
teenth-Century Japan." In *Religion in Japan: Arrows to Heaven and Earth*, ed.
Peter Kornicki and Ian McMullen, 135–55. Cambridge, UK: Cambridge
University Press, 1996.

Notehelfer, Fred G. *Japan Through American Eyes: The Journal of Francis Hall, 1859–
1866.* Boulder, CO: Westview Press, 2001.

Okazaki, Jōji. *Pure Land Buddhist Painting.* Tokyo: Kōdansha, 1977.

Ooms, Herman. *Tokugawa Ideology: Early Constructs, 1570–1680.* Princeton, NJ:
Princeton University Press, 1985.

————. *Tokugawa Village Practice: Class, Status, Power, Law.* Berkeley, CA, Los
Angeles, and London: University of California Press, 1996.

Ōtō Osamu 大藤修. *Kinsei nōmin to ie, mura, kokka: seikatsushi, shakaishi, no shiza
kara* 近世農民と家・村・国家: 生活史・社会史の視座から. Tokyo:
Yoshikawa kōbunkan, 1996.

Ōto Yoshifuru 大戸吉古 and Yamaguchi Osamu 山口修, eds. *Edo jidai zushi
14: Tōkaidō 1* 江戸時代図誌 14: 東海道 1. Tokyo: Chikuma shobō, 1976.

Ouwehand, Cornelius. *Namazu-e and Their Themes: An Interpretive Approach to Soma Aspects of Japanese Folk Religion.* Leiden: E. J. Brill, 1964.

Ōyamadera engi narabi kiroku 大山寺縁起并記録. Tōkyō daigaku shiryō hensanjo, 1921. Handwritten copy. Orginal document dated early 1700s; copied by Afurijinja in 1877.

Ōyama Afurijinja 大山阿夫利神社, ed. *Sagami Ōyama kaidō* 相模大山街道. Isehara: Ōyama Afurijinja, 1987.

Ōyama chishi shirabe kakiage 大山地誌調書上. Tōkyō daigaku shiryō hensanjo, 1921. Handwritten copy. First compiled in 1835 as "Chishi onshirabe kakiage" 地誌御調書上; copied by Afurijinja in 1877.

Payne, Richard Karl. *The Tantric Ritual of Japan—Feeding the Gods: The Shingon Fire Ritual.* New Delhi: International Academy of Indian Culture, Aditya Prakashan, 1991.

Powell, William. "Literary Diversions on Mount Jiuhua: Cults, Communities, and Culture." In *Sacred Mountains of Asia*, ed. John Einarsen, 22–26. Boston, MA and London: Shambhala, 1995.

Rambelli, Fabio. "*Honji suijaku* at Work: Religion, Economics, and Ideology in Pre-Modern Japan." In *Buddhas and Kami in Japan: Honji Suijaku as a Combinatory Paradigm*, ed. Mark Teeuwen and Fabio Rambelli, 255–86. London and New York: RoutledgeCurzon, 2003.

Ramirez-Christensen, Esperanza. *Heart's Flower: The Life and Poetry of Shinkei.* Stanford, CA: Stanford University Press, 1994.

Reader, Ian and George J. Tanabe Jr. *Practically Religious: Worldly Benefits and the Common Religion of Japan.* Honolulu, HI: University of Hawai'i Press, 1998.

Renondeau, Gaston. *Le Shugendō: Histoire, Doctrine, et Rites des Anachorètes Dits Yamabushi.* Paris: Imprimerie Nationale, 1965.

Rotermund, Hartmut O. *Die Yamabushi.* Hamburg: Kommissionsverlag, Cram, de Gyuter & Co., 1967.

———. *Hōsōgami ou la petit vérole aisément: Matériaux pour l'étude des épidémies dans le Japon des XVIIIe, XIXe siècles.* Paris: Maisonneuve & Larose, 1991.

———. "Demonic Affliction or Contagious Disease: Changing Perceptions of Smallpox in the Late Edo Period." *Japanese Journal of Religious Studies* 28, nos. 3–4 (2001): 373–98.

Ruch, Barbara. "Medieval Jongleurs and the Making of a National Literature." In *Japan in the Muromachi Age*, ed. John Hall and Takeshi Toyoda, 279–309. Berkeley, CA: University of California Press, 1977.

———. "Woman to Woman: Kumano bikuni Proselytizers in Medieval and Early Modern Japan." In *Engendering Faith: Women and Buddhism in Premodern Japan*, ed. Barbara Ruch, 537–80. Ann Arbor, MI: Center for Japanese Studies, University of Michigan, 2002.

Ruppert, Brian O. "Buddhist Rainmaking in Early Japan: The Dragon King and the Ritual Careers of Esoteric Monks." *History of Religions* 42, no. 2 (2002): 143–74.

Sagamihara-shi 相模原市, ed. *Sagamihara shishi* 相模原市史. Vol. 6. Sagamihara: Sagamihara-shi, 1965.

Saitō Gesshin 斎藤月岑. *Bukō nenpyō* 武江年表. Edited by Kaneko Mitsuharu 金子光晴. Tokyo: Heibonsha, 1968.

Sakamoto Masahito (Shōjin) 坂本正仁. "Chūsei Kantō ni okeru Shingonshū kyōdan no tenkai—Hitachi, Kita Shimōsa no Jisshōgata no baai" 中世関東における真言宗教団の展開—常陸・北下総の実勝方の場合. *Nihon bukkyō shigaku* 日本仏教史学 20 (1985): 31–144.

———. "Chūseimatsu minami Kantō ni okeru Kogi Shingonshū no honmatsu kankei: Kongōchōji to Shinpukuji no honmatsu jōron o megutte" 中世末南関東における古義真言宗の本末関係:金剛頂寺と真福寺の本末諍論をめぐって. *Mikkyōgaku kenkyū* 密教学研究 20 (1988): 85–105.

———. "Honmatsuchō ni mieru kinsei no Kogi Shingonshū" 本末帳に見える近世の古義真言宗. *Mikkyōgaku kenkyū* 密教学研究 11 (1979): 20–44.

———. "*Shingonshū shohatto* to Shingon gokohonji no seiritsu ni tsuite: kinsei shoki Shingonshū no ichi sokumen" 「真言宗諸法度」と真言五箇本寺の成立について:近世初期真言宗史の一側面. *Taishō daigaku daigakuin kenkyū ronshū* 大正大学大学院研究論集 3 (1979): 285–96.

Sallnow, Michael. *Pilgrims in the Andes: Regional Cults in Cusco*. Washington, DC: Smithsonian Institution Press, 1987.

Samukawa chōshi henshū iinkai 寒川町史編集委員会, ed. *Samukawa chōshi chōsa hōkokusho 1: Kōyasan Takamuroin shiryō* 寒川町史調査報告書 1: 高野山高室院資料. 2 vols. Samukawa: Samukawa-machi, 1992–1993.

Saso, Michael. *Homa Rites and Mandala Meditations in Tendai Buddhism*. New Delhi: International Academy of Indian Culture, Aditya Prakashan, 1991.

———. *Tantric Art and Meditation*. Honolulu, HI: Tendai Educational Foundation, 1990.

Satō, Hiroo. "Wrathful Deities and Saving Deities." In *Buddhas and Kami in Japan: Honji Suijaku as a Combinatory Paradigm*, ed. Mark Teeuwen and Fabio Rambelli, 95–114. London and New York: RoutledgeCurzon, 2003.

Satō Shunkō 佐藤俊晃. "'Seshū' no shiten kara miru shugen jiin to Sōtōshū jiin: kinsei kindai Akita-han hinai chihō ni okeru jirei hōkoku" 「世襲」の視点から見る修験寺院と曹洞宗寺院: 近世〜近代、秋田藩比内地方における事例報告. *Kyōka kenkyū* 教化研修 37 (1994): 263–68.

Satō Ryōji-ke shozō monjo 佐藤良次家所蔵文書. Isehara shishi hensanshitsu, Kanagawa Prefecture. Microfilm.

Sekimori, Gaynor. "The Separation of Kami and Buddha Worship in Haguro Shugendō, 1869–1875." *Japanese Journal of Religious Studies* 32, no. 2 (2005): 197–234.

Setagaya kuritsu kyōdo shiryōkan 世田谷区立郷土資料館, ed. *Shaji sankei to daisankō* 社寺参詣と代参講. Tokyo: Setagaya kuritsu kyōdo shiryōkan, 1991.

Shinbo Tōru 真保亨. *Besson mandara* 別尊曼荼羅. Tokyo: Mainichi shinbunsha, 1985.

Shinjō Tunezō 新城常三. *Shaji to kōtsū: Kumano mōde to Ise mairi* 社寺と交通: 熊野詣でと伊勢参り. Tokyo: Shinshūsha, 1960.

———. *Shinkō shaji sankei no shakai-keizaishiteki kenkyū* 新稿社寺参詣の社会経済史的研究. Tokyo: Hanawa shobō, 1982.

Shinkei 心敬. *Oi no kurigoto* 老のくり言. In *Gunsho ruijū: renga bu* 群書類従: 連歌部, vol. 10, 1075–83. Tokyo: Keizai zasshisha, 1900.

Shinmei jisho 神名辞書. Tokyo: Seishidō shoten, 1912.

Shinno Junko 真野純子. "Shozan shosha sankei senadatsushoku o meguru yamabushi to shake—Yoshidake no shokoku shake shihaika e no joshō" 諸山諸社参詣先達職をめぐる山伏と社家—吉田家の諸国社家支配化への序章. In *Ronshū Nihon bukkyō shi 7: Edo jidai* 論集日本仏教史 7: 江戸時代, ed. Tamamuro Fumio 圭室文雄, 105–31. Tokyo: Yūzankaku, 1986.

Shinno Toshikazu 真野俊和. *Seinaru tabi* 聖なる旅. Tokyo: Tōkyōdō shuppan, 1991.

Shinzō 心蔵, ed. *Ōyama Fudō reigenki* 大山不動霊験記. N.p.: Sagami Ōyama Yōchiin, 1792.

Shintō taikei hensankai 神道大系編纂会, ed. *Shintō taikei: jinja hen* 神道大系: 神社編 Vol. 16. Tokyo: Shintō taikei hensankai, 1982.

Smyers, Karen A. *The Fox and the Jewel: Shared and Private Meanings in Contemporary Japanese Inari Worship.* Honolulu, HI: University of Hawai'i Press, 1999.

"Shoshū kaikyū" 諸宗階級. In *Zokuzoku gunsho ruijū* 続々群書類従, vol. 10, 356–448. Tokyo: Kokusho kankōkai, 1907.

Soja, Edward. *Postmodern Geographies: The Reassertion of Space in Critical Social Theory.* London and New York: Verso, 1989.

Sōshū Ōyamadera engi narabi Myōōtarō raiyu 相州大山寺縁起並明王太郎来由. Kokuritsu kōmonjokan, Tokyo.

Sudō Shigeo 須藤重雄. *Afurijinja kodenkō* 阿夫利神社古伝考. Tōkyō daigaku shiryō hensanjo, 1921. Handwritten copy. Original document dated 1849; copied by Afurijinja in 1877.

Sugane Yukihiro 菅根幸裕. "Kinsei no Ōyamakō to Ōyama oshi—Kazusa no kuni Sakuda-mura no Ōyamakō shiryō o chūshin ni" 近世の大山講と

大山御師—上総国作田村の大山講史料を中心に. *Sangaku shugen* 山岳 修験 18 (1996): 30–46.

Suzuki Heikurō 鈴木平九郎. *Kōshi nikki* 公私日記. Vols. 4 and 6, ed. Mizuno Yū 水野祐 and Itō Yoshiichi 伊藤好一. Tachikawa: Tachikawa-shi kyōiku iinkai, 1980–1981.

Suzuki Masataka 鈴木正崇. *Nyonin kinsei* 女人禁制. Tokyo: Yoshikawa Kōbunkan, 2002.

———. *Yama to kami to hito: sangaku shinkō to shugendō no sekai* 山と神と人: 山岳信仰と修験道の世界. Kyoto: Tankōsha, 1991.

———. "Tateyama shinkō" 立山信仰. *Kikan minzokugaku* 季刊民俗学 75 (1996): 7–21.

Suzuki Michirō 鈴木道郎. "Meiji shoki ni okeru Sagami Ōyama oshi no keizai seikatsu" 明治初期における相模大山御師の経済生活. In *Ōyama shinkō* 大山信仰, ed. Tamamuro Fumio 圭室文雄, 175–91. Tokyo: Yūzankaku, 1992.

Suzuki Shōsei 鈴木章生. "Sagami Ōyama shinkō no seiritsu to tenkai: minshū sankei no kōdō to shinkōken o megutte" 相模大山信仰の成立と展開: 民衆参詣の動向と信仰圏をめぐって. *Hadano shishi kenkyū* 秦野市史 研究 6 (1986): 65–87.

Suzuki Yoshiaki 鈴木良明. "Ōyama shinkō no keimō katsudō" 大山信仰の 啓蒙活動. *Sangaku shugen* 山岳修験 18 (1996): 20–29.

Takano Toshihiko 高埜利彦. "Idō suru mibun: shinshoku to hyakushō no aida" 移動する身分: 神職と百姓の間. In *Nihon no kinsei 7: mibun to kaku-shiki* 日本の近世 7: 身分と格式, ed. Asao Naohiro 朝尾直弘, 345–77. Tokyo: Chūō kōronsha, 1992.

Takao Isao-ke shozō monjo 高尾勲家所蔵文書. Isehara shishi hensanshitsu, Kanagawa Prefecture. Microfilm.

Tamamuro Fumio 圭室文雄. *Nihon bukkyō shi: kinsei* 日本仏教史: 近世. To-kyo: Yoshikawa kōbunkan, 1987.

———. *Nihonjin no kōdō to shisō 16: Edo bakufu no shūkyō tōsei* 日本人の行動と 思想 16: 江戸幕府の宗教統制. Tokyo: Hyōronsha, 1971.

———. *Shinbutsu bunri* 神仏分離. Tokyo: Kyōikusha, 1971.

———. "Bakuhan taisei to bukkyō-kirishitan dan'atsu to danka seido no ten-kai" 幕藩体制と仏教-キリシタン弾圧と檀家制度の展開. In *Ronshū Nihon bukkyō shi 7: Edo jidai* 論集日本仏教史 7: 江戸時代, ed. Tamamuro Fumio 圭室文雄, 1–40. Tokyo: Yūzankaku, 1986.

———. "Jiin honmatsuchō no seikaku to mondaiten" 寺院本末帳の性格と 問題点. In *Edo bakufu jiin honmatsuchō shūsei* 江戸幕府寺院本末帳集成, Vol. 3, ed. Jiin honmatsuchō kenkyūkai 寺院本末帳研究会, 5–26. Tokyo: Yūzankaku, 1981.

———. "Ōyama Fudō no kidachi no rieki ni tsuite" 大山不動の木太刀の利益について. *Isehara no rekishi* 伊勢原の歴史 6 (1991): 86–93.

———. "*Ōyama Fudō reigenki* ni miru Ōyama shinkō" 「大山不動霊験記」にみる大山信仰. In *Ōyama shinkō* 大山信仰, ed. Tamamuro Fumio 圭室文雄, 127–47. Tokyo: Yūzankaku, 1992.

———. "Ōyama shinkō" 大山信仰. In *Kanagawa kenshi kakuronhen 3: bunka* 神奈川県史 各論編 3: 文化, 363–75. Yokohama: Kanagawa-ken, 1980.

———. "Ōyama shinkō no kenkyū dōkō" 大山信仰の研究動向. In *Ōyama shinkō* 大山信仰, ed. Tamamuro Fumio 圭室文雄, 369–78. Tokyo: Yūzankaku, 1992.

———. "Shinbutsu bunri rei" 神仏分離令. In *Kokushi daijiten* 国史大辞典, vol. 7, ed. Kokushi daijiten henshū iinkai 国史大辞典編集委員会, 920. Tokyo: Yoshikawa kōbunkan, 1983.

———. "Shūshō: shinbutsu bunri" 終章: 神仏分離. In *Zusetsu Nihon no bukkyō 6: shinbutsu shūgō to shugendō* 図説日本の仏教 6: 神仏習合と修験, ed. Tanabe Saburōsuke 田辺三郎助, 335–54. Tokyo: Shinchōsha, 1989.

———, ed. *Zusetsu Nihon bukkyō no rekishi: Edo jidai* 図説日本仏教の歴史: 江戸時代. Tokyo: Kōsei shuppansha, 1996.

Tamamuro Taijō 圭室諦成. "Kaichō" 開帳. In *Nihon rekishi daijiten* 日本歴史大辞典, vol. 2, 508–9. Tokyo: Kawade shobō, 1968.

Tamayama Jōgen 玉山成元. "Kantō jūhachi danrin no seiritsu" 関東十八檀林の成立. *Taishō daigaku kenkyū kiyō* 大正大學研究紀要 52 (1967): 207–16.

Tanaka Sen'ichi 田中宣一. "Meiji shoki ni okeru Ōyamakō no bunpu" 明治初期における大山講の分布. In *Ōyama shinkō* 大山信仰, ed. Tamamuro Fumio 圭室文雄, 193–204. Tokyo: Yūzankaku, 1992.

———. "Sagami Ōyama no Chatōdera mairi ni tsuite" 相模大山の茶湯寺参りについて. *Seijō bungei* 成城文芸 91 (1980): 21–41.

———. "Sōshū Ōyamakō no oshi to danka: Edo makki no dankai to natsuyama tōhai o megutte" 相州大山講の御師と檀家:江戸末期の檀廻と夏山登拝をめぐって. *Nihon jōmin bunka kiyō* 8 (1982): 157–91.

———. "Sōshū Ōyamakō no oshi to danka: Edo makki no dankai to natsuyama tōhai o megutte" 相州大山講の御師と檀家:江戸末期の檀廻と夏山登拝をめぐって. In *Ōyama shinkō* 大山信仰, ed. Tamamuro Fumio 圭室文雄, 63–90. Tokyo: Yūzankaku, 1992.

Tanba Kunio 丹羽邦男. "Sendōshi no machi: Meiji zenki no Ōyama-chō" 先導師の町: 明治前期の大山町. In *Ōyama shinkō* 大山信仰, ed. Tamamuro Fumio 圭室文雄, 205–40. Tokyo: Yūzankaku, 1992.

Teeuwen, Mark. "The Creation of a *honji suijaku* Deity: Amaterasu as the Judge of the Dead." In *Buddhas and Kami in Japan: Honji Suijaku as a Combinatory*

Paradigm, ed. Mark Teeuwen and Fabio Rambelli, 115–44. London and New York: RoutledgeCurzon, 2003.

———, trans. *Motoori Norinaga's "The Two Shrines of Ise: An Essay of Split Bamboo" (Ise Nikū Sakitake no Ben)*. Wiesbaden: Harrossowitz Verlag, 1995.

Teeuwen, Mark and Fabio Rambelli. "Introduction: Combinatory Religion and the *honji suijaku* Paradigm in Pre-Modern Japan." In *Buddhas and Kami in Japan: Honji Suijaku as a Combinatory Paradigm*, ed. Mark Teeuwen and Fabio Rambelli, 1–53. London and New York: RoutledgeCurzon, 2003.

Teeuwen, Mark and Hendrik van der Veere. *Nakatomi harae kunge: Purification and Enlightenment in Late Heian Japan*. Munich: Iudicium Verlag, 1998.

Tenaka Myōōtarō Kagemoto 手中明王太郎影元. *Ōyama miyadaiku Myōōtarō nikki* 大山宮大工明王太郎日記. 2 vols, ed. Tenaka Tadashi 手中正. Yamato-shi: Tenaka Tadashi, 1992–1993.

———. "Ōyama Afurijinja shinchikuzu" 大山阿夫利神社新築図. N.p.: N.d.

Tenaka Tadashi 手中正. "Ōyama no shinbutsu bunri" 大山の神仏分離. Paper presented at the forty-ninth annual meeting of the Chihōshi kenkyū kyōgikai 地方史研究協議会. November 1, 1998, handout, document 4.

Ten Grotenhuis, Elizabeth. *Japanese Mandalas: Representations of Sacred Geography*. Honolulu, HI: University of Hawai'i Press, 1999.

Teiser, Stephen. *The Ghost Festival in Medieval China*. Princeton, NJ: Princeton, University Press, 1988.

Thal, Sarah E. *Rearranging the Landscape of the Gods: The Politics of a Pilgrimage Site in Japan, 1573–1912*. Chicago, IL: University of Chicago Press, 2005.

———. "Rearranging the Landscape of the Gods: A History of Konpira Pilgrimage in the Meiji Period." Ph.D. diss., Columbia University, 1999.

———. "Redefining the Gods: Politics and Survival in the Creation of Modern Kami." *Japanese Journal of Religious Studies* 29, nos. 3–4 (Fall 2002): 379–404.

Thornton, Sybil. *Charisma and Community Formation in Medieval Japan: The Case of the Yugyō-ha (1300–1700)*. Ithaca, NY: Cornell University, 1999.

Togawa Anshō 户川安章, ed. *Yamagata-ken bunkazai chōsa hōkokusho 16: Dewasanzan no shugendō to shinbutsu bunri* 山形県文化財調査報告書 16: 出羽三山の修験道と神仏分離. Yamagata: Yamagata-ken kyōiku iinkai, 1969.

Toki Masanori 土岐昌訓. "Kinsei no shinshoku soshiki: Musashi no kuni no jirei" 近世の神職組織: 武蔵国の事例. *Nihon bunka kenkyūjo kiyō* 日本文化研究所紀要 12 (March 1963): 191–254.

———. "Shirakawa, Yoshida no shinshoku shihai: kinsei ni okeru Musashi, Sagami no ryōkoku o chūshin ni" 白川・吉田の神職支配: 近世に於ける武蔵・相模の両国を中心に. *Kokugakuin zasshi* 3 (1979): 56–68.

Tokugawa kinrei kō 徳川禁令考, vol. 5. Tokyo: Yoshikawa kōbunkan, 1932.

Tōkyō daigaku shiryō hensanjo 東京大学史料編纂所, ed. *Dainihon Kinsei shiryō: Shichū torishimari ruishū 16* 大日本近世史料:市中取締類集 16. Tokyo: Tōkyō Daigaku shuppankai, 1984.

Tōkyō-to kōbunshokan 東京都公文書館, ed. *Tōkyō shishi kō 6: sangyōhen* 東京市史稿 6: 産業篇. Tokyo: Tōkyō-to kōbunshokan, 1958.

Tōkyō-to kōbunshokan 東京都公文書館, ed. *Tōkyō shishi kō 7: sangyōhen* 東京市史稿 7: 産業篇. Tokyo: Tōkyō-to kōbunshokan, 1960.

Tōkyō-to Setagaya-ku kyōiku iinkai 東京都世田谷区教育委員会, ed. *Ise dōchūki shiryō* 伊勢道中記史料. Tokyo: Tōkyō-to Setagaya-ku kyōiku iinkai, 1985.

———, ed. *Karei nenjū gyōji: kōyaku Kamimachi Ōba-ke* 家例年中行事: 口訳上町大場家. Tokyo: Tōkyō-to Setagaya-ku kyōiku iinkai, 1989.

Tōma Yūchō 十摩宥長. "Ōyama shi" 大山史. In *Ōyamadera engi* 大山寺縁起, 1–138. Isehara: Taisanji, 1984.

Tonomura, Hitomi. *Community and Commerce in Late Medieval Japan: The Corporate Villages of Tokuchin-ho.* Stanford, CA: Stanford University Press, 1992.

Toyoda Takeshi 豊田武. *Kaitei Nihon shūkyō seidoshi no kenkyū* 改訂・日本宗教制度史の研究. Tokyo: Daiichi shobō, 1973.

———. *Myōji no rekishi* 苗字の歴史. Tokyo: Chūō kōronsha, 1971.

Tremlett, Paul. "The Problem of Belief: A Response to Matthew Engelke (*AT* 18, 6)." *Anthropology Today* 19, no. 4 (2003): 24.

Tsuji Zennosuke 辻善之助. *Nihon bukkyō shi* 日本仏教史. 10 vols. Tokyo: Iwanami shoten, 1944–1955.

Turner, Victor Witter. *Image and Pilgrimage in Christian Culture.* New York: Columbia University Press, 1978.

Tyler, Royall. "A Glimpse of Mt. Fuji in Legend and Cult." *Journal of the Association of Teachers of Japanese* 16, no. 2 (1981): 140–65.

———. "The Tokugawa Peace and Popular Religion: Suzuki Shōsan, Kakugyō Tōbutsu, and Jikigyō Miroku." In *Confucianism and Tokugawa Culture*, ed. Peter Nosco, 92–119. Princeton, NJ: Princeton University Press, 1984.

Udaka Yoshiaki 宇高良哲. *Edo bakufu no bukkyō kyōdanshi tōsei* 江戸幕府の仏教教団統制. Tokyo: Tōyō bunka shuppan, 1987.

———. *Tokugawa Ieyasu to Kantō bukkyō kyōdan* 徳川家康と関東仏教教団. Tokyo: Tōyō bunka shuppan, 1987.

Ushiyama Yoshiyuki 牛山佳幸. "'Nyonin kinsei' sairon" 「女人禁制」再論. *Sangaku shugen* 山岳修験 17 (1996): 1–11.

Utsumi Benji 内海弁次. *Sōshū Ōyama* 相州大山. Yokohama: Kanagawa shinbunsha, 1996.

Utsumi Teruo (Shikibu)-ke shozō monjo 内海輝雄(式部)家所蔵文書. Isehara shishi hensanshitsu, Kanagawa Prefecture. Microfilm.

Vaporis, Constantine Nomikos. *Breaking Barriers: Travel and the State in Early Modern Japan*. Cambridge, MA: Council on East Asian Studies, Harvard University, 1994.

Vesey, Alexander Marshall. "The Buddhist Clergy and Village Society in Early Modern Japan." Ph.D. diss., Princeton University, 2003.

Wada Mitsuko-ke shozō monjo 和田美寿子家所蔵文書. Isehara shishi hensanshitsu, Kanagawa Prefecture. Microfilm.

Wakabayashi, Haruko Nishi. "Tengu: Images of Buddhist Concepts of Evil in Medieval Japan." Ph.D. diss., Princeton University, 1995.

Walthall, Anne. "Nativism as a Social Movement: Katagiri Harukazu and the *Hongaku reisha*." In *Shinto in History: Ways of the Kami*, ed. John Breen and Mark Teeuwen, 205–29. Honolulu, HI: University of Hawai'i Press, 2000.

Washio Junkei 鷲尾順敬. "Sagami Ōyama Afurijinja chōsa hōkoku" 相模大山阿夫利神社調査報告. In *Shinpen Meiji ishin shinbutsu bunri shiryō* 新編明治維新神仏分離史料, vol. 3, ed. Tsuji Zennosuke 辻善之助 et al., 564–83. Tokyo: Meichō shuppan, 1983.

Williams, Duncan. *The Other Side of Zen: A Social History of Sōtō Zen Buddhism in Tokugawa Japan*. Princeton, NJ: Princeton University Press, 2005.

―――. "Representations of Zen." Ph.D. diss., Harvard University, 2000.

Yamamoto Mitsumasa 山本光正. "Kinsei ni okeru Edowan kōtsū ni tsuite" 近世における江戸湾交通について. In *Ōyama shinkō* 大山信仰, ed. Tamamuro Fumio 圭室文雄, 286–303. Tokyo: Yūzankaku, 1992.

Yamasaki, Taikō. *Shingon: Japanese Esoteric Buddhism*. Boston, MA: Shambhala, 1988.

Yamashita Kazumasa 山下和正. *Chizu de yomu Edo jidai* 地図で読む江戸時代／*Japanese Maps of the Edo Period*. English translation by Charles De Wolf. Tokyo: Kashiwa shobō, 1998.

Yasuike Hiroyuki 安池尋幸. "Chūsei, kinsei ni okeru Edo naikai tosen no tenkai" 中世·近世における江戸内海渡船の展開. In *Ōyama shinkō* 大山信仰, ed. Tamamuro Fumio 圭室文雄, 251–65. Tokyo: Yūzankaku, 1992.

Yoshida, Nobuyuki. "Osaka's Brotherhood of Mendicant Monks." In *Osaka: The Merchants' Capital of Early Modern Japan*, ed. James L. MacClain and Wakita Osamu, 158–79. Ithaca, NY and London: Cornell University Press, 1999.

Yoshida, Kazuhiko. "Religion in the Classical Period." In *Nanzan Guide to Japanese Religions*, ed. Paul Swanson and Clark Chilson, 144–62. Honolulu, HI: University of Hawai'i Press, 2006.

Zhao, Qiguang. *Asian Thought and Culture: A Study of Dragons, East and West*. New York: Peter Lang, 1992.

List of Characters

Afurijinja　阿夫利神社
Afurijinja kodenkō　阿夫利神社
　　古伝考
Afurisan　阿部利山 or
　　阿夫利山 or 雨降山
Afurisan ryaku engi
　　雨降山略ゑんぎ
ainoyama　間の山
Aizen Myōō　愛染明王
Akiba　秋葉
Amaterasu　天照
Amefuriki　雨降木
Ame no Hanasakuya Hime
　　天咲哉姫
Ame no Minakanushi no Kami
　　天御中主神
Ame no Torifune　天鳥船
Andō Hiroshige　安藤広重
Anrakuji　安楽寺
arafurukami　荒振神
Asama　浅間
ashi　葦
Atago　愛宕
Atsuta　熱田

bakufu　幕府

Bandō　坂東
bekkakusha　別格社
bettō　別当
Bikisho　鼻皈書
Bishamonten　毘沙門天
-bō　坊
bon'yama　盆山
bosatsu　菩薩
Boshin　戊辰
Bōsō　房総
Bukō nenpyō　武江年表
Byakuryaku Raidenjin
　　霹靂雷電神

cha　茶
Chatōdera　茶湯寺
chōgotai　懲胡隊
Chōjunbō　長順坊
chūkōgi　中講義
Chūkyōin　中教院
chūsei　中世
chūsentō　中先頭
Chūsha　忠車

Daibonten　大梵天
Daifukuzan　大福山

Daigoji 醍醐寺

Daihannyakyō 大般若経

daijin 大神

daikan 代官

Daikanjin 大勧進

Daikakubō 大覚坊

Daikakuji 大覚寺

daikōgi 大講義

daikyōshō 大教正

Dainichi 大日

Dainichikyō 大日経

daisendatsu 大先達

daisentō 大先頭

Daitenma 大天魔

Daitengu 大天狗

Daiyūzan 大雄山

Daizōin 大蔵院

Dajōkan 大政官

danchū 檀中

dangisho 談義所

danka 檀家 or 旦家

dankai 檀回

danna 檀那 or 旦那

dannachō 檀那帳 or 旦那帳

danrin 談林 or 壇林

dan'otsu 檀越

degaichō 出開帳

Dewa Sanzan 出羽三山

dōji 童子

Dontei Robun 鈍亭魯文

dōsojin 道祖神

Edo shokōchū chōtō kōchū fuda
hikaechō 江戸諸講中挑灯
講中札控帳

Edo sōganoko meisho taizen
江戸惣鹿子名所大全

Eiyo 栄誉

Eizō 栄増

Engi shiki 延喜式

Enkōin 圓光院

Enma 閻魔

ennichi 縁日

En no Gyōja 役行者

Enoshima 江ノ島

Enoshima Benten 江ノ島弁天

Enzōbō 円蔵坊

etoki 絵解き

fuda 札

Fudō Myōō 不動明王

Fudōson sairei 不動尊祭礼

Fuji 富士

Fuji Ōyama dōchū zakki
富士大山道中雜記

Fukuhara Jōjirō 福原定次郎

furegashira 触頭

Fūhaku 風伯

Fukuba Bisei 福羽美静

Fūugū 風雨宮

Gangyō Shōnin 願行上人

Gangyō 願行

gannin bōzu 願人坊主

Genkō shakusho 元享釈書

Gion 祇園

Godaiin Hachidaibō
伍大院八大坊

Godai Myōō 五大明王

goma 護摩

gomakō 護摩講

Gonda Naosuke 権田直助

gongen 権現

gonshōkōgi 権小講義

gonshō kyōshō 権小教正

goō 牛王

goōhōin 牛王宝印

Gozu Tennō 牛頭天王

Gozu Tennō rekijinben
牛頭天王歴神弁

gūji 宮司
Gyōjitsu 尭実
Gyōki 行基
Gyokurōbō 玉瀧坊

Hachidaibō 八大坊
Hachidai Kongō Dōji
　八大金剛童子
Haguro 羽黒
haibutsu kishaku 廃仏棄釈
haiden 拝殿
Hakone Enoshima Kamakura
　dōchūki 箱根江ノ島鎌倉
　道中記
Hakonesan Kongōōin
　箱根山金剛王院
Hakusan 白山
Haruna 榛名
Hashimotobō 橋本坊
Hasuge 八管
hatagoya 旅籠屋
hatamoto 旗本
hatsuho 初穂
hatsuyama 初山
hatto 法度
Hayashi Razan 林羅山
hibutsu 秘仏
Hie 日吉
hijiri 聖
Hiko 英彦
Hinata 日向
Hirata Atsutane 平田篤胤
Hirata Kanetane 平田銕胤
Hishikawa Moronobu 菱川師宣
hōdanjo 法談所
Hōjuin 宝寿院
Hōkongōji 宝金剛寺
Honchō kōsōden 本朝高僧伝
Honchō jinjakō 本朝神社考
Hondaibō 本大坊

honden 本殿
hondō 本堂
honji 本地
honji suijaku 本地垂迹
honmatsu seido 本末制度
hōnō 奉納
Hōnobō 宝之坊
Hōnyo 法如
Honzanha 本山派
hōraku 法楽
hyakumikō 百味講

Ideha 出羽
ie 家
igaichō 居開帳
Iiyama 飯山
Iizumi 飯泉
Ikazuchidake 雷岳
Imagawa Yoshimoto 今川義元
-in 院
Inaba Masakuni 稲葉正邦
Inari 稲荷
Ina Tadatsugu 伊奈忠次
Inbe 忌部
Inomata Gidayū 猪俣義大夫
Ise 伊勢
Ise nikū sakitake no ben
　伊勢二宮さき竹の弁
Ishikawa Hōshōji 石川宝生寺
Itō Jinsai 伊藤仁斎
Iwashimizu Hachiman
　石清水八幡
Izanagi 去来諾 or 伊弉諾
Izanami 去来冉 or 伊弉冉
Izusan Hannyain 伊豆山般若院

Jakudō 寂道
Jakushin 寂信
Jikigyō Miroku 食行身禄
jiku no shu 慈救祝

Jingikan　神祇官

Jingishō　神祇省

jingitai　神祇隊

Jingūkyō　神宮教

Jinnō hongi　神皇本紀

Jippensha Ikku　十返舎一九

Jitsuei　実榮:

Jitsujō　実乗

Jitsujōbō　実城坊

Jitsuō　実雄:

jōdo　浄土

Jōdoshin　浄土真

jōe　浄衣

Jōenbō　常円坊

jōhōdanjo　常法談所

Jutokuin　授徳院

kabuki　歌舞伎

kagura　神楽

Kagutsuchi　迦具土

kaichō　開帳

kaidō　街道

Kaidōki　開導記

kaihi　開扉

Kaiun　快運

Kaizō　開蔵

Kakkyoku　覚昶

Kakugyō Tōbutsu　角行藤仏

Kamakura Enoshima Ōyama
　　shinpan ōrai sugoroku　鎌倉
　　江ノ島大山新板往来双六

Kamei Koremi　亀井茲監

kami　神

Kamikasuya　上粕屋

Kaminobō　上之坊

kami no yo　神界

Kamo no Mabuchi　賀茂真淵

Kanamaru Monkan　金丸文観

Kanayamabiko　金山昆古

Kanga　貫雅

kanji　幹事

kannagi　覡巫 or 巫 or 覡

Kannon　観音

Kannonji　観音寺

kannushi　神主

kanpeisha　官幣社

Kantōchū honji hōrongi
　　shokeshū sadamesho　関東中
　　本寺法論義所化衆定書

karoku　家禄

Kashima　鹿島

Kasō mitsuden　家相密伝

Kasuga　春日

Kasuga no Tsubone　春日局

Katsushika Hokusai　葛飾北斎

Kazesaburō　風三郎

kechien　結縁

keigan　啓龕

Keisokusan　鶏足山

kekkai　結界

Ken'a　釼阿

Kenjō　憲静

Kenryū　賢隆

kessha　結社

ki　気

Kikuri Hime　菊理媛

Kirakubō　喜楽坊

Kiri Ōji　霧王子

kitō　祈祷

kitōdera　祈祷寺

kitōshi　祈祷師

kō　講

Kōbō Daishi　弘法大師

kōchū　講中

Kōenbō　光円坊

kofun　古墳

kōsha　講社

Kōga　吽雅

kōgashira　講頭

Kogidō　古義堂

Kogi Shingon　古義真言

Kojiki　古事記

kōkanban　講看板

Kokoro no hashira　心の柱 or
　古故路乃波志良

koku　石

kokuheisha　国幣社

Kokumei fudoki

Kokuzō hongi　国造本紀

Kominoge　小蓑毛

kōmoto　講元

Kōmyōin　光明院

Kongara Dōji　矜迦羅童子

Konjikisenkutsu　金色仙窟

Konjōin　金乗院

Konohanasakuya Hime
　木花咲耶姫

Konpira　金毘羅

Konshōin　根生院

Kōshin　庚申

Kōshū Kaidō　甲州街道

Kōten Kōkyūsho　皇典講究所

Kotohira　金刀比羅

Kōtokuin　広徳院

Kōyasan Henshōkōin
　高野山遍照光院

Koyasu　子易

Kōzō　光増

Kūben　空弁

Kūkai　空海

Kumano　熊野

Kurama　鞍馬

kumi　組

Kuni no Tokotachi no Mikoto
　国常立尊

Kunlun　崑崙

Kurikara　倶利迦羅

kusu　楠

kusuri　薬

Kyōbushō　教部省

kyōdōshoku　教導職

kyōha shintō　教派神道

machiyado　町宿

Maefudōdō　前不動堂

Maiasa shinpai norito
　毎朝神拝詞

Masuda Inamaro　増田稲麿

Matsuya Jinshirō　松屋甚四郎

Meguro Fudō　目黒不動

Miroku　弥勒:

Mishima Taisha　三嶋大社

maneki　招き

Manihōden　摩尼宝殿

mappō　末法

Matsubara　松原

Miketsukami　御饌都神

miki　神酒

mikoshi　御輿

Minamoto　源

mine'iri　峰入

Minobu　身延

Minoge　蓑毛

Miroku　弥勒

Mitake　御岳

Miura　三浦

mochiba　持場

monzenmachi　門前町

Motoori Norinaga　本居宣長

mujinkō　無尽講

Murayama Hachidayū
　村山八太夫

Myōjū　妙住

myōō　明王

Myōō Gongen　明王権現

Myōōji　明王寺

Myōōtarō raiyu　明王太郎来由

Nagare no Ōmoto no Mikoto
　流の大元尊

naiin　内院

Nakanoin　中之院

Naniwakō　浪花講

nanokadō　七日堂

Nan'yō no michi no ki
　南陽の道の記

naorairyō　直会

Narita Fudō　成田不動

negi　禰祇

Nenjū gyōji　年中行事

Nichiren　日蓮

Nihongi　日本紀

Nihon kokumei fudoki
　日本国名風土記

Nihon sōkoku fudoki
　日本総国風土記

Nijū no Taki　二重滝

Ninigi no Mikoto　瓊瓊杵尊

Ninnaji　仁和寺

Nishikawa Sugao　西川須賀雄

nōke　能化

norito　祝詞

nukemairi　抜け参り

nyoishu　如意珠

Nyoizan　如意山

nyonin kekkai　女人結界

nyonin kinsei　女人禁制

ōbaku　黄檗

odachi　御刀

odachikō　御刀講

Oda Nobunaga　織田信長

Ogyū Sorai　荻生徂徠

Ōhirume no Muchiwake Mitama
　no Kami
　大日霊貴別御霊の神

Ōikazuchi no Kami　大雷神

Ōji Konrinji　王子金輪寺

Ōjū　応住

Okami no Kami　於加美神
　also Kuraokami no Kami
　闇於加美神 or Takaokami no
　Kami　高龗神

ōkan　往還

Ōki Gen'ichirō　大木源一郎

Ōkuni Takamasa　大国隆正

ōmikagura　大御神楽

omiki　御神酒

omikikō　御神酒講

omikiwaku　御神酒枠

Ōmine　大峰

Ōmononushi　大物主

onmyōdō　陰陽道

oshi　御師

oshi ari no dōsha
　御師有之道者

Ōyama　大山

Ōyamadera　大山寺

Ōyamadera engi　大山寺縁起

Ōyama dōchū chōkō zue
　大山道中張交図会

Ōyama Fudō reigenki
　大山不動霊験記

Ōyama Isamu　大山勇

Ōyama jiki　大山事記

Ōyama keishin kōsha chōkai
　kiyaku
　大山敬慎講懲戒規約

Ōyama keishin kōsha kisoku
　大山敬慎講社規則

Ōyama keishin kōsha teikyūhaku
　kisoku　大山敬慎講社定休
　泊規則

Ōyama Keishin Kōsha
　大山敬慎講社

Ōyamamichi　大山道

Ōyama no Mikoto　吾路山命

Ōyamazumi no kami　大山積神

Ōyamazumi no Mikoto
大山跡祇命

Penglai 蓬萊

Raigōin 来迎院
Raikei 頼慶
Renjōin 蓮乗院
Rinzai 臨済
rokkon shōjō 六根精浄
Rokuharamitsuji 六波羅蜜寺
Rokusho Shrine 六所神社
Rōben 良弁
Rōsekisan 狼跡山
Ryōbu Shinto 両部神道
Ryōzenji 霊山寺
ryūjin 龍神
Ryūkei 隆慶
Ryūtei Rijō 滝亭鯉丈

Saiganji 西岸寺
Saigōji 西迎寺
Saisei itchi 祭政一致
Saiten shūrei kogoto
祭典習礼小言
Saiten shūrei shiki
祭典習礼私記
Saitō Gesshin 斎藤月岑
Sakamoto 坂本
Sanbōin 三宝院
sangaku shinkō 山岳信仰
sanmai 三昧
Sannō Gongen 山王権現
Sarutahiko 猿田彦
Satō Chūmu 佐藤中務
Seijun 盛順
Seinyo 性如
Seitaka Dōji 勢多迦童子
sekisho 関所

Sekison Daigongen 石尊大権現
Sekison Gongen 石尊権現
Sekison Myōō 石尊明王
Senchōbō 泉長坊
Sendai kuji hongi 先代旧事本紀
Sendai kuji hongi taiseikyō
先代旧事本紀大成経
sendatsu 先達
sendōshi 先導師
Sengen 浅間
Sensōji 浅草寺
sentō 先頭
sewa'nin 世話人
Shigōkō 諡号考
shajin 社人
shido kekkai 四土結界
shigikizami 神木剋
shigitate 神木立て or 神木起
shijūkuin 四十九院
shikan 祠官
shimeharai 七五三祓 or 注連祓
shinbutsu bunri 神仏分離
shinbutsu shūgō 神仏習合
Shingi Shingon 新義真言
Shingon 真言
Shingon Ritsu 真言律
Shingonshū shohatto
真言宗法度
Shinja Daiō 震蛇大王
Shinjashinja 深砂振邪
shinjisai 神事祭
shinke 神家
Shinkyō kafu 神教歌譜
Shinmyō 神明
shinpai 神拝
Shinpen Musashi no kuni fudoki
kō 新編武蔵国風土記稿
Shinpen Sagami no kuni fudoki kō
新編相模国風土記稿

Shinrikibō 神力坊
shintai 神体
Shintō Honkyoku 神道本局
Shintō Jimukyoku 神道事務局
Shintō Taikyō 神道大教
Shinzō 心蔵:
Shirakawa 白川
shishoku 祠職
shishoku 師職
Shōgoin 聖護院
Shōgon'in 荘厳院
shōjin ochi 精進落ち
shoke 所化
Shōdō 照道
Shōkyōin 小教院
shōsentō 小先頭
Shōtengu 小天狗
shugendō 修験道
shugenja 修験者
Shusō 守操
shūto 衆戸
Sōden mitsuji 相伝密事
Sōgishiki 葬儀式
sonnō jōi 尊王攘夷
Sonshō 尊勝
Sonshō darani 尊勝陀羅尼
Sōtō 曹洞
Sōyō Ōyamafu 相陽大山譜
Sudō Shigeo 須藤重雄
Suika Shintō 垂加神道
Sujin 崇神
Sumemima no Mikoto 皇御孫命
Susanoo no Mikoto 須佐之男命
Sutoku 崇徳
Suwa 諏訪

Taga 多賀
Taikyōin 大教院
taikyō senpu undō
　大教宣布運動

Taisanji 大山寺
Takao 高尾
Takaosanji 高雄山寺
Takeda Shingen 武田信玄
ta no kami 田の神
Tateyama 立山
tayū 大夫
tenaga 手長
tenagakō 手長講
Tenaka Myōōtarō Kagemoto
　手中明王太郎景元
Tenaka Myōōtarō Kagenao
　手中明王太郎景直
Tendai 天台
tengu 天狗
tenma 天魔
Tenmu 天武
terauke seido 寺請制度
tobi 鳶
Tōji 東寺
Tōkaidō 東海道
Tōkaidō bunken ezu
　東海道分間絵図
Tōkaidō gojūsantsugi saiken zue
　東海道五十三次細見図会
Tōkaidō meisho zue
　東海道名所図会
tokoyo 常世
Tokoyo Ugokazu no Mikoto
　常世不動尊
Tokugawa Iemitsu 徳川家光
Tokugawa Ietsuna 徳川家綱
Tokugawa Ieyasu 徳川家康
Tokuichi 徳一
torii 鳥居
tōnin 頭人
toritsugi 取次
Tori no Iwakusufune no Mikoto
　鳥石楠船命
toshigoi no matsuri 祈年祭

Tōshō Gongen　東照権現
Toyouke Hime　豊受媛
Tōzanha　当山派
Tsuchimikado　土御門
Tsūga　通雅
Tsukuba　筑波
tsumado　妻戸
tsurugi　剣
Tsushima　津島
Tōsei zamochi banashi
　当世座持話
Tosotsuten　兜率天
Tōto saijiki　東都歳時記

Ugū　雨宮
Ukōzan　雨降山
ujiko　氏子
Uranai ninsō den
　うらない・にんそう伝
Ushi　雨師
Utagawa Kuniyoshi　歌川国芳
Utagawa Sadahide　歌川貞秀
Utsumi Shikibu　内海式部
Utsumi Yūkei　内海祐慶

waka　和歌
wakibō　脇坊
wakiōkan　脇往還

Yakushi Nyorai　薬師如来
yamabiraki　山開
yamabushi　山伏
Yamada Hyōma　山田平馬
Yamaga Sokō　山鹿素行
yama no kami　山の神
yamashita　山下
Yamato Takeru no Mikoto
　日本武尊 or 倭建命
Yamazaki Ansai　山崎闇斎
Yano Seitayū　矢野清大夫
Yōchiin　養知院
yonaoshi　世直し
Yoshida　吉田
yugyōsha　遊行者
Yuiitsu Shinto　唯一神道
Yūjunbō　祐順坊
yu lan pen　芋蘭盆
Yūryaku　雄略
Yūtenji　祐天寺

Zaō Gongen　蔵王権現
Zen　禅
Zenkōji　善光寺
Zenshūin　善集院
Zoku Edo sunago onko meisekishi
　続江戸砂子温故名跡志

Index

Harvard East Asian Monographs
(*out-of-print)

Harvard East Asian Monographs

Harvard East Asian Monographs

Harvard East Asian Monographs